Getting Started With Alpha Five Desktop Applications

By Dr. Indera E. Murphy

Tolana Publishing
Teaneck, New Jersey

Published By:
Tolana Publishing
PO Box 719
Teaneck, NJ 07666 USA

Find us online at www.tolanapublishing.com
Inquiries may be sent to the publisher: tolanapub@yahoo.com

Our books are available online at www.barnesandnoble.com. They can also be ordered from Ingram.

Quantity discounts are available for corporations, non-profit organizations and educational institutions for educational purposes, fundraising or resale. www.tolana.com/wholesale.html

ISBN-13: 978-1-935208-23-5
ISBN-10: 1-935208-23-3

Library of Congress Control Number: 2013940467

Printed and bound in the United States Of America

Cover by Mary Kramer, owner of Milkweed Graphics, www.milkweedgraphics.com

v1.0

About The No Stress Tech Guide Series

Getting Started With Alpha Five Desktop Applications is part of the growing series of computer software books that are designed to be used as a self-paced learning tool. Our books can also be used in a classroom setting or in an online class. The books in this series contain an abundance of step-by-step instructions and screen shots to help reduce the "stress" often associated with learning new software.

This book is geared towards the beginner and intermediate user, while the Alpha Five Beyond The Basics book is for the intermediate user. The other audience for this book is people that have created applications in another database tool and now want to learn Alpha Five.

Titles In The Series

	ISBN
ACT! 2007	978-0-9773912-5-7
ACT! 2009	978-1-935208-07-5
ACT! 2010	978-1-935208-09-9
ACT! Pro 2011	978-1-935208-13-6
ACT! Pro 2012	978-1-935208-17-4
Sage ACT! Pro 2013	978-1-935208-22-8
Using Crystal Reports 2008 With ACT! 2010 Databases	978-1-935208-10-5
Getting Started With Alpha Five Desktop Applications	978-1-935208-23-5
Alpha Five Desktop Applications Beyond The Basics	978-1-935208-24-2
Creating Reports & Charts For Alpha Five Desktop Applications Made Easy	978-1-935208-26-6
Using SAP Crystal Reports With Alpha Five Databases Made Easy	978-1-935208-25-9
Crystal Reports XI For Beginners (2nd Edition)	978-1-935208-00-6
What's New In Crystal Reports 2008	978-1-935208-01-3
Crystal Reports 2008 For Beginners	978-0-9773912-9-5
Crystal Reports 2011 For Beginners (2nd Edition)	978-1-935208-15-0
Crystal Reports Beyond The Basics	978-1-935208-18-1
Crystal Reports For Visual Studio 2005	978-0-9773912-6-4
Crystal Reports Basic For Visual Studio 2008	978-0-9773912-8-8
Crystal Reports For Visual Studio 2010	978-1-935208-12-9
Crystal Xcelsius 4.5	978-1-935208-02-0
Xcelsius 2008	978-1-935208-05-1
SAP Crystal Dashboard Design 2011 For Beginners	978-1-935208-11-2
OpenOffice.org 2 Writer	978-0-9773912-4-0
OpenOffice.org 3 Writer	978-1-935208-08-2
Microsoft Office Starter 2010 (Word & Excel)	978-1-935208-14-3
Microsoft PowerPivot For Excel 2010	978-1-935208-16-7
Microsoft Works 7	978-0-9773912-2-6
Microsoft Works 8 & 8.5	978-0-9773912-1-9
Microsoft Works 9	978-0-9773912-7-1
Windows XP	978-0-9773912-0-2

Why I Wrote This Book

There are a few reasons that I decided to write this book, as discussed below.

⇒ There are not a lot of books with hands-on exercises for this complex software package.
⇒ I felt that users, especially new application designers would prefer to have more assistance in learning how to create desktop applications in Alpha Five.
⇒ I have written several beginners books that help people get started using the software. The goal of this book is to help people learn how to design Alpha Five desktop applications.

About The Author

Dr. Indera Murphy is an author, educator and IT professional that has over 20 years of experience in the Information Technology field. She has held a variety of positions including technical writer, programmer, online adjunct professor, consultant, web designer, course developer and project leader. Indera has designed and developed software applications and websites, as well as, manage technology driven projects in several industries. In addition to being an Executive Director, she has taught courses in a variety of areas including project management, technical writing, Crystal Reports, information processing, Access, HTML, Windows, Excel, Dreamweaver and critical thinking.

Thank you for purchasing this book!

CONTENTS

GETTING STARTED WITH ALPHA FIVE

After reading this chapter and completing the exercises you will be able to:

- ☑ Have a better understanding of Alpha Five and what you can use it for
- ☑ Check for Alpha Five updates
- ☑ View a sample Alpha Five application
- ☑ Download the practice files

CHAPTER 1

Welcome To Alpha Five!

Alpha Five is a Windows based software package that is used to develop relational database applications. Not so long ago, developing applications was only done by programmers and other IT professionals. Alpha Five allows non programmers to develop database driven applications for the desktop, the web and mobile devices.

Databases created in Alpha Five use the **.DBF** file format. Alpha Five can use databases of almost any file size. Alpha Five also provides the ability to connect to and use data from a variety of database types without importing the data, including, Microsoft Access, Microsoft SQL Server, FileMaker Pro, Pervasive, Oracle, Paradox and more. Databases that have an **ODBC DRIVER** can also be used.

This is possible because Alpha Five has two types of tables (Passive-Link and Active-Link) that are specifically for connecting to what I call external or remote databases. This means that it is not a requirement to import data from these types of data sources into Alpha Five, to be able to access and update the data in external databases. While you can use an ODBC driver, the preferred way to connect to external databases is to use passive and active link tables.

The primary goal of Alpha Five is to allow a wide range of non programmers, as well as programmers, to have the ability to create and maintain database applications. Alpha Five makes creating basic reports easier through the use of Genies, which are similar to wizards that you may have used in other software packages. In addition to reports printed on paper, Alpha Five reports can be exported to Word, Excel, HTML and PDF formats. You can also create complex reports that include subreports, formulas, charts and much more.

I suspect that the majority of non programmers have not written any code. In some cases, this can severely limit ones ability to add the functionality that they need for the application. Alpha Five has Genies and Builders that create code automatically, behind the scenes.

Not including the Alpha Five server bundles, there are two editions of Alpha Five: The **DESKTOP EDITION**, which is used to develop PC-based desktop applications and the **DEVELOPER EDITION**, which is used to develop web based and mobile applications in addition to PC-based applications.

The best way that I can describe Alpha Five is that it is a relatively easy to use **RAD (RAPID APPLICATION DEVELOPMENT) TOOL** that is used to create and manage desktop and web based applications. One reason that it is relatively easy to use is because the software is menu driven. As you will see, the software has a lot of options. You will also see that there is often more than one way to access the same option.

It is my sincere hope that whatever your current skill level is with Alpha Five, that you will learn more about features that you are already familiar with as you go through this book and that you learn about features that you did not know existed. Learning new tips and shortcuts will let you work faster and smarter. The more you know about Alpha Five, the easier your day to day application design experiences will be.

So sit back, relax and lets get started!

How This Book Is Organized

Topics and exercises in one chapter build on ones covered in previous chapters. To get the most out of this book, it is not advised that you skip around. The first reason is because some of the files used in later chapters are based on files created in exercises earlier in the book.

The other reason is that a topic or option may have been covered in more detail earlier in the book. If you decide to skip around and cannot complete an exercise because there is something that you do not understand, you will have to go back and find the section that covers the topic in question. Below is an overview of what is covered in each chapter.

Chapter 1, Getting Started With Alpha Five covers background information about Alpha Five, conventions that I use in this book, a tour of an application that was created in Alpha Five and downloading the practice files.

Chapter 2, Exploring The Alpha Five Workspace covers options on the menu and toolbar. The Control Panel and options on each tab are covered, including the options on the shortcut menus. You will also learn about the workspace customization options.

Chapter 3, Creating Your First Database covers creating a database and tables.

Chapter 4, Field Rules covers learning about and creating field rules for tables.

Chapter 5, Using The Append Genie And Append Builder covers using the Append Genie and Append Builder to add (append) data to tables.

Chapter 6, Using The Set Editor covers learning about and creating sets for a database. Sets allow you to use multiple tables as if they were one.

Chapter 7, Using The Layout Editor covers the features of the Layout Editor that are common to forms, browses, reports, letters and labels.

Chapter 8, Creating Forms covers creating basic forms, using the form Genie, understanding form and object properties, the layout workspace and style sheets.

Chapter 9, Creating Browses covers creating custom browses (a type of form), adding a browse to a form and browse properties.

Chapter 10, Enhancing Forms Part 1 covers adding system fields to a form, setting up non scrollable regions and adding an embedded browse to a form.

Chapter 11, Enhancing Forms Part 2 covers creating a form with tabs, creating and managing styles and using Smart Fields.

Chapter 12, Data Entry Tips And Tools covers features that make data entry easier.

Chapter 13, Using PowerPivot (Bonus) This bonus chapter covers some of the basics of creating Pivot Tables and Pivot Charts with PowerPivot For Excel, which is a free add-on for Excel.

Objectives Of This Book

This book is written to accommodate self-paced, classroom and online training. While there are no required prerequisites to successfully complete the exercises in this book, having a general knowledge of any of the following would be helpful.

- ☑ Database structures
- ☑ Creating basic formulas
- ☑ Report design

There seems to be a growing trend of Access developers switching to Alpha Five. As one that has used Access to develop applications, I understand. The good news for you is that you have a slight advantage to learning Alpha Five. This book will help you also because the Alpha Five interface is different then the Access interface and Alpha Five uses slightly different terminology.

If you have used another database package like Access, the biggest thing that you will have to get use to in Alpha Five, in my opinion, is the difference in terminology. By that I mean, Access and many other databases will collectively refer to something one way and Alpha Five will refer to the same topic with a different name. For example, in most software, there is something called a wizard, which is used to help you create something. In Alpha Five, wizards are called Genies.

This book is a visual guide that shows you how to use a large number of the features in Alpha Five. There are over 400 illustrations that practically eliminate the guess work and let you know that you are doing the steps correctly.

Step-by-step instructions are included throughout this book. This book takes a hands-on approach to teaching you how to use features in Alpha Five to provide the skills required to create desktop applications. After completing the exercises in this book, you will be able to perform the following tasks and more:

- ☑ Create databases and tables
- ☑ Create forms
- ☑ Link tables by creating a set
- ☑ Create field rules
- ☑ Use many of the Genies
- ☑ Create and customize a browse
- ☑ Use operations

Conventions Used In This Book

I designed the following conventions to make it easier for you to follow the instructions in this book.

- ☑ The `Courier` font is used to indicate what you should type.
- ☑ **Drag** means to press and hold down the left mouse button while moving the mouse.
- ☑ **Click** means to press the left mouse button once, then release it immediately.
- ☑ **Double-click** means to quickly press the left mouse button twice, then release the mouse button.
- ☑ **Right-click** means to press the right mouse button once, which will open a shortcut menu.
- ☑ **Press Enter** means to press the Enter key on your keyboard.
- ☑ **Press Tab** means to press the Tab key on your keyboard.

☑ **Click Save** means to click the Save button on the dialog box.

☑ **Click Finish** means to click the Finish button on the dialog box.

☑ **SMALL CAPS** are used to indicate an option to click on or to bring something to your attention.

☑ This icon indicates a shortcut or another way to complete the task that is being discussed. It can also indicate a tip or additional information about the topic that is being discussed. Some of this information comes from my personal experience using Alpha Five.

☑ This icon indicates a warning, like a feature that has been removed or information that you need to be aware of. This icon can also represent what I call a quirk, meaning a feature did not work as I expected it to.

☑ This icon represents what I call an "Alpha Five-Ism". This means that the term or concept being presented is called something different in Alpha Five then it is commonly known as or called in many other database software packages. Hopefully, this will help in the transition, if you have used other database software.

☑ [See Chapter 3, Database Concepts] refers to a section in a chapter that you can use as a reference for the topic that is being discussed.

☑ [See Chapter 2, Figure 2-8] refers to an illustration (screen shot) that you can use as a reference for the topic that is being discussed.

☑ When you see "**YOU SHOULD HAVE THE OPTIONS SHOWN IN FIGURE X-X**", or something similar in the exercises, check to make sure that your screen does look like the figure. If it does, continue with the next set of instructions. If your screen does not look like the figure, redo the steps that you just completed so that your screen does match the figure. Not doing so may cause you problems when trying to complete exercises later in the book.

☑ The section heading **EXERCISE X.Y:** (where X equals the chapter number and Y equals the exercise number) represents exercises that have step-by-step instructions that you should complete. You will also see sections that have step-by-step instructions that are not an exercise. Completing them as you go through the book is optional, but recommended.

☑ Many of the dialog boxes in Alpha Five have OK, Cancel and Help buttons on the right side or bottom. Viewing these buttons on all of the screen shots adds no value, so they are not shown in the figures.

☑ As you will see, when you use a space in a file or field name, Alpha Five will replace it with an underscore. For example, "first name" becomes "first_name". The only time that I use the underscore is if you have to type in the field name.

☑ **TOOLS ⇒ FEATURE PACKS ⇒ INSTALL OPTIONAL FEATURE PACKS** means to open the **TOOLS** menu, select the option **FEATURE PACKS**, then select the **INSTALL OPTIONAL FEATURE PACKS** option, as shown in Figure 1-1.

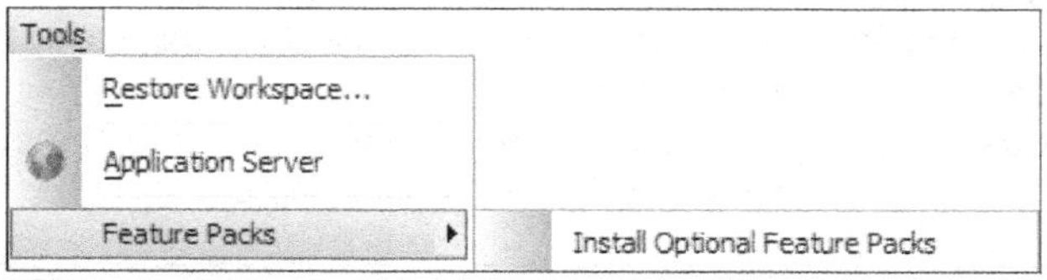

Figure 1-1 Menu navigation technique shown

Assumptions

Yes, I know one should never assume anything, but the following assumptions have been made. It is assumed that you . . . .

☑ Have Alpha Five version 11 or higher installed on your computer. If you are not sure what version of Alpha Five that you have installed, open Alpha Five, then select Help ⇒ About Alpha Five, as illustrated on the dialog box shown in Figure 1-2. You will see the version that is installed.

Figure 1-2 About Alpha Five dialog box

☑ Know that the version of Alpha Five used to write this book is Alpha Five, version 11.

☑ Know that the operating system used to write this book is Windows 7. If you are using a different version of Windows, any or all of the following can apply:

① Some of the screen shots may have a slightly different look.

② Some of the instructions for Windows tasks may be different.

③ The path to folders and files on your computer may be different then the paths listed in this book.

☑ Are familiar with the Windows environment, including Windows Explorer and that you are comfortable using a mouse.

☑ Know that when you see <smile> in this book, it signifies my attempt of adding humor to the learning process.

☑ Understand that the term **OBJECT** refers to the tables, sets, browses, forms and reports that you create, as well as, items like buttons or images that you add to a layout.

☑ Understand that from time to time, I will point out functionality that may not work as expected. When I do this, I am not complaining, merely pointing out things that you should be aware of.

☑ Have access to the Internet to download the practice files needed to complete the exercises in this book and to download any updates to Alpha Five that are available.

☑ Understand that there will be options on dialog boxes that will not be referenced in the step-by-step instructions. When that is the case, accept the default value.

☑ Know that I am not perfect and sadly, you may find minor mistakes in this book. It is not intentional and I apologize for any inconvenience.

☑ Optional: That you have Excel 2010 or higher installed if you want to work on the exercises that are in Chapter 13, Using PowerPivot, the bonus chapter.

Because this software is updated frequently, it is very possible that what you see in the screen shots in this book will be different then what you see on your screen because option names will change, be deleted and new options added.

Getting Help With Alpha Five

As explained below, there are four primary ways to get help if you have a question on how to use a feature or option in Alpha Five.

① Read this book from cover to cover and complete the exercises. Many of the basic questions that you may have are probably covered in this book.
② The Help file. It is helpful for the basic definitions of features. The help file is accessed through the Documentation Viewer.
③ Alpha Five forum. You can post questions and learn how other people are using the software. The forum is also a great way to keep current on the latest Alpha Five trends and for getting ideas on how to enhance the reports that you create. The name of the forum is Alpha Five Version 11 Desktop Applications. If you do not already have a free account, you will have to create one to be able to post and answer questions. The website is http://msgboard.alphasoftware.com/alphaforum/.
④ Hire an Alpha Five consultant. Need I say that this is the most expensive option and you probably will not get an answer to your question as fast as you would like. Never mind the cost <smile>.

How To Check For Software Updates

There are three ways to check for updates when Alpha Five is open, as explained below. The last two options are on the Help menu.

① On the **NEWS & UPDATES TAB** on the Select Workspace dialog box. [See Chapter 2, Select Workspace Dialog Box]
② **CHECK FOR NEW VERSION** This option checks to see if you have the latest build of the software. You will see the message shown in Figure 1-3 if there is a more current version of the software. Click on the Download Patches link. You will see a web page similar to the one shown in Figure 1-4.
③ **DOWNLOAD PATCHES** displays a page similar to the one shown in Figure 1-4. As shown, this page displays the current build number and link to the release notes.

> If you click on the **VIEW RELEASE NOTES LINK** on the Help menu or on the web page shown in Figure 1-4 and scroll down, you will see that the software is updated more frequently then most software. The good news is that the software is maintained. The bad news is that it is possible that some of the Alpha Five interface may look different on your computer then the screen shots in this book.

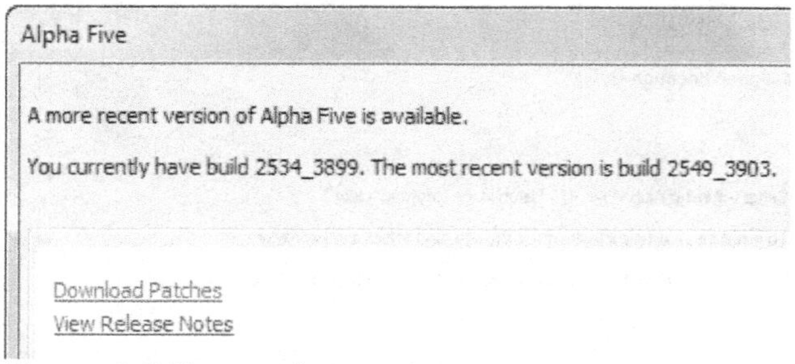
Alpha Five
A more recent version of Alpha Five is available.
You currently have build 2534_3899. The most recent version is build 2549_3903.
Download Patches
View Release Notes

Figure 1-3 New version message

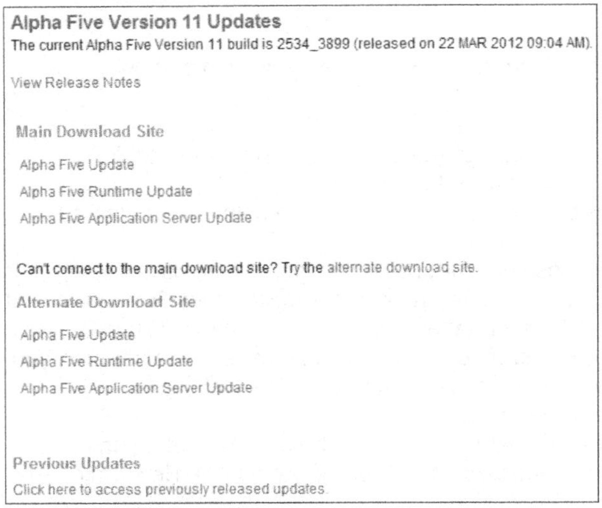
Alpha Five Version 11 Updates
The current Alpha Five Version 11 build is 2534_3899 (released on 22 MAR 2012 09:04 AM).
View Release Notes
Main Download Site
Alpha Five Update
Alpha Five Runtime Update
Alpha Five Application Server Update
Can't connect to the main download site? Try the alternate download site.
Alternate Download Site
Alpha Five Update
Alpha Five Runtime Update
Alpha Five Application Server Update
Previous Updates
Click here to access previously released updates.

Figure 1-4 Download web page

How To Download An Update File

1. On the web page shown above in Figure 1-4, click on the **ALPHA FIVE UPDATE** link.

2. On the File Download dialog box, click the Save button.

3. On the Save As dialog box, navigate to the location where you want to save the file. I recommend saving the file to your desktop, so that it is easy to find. You can move the file after you install it or you can delete it. Once you have selected the location, click the Save button.

4. At a minimum, close Alpha Five. It is recommended that all applications be closed before installing the update.

Install The Update File

1. When the file has finished downloading, double-click on it. If prompted, click the **RUN** button.

2. On the first screen, click Next.

3. On the screen shown in Figure 1-5, the path where Alpha Five is installed should be in the Destination Folder field.

   This is the best place to install the update.

   Click Next.

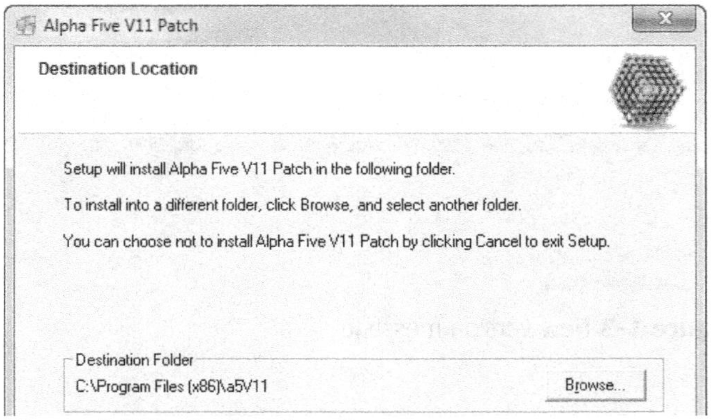
Alpha Five V11 Patch
Destination Location
Setup will install Alpha Five V11 Patch in the following folder.
To install into a different folder, click Browse, and select another folder.
You can choose not to install Alpha Five V11 Patch by clicking Cancel to exit Setup.
Destination Folder
C:\Program Files (x86)\a5V11
Browse...

Figure 1-5 Destination Location screen

4. Click Next on the Start Installation screen unless you need to change the destination location.

   The update will now be installed, as shown in Figure 1-6.

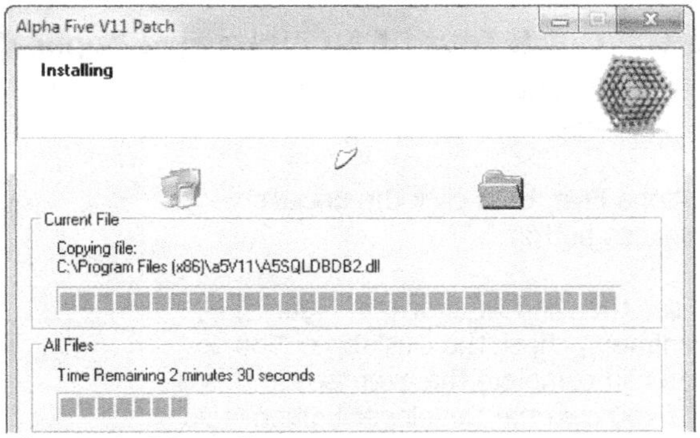

Figure 1-6 Installing screen

5. When the update is finished, the dialog box will display a message saying that patch was successfully installed. Click the Finish button. You can re-open Alpha Five now.

Exercise 1.1: Create A Folder For Your Application And Download The Practice Files

In this book, you will learn how to create several types of objects that would be used in a database application. It is a good idea to store all of the files in the same folder on your computers hard drive so that you can find them easily. I will refer to this folder as "your folder" throughout the book. The instructions below show you how to create the folder at the root of the C drive. If you want to create the folder in another location or under an existing folder, navigate to that location prior to starting step 2.

1. Open Windows Explorer, then click on the C drive.
2. File ⇒ New ⇒ Folder.
3. Type `Alpha 5 Book` as the folder name, then press Enter.
4. The practice files for this book are in a zip file named a5.zip. To have the link for the zip file sent to you, send an email to alpha5@tolanapublishing.com. If you do not receive an email in a few minutes with the subject line Alpha 5 Desktop Application Files, check the spam folder in your email software.
5. When you have the zip file, download it to your folder.

> **Practice Files**
> The practice files are in the zip file. You have to unzip (open and extract) the practice files. If you have the WinZip© software or a similar package installed on your computer, you can go to the next step below. If you do not have WinZip, Windows 7 will let you view a list of the files in the zip file in Windows Explorer. In Windows Explorer, click on the zip file and then drag the files in the zip file to the folder that you created in step 3 above.

6. Open Windows Explorer, then click on the folder that you just created. Right-click on the zip file and select **EXTRACT TO HERE**, as shown in Figure 1-7.

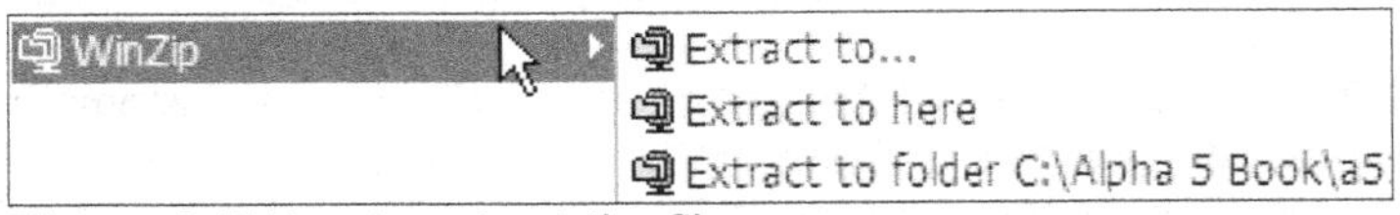

Figure 1-7 How to extract the files

Exercise 1.2: Quick Tour Of An Alpha Five Application

In this exercise you will open the sample database the comes with Alpha Five to get a feel of what Alpha Five is capable of.

1. Open Alpha Five, then click the **RECENT WORKSPACES** button.

   If you see the window shown in Figure 1-8, at a minimum, check the Desktop option so that you can complete the exercises in this book. If you own the Developer Edition, also check the Web option.

   You should now see the options shown in Figure 1-9.

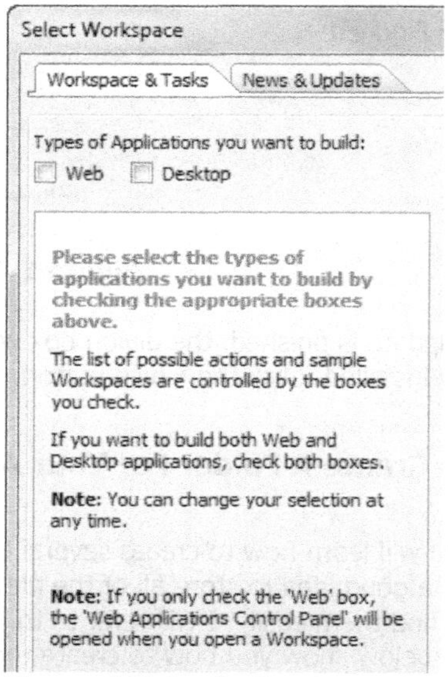

Figure 1-8 Application types

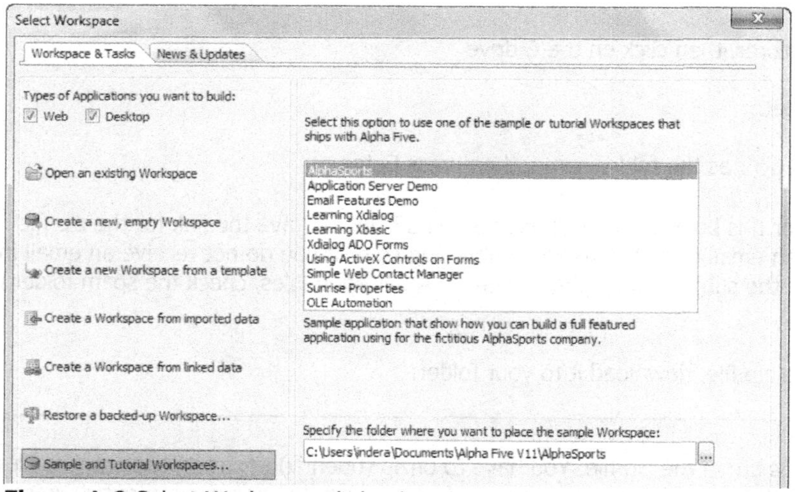

Figure 1-9 Select Workspace dialog box

2. Click on the Sample and Tutorial Workspaces option on the left, then select Alpha Sports on the right, if necessary. Click OK. You will see the application shown in Figure 1-10. This is the first screen that users will see when they open the Alpha Sports application.

Quick Links The links in this section are used to create customer records, edit existing customer records and create new invoices. When you click on one of these links, the associated form opens on a new tab, as shown in Figure 1-11.

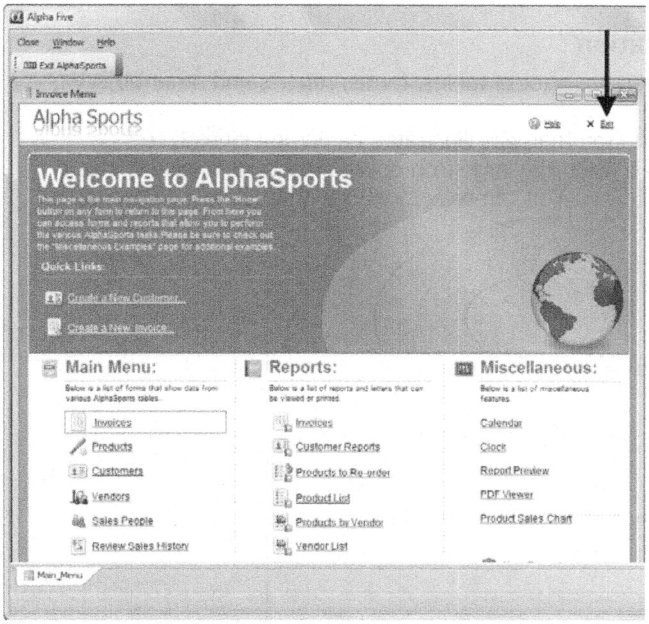

Figure 1-10 Alpha Sports application

Figure 1-11 Form tab in the Window bar

Main Menu The links in this section are used to view data on a form. The difference between these links and the one in the Quick Links section is that these do not open and automatically display a new record. You can add new records from these links.

Reports The links in this section are used to run reports. Most reports have selection criteria to let the person running the report select the records that they want to see. Figure 1-12 shows the selection criteria for an Invoice report. Figure 1-13 shows the selection criteria for a customer report. You can run some of the reports now to see how they work.

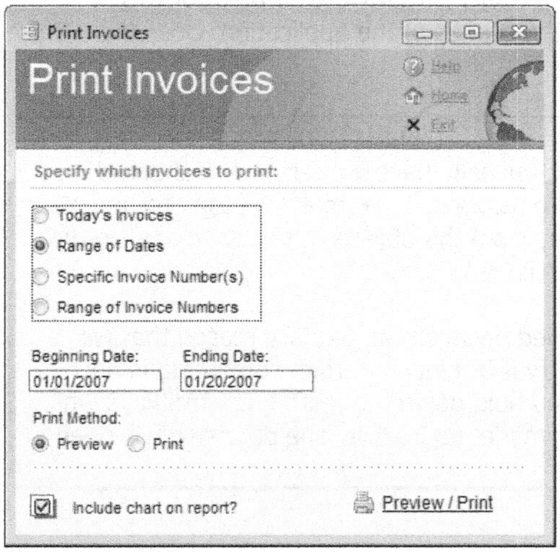

Figure 1-12 Invoice report selection criteria

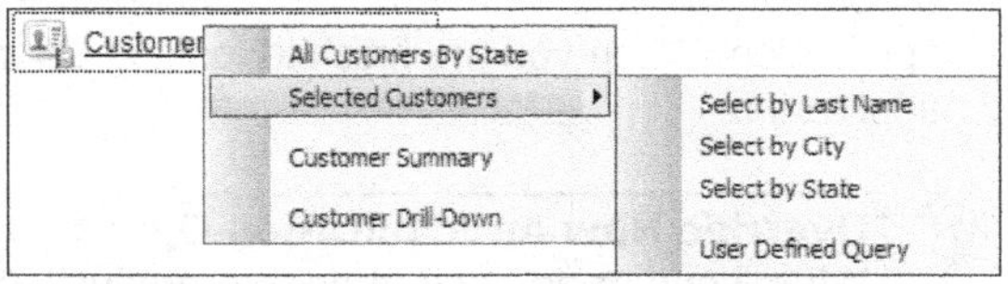

Figure 1-13 Customer report selection criteria

Behind The Scenes Of The Application

As you can imagine, this sample application has a lot of tables, forms, reports and other objects.

1. To view these objects, click the Exit button that was illustrated earlier in Figure 1-10. Figure 1-14 shows the Tables/Sets tab using the large icon option. Figure 1-15 also shows the Tables/Sets tab. This is the Detail view. You can select the view that is most comfortable for you.

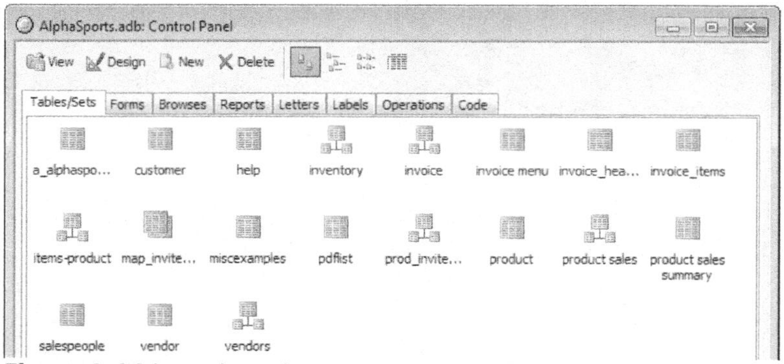

Figure 1-14 Large icon view

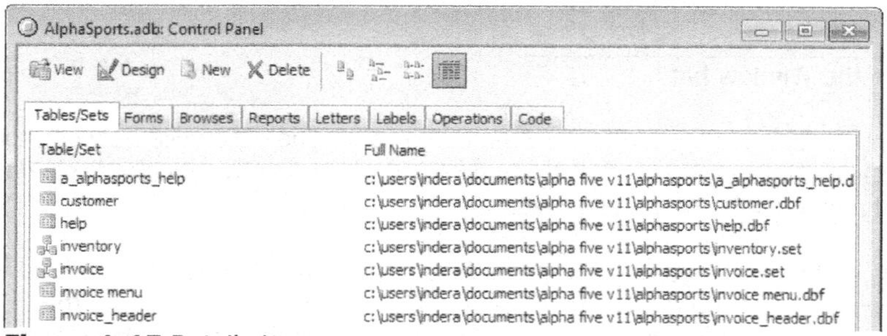

Figure 1-15 Detail view

2. If you click on each of the tabs, you will see all of the objects that were created for this application. When you are finished looking behind the scenes of the application, close the application.

Override How An Application Opens

When you put an application into production, you usually have it open to a dashboard, as shown earlier in Figure 1-10. This is done for two reasons: 1. To make it easier for people to use the application and 2. To keep users away from the objects in the database, so that they cannot delete or mess anything up. Yes, I said it.

For the rest of us, this is annoying and not needed because the primary reason that we open an application is because we need to modify it or heaven forbid, something is not working <smile>. In either case, if you press and hold down the Shift + Control keys while the database is opening, it will not open in user mode, as I call it. The database will open in what is known as **DEBUG MODE**.

Override How An Application Opens (Continued)
If you open the File menu, press the Shift + Control keys, then select a database, you will see the dialog box shown in Figure 1-16, whether or not the database has a startup form.

Yes, I know what you are thinking, "Great, there is nothing stopping users from doing this". Fortunately, you can prevent users from trying to bypass the Startup form. You will learn how in Chapter 2.

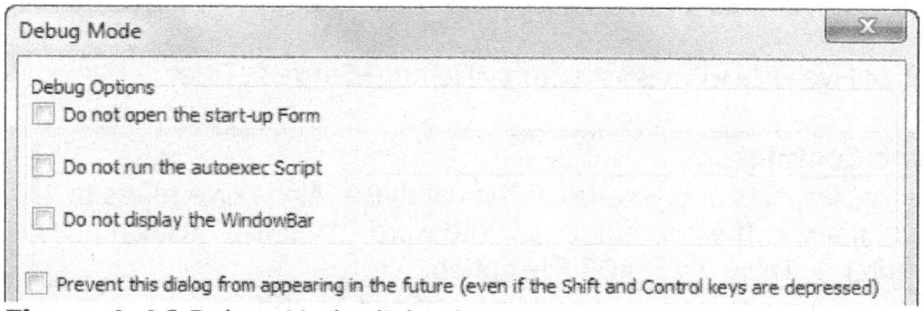

Figure 1-16 Debug Mode dialog box

Having More Than One Database Open At The Same Time
As time goes on, you may have the need to have more than one Alpha Five database open at the same time. To open another database, open another instance of Alpha Five.

Alpha Five Database Limits

While the sample database that you just viewed has a lot of objects, databases created in Alpha Five have some limits, as explained in Table 1-1. Don't boo me! I just wanted to let you know what some of the limits are. Don't worry, they aren't severe. <smile> This link has the full list of limits.
http://wiki.alphasoftware.com/Database+Specifications&structure=Alpha+Five+User+Guide+Title

Feature	Limit
Tables that can be open at the same time	100
Field name length	32 (1)
Character field length	255
Index name length	32 (1)
Layout name length	24
Object name length	63
Saved setting name length	24
Characters in a password	8
Fields per record	1,023
Records per table	2 million
Calculated fields per table	512
Tables in a set	40
Indexes in a table	40
Index key characters	240
Active query lists per table or set	4
Characters in an expression	1,024

Table 1-1 Alpha Five database limits

(1) 10 is recommended.

File Types

When you view a database in Windows Explorer, you will see several file types. File types are denoted by their three digit extension. If you want to view the file types for the Alpha Sports database, open Windows Explorer, then navigate to this path if you have Windows 7.
C:\Users\Your User Name\My Documents\Alpha Five V11\AlphaSports

Personally, I was shocked to see the **.SEX** file extension. Table 1-2 explains some of the file types that I think you would probably have to most need for. You can view the entire list of file types, at the link below.
http://wiki.alphasoftware.com/Alpha+Five+File+Types&structure=Getting+Started+Title

File Type	What The File Type Contains . . .
.adb	The file names of all tables, sets and libraries in the database. Alpha Five refers to this file type as a **WORKSPACE**. If you prefer to see the word "database" instead of workspace, See Chapter 2, Table 2-16, ADB File option.
.alm	Scripts, menus, toolbars, import definitions and user defined functions.
.dbf	A tables data.
.cdx	The tables index(es).
.set	A sets data dictionary, which has a list of forms, report designs and operations that use the set.

Table 1-2 File types explained

EXPLORING THE ALPHA FIVE WORKSPACE

In this chapter you will learn about what I call the "Alpha Five workspace". This includes the options on the menu and toolbar, as well as, options on the Control Panel. You will also learn about the workspace customization options. This workspace is the software window, which is different then Alpha Five referring to a database as a workspace.

CHAPTER 2

Overview

Alpha Five has hundreds, may be thousands of options. Each object type (the tabs on the Control Panel) has its own menu and toolbar options.

For example, the top of Figure 2-1 shows the menu and toolbar when no database is open. These are the menu and toolbar options that all of the objects share.

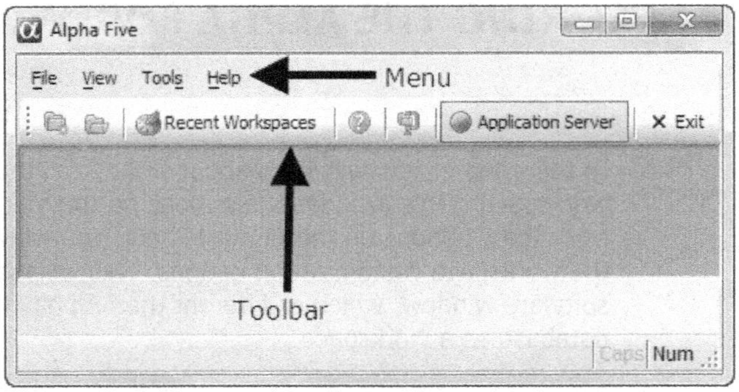

Figure 2-1 Menu and toolbar with no database open

Figure 2-2 shows the menu and toolbar when a form is opened in design mode. The common toolbar options are explained later in Table 2-6.

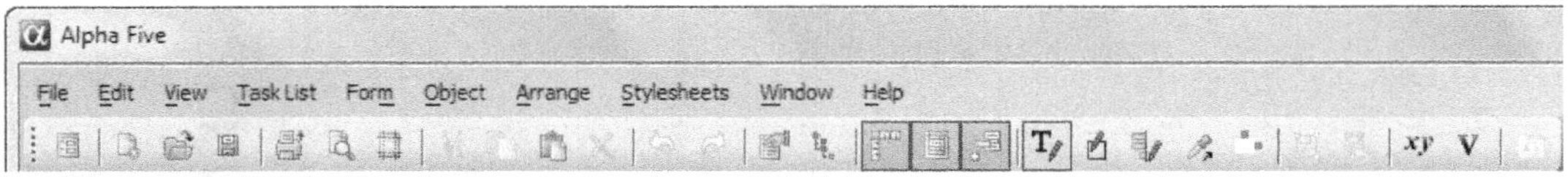

Figure 2-2 Menu and toolbar when a form is open in design view

Select Workspace Dialog Box

As shown earlier in Figure 2-1, when you first open Alpha Five, there is not much going on.

By default, the dialog box shown in Figure 2-3 does not open when Alpha Five is first opened.

There are two options for opening this dialog box, as explained below.

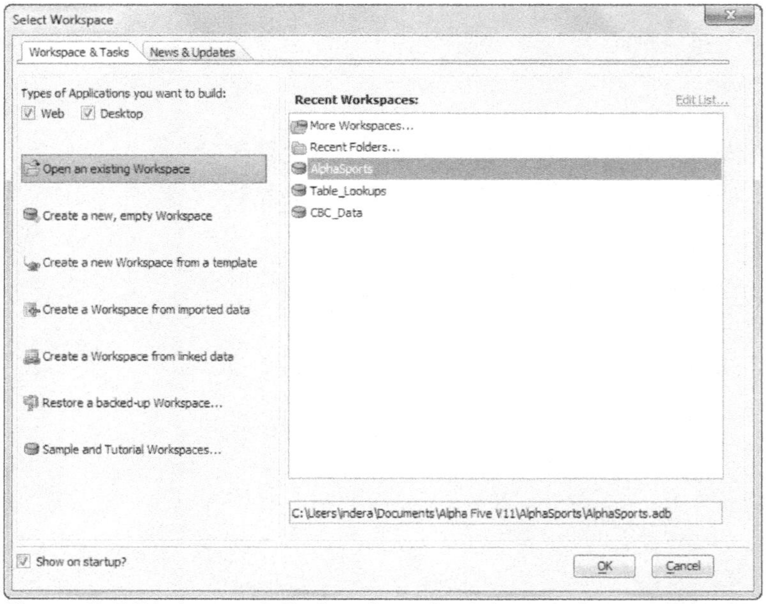

Figure 2-3 Workspace & Tasks tab on the Select Workspace dialog box

① Click the **RECENT WORKSPACES BUTTON** on the toolbar shown earlier in Figure 2-1.

② If you want to have this dialog box automatically open every time that Alpha Five is opened, check the **SHOW ON STARTUP?** option in the lower left corner of Figure 2-3 above.

Workspace & Tasks Tab

The options on this tab are explained below.

The **EDIT LIST LINK** option (below the red X in the upper right corner of the Select Workspace dialog box) opens the dialog box shown in Figure 2-4. This is a list of the databases that you have opened and the order that you have opened them in.

Figure 2-4 Edit Recent Workspace List dialog box

You can add, edit or delete items in this list. You can also change the order of the databases. Changing the order, changes the order that the databases are displayed in the Recent Workspaces list shown earlier in Figure 2-3.

The default number of recently opened databases is eight, which is the same default number of databases that can be displayed at the bottom of the File menu. You can change this default on the Settings dialog box, which you will learn more about later in this chapter. There really is no maximum limit to the number of databases that can be displayed. However, the text file (shown above in Figure 2-4) that the paths to the databases are stored in, has a 2 GB limit.

OPEN AN EXISTING WORKSPACE Is used to open an existing database. The options in the Recent Workspaces section on the right of Figure 2-3 are explained below. The databases that you opened recently are displayed in this section at the bottom of the list.

The **MORE WORKSPACES** option opens the Open Database dialog box so that you can select the database that you want to open. (1)

The **RECENT FOLDERS** option is used to open a folder that has a database that you have already opened. (1)

CREATE A NEW, EMPTY WORKSPACE Select this option when you want to create a new database.

CREATE A NEW WORKSPACE FROM A TEMPLATE Alpha Five comes with the database templates shown in Figure 2-5. Select this option if one of the templates has some of the objects that you need to create a database.

CREATE A WORKSPACE FROM IMPORTED DATA Select this option if there is data in a non Alpha Five data source that you want to import and use as the basis for a new Alpha Five database.

CREATE A WORKSPACE FROM LINKED DATA Select this option when you want to create a new Alpha Five database and link it to data in another data source. This option is different from the import data option because changes made to the data in Alpha Five will also be made in the original data source when the data is linked. For example, if there is data in a spreadsheet, you can link to the spreadsheet, create a form or two in Alpha Five and do the data entry for the spreadsheet in Alpha Five. Another use is to create reports in Alpha Five from data in the linked data source.

(1) Select this option if the database that you want to open is not displayed in the Recent Workspaces list.

RESTORE A BACKED-UP WORKSPACE Is used to bring back a copy of a database that was previously backed up in Alpha Five. There is also an option to select specific files in the database to restore.

SAMPLE AND TUTORIAL WORKSPACES Displays the list of sample databases and tutorials that you have access to, as you saw in the quick tour of an application in Chapter 1.

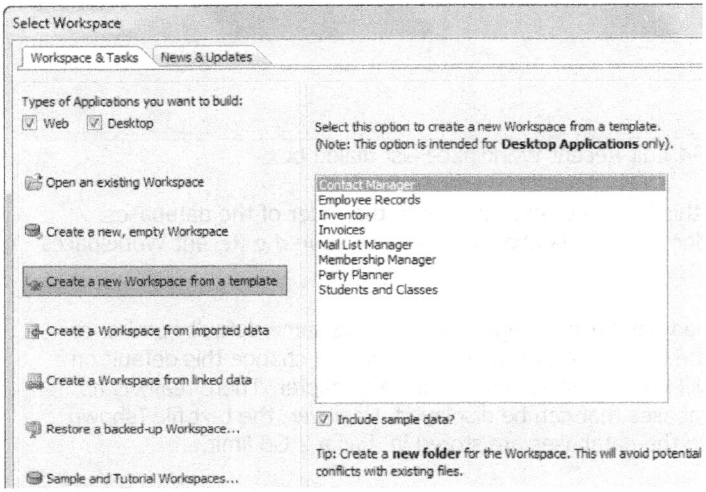

Figure 2-5 Database templates

News & Updates Tab

The options shown in Figure 2-6 let you know whether or not there are software updates that you can install.

You can check the **AUTOMATICALLY CHECK FOR NEWS AND UPDATES OPTION ON STARTUP** option if you want the software to check for updates every time that you open it. Doing this causes Alpha Five to take longer to open.

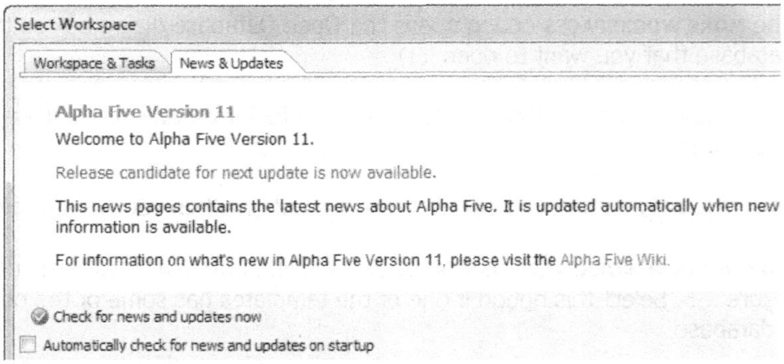

Figure 2-6 News & Updates tab

Alpha Five Common Menu Options

As shown earlier in Figure 2-1, there are four menu options (File, View, Tools and Help). As long as the selected object is not in design mode, all of these menu options are available. The one that is not available in design mode is the Tools menu. Depending on the object selected, additional options will be on these menus. The options on each menu are explained in Tables 2-1 to 2-4.

File Menu

The options on the menu shown in Figure 2-7, are used to open, close, print, import/export data and save databases. The options are explained in Table 2-1.

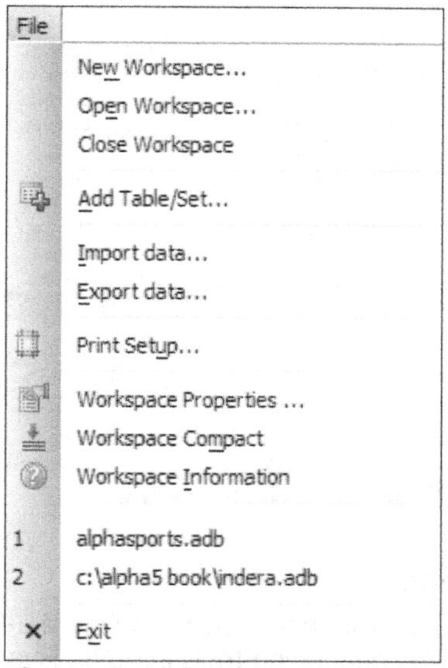

Figure 2-7 File menu

Option	Is Used To . . .
New Workspace	Create a new database.
Open Workspace	Open an existing database.
Close Workspace	Close the database.
Add Table/Set	Add a table or set to the database that is open.
Import Data	Add data from another data source to the database that is open.
Export Data	Copy data from the database that is open to another data source.
Print Setup	Select options for the printer that will be used.
Workspace Properties	Open the Workspace Properties dialog box, which is used to set options for the database.
Workspace Compact	Remove empty space from the database. Space is automatically added to the database when data is added or deleted. Compacting a database makes the file size smaller. Under certain conditions, this can make the database run faster.
Workspace Information	Open the dialog box shown in Figure 2-8. The options are used to view information about the tables, fields and indexes in the database. You can also view records in the table or set by clicking the View Records button.
Exit	Close Alpha Five.

Table 2-1 File menu options explained

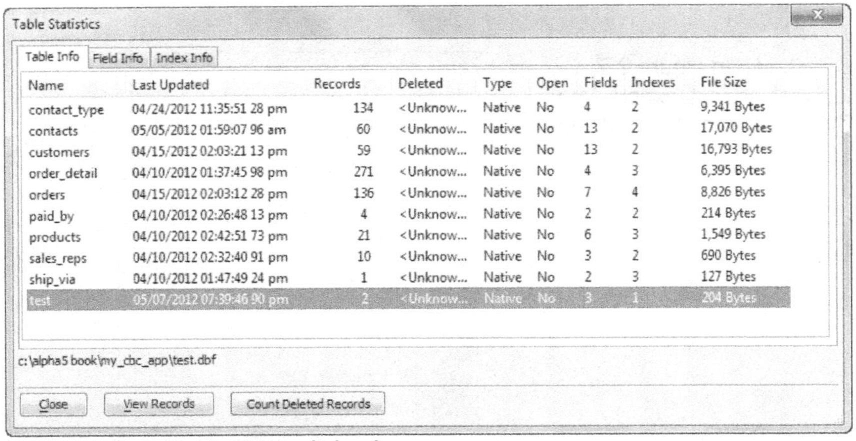

Figure 2-8 Table Statistics dialog box

View Menu

The options on the menu shown in Figure 2-9, are many of the developer and debugging tools in Alpha Five that are used to resolve logic, code and other types of problems. The options are explained in Table 2-2.

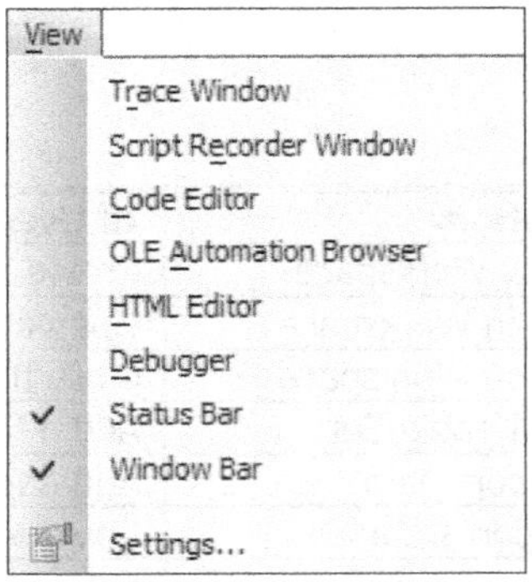

Figure 2-9 View menu

Option	Is Used To . . .
Trace Window	Open the Trace Window, which is used to view errors, monitor events, debugging scripts and more. Messages are sent to this window when an application is running.
Script Recorder Window	Record your actions when you are using Alpha Five and creates the Xbasic code based on the actions that you are doing. Using this option will remind you of creating a macro in Excel.
Code Editor	Open the Code Editor window. This option is used to write or edit code for the object that is selected in the Control Panel.
OLE Automation Browser	Open the OLE Automation Object Browser. The options are used to look at the properties of Active X Controls on your computer.
HTML Editor	Open the HTML Editor. This editor is used to write HTML (**HYPERTEXT MARKUP LANGUAGE**) code, usually for an Xdialog form or web page.
Debugger	Open the **XBASIC DEBUGGER**. This tool is mainly used to view Xbasic code when the code is not working as expected.
Status Bar	Display and hide the panel at the bottom of the workspace.

Table 2-2 View menu options explained

Option	Is Used To . . .
Window Bar	Display and hide the panel above the Status bar. This panel displays a tab for each object that is open. This provides an easy way to navigate between the open objects. Right-clicking on a tab in the Window bar displays the shortcut menu shown in Figure 2-10. [See Chapter 1, Figure 1-11 to view the Window bar]
Settings	Explain the options on the **SETTINGS DIALOG BOX** shown later in Figure 2-56. This dialog box is used to set default options and preferences for features in Alpha Five.

Table 2-2 View menu options explained (Continued)

The options on this menu work the same way that they do in Windows.

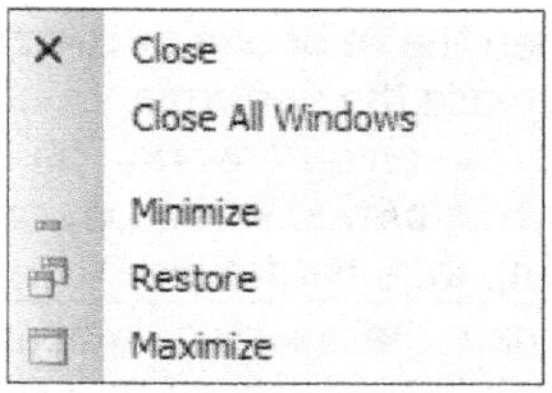

Figure 2-10 Object tab shortcut menu

Tools Menu

The options on the menu shown in Figure 2-11, are used to enhance and maintain the database.

There are also external applications, like Alpha Mailer on the menu, that are used to provide additional functionality for databases. The options are explained in Table 2-3.

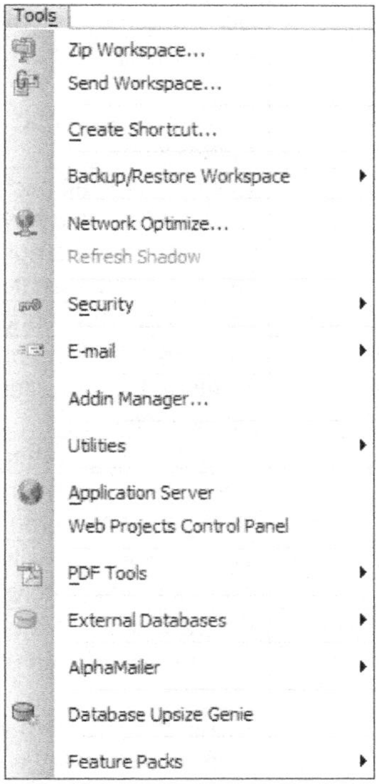

Figure 2-11 Tools menu

Option	Is Used To . . .
Zip Workspace	Create a zip file of all of the objects (tables, forms, etc.) in the current database.
Send Workspace	Create a zip file of the database, which will be sent as an attachment in an email.
Create Shortcut	Open the **CREATE SHORTCUT GENIE**, which is used to create a shortcut to open Alpha Five and a particular database at the same time. This is helpful when you are creating an application because it requires one less step to open the database.
Backup/Restore Workspace	Create a backup copy of a database, restore a database from a backup copy and view the backup log.
Network Optimize	Open the **NETWORK OPTIMIZATION DIALOG BOX**. The options are used to increase the performance of an Alpha Five database if the database is running on a network. The database on the network drive is called the **MASTER DATABASE**. A copy of the database is created and placed on your computers hard drive. This copy is called the **SHADOW DATABASE**.
Refresh Shadow	Update the selected database if it is a Shadow database. This is necessary when the database is stored on a server and you have a copy of the database (the Shadow database) on your computers hard drive.
Security	Create, change and remove passwords from a database, as well as, set up users and groups for the database.
E-mail	Send and read e-mail.
Addin Manager	Open the Addin Manager dialog box to view the addins that are installed or disabled. Installed addins have a check mark. An addin is a library of functions and scripts. Global functions and scripts are stored in a **.ALB LIBRARY FILE**.
Utilities	Create an install package for the database that you created. This feature only works if you have the **RUN-TIME EDITION** of Alpha Five installed. You can also limit the number of users for a run-time application by selecting the **THROTTLE RUNTIME USER COUNT** option on the submenu.
Application Server	Start, stop and configure the application server.
Web Projects Control Panel	Displays the Web Projects Control Panel if you have the **DEVELOPER EDITION** of Alpha Five installed. This control panel is used to create web based applications.
PDF Tools	Create PDF files, merge files, **EXPORT DATA TO RTF**, **HTML** and **TEXT FORMATS**.
External Databases	Select connection strings, open the Database Explorer, use connection strings and open the **SQL QUERY GENIE**.
Alpha Mailer	Open the Alpha Mailer software program. This program is used to send emails in bulk. There is a trial version that you can use to see if you like it.
Database Upsize Genie	Convert Alpha Five tables to an SQL database. The original database is left un-touched. Once converted, **ACTIVE-LINK TABLES** are automatically created.
Feature Packs	Install the feature packs that come with version 11 (This is all feature packs from Alpha Five version 10, which are now included for free.) or feature packs that you purchase. Feature packs add functionality to Alpha Five.

Table 2-3 Tools menu options explained

Help Menu

The options on the menu shown in Figure 2-12 provide assistance in using Alpha Five. The options are explained in Table 2-4.

Many of the options on this menu require Internet access to use.

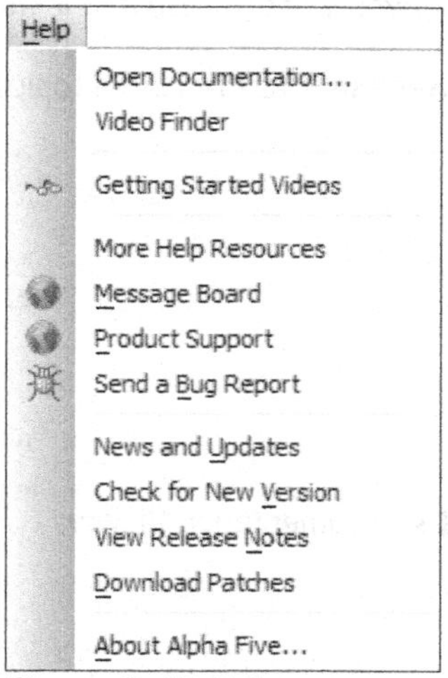

Figure 2-12 Help menu

Option	Description
Open Documentation	Opens the dialog box shown in Figure 2-13. This tool is used to search the help file.
Video Finder	Opens the Video Finder dialog box, which is used to view a list of the videos that have been created to help you learn Alpha Five. You can also watch the videos from this dialog box.
Getting Started Videos	Displays the web page that has links to the Getting Started Videos for Alpha Five.
More Help Resources	Displays the home page of the online help file. This is the online version of the documentation.
Message Board	Displays the home page for the **ALPHA FIVE FORUMS**.
Product Support	Displays the web page that lists all of the support options for Alpha Five.
Send a Bug Report	Opens the Sending a Bug Report dialog box, which lets you submit information to Alpha Software when you find something that may not be working properly in the software.
News and Updates	Opens the News & Updates tab on the Select Workspace dialog box.
Check for New Version	Opens the dialog box shown earlier in Chapter 1, Figure 1-3, if there is a new version of the software. Otherwise, you will see a notice message letting you know that you have to most current version.
View Release Notes	Displays the Release Notes web page.
Download Patches	Displays the web page for downloading updates to the software.
About Alpha Five	Opens the About Alpha Five window. [See Chapter 1, Figure 1-2]

Table 2-4 Help menu options explained

Using The Documentation Viewer

The help file is displayed in the documentation viewer shown in Figure 2-13. The viewer can be used without being connected to the Internet.

The **TOPIC LIST TAB** contains the help topics in the documentation. You can scroll down the list or type in the topic that you want to read about.

The **TABLE OF CONTENTS TAB** has the topics grouped by subject, as shown in Figure 2-14. Click on the topic that you want to read and it will be displayed on the right on a new tab.

The **FAVORITES TAB** is used to store topics that you want to view again.

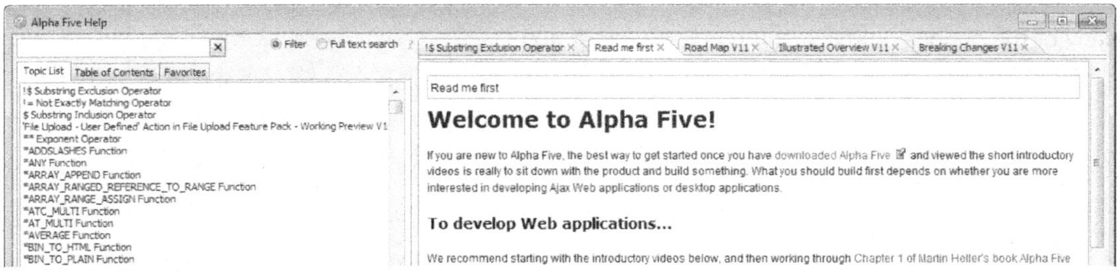

Figure 2-13 Documentation Viewer

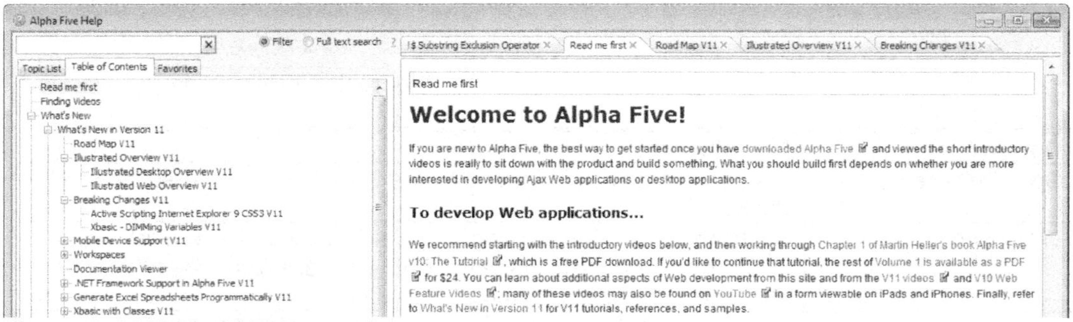

Figure 2-14 Table Of Contents tab

> If you use the viewer without being connected to the Internet, you will not be able to view the screenshots or watch the videos that have a link in the documentation.

How To Search The Documentation

In addition to being able to type in the topic that you want to read about, you can use the **FILTER** option, which is used to search in real time, as you type in the topic.

The **FULL TEXT SEARCH** option searches the body of the topics to retrieve all of the matches. After you type in the topic, click the Go button.

Documentation Viewer Toolbar

The toolbar shown in Figure 2-15 provides additional functionality for the documentation viewer. The options are explained in Table 2-5.

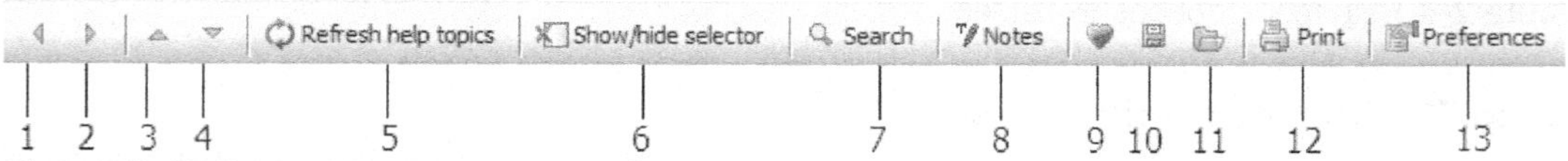

Figure 2-15 Documentation Viewer toolbar

Button	Description
1	Displays the previous topic that you viewed.
2	Displays the next topic that you viewed.
3	Displays the topic before the one currently displayed on the tab. (2)
4	Displays the next topic after the one currently displayed on the tab. (2)
5	Updates the copy of the help file that is on your computers hard drive. You will see the message shown in Figure 2-16. It lets you know how many existing topics were updated, the number of new topics added and how many topics were deleted.
6	Displays or hides the left side of the viewer.
7	Opens the dialog box shown in Figure 2-17. The options are used to create multiple search criteria. This will be helpful if you want to search for two or more topics at the same time.
8	Displays the options shown in Figure 2-18. The options are used to add or edit notes for the selected topic, create your own help topic and manage the notes for the selected topic. To add notes, you have to set up a table, which you will learn how to do later in this chapter.
9	Adds the topic displayed on the right side of the viewer to your Favorites list.
10	Opens the dialog box shown in Figure 2-19. This feature is used to save all off the topics that are displayed on tabs at one time, so that they can be retrieved. Type in a name for the list, then click OK.
11	Opens the dialog box shown in Figure 2-20. The lists that you created are on the left and the topics in the list are displayed on the right.
12	Prints the topic that is displayed.
13	[See Documentation Viewer Preferences, later in this chapter]

Table 2-5 Documentation Viewer toolbar buttons explained

(2) This is based on entries on the Table of Contents tab.

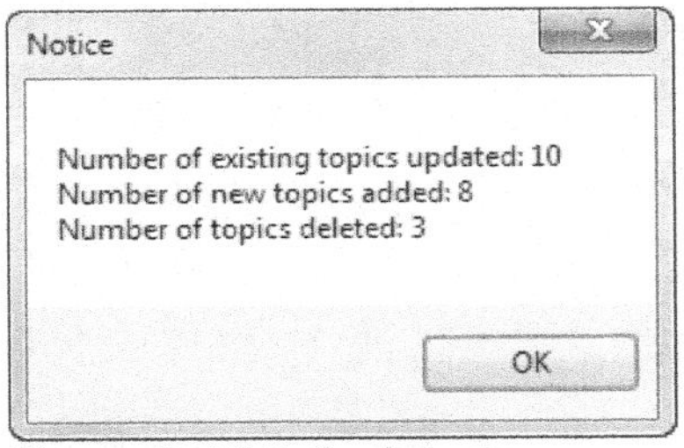

Figure 2-16 Refresh topics message

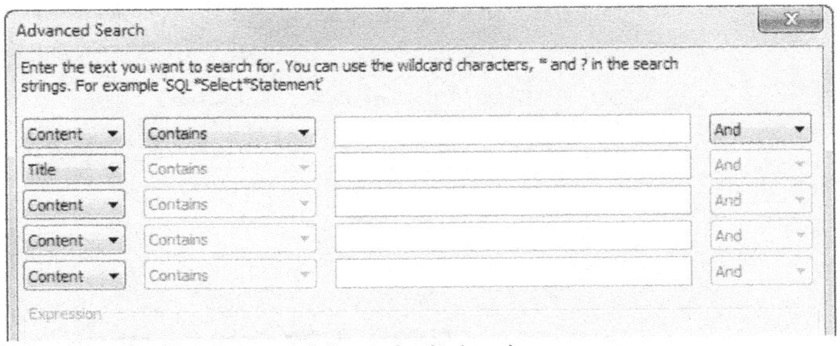

Figure 2-17 Advanced Search dialog box

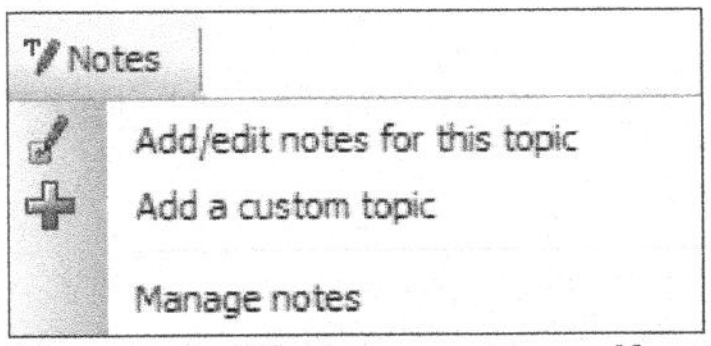

Figure 2-18 Notes options (for topics)

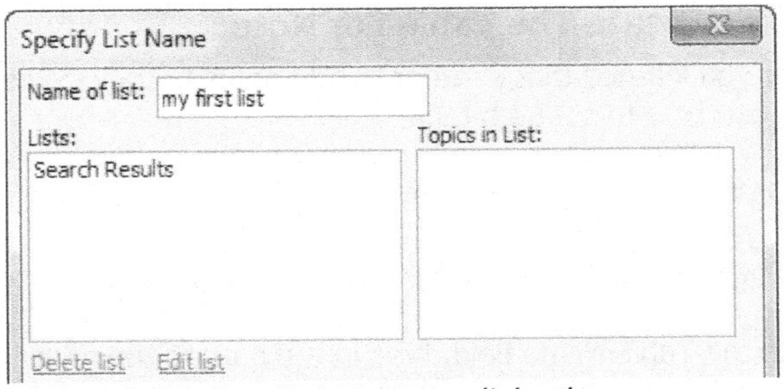

Figure 2-19 Specify List Name dialog box

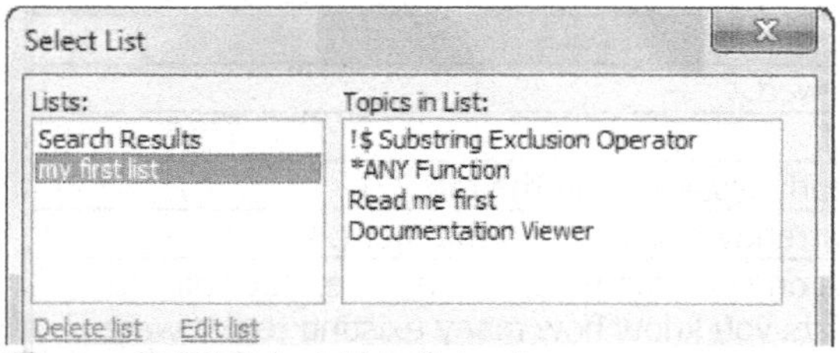

Figure 2-20 Select List dialog box

Documentation Viewer Shortcut Menu

The shortcut menu shown in Figure 2-21 allows access to options that you may use the most.

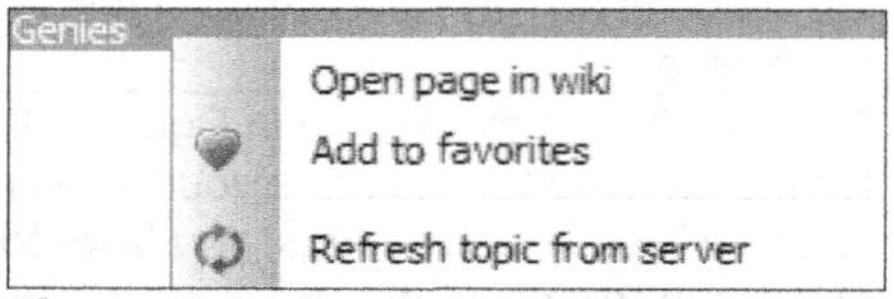

Figure 2-21 Documentation viewer shortcut menu

The **OPEN PAGE IN WIKI** option displays the web page for the selected topic in your web browser if the computer is connected to the Internet.

The other two options on the shortcut menu were explained earlier in Table 2-5, Buttons 5 and 9.

Documentation Viewer Preferences

The options shown in Figure 2-22 are used to configure the Documentation Viewer.

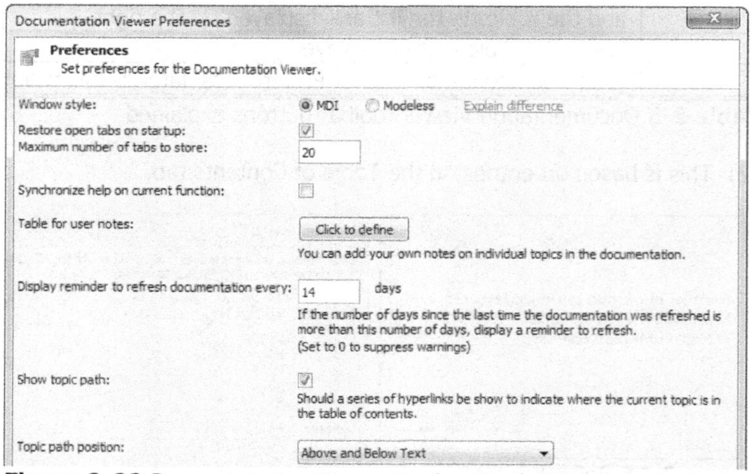

Figure 2-22 Documentation Viewer Preferences dialog box

How To Create The Table For Notes

Earlier you learned that in order to add notes to topics, you have to set up a table. The steps below show you how to set up a table.

1. On the Documentation Viewer Preferences dialog box, click the **CLICK TO DEFINE BUTTON**.

2. Open the Table type drop-down list and select the type of table that you want to create.

3. In the Table Name field, type in the path to the folder where you want the table created, then type the name that you want to use for the Notes table, similar to what is shown in Figure 2-23.

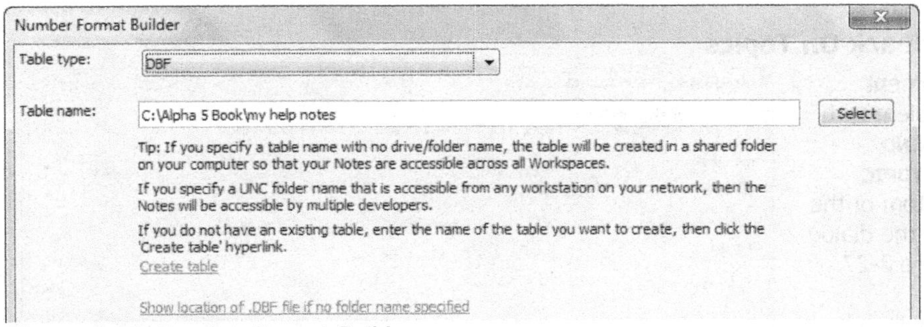

Figure 2-23 Number Format Builder

4. Click the **CREATE TABLE** link to create the table.

How To Add A Note To A Topic

The steps below show you how to add a note to a topic.

1. Scroll to the bottom of the topic that you want to add a note to, then click the **ADD NOTE BUTTON**.

2. On the dialog box shown in Figure 2-24, select the Note type, then type in your note.

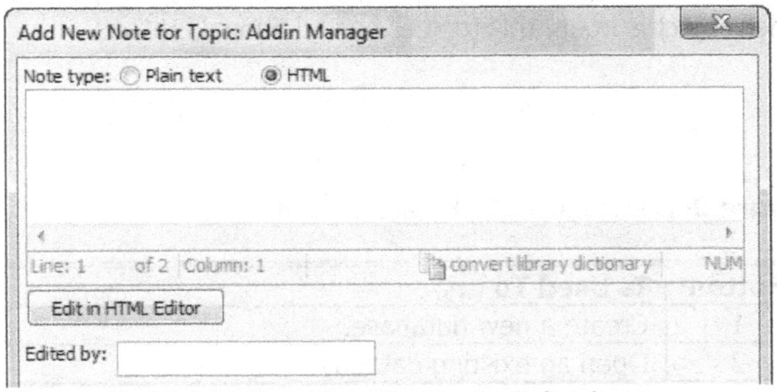

Figure 2-24 Add New Note for Topic dialog box

3. Click OK. At the top of the help topic in the right corner, you will see a link for **USER NOTES**.

   If you click on this link, at the bottom of the topic, you will see your note, as illustrated in Figure 2-25.

Figure 2-25 User notes on a help topic

Managing Notes

The dialog box shown in Figure 2-26 is used to edit and delete notes.

Notes button on the toolbar ⇒ Manage Notes, opens this dialog box.

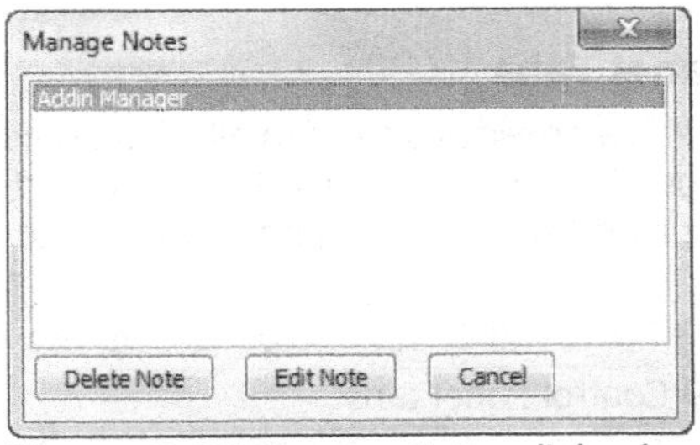

Figure 2-26 Manage Notes dialog box

Providing Feedback On Topics

If you have a comment, suggestion or problem with a topic, click the **SEND FEEDBACK ON THIS TOPIC BUTTON** at the bottom of the topic. You will see the dialog box shown in Figure 2-27.

Use this dialog box to submit your feedback.

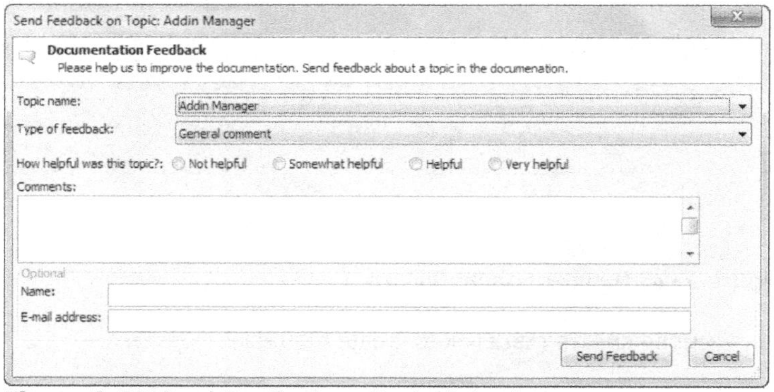

Figure 2-27 Send Feedback on Topic dialog box

Common Workspace Toolbar

Figure 2-28 shows the toolbar that is available when the Control Panel is open. Compare this to the toolbar shown earlier in Figure 2-1. The buttons are explained in Table 2-6. When a table, form or other object is open, this toolbar has additional buttons.

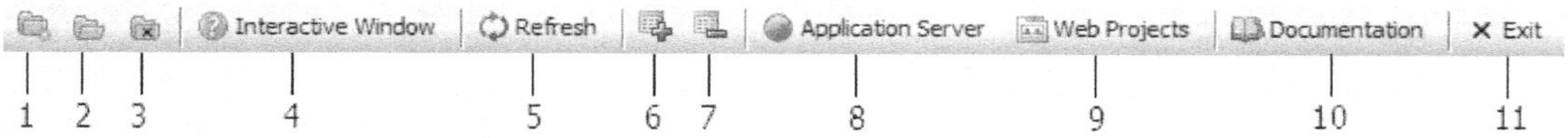

Figure 2-28 Common workspace toolbar

Button	Is Used To . . .
1	Create a new database.
2	Open an existing database.
3	Close the current database.
4	Open the Code Editor window.
5	Refresh the Control Panel.
6	Add tables or sets to the database.
7	Remove the selected table or set from the database.
8	Start and stop the application server.
9	Open the Web Projects Control Panel. This button does not work if you have the Desktop Application Developer Edition of Alpha Five installed.
10	Opens the Documentation viewer.
11	Close Alpha Five.

Table 2-6 Common workspace toolbar buttons explained

Control Panel Tabs

The Control Panel provides access to all of the objects in the database. The tabs shown in Figure 2-29 provide easy access to all of the objects that you create for the database. Table 2-7 explains the type of object that is stored on each tab.

Figure 2-29 Control Panel tabs

Tab	The Tab Contains . . .
Tables/Sets	Tables and sets in the database and tables or sets that are linked to.
Forms	Data entry forms, which are used to view, add and edit data in the database.
Browses	Data entry forms, which are used to view, add and edit data in the database. A Browse looks like a spreadsheet.
Reports	Layouts that are used to print or display data in a meaningful way.
Letters	Layouts that are used to print letters, that are often mailed.
Labels	Layouts that are used to print labels. This layout type can also be used to print envelopes.
Operations	Mini programs if you will, that provide more functionality to the tables, sets, forms browses, reports and letters that you create. This functionality includes importing and exporting data, modifying data and querying records. This is done by selecting options on a genie or dialog box that is specific for the type of operation that you want to create.
Code	A series of actions that you create that will be used to modify or customize the data.

Table 2-7 Control Panel tabs explained

Displaying Tabs
If you do not see all of the tabs shown above in Figure 2-29, right-click on any tab. On the shortcut menu shown in Figure 2-30, clear the check mark next to the Layouts option.

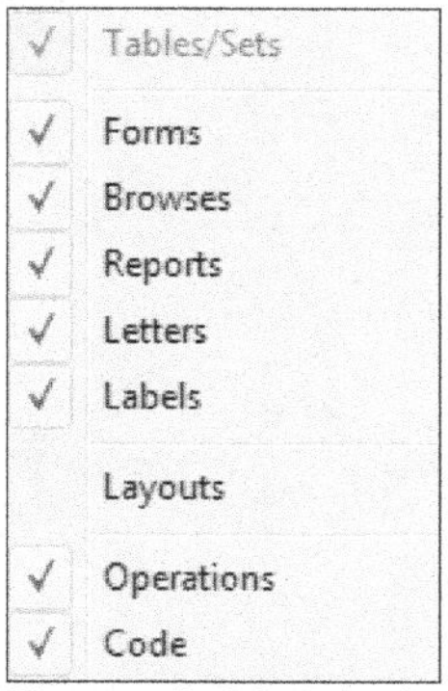

Figure 2-30 Tab shortcut menu

Control Panel Toolbar

In addition to the toolbar shown in Figure 2-31, the files on each tab have a shortcut menu that has options specific for the object type. Some object types cause the toolbar shown in Figure 2-31 to change.

Table 2-8 explains the buttons on the Control Panel toolbar.

These options are available when any of the following tabs are selected: Table/Sets, Forms or Browses.

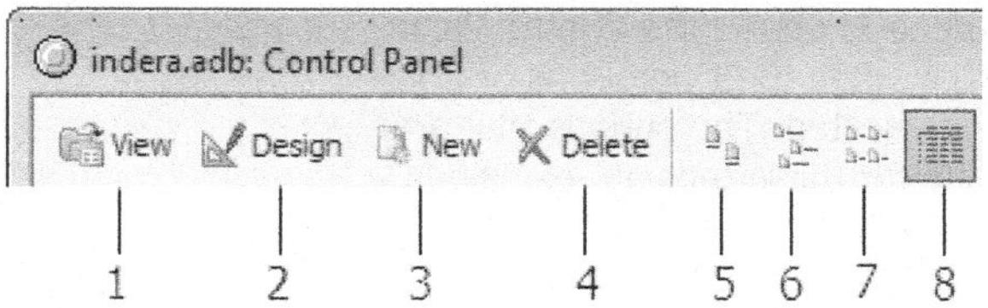

Figure 2-31 Control Panel toolbar

Button	Is Used To . . .
1	View the selected object. (3)
2	Open the object in design mode so that it can be edited.
3	Create a new object.
4	Delete the selected object.
5	Display the objects on the tab with large icons. (4)
6	Display the objects on the tab with small icons. (4)
7	Display the objects on the tab in a list view. (4)
8	Display the objects on the tab in a detail view. (4)

Table 2-8 Control Panel toolbar buttons explained

(3) On the Table/Sets tab, this button is used to view the table or set in a variety of ways, as shown in Figure 2-32. The **DEFAULT BROWSE** and **DEFAULT FORM** options are available for all tables and sets. They are created automatically. They are helpful when you want to quickly view the data as it appears in the table, with any field rules that have been applied. The options after the two default options appear, based on whether or not the table or set was used as the basis for another object. In this example, the selected table or set was used to create forms, reports and labels. You can select any of these options on this menu to view the data.
(4) This is the same functionality that is in Windows Explorer.

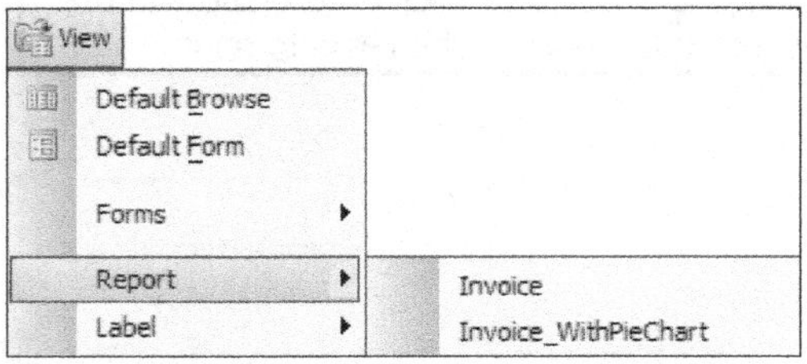

Figure 2-32 View button options for tables and sets

Figure 2-33 shows the Control Panel toolbar when the Reports, Letters or Labels tab is selected. The options that are unique for these tabs are explained in Table 2-9.

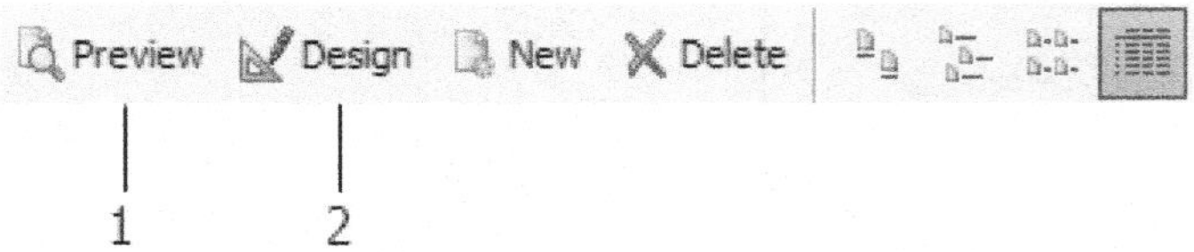

Figure 2-33 Control Panel toolbar for Reports, Letters and Labels

Button	Is Used To . . .
1	Preview the file or open the Print Genie.
2	Open the object in design view.

Table 2-9 Control Panel toolbar buttons for Reports, Letters and Labels explained

Figure 2-34 shows the Control Panel toolbar when the Operations or Code tab is selected. The options that are unique for these tabs are explained in Table 2-10.

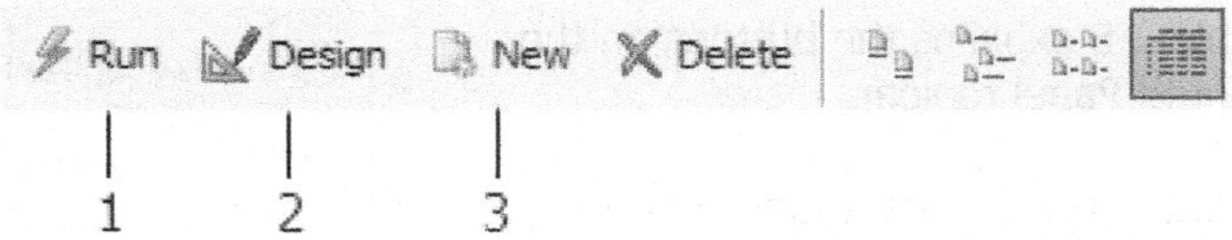

Figure 2-34 Control Panel toolbar for Operations and Code

Button	Is Used To . . .
1	Run the operation.
2	Modify the operation.
3	Create a new operation.

Table 2-10 Control Panel toolbar buttons for Operations and Code tabs explained

Control Panel Menu

The objects on each tab in the Control Panel have a shortcut menu. The options that are specific to the tab are explained in the tables below. Each tab also has at least two menus. One menu is displayed when no objects on the tab selected. When an object on the tab is selected, a different menu appears.

For example, if the Forms tab is selected without a form being selected, the menu shown in Figure 2-35 is displayed. Notice that it has the Layout menu. If a form is selected, the menu shown has the Form menu shown in Figure 2-36. Compare the menus shown in Figures 2-35 and 2-36 to the menu shown earlier in Figure 2-1.

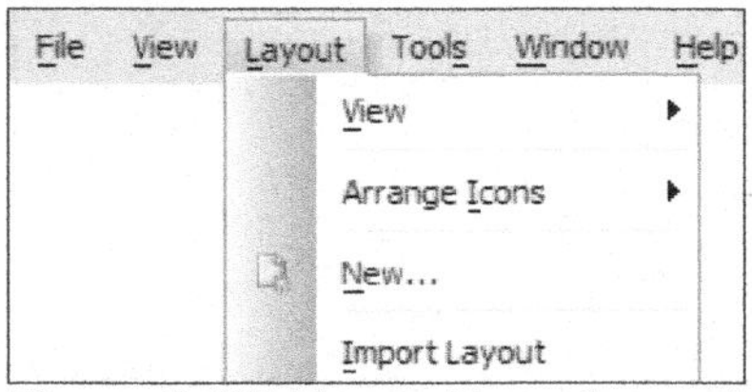

Figure 2-35 Menu with no form selected on the Forms tab

Figure 2-36 Menu with form selected on the Forms tab

Control Panel Shortcut Menus

Keep in mind that the shortcut menus shown in this section are only available when you right-click on an object on the tab. If you right-click on a blank space on the tab, you will see a different shortcut menu. If you click on an object and open the corresponding menu option, you will see the same options that are on the shortcut menu.

Tables/Sets Shortcut Menu

The options shown in Figure 2-37 are available when you right-click on an object on the Tables/Sets tab. The options are explained in Table 2-11.

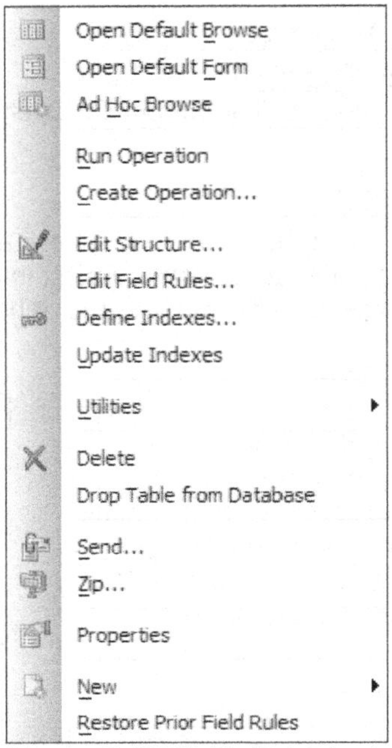

Figure 2-37 Table/Sets shortcut menu

Option	Description
Open Default Browse	Displays the data in the table or set in a generic browse.
Open Default Form	Displays the data in the table or set in a generic form.
Ad Hoc Browse	Opens the **AD-HOC DIALOG BOX**, which is used to create a browse or form layout. You can select the fields, the order that the fields appear in and create a filter for the records that will be displayed. Layouts created using this option can be saved.
Run Operation	Opens the **RUN OPERATION GENIE**, which is used to select the operation(s) that you want to run for the selected table or set. For any table or set in the database, select the **SHOW OPERATIONS FOR ALL TABLES/SETS** option, then click on the operation type that you want to run.
Create Operation	Opens the dialog box shown in Figure 2-38, which is used to create an operation manually or with the genie.
Edit Structure/Edit Set	Opens the **RESTRUCTURE TABLE WINDOW** for tables or the **SET EDITOR DIALOG BOX** for sets. These dialog boxes are used to change some aspect of the fields in the table or set.
Edit Field Rules	Opens the **FIELD RULES DIALOG BOX**.
Define Indexes	Opens the **INDEX BUILDER**, which is used to create, edit or rebuild indexes for the table or set.
Update Indexes	Automatically updates the indexes in the table or set. Use this option after you have added or modified indexes in the database. This will help the database run faster.

Table 2-11 Tables/Sets shortcut menu options explained

Option	Description
Utilities	Displays the submenu shown in Figure 2-39 for tables or the submenu shown in Figure 2-40 for sets. The options on these submenus provide additional options to maintain the table or set.
Delete	Deletes the selected table or set.
Drop Table from Database/ Drop Set From Database	Is used to remove the selected table or set from the database.
Send	Opens the **SEND TABLE DIALOG BOX** or the **SEND SET DIALOG BOX**. These dialog boxes are used to send the table or set via email. A zip file containing the table or set can also be created from these dialog boxes to be sent via email.
Zip	Opens the **ZIP TABLE DIALOG BOX** or the **ZIP SET DIALOG BOX**. These dialog boxes are used to create a zip file that contains the table or set.
Properties	Opens the **TABLE INFORMATION DIALOG BOX**, which displays information for the selected table or the **SET INFORMATION DIALOG BOX**, which displays information for all of the tables in the set. These dialog boxes display field, index and statistic information.
New	Is used to create a new table or set.
Restore Prior Field Rules	This option is only available if you created a field rule and then changed the structure of the field, like changing the name of the field. Selecting this option opens the dialog box shown in Figure 2-41. The options on this dialog box are used to restore the field rules for the selected table from a backup file. Doing this is optional. This process is similar to restoring a database.

Table 2-11 Tables/Sets shortcut menu options explained (Continued)

The **MORE OPTION?**, if checked, displays all of the operation types. Clearing this option only displays the most used operations.

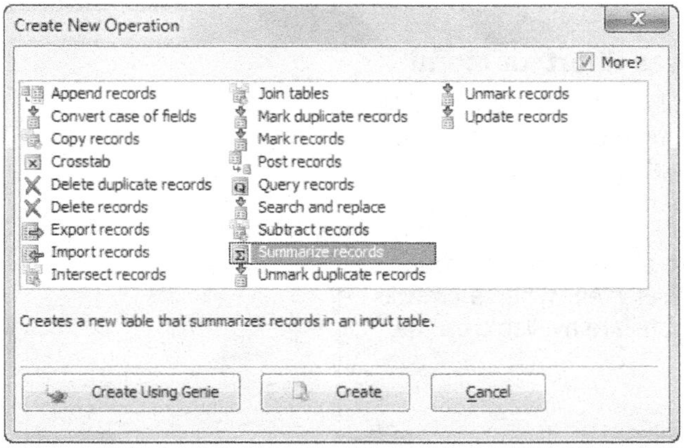

Figure 2-38 Create New Operation dialog box (Tables/Sets shortcut menu)

Figure 2-39 Utilities submenu options for tables

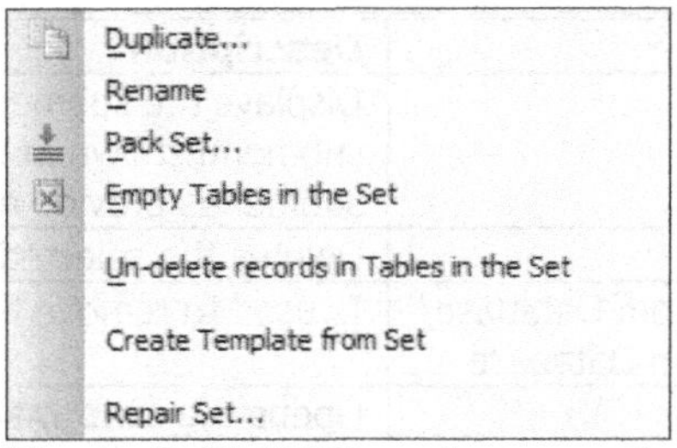

Figure 2-40 Utilities submenu options for sets

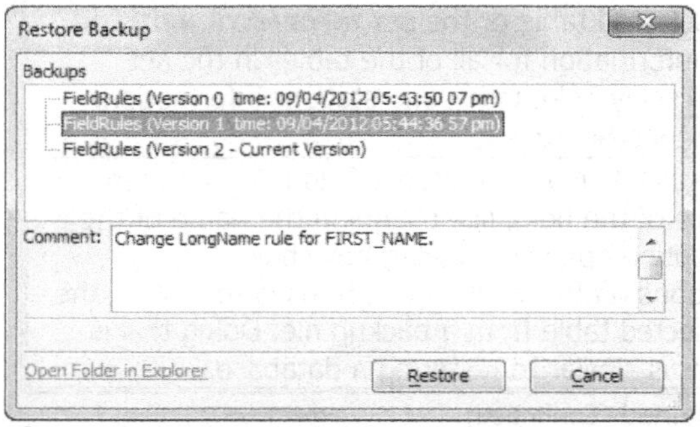

Figure 2-41 Restore Backup dialog box (for field rules)

Forms And Browses Shortcut Menu

The options shown in Figure 2-42 are available when you right-click on an object on the Forms or Browses tab. The options are explained in Table 2-12.

These options are also available on the Form menu when a form is selected. When a browse is selected, these options are available on the Browse menu.

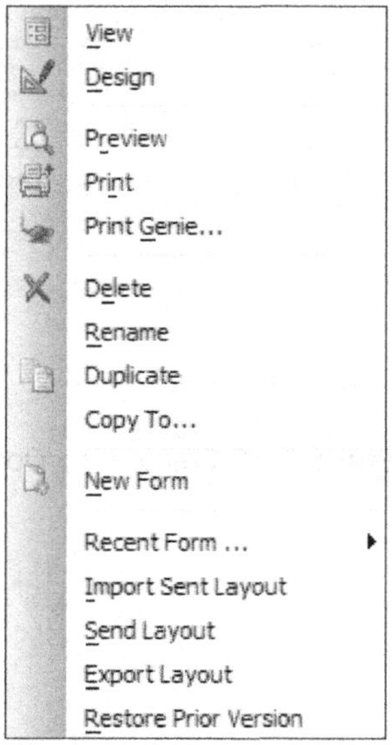

Figure 2-42 Forms and Browses shortcut menu

Option	Description
View	Displays the data from the table or set as it will appear on the form or browse that you created.
Design	Opens the form or browse so that it can be modified.
Preview	Displays the form or browse in the window shown in Figure 2-43. Select this option when you want to print the form or browse.
Print	Opens the **PRINT DIALOG BOX** to select the print options for the object that was selected before opening this dialog box.
Print Genie	Opens the **PRINT GENIE**, which is used to select the Print Method (print, preview, e-mail, save to file or fax). A filter can also be selected to limit the number of records that will be printed. The majority of options on this dialog box are the same as the ones on the Select Filter dialog box. [See Chapter 12, Select Filter Dialog Box]
Copy To	Opens the **COPY LAYOUT TO DIALOG BOX**, which is used to select a table or set (that has the same field names as the current table or set) that the selected layout will be copied to. The table and set can be in the current database or in another database.
New Form/Browse	Opens the **NEW FORM DIALOG BOX** or **NEW BROWSE DIALOG BOX**, so that a new form or browse can be created.
Recent Form/Browse	Is used to open an existing form or browse in design mode.
Import Sent Layout	Is used to import a layout package into the database that is currently open.
Send Layout	Is used to create a **PACKAGE FILE** that contains the selected layout. This allows the layout to be emailed to another person, so they can view the layout. (5)
Export Layout	Is used to export (save a copy) the selected layout to a package file. (5)
Restore Prior Version	This option is only available once you have created a form. It opens the **RESTORE BACKUP DIALOG BOX**. The options are used to restore a previous version of the form. Some of the backup copies of the form display comments, which will tell you what changes were made.

Table 2-12 Forms and Browses shortcut menu options explained

(5) Once this package file has been imported into a database, the layout can be viewed. The file extension for package files is **(.A5PKG)**.

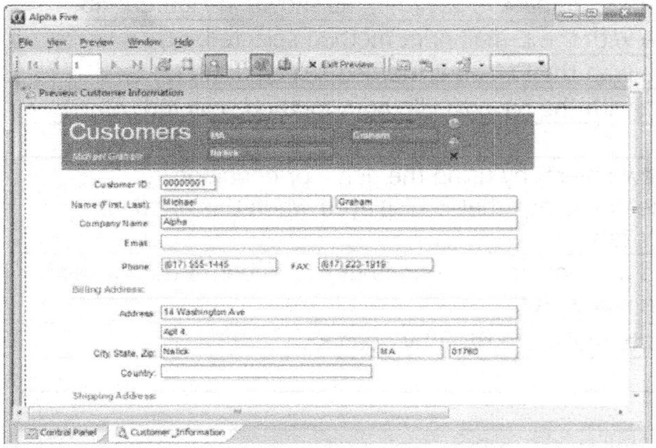

Figure 2-43 Preview window

Reports, Letters And Labels Shortcut Menu

The options shown in Figure 2-44 are available when you right-click on an object on the reports, letters or labels tab. The options are explained in Table 2-13.

These options are also available on the Reports, Letters and Labels tabs on the Control Panel menu with the same name, when an object on the tab is selected.

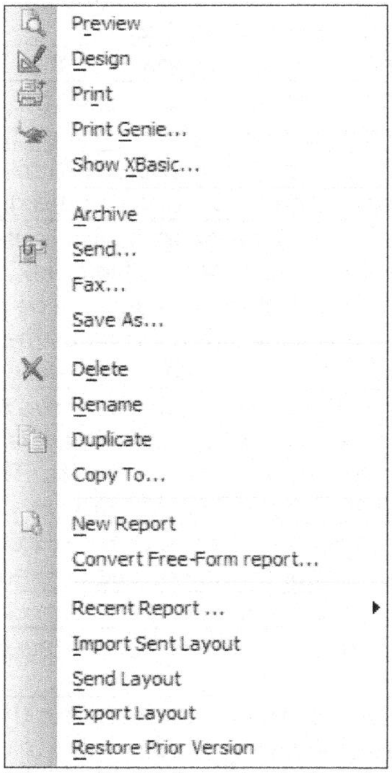

Figure 2-44 Reports, Letters and Labels shortcut menu

Option	Description
Preview	Displays the report, letter or label.
Design	[See Table 2-12]
Print	[See Table 2-12]
Print Genie	[See Table 2-12]
Show XBasic	Displays the Xbasic code for the reports print, preview, save as and send features shown in Figure 2-45. (6)
Archive	Automatically saves the report in PDF format in a folder named Archive under the folder that the database is saved in, as shown in Figure 2-46.
Send	Opens the Print Genie with the E-mail print method selected. (7)
Fax	Opens the Print Genie with the Fax print method selected. (6) (7)
Save As	Opens the Print Genie with the Save to File print method selected. (7)
Copy To	[See Table 2-12]
New <Object>	Is used to create a new object, by using the genie or definition. Figure 2-47 shows the dialog box that is displayed when this option is selected on the Labels tab.
Convert Free-Form report	I could not find any documentation about this option. I do not think that this option works. (6)
Recent Report	Displays a list of reports that were recently opened.
Import Sent Layout	[See Table 2-12]
Send Layout	[See Table 2-12]

Table 2-13 Reports, Letters and Labels shortcut menu options explained

Option	Description
Export Layout	[See Table 2-12]
Restore Prior Version	[See Table 2-12] The only difference is that a report will be restored.

Table 2-13 Reports, Letters and Labels shortcut menu options explained

(6) This option is not available for letters and labels.
(7) Filter criteria can be selected on the dialog box. Maybe it's me, but I do not understand the purpose of this option, when the Print Genie option that is on the shortcut menu opens the same dialog box.

> **What Is XBasic?**
> This is Alpha Five's programming language.

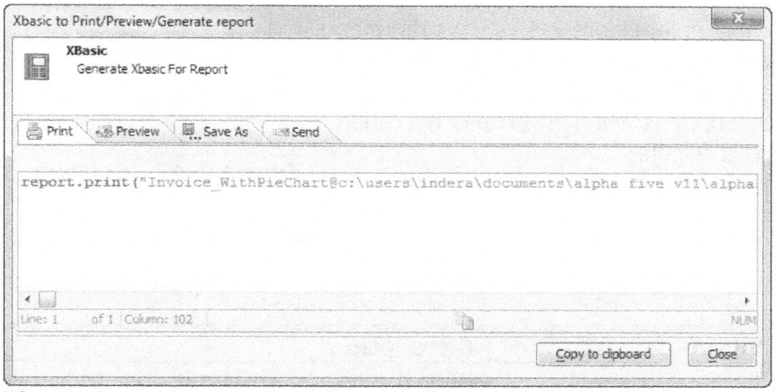

Figure 2-45 XBasic to Print/Preview/Generate report dialog box

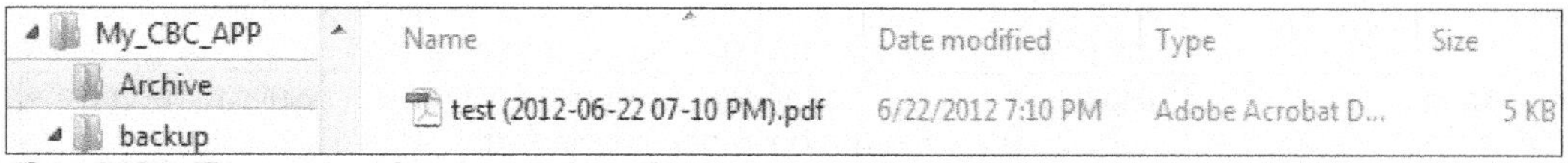

Figure 2-46 Location of report archive file

As shown in Figure 2-47, in addition to creating labels, envelopes can also be created from the Mailing Genie.

The **LABEL DEFINITION** option (the last option) opens the **LABEL SIZE DIALOG BOX**.

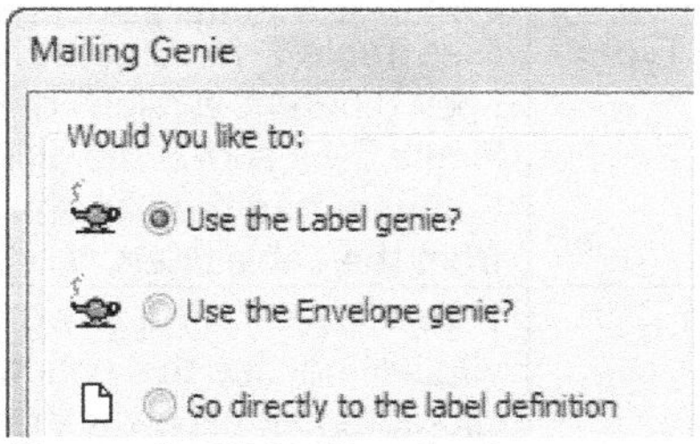

Figure 2-47 Mailing Genie

> When I tested the **LABEL DEFINITION** option (shown above in Figure 2-47), it did not work on the Letter and Report Genies. If the option would have worked, my guess would be that the option would open a blank report or letter layout in the editor.

> **What Are Operations?**
> Operations are a way of changing data in more than one record at the same time, based on criteria. Operations are the equivalent of queries in other database software.

Operations Shortcut Menu

The options shown in Figure 2-48 are available when you right-click on an object on the Operations tab. The options are explained in Table 2-14.

These options are also available on the menu when an operation is selected. The name of the menu changes to match the type of operation that is selected.

For example, Figure 2-49 shows the menu options when a **SUMMARY** operation type is selected and Figure 2-50 shows the menu options when an **EXPORT** operation type is selected.

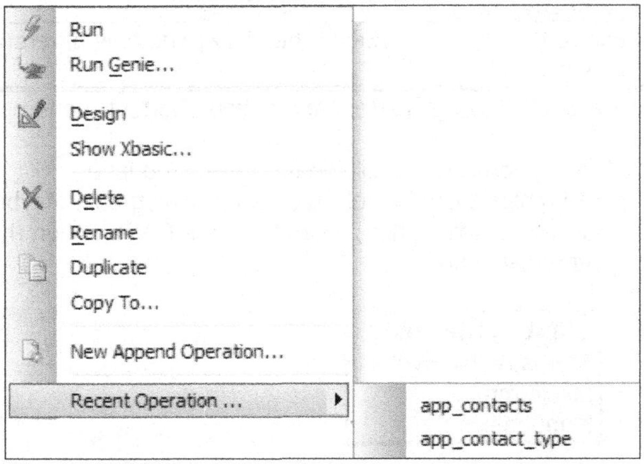

Figure 2-48 Operations shortcut menu

Figure 2-49 Summary operation menu

Figure 2-50 Export operation menu

Option	Description
Run	Runs the operation. This is done to live data.
Run Genie	[See Table 2-11, Run Operation]
Design	Opens the appropriate builder (based on the type of operation that was selected) so that the operation can be modified.
Show Xbasic	Displays the dialog box shown in Figure 2-51, which displays the code that will run when the operation is selected.
Copy To	Opens the **COPY OPERATION TO DIALOG BOX**. The options are used to copy the operation to a table or set.
New <Operation Type> Operation	[See Table 2-11, Create Operation] The difference is that the options open different versions of the **CREATE NEW OPERATION DIALOG BOX**. Figure 2-52 shows the dialog box when this option is selected. Compare it to the one shown earlier in Figure 2-38, which is opened from the Tables/Sets shortcut menu.
Recent Operation	If you have not run any of the type of operation that is selected, you will not see this option on the shortcut menu. For example, if you clicked on an export operation, you would not see this option. This option displays the operations that you have run, as shown earlier at the bottom of Figure 2-48.

Table 2-14 Operations shortcut menu options explained

Chapter 5, Figure 5-19 shows another version of the Xbasic dialog box for operations.

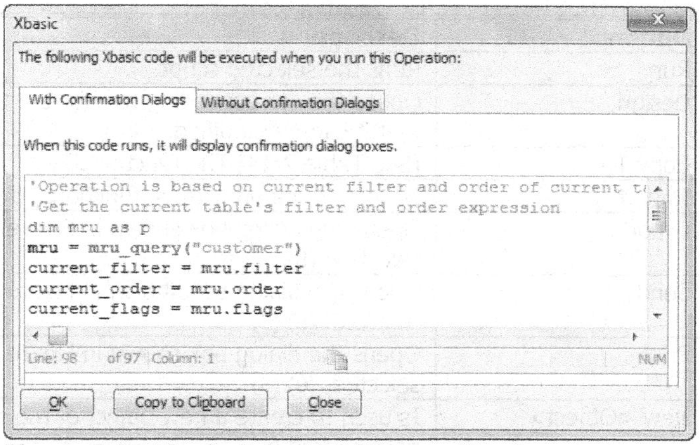

Figure 2-51 Xbasic dialog box (for operations)

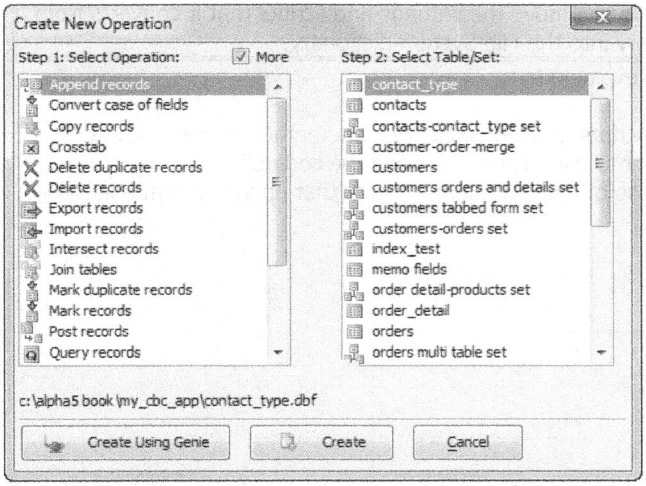

Figure 2-52 Create New Operation dialog box (Operations shortcut menu)

Code Shortcut Menu

The options shown in Figure 2-53 are available when you right-click on an object on the Code tab.

The options vary depending on the type of code (bitmap, function, menu, script or toolbar) that is selected. The options are explained in Table 2-15.

These options are also available on the menu when code is selected. The name of the menu changes to match the type of code that is selected.

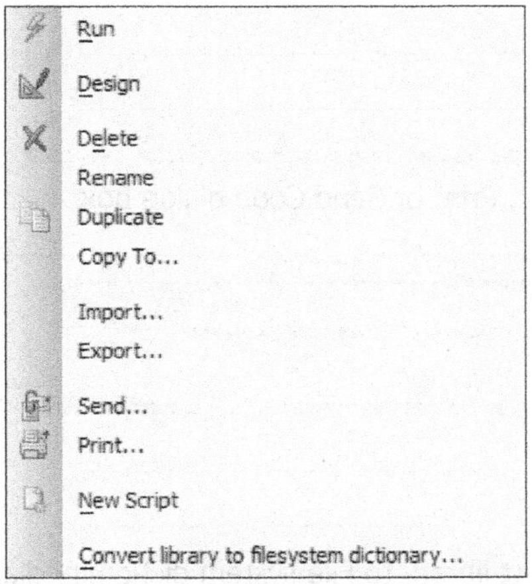

Figure 2-53 Code shortcut menu for a script

Option	Description
Run	Runs the selected script.
Design	Opens the corresponding tool for the type of code that is selected, so that it can be modified.
Copy To	[See Table 2-14] The functionality is the same, just applied to code.
Import	Is used to import scripts, functions, classes, menus and more.
Export	Opens the dialog box shown in Figure 2-54 with the Export option selected. (8)
Send	Opens the dialog box shown in Figure 2-54 with the Send option selected. (8) (9)
Print	Opens the dialog box shown in Figure 2-54 with the Print option selected. (8) (9)
New <Object>	Is used to create a new object of the same type as the one that you right-clicked on.
Convert library to file system dictionary	Opens the dialog box shown in Figure 2-55. It is used to select a folder where Alpha Five can move the settings and scripts that it converts from a standard library into the File System dictionary.

Table 2-15 Code shortcut menu options explained

(8) This dialog box is used to select the scripts, functions, classes, enumerations, menus and toolbars in the database that you want to export, print or send the code of.

(9) Again, I do not understand the purpose of multiple menu options that open the same dialog box.

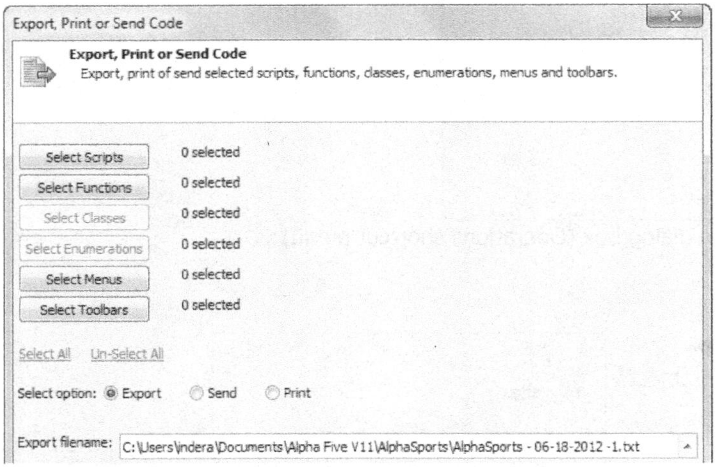

Figure 2-54 Export, Print or Send Code dialog box

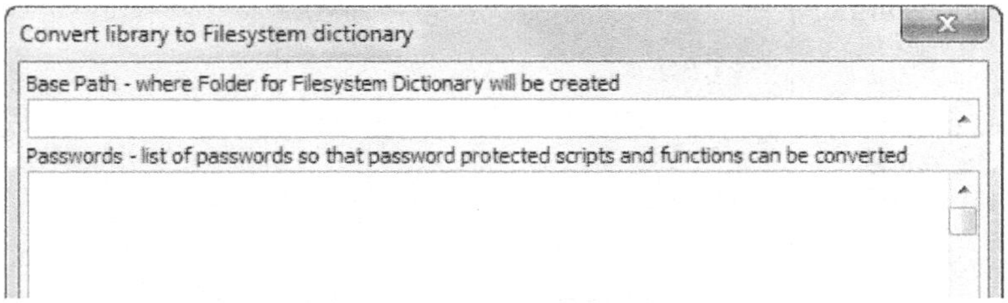

Figure 2-55 Convert library to File system dictionary dialog box

Customizing The Workspace

The dialog box shown in Figure 2-56 is used to change the default options for Alpha Five.

View ⇒ Settings, opens this dialog box.

As you can see, there are a lot of options. The ones explained later in Table 2-16 are ones that I think that you may have a need to change when you have finished this book and are creating databases on your own.

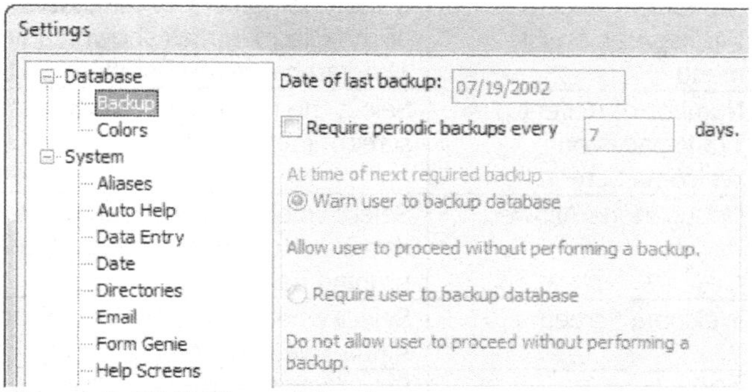

Figure 2-56 Settings dialog box

System Preferences

The System Preferences section shown in Figure 2-57 is where the options are that you may want to change.

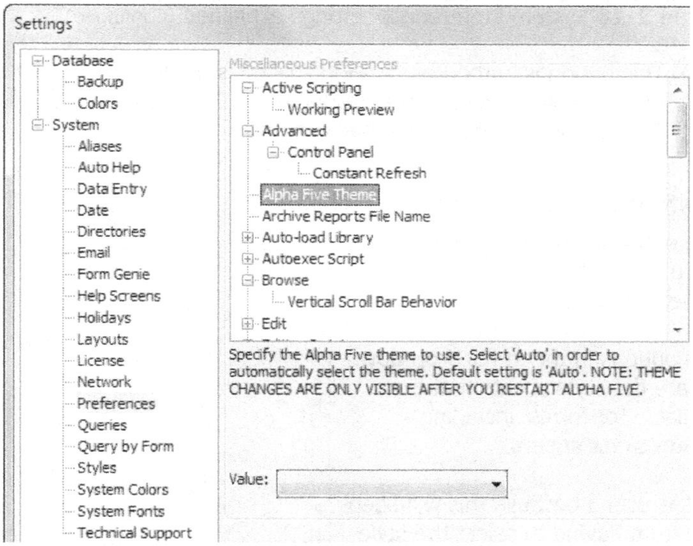

Figure 2-57 System Preference settings

Option	Is Used To . . .
Alpha Five Theme	Change the color scheme of the workspace.
Execute the Auto Exec Script (In the Autoexec Script folder)	Enable the Autoexec script for the database. If modified, this script can be used to hide the Control Panel in an application that will be used by other people.
Scroll Wheel (In the Edit folder)	Select the number of lines that the mouse scroll wheel scrolls in the editors.
Background Internet Access (In the Internet folder)	Enable or disable Alpha Five checking for news or updates when the software is opened.

Table 2-16 System Preferences settings explained

Option	Is Used To . . .
Number of Recent Workspaces on File menu	Select the number of databases that will be displayed at the bottom of the File menu, as shown earlier at the bottom of Figure 2-7. The databases are numbered. The default is eight. (10)
Number of Recent Workspaces on Welcome Screen	Select the number of databases that will be displayed on the Welcome screen. (10) (11)
Debug Mode Allowed	Select whether a user can use the Ctrl + Shift keys when opening a database to prevent the startup form and autoexec script from running. (12)
Welcome Screen	Select whether or not the Welcome screen will be displayed when Alpha Five is opened. (11) (12)
ADB File (In the Terminology folder)	Select whether the term "Workspace" or "Database" is displayed in the software. For example, if Database is selected, the Number of Recent options above in this table would display the word "Databases" instead of "Workspaces".

Table 2-16 System Preferences settings explained (Continued)

(10) This option is in the Recent Workspace List folder.
(11) The Welcome screen is the Workspace & Tasks tab on the Select Workspace dialog box.
(12) This option is in the **STARTUP FOLDER**.

System Styles

The options shown in Figure 2-58 are used to change the default values for forms.

The options in the **STYLE** drop-down list are the style sheets that are available for forms, including **LEGACY STYLE SHEETS**.

This is useful because this will keep you from having to select the style sheet for each form that you create.

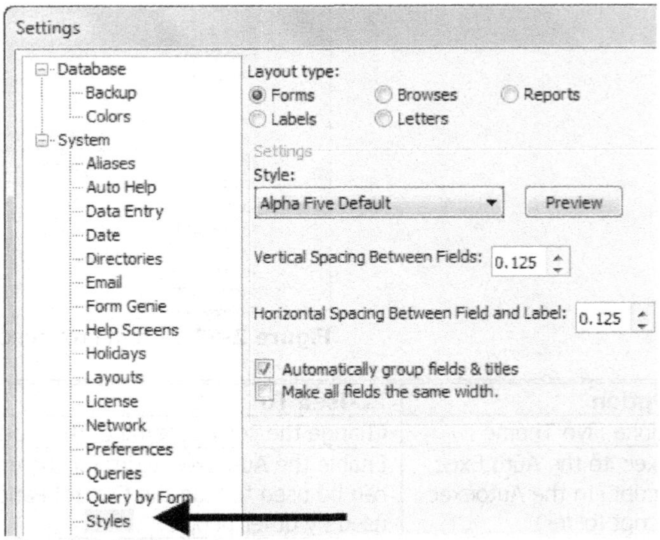

Figure 2-58 Form layout options

System Data Entry Options

The options shown in Figure 2-59 are used to select the default data entry mode for forms and browses.

The default option can be changed on a form by form and browse by browse basis.

[See Chapter 8, Data Entry Tab For Forms and Chapter 9, Data Entry Tab For Browses] The options are explained below.

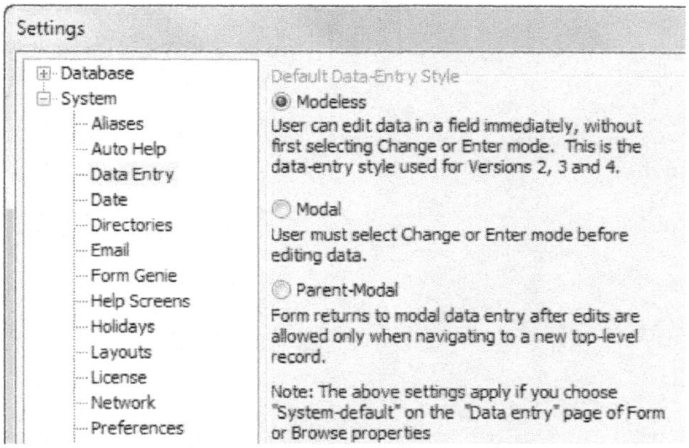

Figure 2-59 Default Data Entry options

① **MODELESS** This is the default data entry mode. It does not require the user to take any action to be able to enter or edit data on the form. This means that a user could add or modify data without knowing it.

② **MODAL** Requires the user to take an action, like select a command or press a key to be able to enter or edit data on a form. This option is used when you want to ensure that the user is aware that they are about to enter or modify data.

③ **PARENT-MODAL** This option can be used when the form is based on a set that has a one-to-many link. It is similar to the modal option.

System Directories

The options shown in Figure 2-60 are used to select the default folders where Alpha Five will save files.

The **PRIVATE PATH** option is where temporary files and files that are automatically created by Alpha Five, like the **EXPORT TO EXCEL** option (in the form view) creates.

To change this folder, clear the check mark for the **USE WINDOWS TEMPORARY FOLDER** option, then open the drop-down list and select the folder that you want to use for the temporary folder.

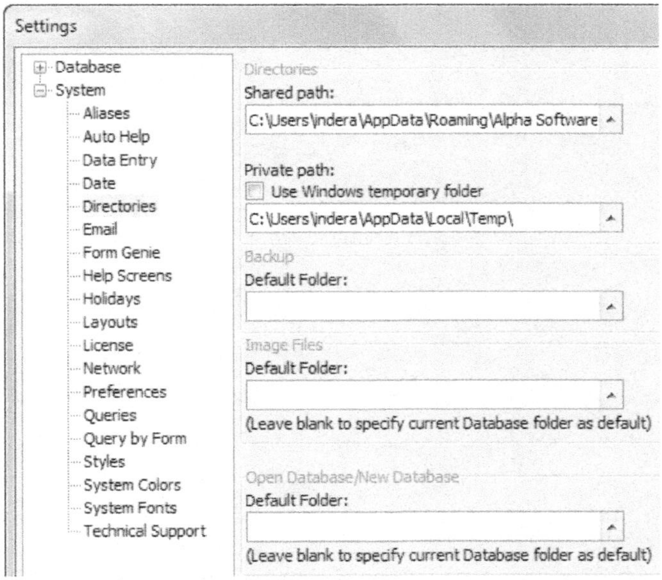

Figure 2-60 Directories options

CREATING YOUR FIRST DATABASE

After completing the exercises in this chapter you will be able to:

- ☑ Understand database terminology, database concepts and field types
- ☑ Create a database
- ☑ Create tables using different genie options

CHAPTER 3

Overview

Chapters 3, 4 and 5 are probably the most important chapters in this book for you to understand because tables are the foundation of any database application you will develop. If you do not configure your tables and sets properly, you will encounter many difficulties later on in the application development process. These are some of the tables that you will create in this chapter.

☑ Contacts ☑ Customers ☑ Orders ☑ Products ☑ Sales Reps

What Is A Database Application?

A database application contains data, forms, reports, queries and more for the purpose of being able to view, maintain and report on a related set of data. If you have used an ATM machine, you have used an application. The ATM application prompts you for things like deposit or withdrawal, how much you want to withdraw and which account you want to withdraw the money from.

Learning To Create Database Applications

For some, learning to create database applications can be intimidating. **LEARNING TO CREATE DATABASE APPLICATIONS REQUIRES TIME, PATIENCE, DEDICATION AND ATTENTION TO DETAIL.** Alpha Five is a very robust package and has a lot of features and options. As you go through the exercises in this book, take your time and try to understand how the concepts that you are learning can be applied to applications that you will create on your own. It is possible to go through this entire book in a few days if you already have above average database design experience with another database development software package or if you have used a previous version of Alpha Five and have a solid foundation of relational databases.

The reality is that you will make some mistakes along the way. If you have a fear of making mistakes, this is the time to let go of the fear because the fear will prevent you from learning. It is also normal to initially get confused on what to do next. Even though you may not understand why you are being instructed to do something, the steps in each exercise will allow you to achieve the expected result. This is how you will begin to build a foundation for creating applications and learning Alpha Five.

The first time that a concept or technique is presented, a lot of information is provided. Each subsequent time that you have to perform the same task, less and less information (aka hand holding) will occur. As you will see, there are a lot of repetitious tasks involved in creating applications. These are the tasks that less and less information will be provided for as you go through the book. The purpose behind this learning technique is to allow you to rely more on your knowledge, instead of flipping through this book to find the answer, which in turn allows you to complete projects on your own, in less time.

Database Terminology

Below are key terms that would be helpful to understand about databases, in order to work with them effectively.

Field A field contains one piece of information and is stored in a record. Examples of fields include customer name and product number.

Record A record has one or more fields. Each of the fields in a record are related. A record looks like a row of data in a spreadsheet.

Table A table is stored in a database and is a collection of records. Most databases have more than one table. Tables are linked on fields. Tables may remind you of a spreadsheet, because SQL databases have rows and columns, which Alpha Five refers to as records and fields. Each table contains information about a specific topic. For example, a customer table would only contain information about customers. The customer table would not contain information about products.

Database A database is a collection of information that is stored in one or more tables. In Alpha Five, tables in other databases or data sources can be linked to.

Relational Database A relational database is a collection of **RELATED** information that is stored in one or more tables in the database. It is important to note that there are different types of physical database structures.

What Is The Difference Between Databases And Tables Anyway?

By now, you have heard both of these terms and may be wondering what the difference is. Databases in Alpha Five are a bit different then some other database packages. A single database in Alpha Five can store the forms, reports and the data itself. You could create an entire database system and store it in one database. As explained in the previous section, tables are where the data is stored. Therefore, the difference between databases and tables in Alpha Five is that tables are one component that makes up a database and the database holds all of the components.

Just What Are Sets, Browses And Operations?

Below are terms that are used in Alpha Five that you need to understand in order to work with databases effectively.

Key Is what other databases calls an **INDEX**. A key is a unique value that each record in a table will have. It is used to identify a record. In some databases, this is known as an ID field or primary key field.

Ordering Is what Alpha Five calls **SORTING**.

Order Criteria Is what Alpha Five calls a **QUERY**, specifically for sorting. This is the criteria that will be used to sort the records in a table.

Expression In Alpha Five, expressions will remind you of formulas because they are used to provide an answer to a question about the data. Expressions can be used to select records that meet the criteria or combine data in two or more fields to create a calculation.

Filter Expressions Are used to create criteria that evaluates to a logical value (like true/false or yes/no). In other databases, this is known as a **BOOLEAN EXPRESSION**.

Sets A set contains linked tables that have related data. In other database types, this is known as a relationship between tables. Unlike tables, sets do not actually have data. This allows data from the linked tables to be displayed as if it was one table. This is often known as a **VIRTUAL TABLE**.

Layout Is a term that is used to reference how data in displayed. Examples of layouts are reports and forms.

Browse Is a layout that is used to view and edit data. A Browse will remind you of a spreadsheet, because it displays data in rows and columns. Unlike a form, a browse displays multiple records at the same time.

Operations Are used to provide more functionality to an object.

Selection Criteria Is used to select which records will be displayed.

Index Is a list of records that are in a particular order, like when records in a table are sorted on a specific field.

Why I Keep Tables In A Different Database From The Forms, Reports, Queries And Other Objects

The best reason in my opinion, to store your tables (data) in a different database then the other objects is because even though you are an "ace" developer and have designed the best relational database system on the planet, sooner or later, someone will want to add something new to the application like a report. Granted, adding to or modifying the database is not the problem. Preventing too much down time and protecting the data is.

By this I mean, if you have all of the objects (the tables, forms, queries, reports etc.) stored in one database, you should not allow anyone to use the database while you are making and testing your changes.

Why you ask? Because if you are making changes and someone else is entering data, you stand a really good chance of over writing the data they are entering.

If your tables (data) are stored in one database - for example, the CUSTDATA database, and the other objects are stored in another database, CUSTAPPS, you can make a copy of the CUSTAPPS database. This will let you make all the changes that you want to the objects in the copy of the CUSTAPPS database, as well as create new objects without forcing the users to get out of the database or affecting the live CUSTAPPS database. This way, the people that are working on the "live" version of the CUSTAPPS database can continue to work.

When you are finished making and testing your changes, all you have to do is copy the version of the CUSTAPPS database you made the changes to back to the live system. The people using the database will automatically get the changes you made, the next time the they open the database, and you will not overwrite the data. In this chapter, you will go over all of the components of a table before you create one, to have a better understanding of them. Many people disagree and prefer to keep everything in one database. The choice is yours.

What Are Genies And How Can They Help Me With Alpha Five?

GENIES are what Alpha Five calls Wizards.

Genies prompt you to make a few selections about the type of object you are creating. Based on your selections, the genie will create what you asked for. A lot of people use genies. Expert developers use them, especially for forms and reports, as they can save some time.

Genies can make things easier. All of the tasks that you do with the genies, you can do on your own, it may just take you longer. One neat feature about the objects that genies create, is that you can modify them, if they do not produce the exact result that you are looking for.

Naming Conventions

One reason to use naming conventions is to make finding the right object easier. For example, on the Tables/Sets tab, tables and sets are displayed. Unless you look at the icon in front of the name, you will not know if an object is a table or a set. An example of a naming convention would be to start all table names with t_ and all sets with s_. This would list all of the tables together and all sets together on the tab.

For the most part, you can name your database and its objects anything you want, as long as the name does not include any of the following:

① **RESERVED WORDS** These are words like field, that Alpha five uses. If you use a reserved word as part of the name, Alpha Five will automatically rename it.
② **SPACES** Do not use spaces in a name. If you do, Alpha Five will replace the space with an underscore. (1)
③ **SPECIAL CHARACTERS** These are characters like #, ^ and *. Use the underscore, A to Z and zero to 9. (1)

(1) Alpha Five sometimes has trouble figuring out what to do with spaces and special characters. If you plan to write Xbasic code, it is easier if there are no spaces in names.

Tables Overview

Believe it or not, there are more than two ways to create a table, as shown on the shortcut menu in Figure 3-1. No, you are not crazy. This is a different shortcut menu then the one that you learned about earlier. [See Chapter 2, Tables/Sets Shortcut Menu]

New Table Shortcut Menu

The shortcut menu shown in Figure 3-1 appears when you do not select an object on the tab before right-clicking.

The options on this shortcut menu are explained in Table 3-1.

The New Table creation options are explained in Table 3-2.

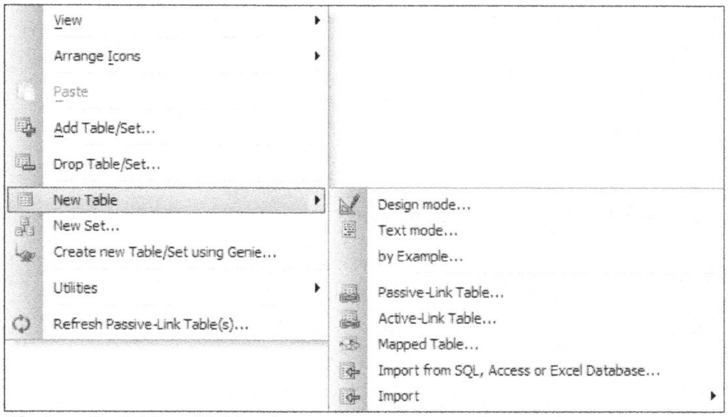

Figure 3-1 New Table shortcut menu creation options

Option	Is Used To . .
View	Select how the tables and sets are displayed on the Tables/Sets tab. The options are large icons, small icons, list and details.
Arrange Icons	Select the order (by name or full name) that the tables and sets are displayed on the tab. **NAME** is the object name in the Table/Set column. **FULL NAME** is the path to the object in the Full Name column. (2)
Paste	 This option does not seem to work.
Add Table/Set	Add a table or set from another database to the database that you currently have open.

Table 3-1 Tables/Sets tab shortcut menu options explained

Option	Is Used To . .
Drop Table/Set	Remove a table or set from the Tables/Sets tab. Doing this does not delete the table or set from the database.
New Table	Create a new table. [See Table 3-2]
New Set	Create a new set.
Create new Table/Set using Genie	Create a table or set using the Genie.
Utilities	Check indexes on the dialog box shown in Figure 3-2, find tables that have a specific value on the dialog box shown in Figure 3-3 or field name on the dialog box shown in Figure 3-4.
Refresh Passive-Link Table(s)	Refresh the contents of a Passive-Link table. This type of table is created (populated) by an SQL statement that retrieves records from an SQL database, which is external to the Alpha Five database. This is one way to use data that is not in an Alpha Five database without importing it.

Table 3-1 Tables/Sets tab shortcut menu options explained (Continued)

(2) The columns are on the Tables/Sets tab.

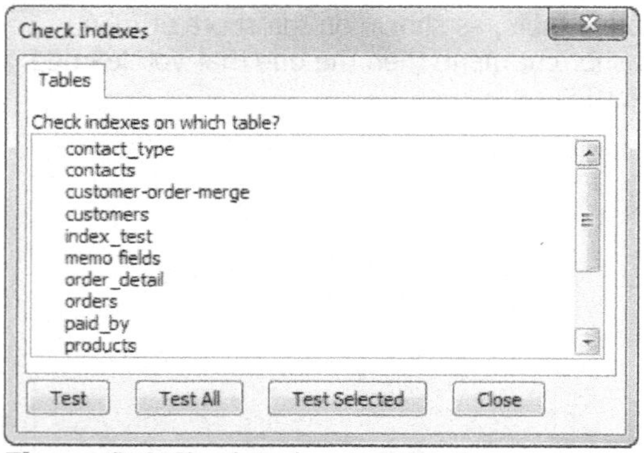

Figure 3-2 Check Indexes dialog box

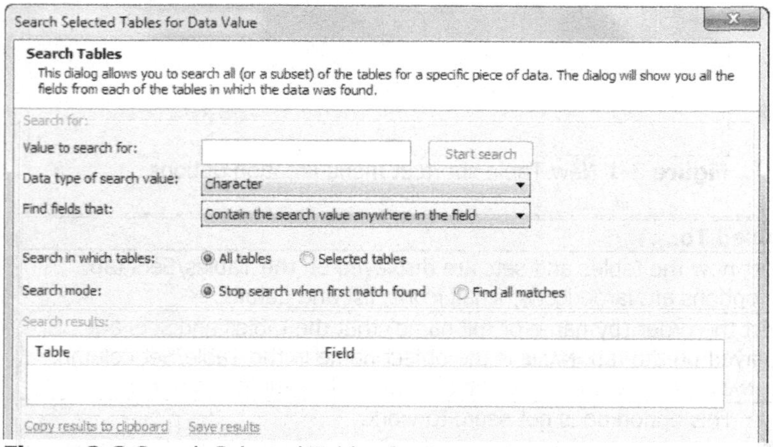

Figure 3-3 Search Selected Tables for Data Value dialog box

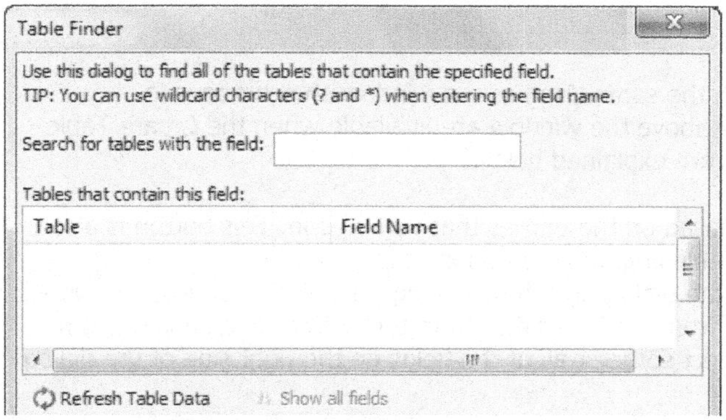

Figure 3-4 Table Finder dialog box

New Table Creation Options

Option	Description
Design mode	Opens the window shown in Figure 3-5. This may be the easiest option to use to create a table.
Text mode	Opens the window shown in Figure 3-6. This option is used to type in the first four fields shown in Figure 3-5. The **FIELD CODES DIALOG BOX** shown on the right side of Figure 3-6 contains the values to enter for the Type. Notice that there is no Index field type. To create an indexed field when using this table creation option, you have to create a field rule or use the **INDEX BUILDER**.
By Example	Creates a table based on the data that you type in, as shown in Figure 3-8.
Passive-Link Table	There is no point in making data changes to this type of table because the changes are not passed back to the remote database. (3)
Active-Link Table	Unlike Passive-Link tables, changes made in Active-Link tables are immediately made in the remote database. (3)
Mapped Table	Is used to create a **VIRTUAL TABLE** with the options shown in Figure 3-9, from two or more physical tables. All of the fields in the physical tables do not have to be used in a mapped table. Calculated fields can also be used. Data can be updated or the virtual table can be set to read only.
Import from SQL, Access or Excel Database	Creates tables based on the data that is imported from an SQL type database.
Import	Creates a table using the **IMPORT GENIE** shown in Figure 3-10 or the **IMPORT BUILDER** shown in Figure 3-11.

Table 3-2 New Table creation options explained

(3) This option creates a table that is populated by a remote database.

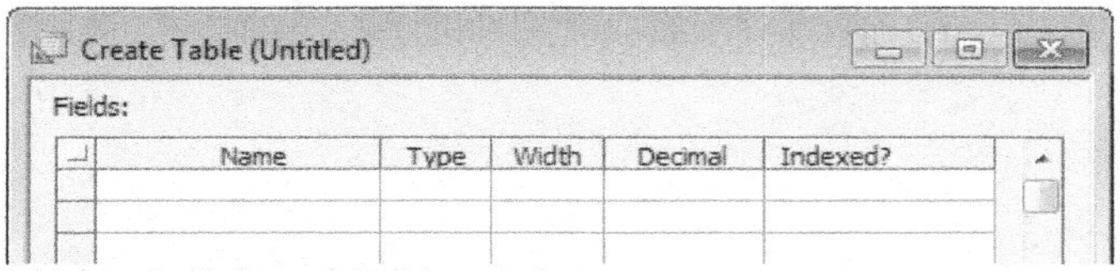

Figure 3-5 Create Table window

Create Table Text Mode Options

The options on this window will accomplish the same thing as the window shown above in Figure 3-5. The two buttons on the toolbar above the window are available when the Create Table Text Mode dialog box is open. The options are explained below.

① **CREATE TABLE** Creates the table based on the entries that you type in. This button is also available when the By Example table creation method is used.

② **IMPORT TABLE STRUCTURE** Opens the dialog box shown in Figure 3-7. The options are used to select a table structure (fields from a table) either from the current database or from a different database. You can select some or all of the fields on the right side of the dialog box to create the new table.

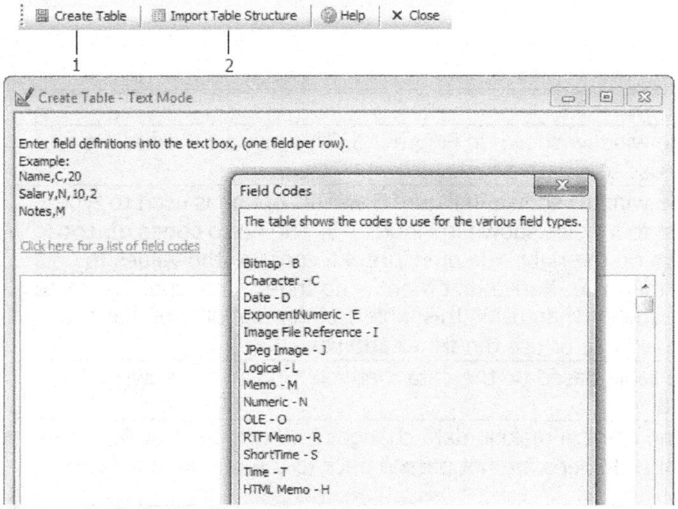

Figure 3-6 Create Table Text Mode window

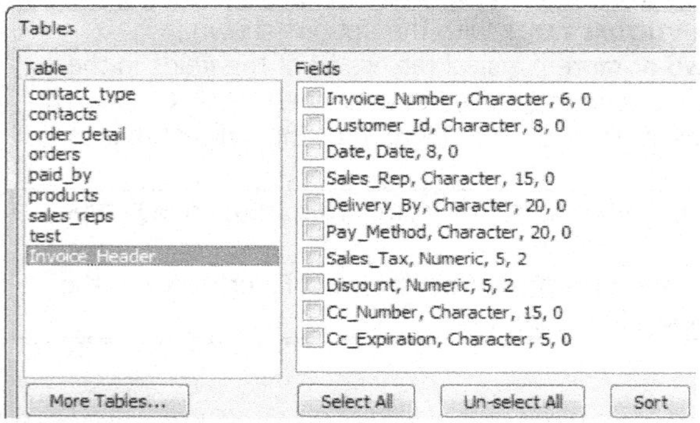

Figure 3-7 Tables dialog box

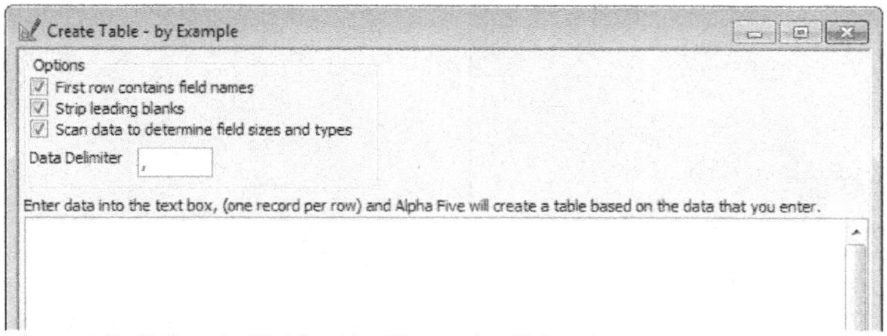

Figure 3-8 Create Table - by Example dialog box

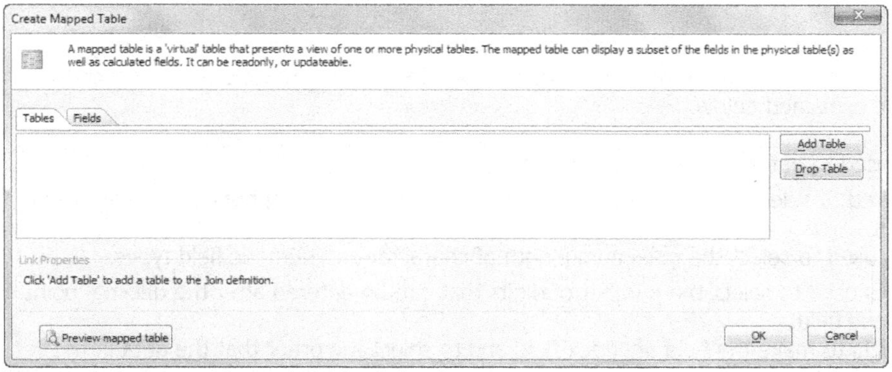

Figure 3-9 Create Mapped Table dialog box

Select this option when the data that you want does not have a connection string.

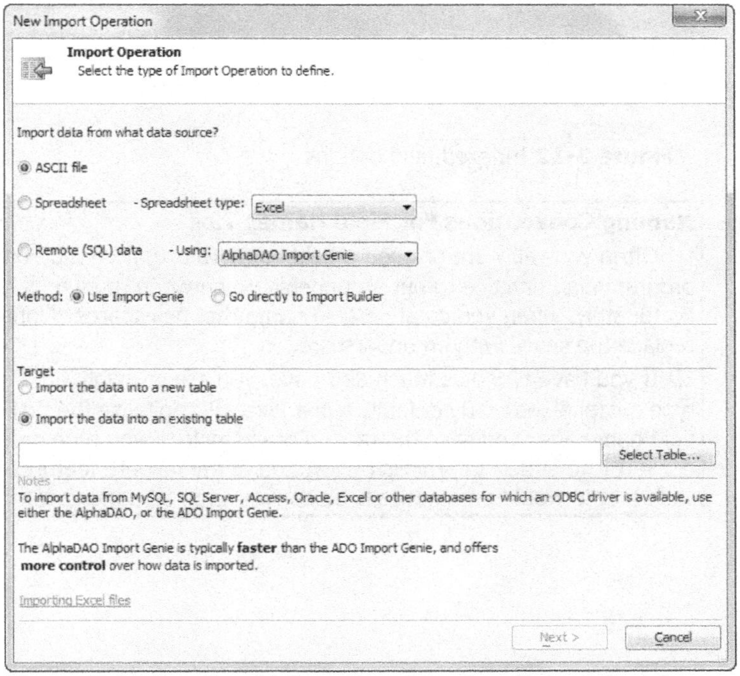

Figure 3-10 New Import Operation dialog box (Import Genie)

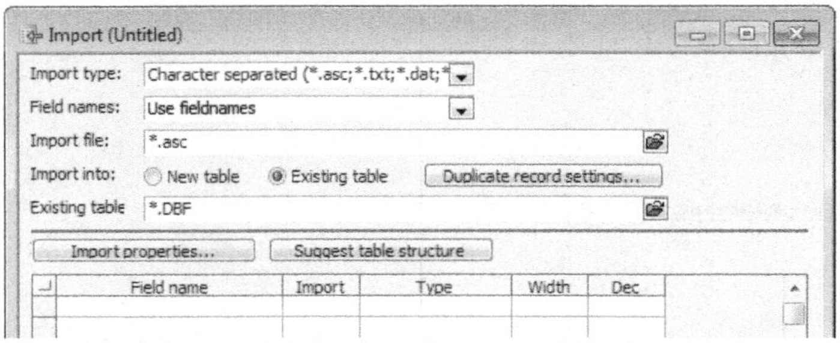

Figure 3-11 Import dialog box (Import Builder for tables)

Table Fields

As you saw earlier in Figure 3-5, there are five fields that you can use to create the records for the table. The fields are explained below.

① **NAME** Is used to enter the name of the field.

② **TYPE** Is used to select the type of field that you are creating. The options are explained in Table 3-3.

③ **WIDTH** Is used to select the maximum length of character and numeric field types.

④ **DECIMAL** Is used to select the number of digits that can be entered after the decimal point in a numeric field.

⑤ **INDEXED?** Is to make the field an index field and to select the order that the data in the field will be sorted by, as shown in Figure 3-12.

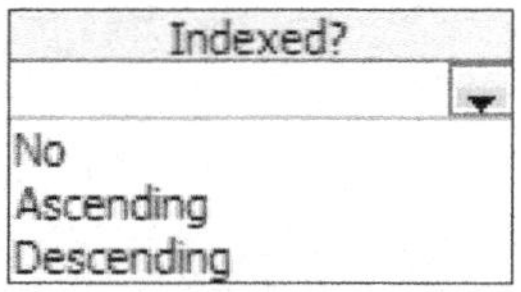

Figure 3-12 Indexed field options

Naming Conventions For Field Names Tips

① Often you will want or need a field name to use more than one word. While it is a good programming practice to put an underscore between the words, doing so can be tedious. Fortunately, when you create a field name that has spaces, Alpha Five will automatically replace the space with an underscore.

② If you have typed as much as I have, you are probably tired of using the Shift key to type a capital letter. By default, Alpha Five will capitalize the first letter of each word in a field name after you save the table. For example, if you type order id, Alpha Five will convert it to Order_Id. This is by far, one of my favorite features of the software. I just wish that id would automatically be converted to all uppercase.

Field Types

Alpha Five has a lot of field types that can be used to store the data that you need. Table 3-3 explains the field types.

Field Type	Description
Character	Is used to store any combination of alphanumeric characters. This is the most used field type. As long as you do not need to do math with the data, you are safest using this field type over the other field types in this table.
Numeric	Stores numbers up to 19 digits. The numbers can have a decimal point, like currency values have and a negative sign. When selecting the field length, include space for the decimal point and a minus sign for negative numbers. Use this field type when you need to do math on the number.
Date	By default, a date field can only accept a date between 01-01-0000 and 12-31-9999. The field width is automatically set to 8.
Logical	Contains one character that represents True or False. You may know this as a **BOOLEAN FIELD**.
Time	Stores the date and time in this format mm/dd/yyyy hh:mm:ss. The width is automatically set to 17.
Short Time	Stores a time. The field width is automatically set to 9.
Exponent Numeric	Stores a fixed precision decimal number. (4)
Memo	Contains a pointer to a memo field file. This field type can contain an unlimited number of characters. You may know this as a **BINARY DATA** (**BLOB**) field. (4) (5)
Bitmap	Stores **.BMP** image files as data in the table. (4) (6)
OLE	Stands for **OBJECT, LINKING** and **EMBEDDING**. This is a way to link to a file created in another application. This means that an OLE field can store a spreadsheet. (4) (6)
Rich Text Memo	Is similar to a Memo field. The differences are: Fields can be added. Character formatting is available. Bitmap files can be stored in this field type. If they are, they are converted to the JPEG file type automatically. (4) (5)
Jpeg Image	Stores image files as data in the table. Bitmap files can be stored in this field type. If they are, they are converted to the JPEG file type automatically. (4) (7)
Image File Reference	Contains a link to an image file. Unlike the Bitmap and Jpeg image field types, this field type does not store the file in the table, which helps keep the size of the database small. (4) (7)
HTML Memo	Is similar to a Memo field. The difference is that HTML code can be used in the field, like the memo field. This field type is for users. (4) (5) (6)
UUID	Stands for **UNIVERSALLY UNIQUE IDENTIFIER**. It is used to create a field that has a unique value, like an ID field.

Table 3-3 Field types explained

(4) This field type is not a data type.
(5) On a form or browse, a button is automatically added to the end of this field type that opens an editor for the user to enter, view and format information.
(6) This is a memo field.
(7) Supports the following image file types: BMP, JPEG, JPG and PNG.

Field Width
If you have used another type of database, you probably know what Alpha Five calls the field width, as the field length.

Character vs Numeric Field Types
Below are some of the benefits of character fields that numeric fields do not support. Character fields can store:
① Letters and numbers.
② Symbols like #, * and %.
③ Leading zeros in a number like zip codes.

Exercise 3.1: Create Your First Database

In this exercise you will create the database for the Capri Book Company application. Before you create the database, you will create a folder to store all of the database files in.

1. In Windows Explorer, create a folder under the Alpha 5 Book folder named `My_CBC_App`.
2. In Alpha Five, File ⇒ New Workspace.
3. On the Create New Workspace dialog box, navigate to the folder that you just created. Type `CBC_APP` in the File name field, then click the Save button. (CBC APP is short for Capri Book Company Application) The database will be created and you will see the Control Panel. Now that the database has been created, you are ready to create tables.

New Table/Set Genie
In addition to the new table creation options shown earlier in Figure 3-1, the New button on the Control Panel Tables/Sets tab has the **CREATE USING GENIE** option. It opens the New Table/Set Genie, which is covered next.

New Table/Set Genie

As the name suggests, this genie is used to create tables and sets. Figure 3-13 shows the table templates that you can select from. If there is a template that meets the majority of your needs, you can use it and make any changes that are needed.

If selected, the **INCLUDE** options below the Preview button will add layouts and sample data to the database for the template that you select. You do not have to use all of the fields in the template.

To view the fields in a template, select the template, then click the Preview button. Figure 3-14 shows the Invoice Header table template fields. The fields could be used for an Order table.

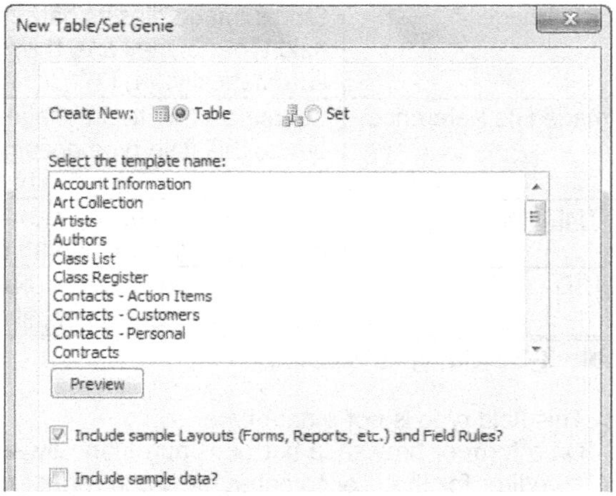

Figure 3-13 Table templates

You are free to pick and choose which fields in the template you want to use once the table is created. Figure 3-15 shows the indexes for the Invoice Header table template.

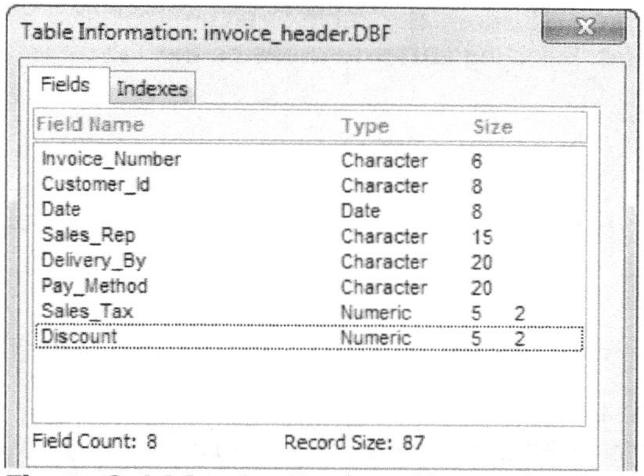

Figure 3-14 Invoice Header table template

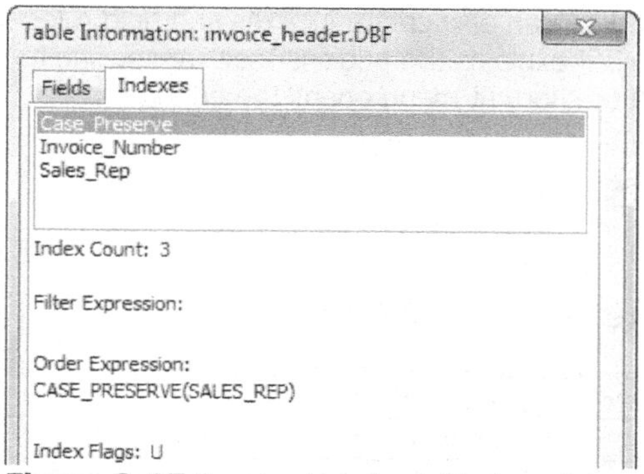

Figure 3-15 Invoice Header table template indexes

> **Table Information Dialog Box**
> Depending on where this dialog box (or the Set Information dialog box) is opened from, it may or may not have the **STATISTICS TAB**. As shown above in Figure 3-15, the dialog box does not have the Statistics tab. In Figure 3-16, the dialog box was opened from the Table ⇒ Properties option on the shortcut menu, which displays the Statistics tab.

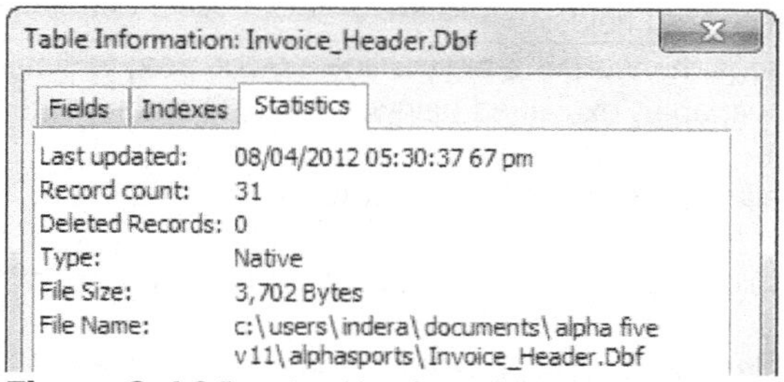

Figure 3-16 Invoice Header table template Statistics tab

Exercise 3.2: Create A Table Using The Genie

In this exercise you will create the Contacts table using the Table genie.

1. Open the New Table/Set Genie, then select the Contacts-Customers template.

2. Clear both Include options shown earlier in Figure 3-13, then click Next.

3. You should see the folder that you created next to the check box on the dialog box shown in Figure 3-17.

   Change the Table Name to `Contacts`, then click Finish.

   The table will now be created and you will see it on the Tables/Sets tab on the Control Panel.

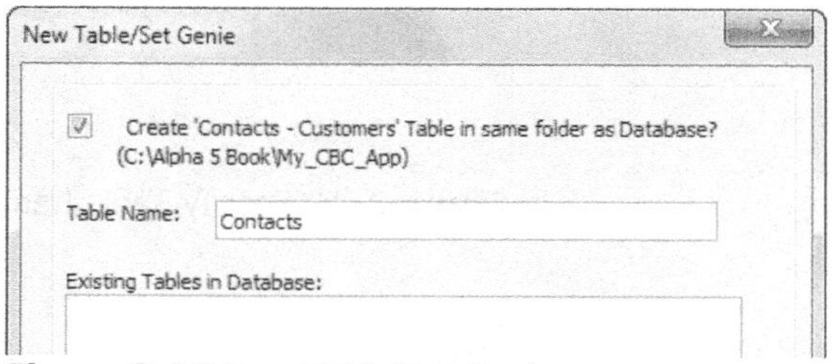

Figure 3-17 New Table/Set Genie

Table Structure Editor

This editor, shown later in Figure 3-21 is used to modify the table. You can add, rename and delete fields. You can also create indexes and field rules. Figure 3-18 shows the Table Structure toolbar. Table 3-4 explains the buttons that are specific to tables. Selecting **EDIT STRUCTURE** on the Table menu or shortcut menu opens the editor.

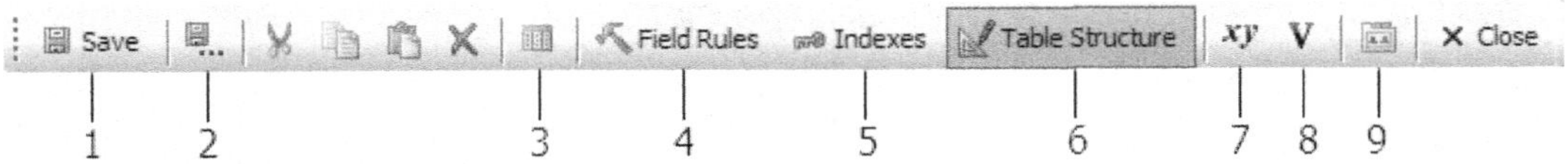

Figure 3-18 Table Structure toolbar

Button	Description
1	The **SAVE** button saves the changes to the table.
2	The **SAVE AS** button is used to save the table with a new name, as shown in Figure 3-19. By default, tables are saved in the same folder as the database.
3	The **BROWSE VIEW** button displays the table in the default browse window.
4	The **FIELD RULES** button opens the Field Rules dialog box.
5	The **INDEXES** button opens the Index Builder.
6	The **TABLE STRUCTURE BUTTON** is a toggle button that displays the Restructure Table window, if the Field Rules dialog box or Index Builder is currently displayed, otherwise, the button is not enabled.
7	The **XY** (Global Calculated Fields) button opens the dialog box shown in Figure 3-20. The options are used to create calculated fields.
8	The **V** (Global Variable) button opens the **VARIABLE DEFINITION DIALOG BOX**, which is used to define the three types of variables explained below, for tables and layouts. ① **LOCAL VARIABLES** are only available for the layout that it is created in and the layouts scripts. ② **SESSION VARIABLES** are available to all layouts (based on the table) and all scripts (based on the layouts). ③ **GLOBAL VARIABLES** are available to all layouts, functions and scripts in the database.
9	When clicked, the **ACTIVATE THE CONTROL PANEL BUTTON** gives the Control Panel the focus.

Table 3-4 Table Structure toolbar buttons explained

The **TABLES IN DATABASE** list displays all of the tables in the database.

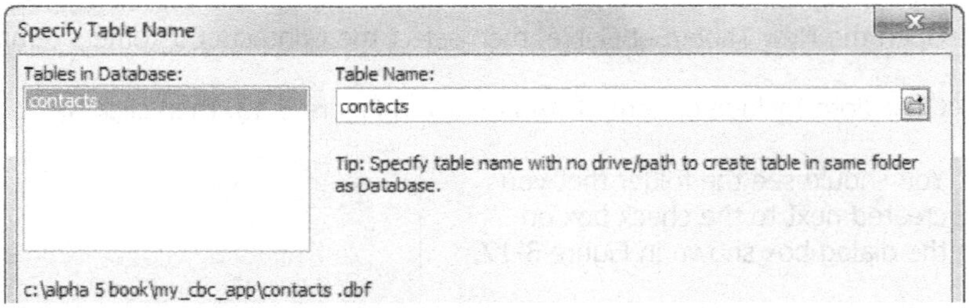

Figure 3-19 Specify Table Name dialog box

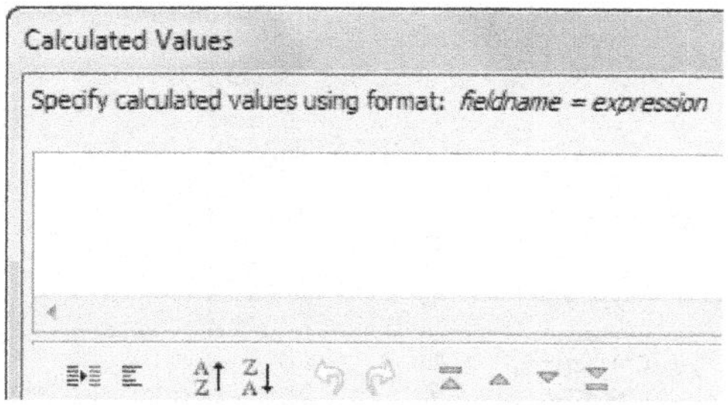
Calculated Values
Specify calculated values using format: fieldname = expression

Figure 3-20 Calculated Values dialog box

Renaming Fields

Often, the field names are not exactly what you want when you create a table from a template. You can rename the fields.

1. Right-click on the Contacts table and select **EDIT STRUCTURE**. You will see the Table Structure Editor.
2. Select the Customer ID field, then type `Contact ID`.
3. Change the Title field to `Email Address`.
4. Change the Other Phone Number field to `Work Phone`.

Deleting Fields In A Table

One of the downsides to using a template to create a table is that there will probably be fields that you do not need. The steps below show you how to delete a field.

1. Click on Middle Initial field row so that it is highlighted, then press the Delete key.
2. Delete the Prefix, Department and Phone Number fields.
3. Click the Save button on the toolbar. When you see the warning message about deleting fields and modifying a fields name, click Yes.

Changing The Field Type

The Contact ID field will be used to link to other tables. It will be the unique value in the table.

1. Change the Type of the Contact ID field to Numeric.

2. Change the width of the field to 6, then click the Save button.

   The table structure should look like the one shown in Figure 3-21.

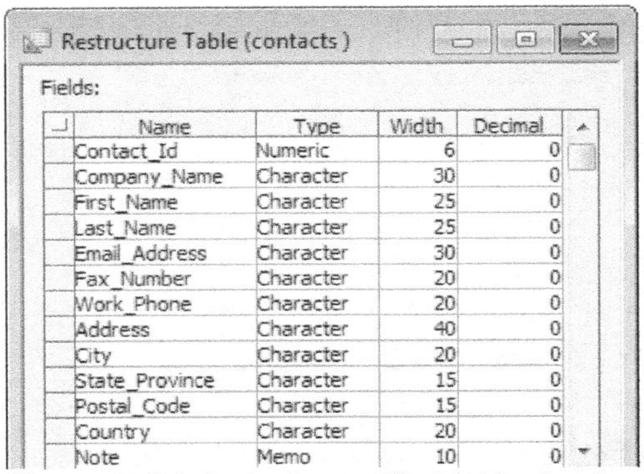

Name	Type	Width	Decimal
Contact_Id	Numeric	6	0
Company_Name	Character	30	0
First_Name	Character	25	0
Last_Name	Character	25	0
Email_Address	Character	30	0
Fax_Number	Character	20	0
Work_Phone	Character	20	0
Address	Character	40	0
City	Character	20	0
State_Province	Character	15	0
Postal_Code	Character	15	0
Country	Character	20	0
Note	Memo	10	0

Figure 3-21 Contacts modified table structure

> **Field Length/Width**
> While it may be tempting to make the field width very large, just in case, keep in mind that the database allocates the space whether or not anything is entered in the field or if the field only uses a small amount of the space allocated for the field. Making the width too large makes the database size larger, which can slow down the database.

Create The Remaining Tables For The Application

There are several tables that need to be created. You will create each table manually. The following tables will be used as Lookup tables in the application: Products, Paid By, Contact Type and Sales Reps. [See Chapter 4, What Are Lookups Used For?] Good software developers will make ID fields numeric, while many non technical people may not. Earlier I stated that ID fields should be numeric, but that it is not a requirement. You will create character ID fields in the Products and Order Detail tables.

> **Indexed? Field Quirk**
> What I discovered about this field is that whether or not you select this option for at least one field in the table, the column disappears after you save the table. While you can click the Indexes button to create indexes, it is strange to me that the column just goes away. I also noticed that a table created with the genie does not have the Indexed column.

Create The Products Table

This table will store all of the information about each product that Capri Book Company sells.

1. Create a table in design mode.

2. Table 3-5 contains the fields for the table.

Name	Type	Width	Decimal	Indexed?
Product ID	Character	6		Ascending
Product Name	Character	35		
Qty In Stock	Numeric	5		
Qty On Order	Numeric	5		
Price	Numeric	6	2	
Reorder Level	Numeric	5	0	

Table 3-5 Products table fields

3. When finished, click the Save button.

   Type `Products` as the table name.

   The table should look like the one shown in Figure 3-22.

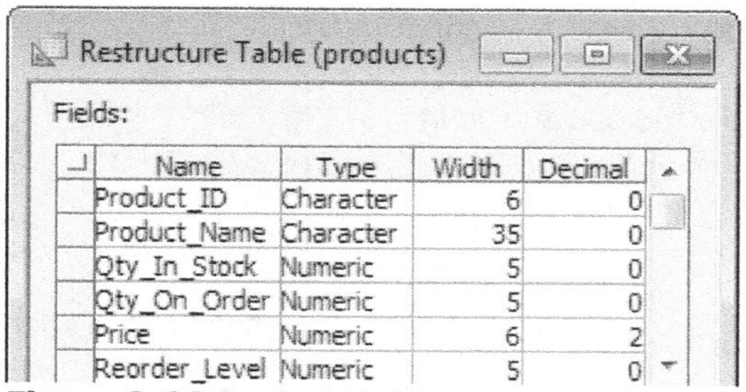

Figure 3-22 Products table

Create The Orders Table

The Orders table will store what is known as order header information for each order, like the Order Number, Customer ID and Order Date.

Table 3-6 shows the fields for the table.

Create the table manually.

Save the table as `Orders`.

It should look like the one shown in Figure 3-23.

Name	Type	Width	Decimal	Indexed?
Order ID	Numeric	6		Ascending
Customer ID	Numeric	6		
SalesRep ID	Numeric	6		
Order Date	Date	8		
PaidBy ID	Numeric	3		
How Shipped	Character	25		
Date Shipped	Date	8		

Table 3-6 Orders table fields

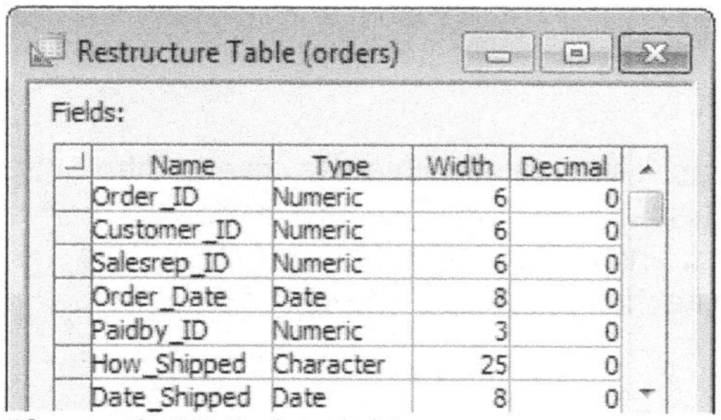

Figure 3-23 Orders table

Create The Order Detail Table

The Order Detail table stores all of the items ordered by customers. This table will store one record for each item that each customer orders.

Table 3-7 shows the fields for the table.

Create the table manually.

Name	Type	Width	Decimal	Indexed?
Order ID	Numeric	6		Ascending
Product ID	Character	6		
Qty	Numeric	4		
Price	Number	6	2	

Table 3-7 Order Detail table fields

Save the table as `Order Detail`.

It should look like the one shown in Figure 3-24.

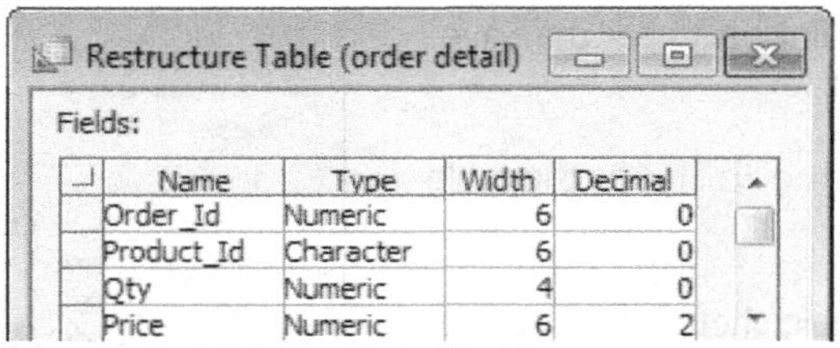

Figure 3-24 Order Detail table

Create The Paid By Table

The Paid By table will store all of the valid ways that Capri Book Company will accept payment for an order. This is a table that will be used as a Lookup table during data entry to validate the method of payment for the order. Table 3-8 shows the fields for the table.

Create the table manually. Save the table as `Paid By`. It should look like the one shown in Figure 3-25.

Name	Type	Width	Decimal	Indexed?
Paid By ID	Numeric	3		Ascending
Paid By	Character	25		

Table 3-8 Paid By table fields

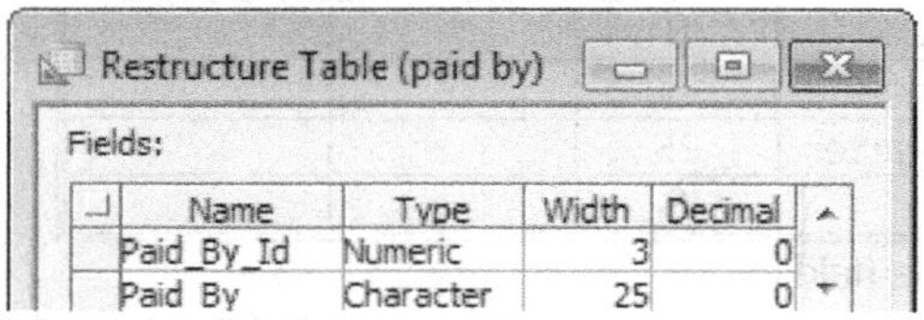

Figure 3-25 Paid By table

Create The Contact Type Table

Capri Book Company wants to track their advertising efforts. They plan to advertise several different ways, like direct mail, online and telephone solicitation. This table will store the information on how each potential customer was contacted, the date of contact and a description of the contact. This table will be used with the Contacts table that you created earlier. Table 3-9 shows the fields for the table.

Create the table manually. Save the table as `Contact Type`. It should look like the one shown in Figure 3-26.

Name	Type	Width	Decimal	Indexed?
Contact ID	Numeric	6		Ascending
Contact Date	Date			
Contact Code	Character	2		
Description	Character	50		

Table 3-9 Contact Type table fields

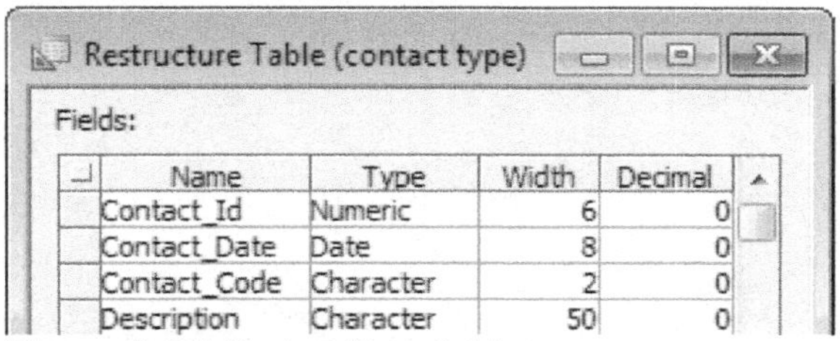

Figure 3-26 Contact Type table

Use The New Table (Text Mode) Option

To change things up a little, you will create the Sales Reps table using the Text Mode table creation option.

Create The Sales Reps Table

This table will store the names of all the Sales Reps. In the real world, more data would be stored in this table, but for this application, the other fields are not needed. Unlike the Restructure Table window shown above in Figure 3-26, the Text Mode table creation method requires you to type the underscore in the field name.

1. New button ⇒ New Table (Text Mode).
2. Type `Sales_Rep_ID,N,5`, then press Enter.
3. Type `Rep_First_Name,C,20`, then press Enter.
4. Type `Rep_Last_Name,C,30`.
5. Your fields should look like the ones shown in Figure 3-27.

   Click the **CREATE TABLE** button on the toolbar.

   Notice that there is no option to designate a field as an index field. You can create a field rule to designate a field as an index by using the **AUTO INCREMENT** Extended field type or you can use the **INDEX BUILDER**.

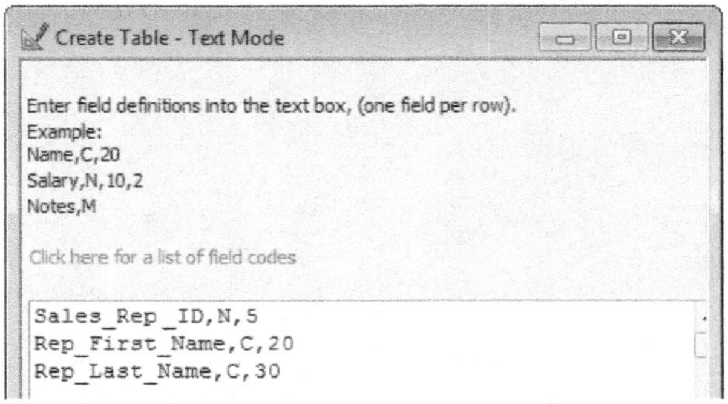

Figure 3-27 Fields for the Sales Reps table

6. Type `Sales Reps` as the table name.

FIELD RULES

In this chapter you will learn about field rules and how they can be used to force data to be entered in a specific way. In particular, you will learn about the following:

- ☑ The difference between table and layout field rules
- ☑ Options on the Field Rules dialog box
- ☑ Create field rules for a variety of field types
- ☑ Lookups
- ☑ Sorting values in a drop-down list

CHAPTER 4

What Are Field Rules And How Useful Are They?

Field rules are criteria and requirements that the data must meet in order to be saved in the table. They can be created at the table or layout level. This chapter covers creating field rules at the table level. Having a solid foundation of table level field rules will be very helpful when the time comes to create field rules at the layout level. Field rules are created primarily for the two reasons explained below.

① **TO MAKE DATA ENTRY EASIER**. For example, on most products ordered, most customers only order one of the product. Instead of having the order taker type a "1" in the Quantity field for the quantity ordered, the Quantity field could default to "1", which means that the person entering the order, does not have to change the value in the Quantity field unless more than one of the product is ordered. Another example would be to supply a list of options for a field that stores how the order will be shipped. The options in the list could be First Class, Media Mail, 2-Day Priority and Overnight.

② **TO PROVIDE CONSISTENCY FROM RECORD TO RECORD IN A TABLE**. For example, I may type "USA" in the Country field and you may type "United States" and someone else may type "US". While they all refer to the same country, it will present a problem if a report needs to display a total dollar amount of sales for the country.

Table Level Field Rules

Because table level field rules trump form level field rules, you should create the majority of field rules at the table level. By trump, I mean that if a field has a rule set at the table level and at the form level, the table level field rule overrules the form level field rule. Another reason to create as many field rules at the table level as possible, is because the rules will be available for all layouts (which includes forms) based on the table.

Layout Level Field Rules

As mentioned earlier, field rules can be created at the layout level. Most of the time, the field rules that you will create at the layout level will be for variables.

> **What Is A Variable And How Is It Different From A Field?**
> A variable is a **VIRTUAL FIELD**, if you will, (that is often the result of a calculation) that is not stored in a table. Only fields are stored in a table.

Field Rules Dialog Box

This is the tool used to create field rules. Field rules are created on a table by tables basis. To open the Field Rules dialog box, click on a table (in the Control Panel), then select **EDIT FIELD RULES** from the Table menu or from the shortcut menu.

The Field Rules dialog box has seven tabs: Field Types, Data Entry, Transformations, Validations, Lookups, Pasting and Events.

It is a good idea to save the field rules frequently and test them. If you have not created a form or browse for the table yet, use the default form or browse to test the rules.

Rules Menu

When you open the Field Rules dialog box, the Rules menu shown in Figure 4-1 is displayed. The options specific to field rules are explained in Table 4-1.

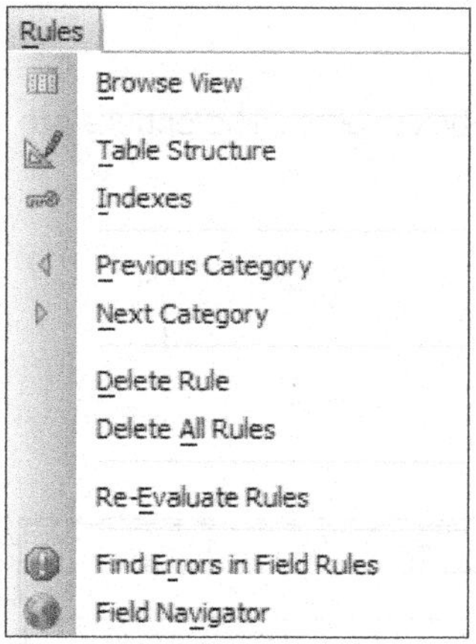

Figure 4-1 Rules menu

> **Re-Evaluate Field Rules**
> In addition to the re-evaluate option on the Rules menu, selecting the following option is also used to re-evaluate field rules. Right-click on the table ⇒ Utilities ⇒ Recalculate field rules.

Option	Description
Previous Category	Sets the focus on the Field Rules dialog box, one tab to the left. (1)
Next Category	Sets the focus on the Field Rules dialog box, one tab to the right. (1)
Delete Rule	Deletes the rule for the field that is displayed in the drop-down list on the Field Rules dialog box.
Delete All Rules	Deletes all of the field rules for the table.
Re-Evaluate Rules	Use this option if you create or change the field rules (on the Field Rules Transformations tab). Running this option reapplies the field rules to the data already in the table. This option works for case conversion rules, validation rules and calculated field rules.
Find Errors in Field Rules	Searches the field rules to see if there are any errors.
Field Navigator	Opens the dialog box shown in Figure 4-2. It is used to search for a field in the current table, by allowing you to create a filter. This feature may be helpful if the table has a lot of fields.

Table 4-1 Rules menu options explained

(1) This is the same as clicking on a tab.

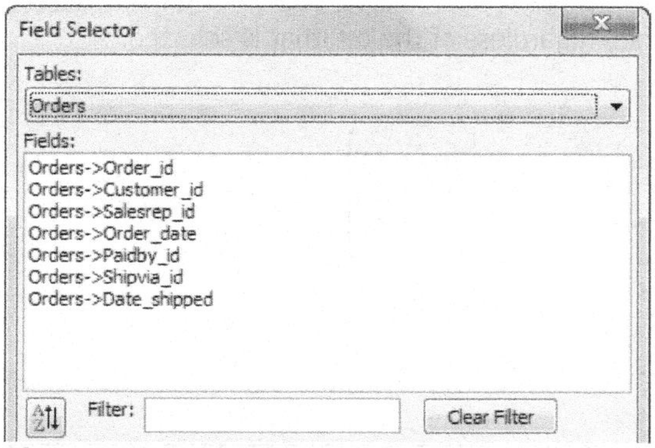

Figure 4-2 Field Selector dialog box

Field Rules Toolbar

The toolbar shown in Figure 4-3 is available when the Field Rules dialog box is open. The options are explained in Table 4-2.

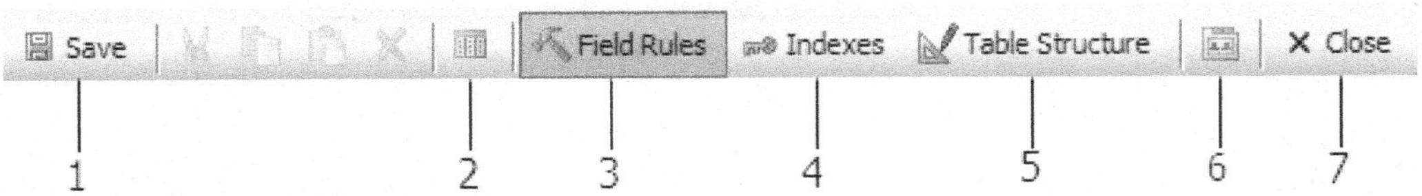

Figure 4-3 Field Rules toolbar

Button	Description
1	Saves the field rules.
2	Displays the data in the table in Browse view.
3	Displays the Field Rules dialog box if the Index Builder or the Restructure Table is currently displayed.
4	Displays the Index Builder shown in Figure 4-4.
5	Displays the Restructure Table window that you used in the previous chapter.
6	Moves the Control Panel on top of the field Rules dialog box.
7	Closes the Field Rules dialog box.

Table 4-2 Field Rules toolbar buttons explained

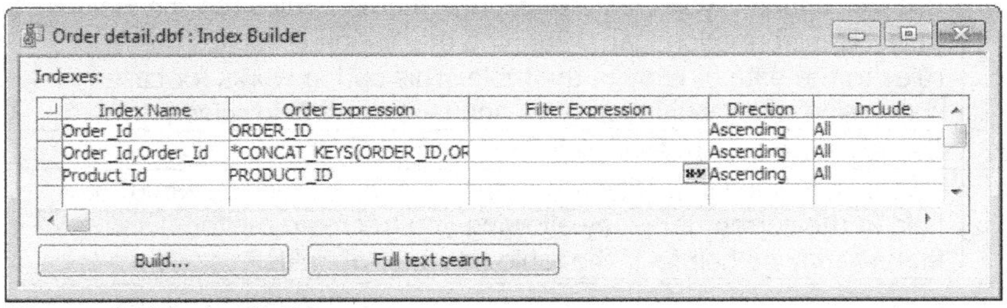

Figure 4-4 Index Builder

Field Rules Dialog Box Common Options

Figure 4-5 shows the options that are always available, regardless of the tab that is selected. The options are explained in Table 4-3.

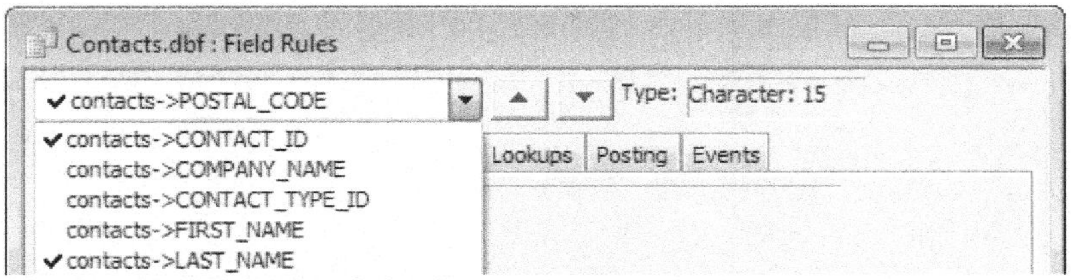

Figure 4-5 Field Rules dialog box common options

> **Check Marks On Tabs**
> I have noticed that even though I did not make any changes on a tab, that a check mark will still appear on the tab. I have also noticed that sometimes a check mark will still be on a tab, even if I delete all of the rules on the tab.

Option	Description
Field Selector List	This drop-down list contains all of the fields in the table. Select the field that you want to apply rules to. Once a rule has been created, a check mark will appear to the left of the field name, as shown above in Figure 4-5.
Up arrow button	Displays the field above the currently selected field in the Field Selector List. (2)
Down arrow button	Displays the field below the currently selected field in the Field Selector List. (2)
Type	This field displays the field type and length of the field.

Table 4-3 Field Rules dialog box common options explained

(2) You can also use the same keys on your keyboard to move up and down the fields in the Field Selector List.

Field Types Tab

The options on the top half of the tab shown in Figure 4-6, are used to select how the field will be filled in. The options are explained below.

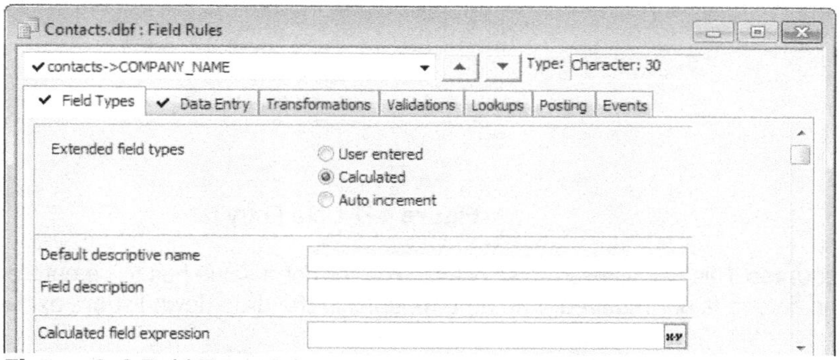

Figure 4-6 Field Types tab

Extended Field Types

① **USER ENTERED** This is the default option for all fields. Use this option when the user should enter the data in the field.

② **CALCULATED** Use this option when you want to create an expression (formula) to add data to the field.

③ **AUTO INCREMENT** Select this option when you want the value in the field to automatically be incremented by a counter. This is mostly used for ID fields. This includes character fields. This means that if the ID value is CH123, it will be incremented to CH124.

DEFAULT DESCRIPTIVE NAME Type in a name for the field as you want it to appear on layouts, including reports. This is the equivalent of a field heading. Make good use of this field because it will keep you from having to change the same field heading each time the field is used on a form, browse or report.

FIELD DESCRIPTION Is used to enter text that will appear on the left side of the Status bar. Usually, this field is used to explain what should be entered in the field during data entry. Fields that will not be used (skipped) during data entry like a field that has the Auto Increment option applied, do not need anything in this field.

The Field Description is not displayed on the Status bar for a browse.

CALCULATED FIELD EXPRESSION As shown above in Figure 4-6, this option is only available when the Calculated Extended field type option is selected. This field is used to create the calculation. The button at the end of the field opens the **EXPRESSION BUILDER**, which is used to create formulas.

Data Entry Tab

The options shown in Figure 4-7 are used to customize the default behavior for the field.

If the Calculated option is selected on the Field Types tab, the only option available on the Data Entry tab is the Skip option.

The options are explained below.

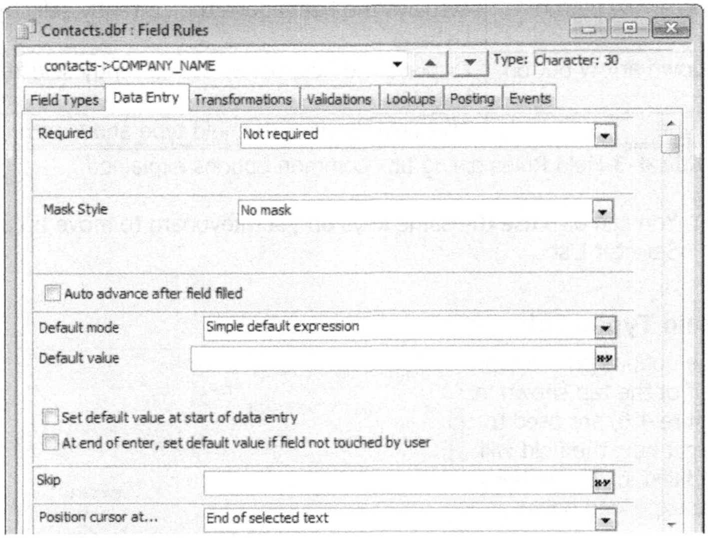

Figure 4-7 Data Entry tab

REQUIRED This field is used to select whether or not a value has to be entered into the field. The default is not required. The other options in the drop-down list are explained below.

① **ALWAYS REQUIRED** If selected, a value has to be entered in the field.

② **CONDITIONALLY REQUIRED** Select this option to create an expression that will be used to determine when a value has to be entered in the field. An example of when to use this option is if you only needed to charge sales tax if the shipping address of an order is in the same state that you are in.

MASK STYLE If the data entered in a field needs formatting, select one of the options explained below.

① **SIMPLE MASK** Is used to select one of the built-in masks. Figure 4-8 shows the masks for phone and zip code fields.

② **CONDITIONAL MASKS** Select this option if the mask should be applied to the field based on a condition (formula) that you create. The options shown in Figure 4-9 are used to create a conditional mask. The options are explained below.

DO NOT STORE MASK LITERALS IN FIELD Check this option if you do not want the template formatting characters to be stored in the field in the table. (3)

PLACE HOLDER CHARACTER Is used to change the character that is displayed in the field on a layout to indicate how much data can be entered. (3)

(3) This option is available when the Simple or Conditional mask option is selected.

Figure 4-8 Input Mask dialog box

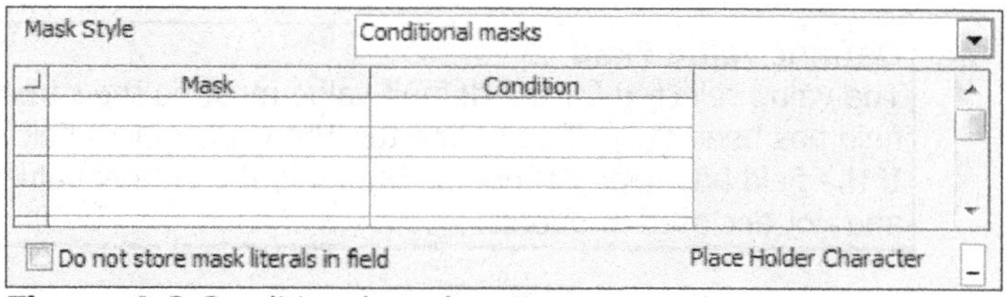

Figure 4-9 Conditional mask options

AUTO ADVANCE AFTER FIELD FILLED Selecting this option causes the insertion point to automatically move to the next field when the current field has been filled to the width defined in the table for the field. A good use of this option is for a middle initial or state field.

DEFAULT MODE Is used to select whether or not the field will have a default value. Setting a default value when appropriate will save time during data entry. The options are explained below.

① **NO DEFAULTS** This is the default option <no pun intended>. If selected, the field will not display a default value on a layout.

② **SIMPLE DEFAULT EXPRESSION** Displays the options shown earlier in Figure 4-7. By default, the default value is displayed when the cursor enters the field.

☑ **DEFAULT VALUE** Is used to type in the default value. (4)

③ **CONDITIONAL DEFAULT VALUE** Displays the options shown in Figure 4-10. (4)

④ **USE PREVIOUS VALUE AS DEFAULT** Select this option when you want to use the value in the field from the previous record, as the default value.

(4) This option is also used to create an expression that will create in the default value.

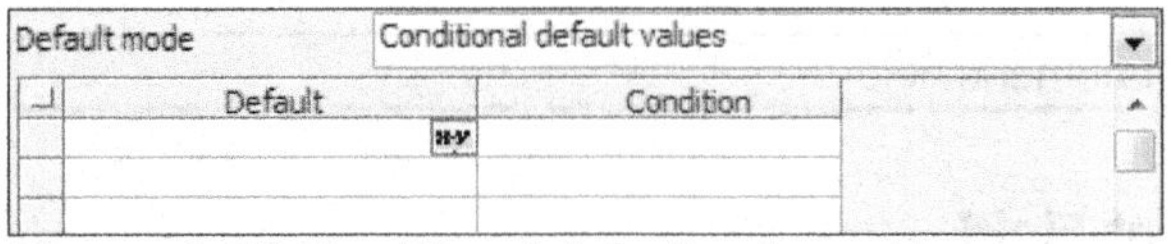

Figure 4-10 Conditional default value options

Check the **SET DEFAULT VALUE AT START OF DATA ENTRY** option if you want the default value added to the field each time a new record is created.

Check the **AT END OF ENTER, SET DEFAULT VALUE IF FIELD NOT TOUCHED BY USER** option if you want the default value applied when the record is saved.

SKIP Is used to create a formula to determine if the field will be skipped over when the Tab or Enter key is pressed. This would mostly be used for an ID field. An expression can also be created to make the skip conditional.

POSITION CURSOR AT . . . Is used to select where the cursor is first placed when the field is being edited. The options are explained below.

① **END OF SELECTED TEXT** This is the default option. Select this option if the entire value in the field will be replaced when edited.

② **START OF UNSELECTED TEXT** Select this option when the value in the field is usually edited.

③ **END OF UNSELECTED TEXT** This option is best suited for fields where more content will be added, like a memo field.

> **Default Value Field**
> The value selected for the default value must be the same as the fields data type. If the field has been defined as Character, the value in this field must be enclosed in quotes. If the field has been defined as Numeric, the default value in this field must be numeric and not enclosed in quotes.

What Is A Mask And What Is It Used For?

In a way, a mask really is a rule that the data in a field must comply with. Masks do this by validating the data before it can be saved. Masks are used to make data entry easier by providing a template of how the data should be entered in the field. This helps prevent data entry errors. The characters explained in Table 4-4 are used to create the mask.

Mask Character	Allows Any . . .
L	Upper case letter.
l	Letter.
#	Sign, number or decimal.
N	Uppercase letter, number, sign or decimal.
n	Letter, number, sign or decimal.
A	Uppercase letter or number.
a	Letter or number.
0	Number (This is a zero).
&	Character.
\	Character after the slash is taken as a literal or template character.

Table 4-4 Mask characters explained

> A mask character cannot be applied to a numeric field.

Exercise 4.1: Create An Auto Increment Field

This functionality is most often applied to ID fields because the value needs to be incremented automatically for each record that is added to the table. Because the field is automatically incremented, it should be skipped, if it will be displayed on a form or browse.

1. Open the Field Rules dialog box for the Contacts table.

2. Select the Contact ID field if it is not already selected in the drop-down list, then select the Auto increment option. Because the field will be skipped, there is no point in filling in the fields at the bottom of the Field Types tab.

Select The Options On The Data Entry Tab

1. Open the Required field drop-down list and select Always Required.

2. Open the Default mode field drop-down list and select Simple default expression.

3. In the Default value field type `000001`. This default value equals the length of the field. Doing this is optional. You could enter 1 or 001 and the field would still be incremented the same.

4. Select the Set default value at start of data entry option.

5. In the Skip field type `.T.`, then click the Save button.

   You should have the options shown in Figure 4-11.

   The options selected on this tab will prevent the user from making any changes to the field because the field will be skipped during data entry.

   The value in the field will automatically be incremented each time a new record is added to the table.

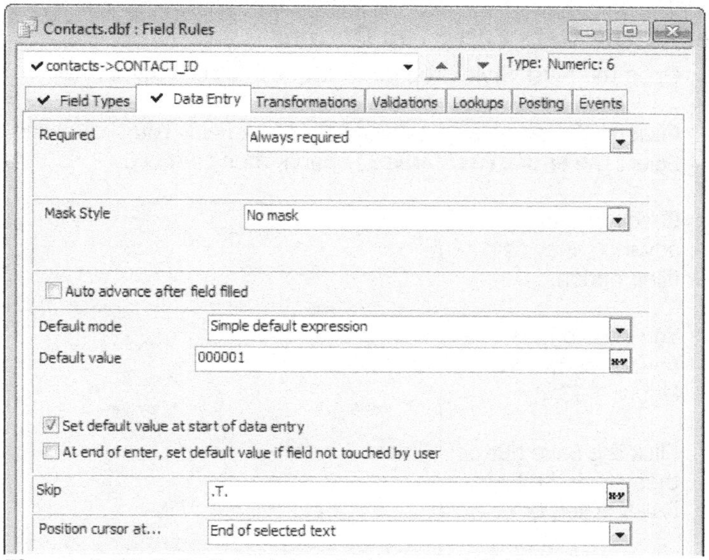

Figure 4-11 Data Entry tab auto increment field options

Logical Expressions

.T. Is a logical expression which equals True.
.F. Is a logical expression which equals False.

Exercise 4.2: Add An Existing Template To A Phone Field

In this exercise you will apply the built-in phone template to a field in the Contacts table. You will also fill in the fields at the bottom of the Field Types tab.

Select The Field Types Tab Options

1. Open the drop-down list at the top of the dialog box and select the Work-Phone field. On the Field Types tab, the User entered option should be selected.

2. In the Default descriptive name field, type `Work Phone`.

3. In the Field description field, type `Type in the contacts work phone number`, as shown in Figure 4-12.

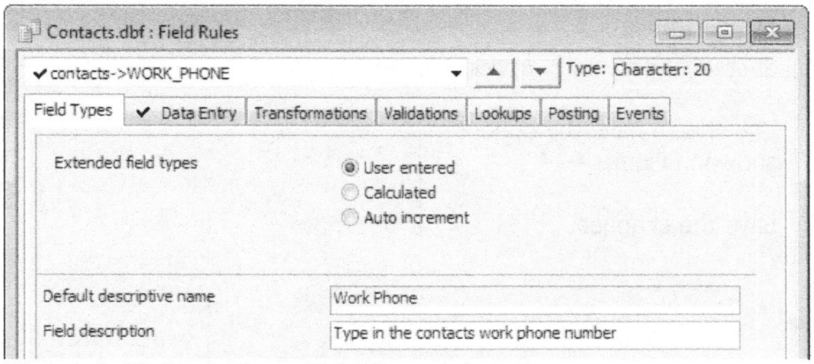

Figure 4-12 Work Phone Field Types tab options

Select The Data Entry Tab Options

1. Open the Mask Style drop-down list and select **SIMPLE MASK**.

2. Click on the arrow at the end of the Mask field. You should see the Input Mask dialog box. Select the **PHONE (US/CANADA)** option, then click OK.

3. Check the Auto advance after field filled option.

   You should have the options shown in Figure 4-13.

   Click the Save button, then close the Field Rules dialog box.

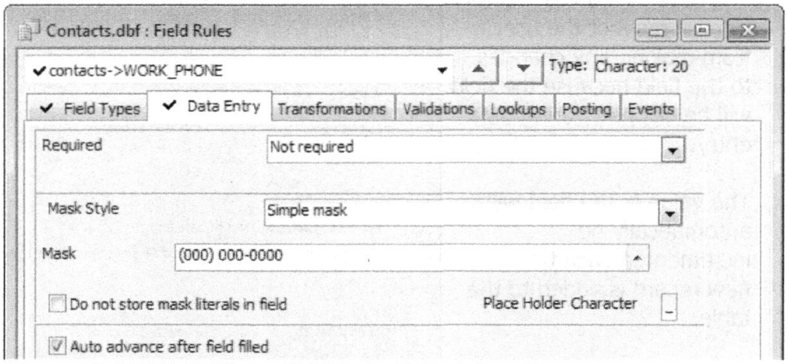

Figure 4-13 Work Phone field Data Entry tab options

Exercise 4.3: Set A Default Value For A Field

In Exercise 4.1 you created a default value that was automatically incremented. In this exercise you will create a default value for the Quantity field, which requires data to be entered. The default value will keep the person from having to enter a value in the field if the default value is the value that they need.

1. Open the Field Rules dialog box for the Order Detail table.

2. Select the Qty field, then enter appropriate content for the two fields at the bottom of the Field Types tab.

3. On the Data Entry tab, open the Required field drop-down list and select Always required.

4. Open the Default mode field drop-down list and select Simple default expression, then type `1` in the Default value field.

5. Check the Set default value at start of data entry option.

   You should have the options shown in Figure 4-14.

   Save the changes.

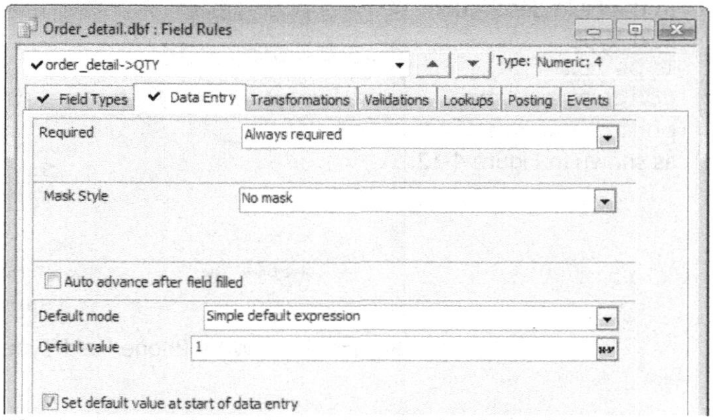

Figure 4-14 Default value options for the Qty field

Exercise 4.4: Create A Custom Mask

In this exercise you will create a mask for the State field so that it will be converted to all capital letters.

1. Open the Field Rules dialog box for the Contacts table.
2. Select the State Province field, then enter appropriate content for the two fields at the bottom of the Field Types tab.
3. On the Data Entry tab, open the Required field drop-down list and select Always required.
4. Open the Mask Style field drop-down list and select Simple mask. In the Mask field type `LL`.
5. Check the Auto advance after field filled option.

   You should have the options shown in Figure 4-15.

   Click the Save button.

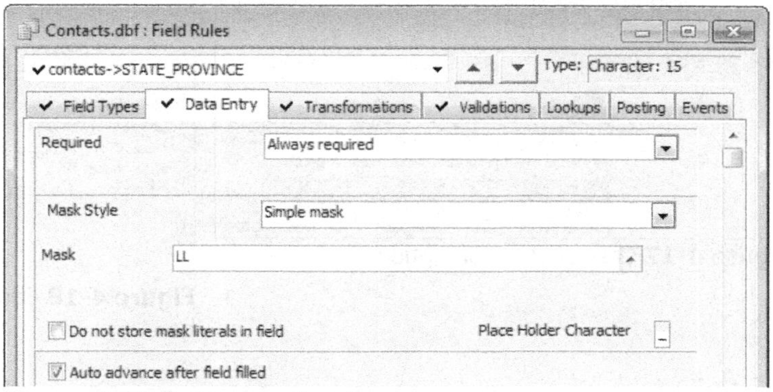

Figure 4-15 Custom mask options

Transformations Tab

The options on this tab are not available for numeric fields.

The options shown at the bottom of Figure 4-16 are used to change the case of words.

Transformation rules will automatically change words to the case that you specify.

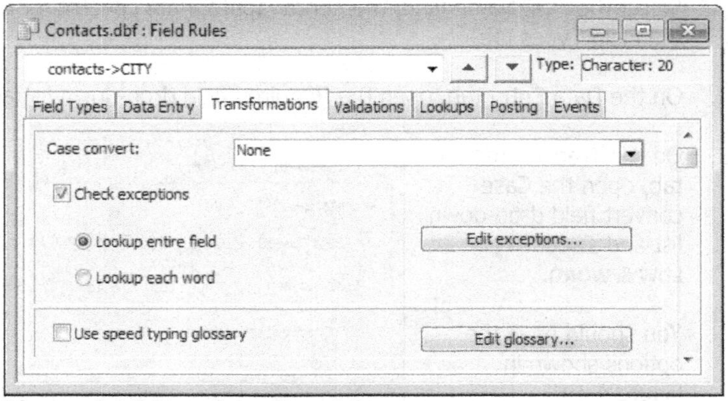

Figure 4-16 Transformations tab

You can also select when the case should not be changed. The options are explained below.

① **CASE CONVERT** The options in this drop-down list are used to select how you want the words converted. The options are shown in Figure 4-17.

② **CHECK EXCEPTIONS** Check this option if you need to define words that you know will not conform to any of the options shown in Figure 4-17.

The **LOOKUP ENTIRE FIELD** and **LOOKUP EACH WORD** options are used to select how to evaluate the data entered in the field.

The **EDIT EXCEPTIONS BUTTON** opens the dialog box shown in Figure 4-18. It is used to enter the words that are exceptions. You would enter words that should be converted, but do not meet the case conversion rules that you set up.

③ **USE SPEED TYPING GLOSSARY** Is used to replace a word or characters that are typed into the field with something else.

The **EDIT GLOSSARY BUTTON** opens the Speed Typing Glossary dialog box. [See Chapter 12, Figure 12-39]

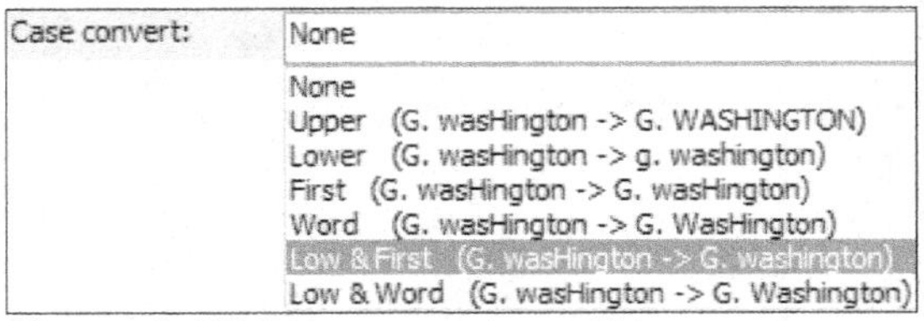

Figure 4-17 Case conversion options

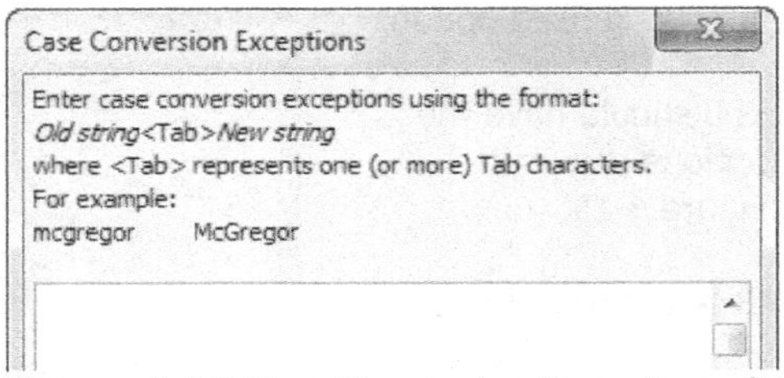

Figure 4-18 Case Conversion Exceptions dialog box

Exercise 4.5: Convert The Case Of A Field

In this exercise you will apply a case conversion transformation to the First Name field.

1. Select the First Name field, then enter appropriate content for the two fields at the bottom of the Field Types tab.

2. On the Data Entry tab, open the Required field drop-down list and select Always required.

3. On the Transformations tab, open the Case convert field drop-down list and select **LOW & WORD.**

   You should have the options shown in Figure 4-19.

   Save the changes.

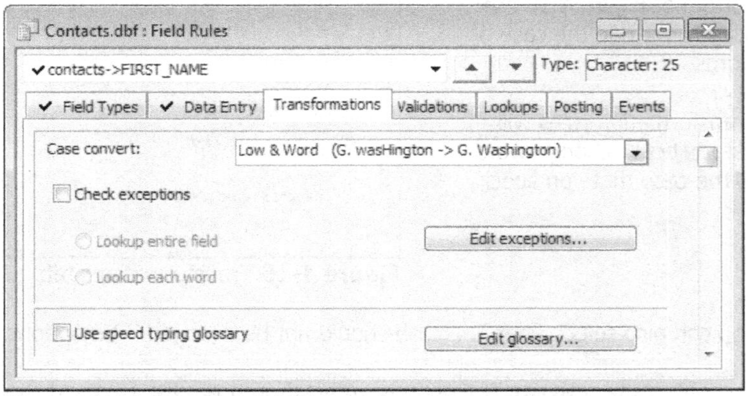

Figure 4-19 First Name field transformations options

Validations Tab

The options shown in Figure 4-20 provide ways to make records unique and to add double data entry rules to fields.

The options are explained below.

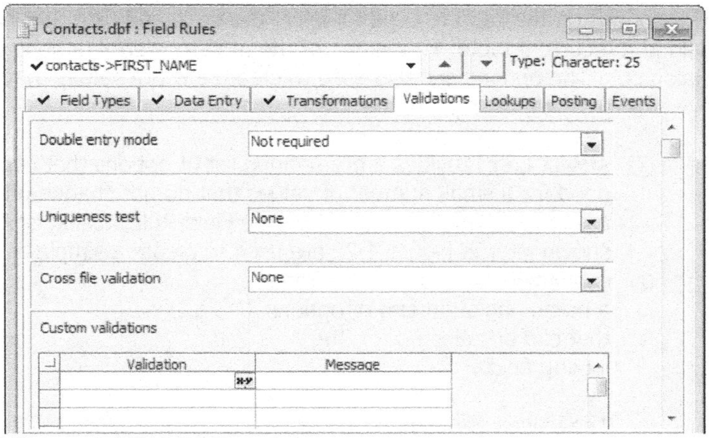

Figure 4-20 Validations tab

① **DOUBLE ENTRY MODE** Selecting this option forces the user to enter the value exactly the same way twice before it will be accepted. An example that comes to mind is entering a social security number.

② **UNIQUENESS TEST** Use this option for a field that has to have unique values. For example, there should not be two records in the table that have the same social security number. The two value options in the drop-down list are used to check to make sure that the value currently being entered does not match a value that is already in the same field in the table.

③ **CROSS FILE VALIDATION** The options shown in Figure 4-21 are used to validate the value in one field in the current table to values in another table. The options shown in Figure 4-22 are used to validate several fields in the current table to values in one or more tables or to validate fields conditionally.

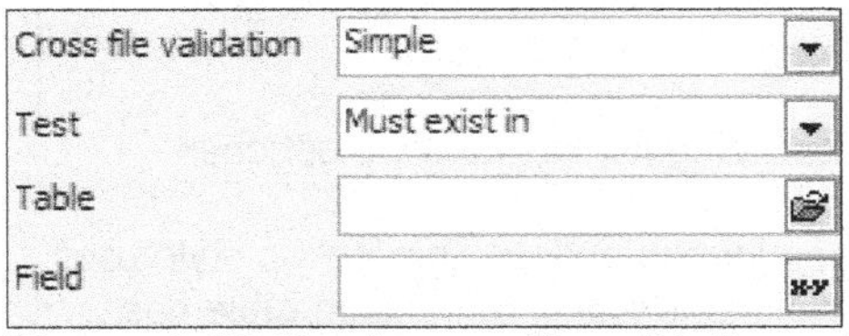

Figure 4-21 Simple cross file validation options

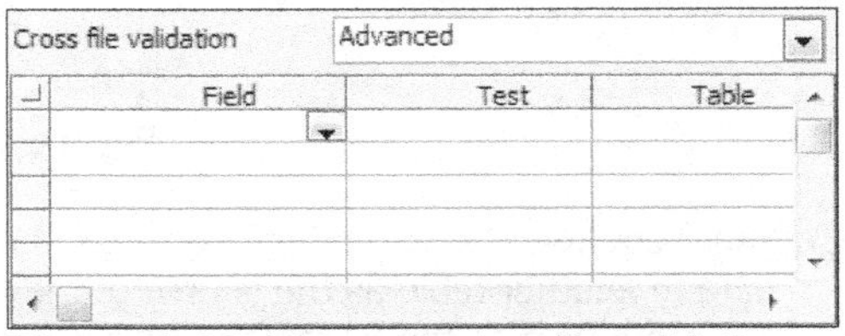

Figure 4-22 Advanced cross file validation options

What Are Lookups Used For?

Lookups are used to find the value for the selected field in a field in another table or in a list.
For example, in the database that you are creating in this book, the Orders table has the Customer ID, Sales Rep ID and Paid By ID fields. Each of these fields in the Orders table should have a lookup because the values that can be stored in each of these fields, already exist in other tables.

Lookup tables are another form of data accuracy and validation. That is because the user selects the value that they need from a list of values, instead of typing the value in. You can give the user the ability to update or add to the lookup tables, but most of the time, updating and adding to lookup tables should be restricted to a few users of the database.

Lookups Tab

The options on this tab are used to select the table and field that has the value needed to fill in a field in the current table. This is one of the more powerful options in my opinion, on the Field Rules dialog box. The options are also used to create a list of values that is attached to a field. There are five lookup styles, as explained below.

① **SIMPLE LIST** Provides a pre-defined list of options that can be selected from. This option is good for a small number of values that do not change often. That is because the values are entered and maintained on the Field Rules dialog box, instead of in a table. The options shown later in Figure 4-28 are used to create a simple list lookup. (5)

② **CASCADING LIST** Is used to create a menu and submenu of options that can be selected for the lookup field.

The values are categorized into a hierarchical structure.

Figure 4-23 shows the options used to create a cascading list lookup.

Figure 4-24 shows the layout to create the cascading list shown in Figure 4-25.

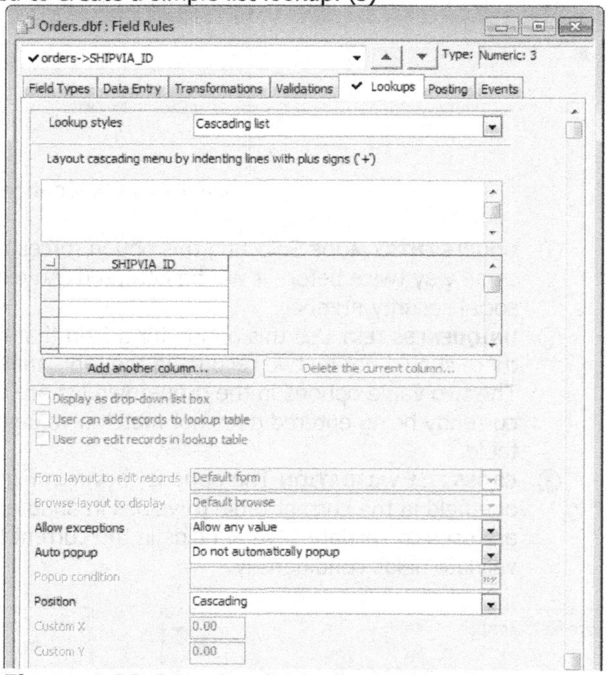

Figure 4-23 Cascading list lookup style options

③ **TABLE LOOKUP** This is the best known and most used lookup option. This lookup style uses data in another table as the source of the lookup values. Usually, the lookup table has the same field as the fill table. A filter can be created to only display certain records in the lookup table (also known as the **SOURCE TABLE**). The fill table (also known as the **DESTINATION TABLE**) is a table that will have a value copied to it. The options shown later in Figure 4-32 are used to create a table lookup. (5)

④ **CONDITIONAL TABLE LOOKUP** This lookup style is similar to the Table lookup style. The difference is that this option supports using multiple source tables. This is accomplished by creating a conditional expression for each table that will be used in the lookup. The options shown in Figure 4-26 are used to create a conditional table lookup.

⑤ **PREVIOUS VALUES** Select this option when you need to dynamically build a list of lookup values from values that have already been entered in the same field in the same table. The options shown in Figure 4-27 are used to create a previous values lookup. (5)

(5) This lookup style can use a drop-down list or pop up dialog box to display the options.

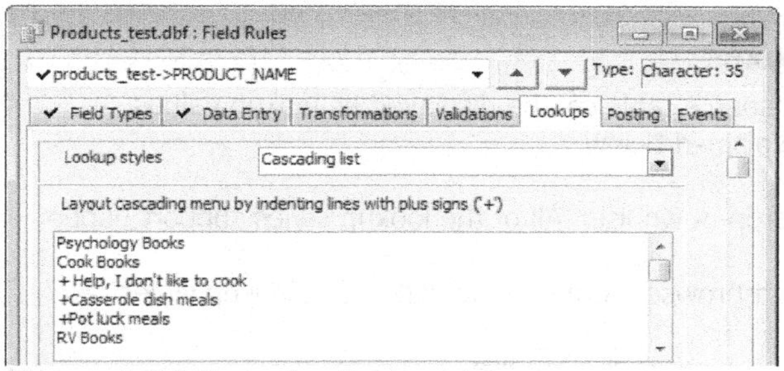

Figure 4-24 Cascading list layout

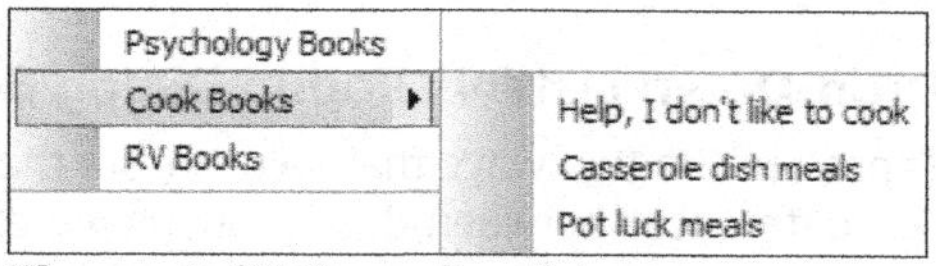

Figure 4-25 Cascading list menu

Conditional Table Lookups Requirement
The tables that will be used for conditional table lookups must have the same field names and types because they will all be mapped to the same field.

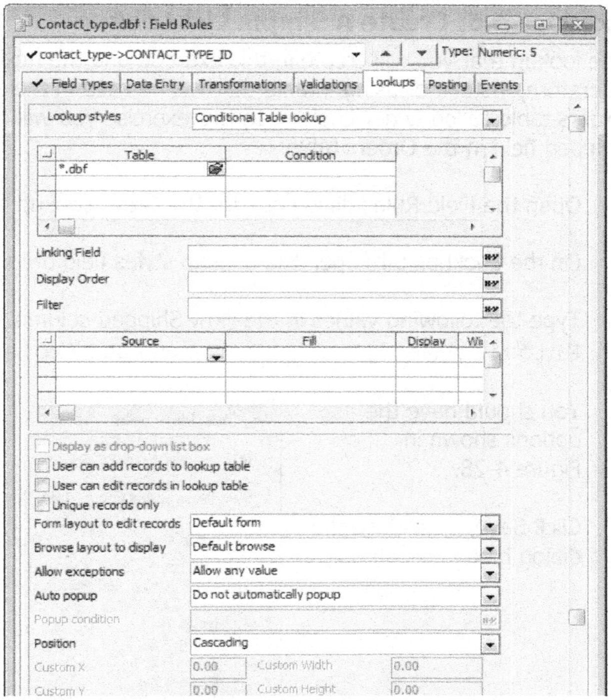

Figure 4-26 Conditional Table lookup options

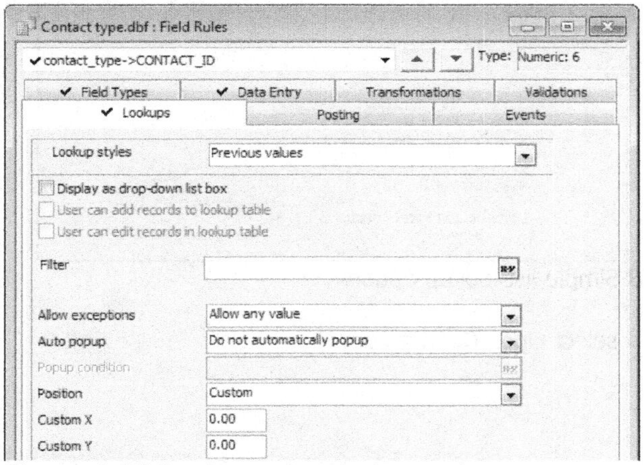

Figure 4-27 Previous values lookup options

Drop-Down Lists vs Popup Dialog Boxes

These are the two ways that values from the source table can be displayed as lookup values. The differences between these options are explained below.

① Many of the lookup styles support drop-down lists. All of the lookup styles support popup dialog boxes.
② Popup dialog boxes can be used on a browse. Some popup dialog box lookup styles can be used with a custom browse.
③ Popup dialog boxes can sort on any column in the browse.

Exercise 4.6: Create A Simple List Lookup

The lookup that you will create in this exercise and the next one are for illustration purposes. Therefore, instead of using a table that will be used in the application, you will use a copy of the Orders table called Order Lookup. In this exercise you will create a simple list lookup for the How Shipped field in the Orders table.

1. Open the Field Rules dialog box for the Order Lookup table, then select the How Shipped field.

2. On the Lookups tab, open the Lookup styles field drop-down list and select **SIMPLE LIST**.

3. Type the following values in the How Shipped column: `First Class Mail`, `Media Mail`, `Priority Mail`, `2-Day Priority` and `Express Mail`.

4. You should have the options shown in Figure 4-28.

   Click Save, then close the dialog box.

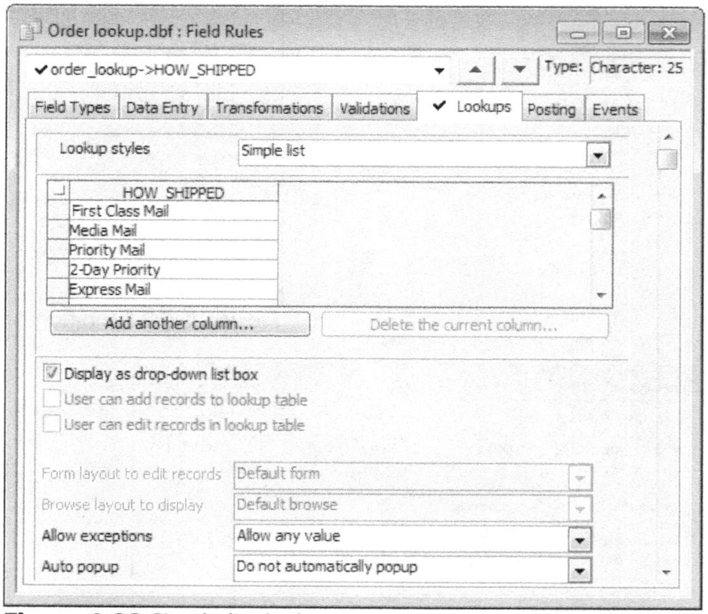

Figure 4-28 Simple list lookup options

5. Right-click on the Order Lookup table and select Open Default Form.

6. Click at the end of the How Shipped field to open the drop-down list.

   You should see the options shown in Figure 4-29.

   Close the form.

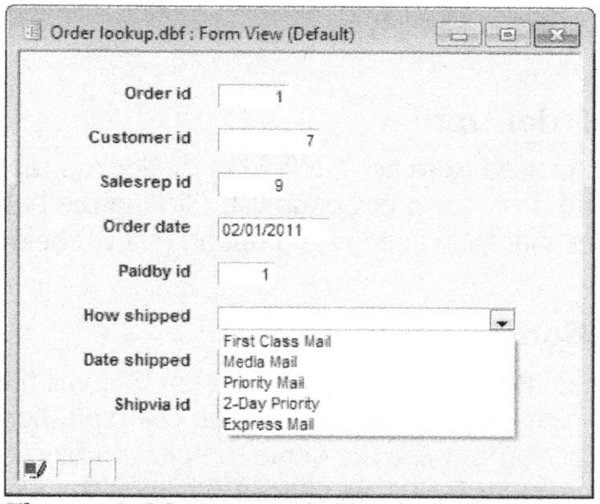

Figure 4-29 Form with Simple list lookup

Exercise 4.7: Create A Table Lookup

In this exercise you will create a lookup drop-down list for the Sales Rep field in the Order Lookup table. The values for the drop-down list will come from a table in a different database. You will then create a table lookup for the Paid By field in the Orders table on your own.

1. Open the Field Rules dialog box for the Order Lookup table, then select the Salesrep ID field.

2. On the Lookups tab, open the Lookup styles drop-down list and select Table lookup.

3. Click the button at the end of the Table field, then select **<MORE FILES ...>**.

4. Navigate to your folder, click on the CBC APP Data folder, then double-click on the Sales Reps.dbf file.

Linking Field Option

This option is used to select the field in the lookup table that has the values that you want the user to select from. If you know the field name, type it in the Linking field. If you do not know the field, click the button at the end of the Linking field. You will see the Expression Builder shown in Figure 4-30.

Click the **CREATE ORDER USING GENIE BUTTON**, then select the linking field in the Sort by drop-down list on the dialog box shown in Figure 4-31.

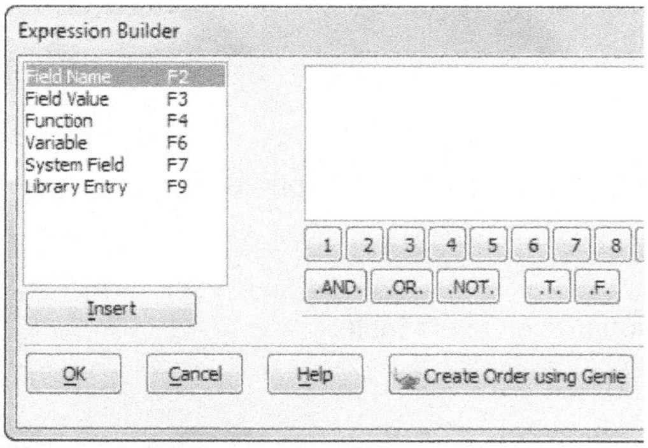

Figure 4-30 Expression Builder

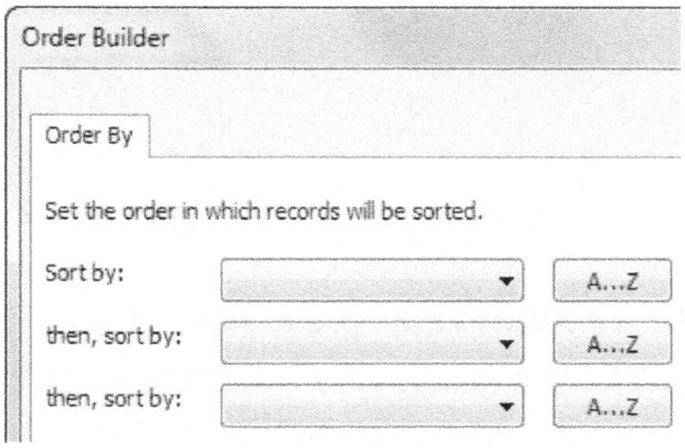

Figure 4-31 Order Builder box

5. In the **LINKING FIELD** type `Rep_ID`.

Display Order Option

This option is used to select the field in the lookup table that will be used to sort the values displayed in the lookup drop-down or popup list. Clicking the button at the end of this field opens the same dialog boxes that the Linking Field option (shown below in Figure 4-32) opens.

Filter Option

This option is used to create an expression that will filter (exclude) records from being displayed in the lookup drop-down or popup list. You can type the expression on the field on the Field Rules dialog box or you can use the genie to help you by clicking the button at the end of the field. Click the **CREATE FILTER USING GENIE BUTTON** on the Expression Builder to open the Filter Builder.

6. In the Source column in the grid, open the drop-down list and select the Rep ID field. Open the Fill field drop-down list and select the Salesrep ID field. Select No in the Display column.

7. On the next row in the grid, open the Source drop-down list and select Rep Full Name. Select Yes in the Display column.

The options selected in step 6 above will add the value in the Rep ID field in the Sales Reps (external) table to the Sales Rep ID field in the Order Lookup table. The ID value will not be displayed in the drop-down list. The options selected in step 7 will display the sales reps full name in the drop-down list, but will not fill any field in the Order Lookup table with this data.

8. Select the **DISPLAY AS DROP-DOWN LIST BOX** option.

   You should have the options shown in Figure 4-32.

   Click the Save button.

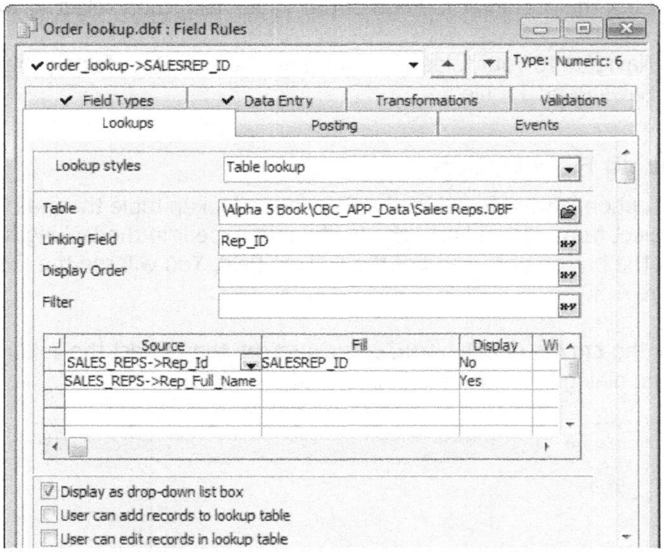

Figure 4-32 Table lookup drop-down list options

Create A Table Lookup On Your Own

In this part of the exercise you will create a Table Lookup in the Orders table.

1. Follow the steps above to create a table lookup for the Paid By ID field in the Orders table.

   Use the Paid By table in the CBC App Data folder to fill the Paid By ID field in the Orders table.

   You should have the options shown in Figure 4-33.

   Save the changes, then close the Field Rules dialog box.

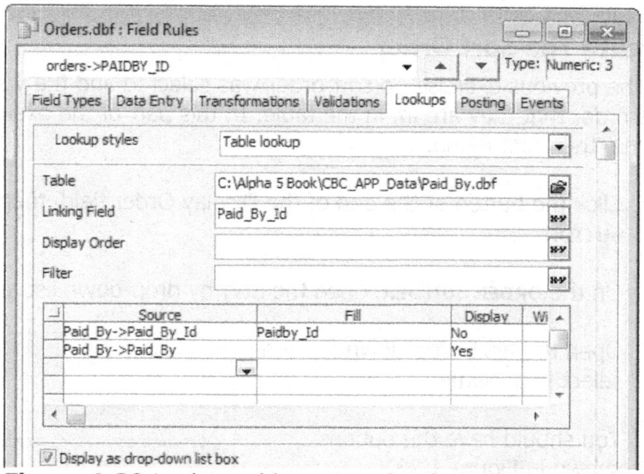

Figure 4-33 Lookup table options for the Paid By ID field

2. Open the Default form for the Orders table. The Paid By ID field should display the options shown in Figure 4-34. Open the Default form for the Order Lookup table, then click at the end of the Sales Rep ID field. You should see the drop-down list shown in Figure 4-35.

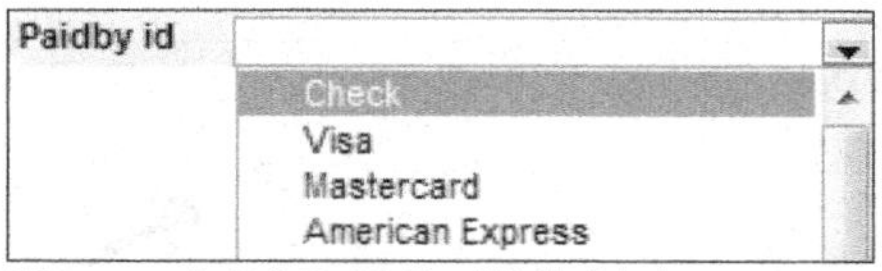

Figure 4-34 Paid By ID field drop-down list options

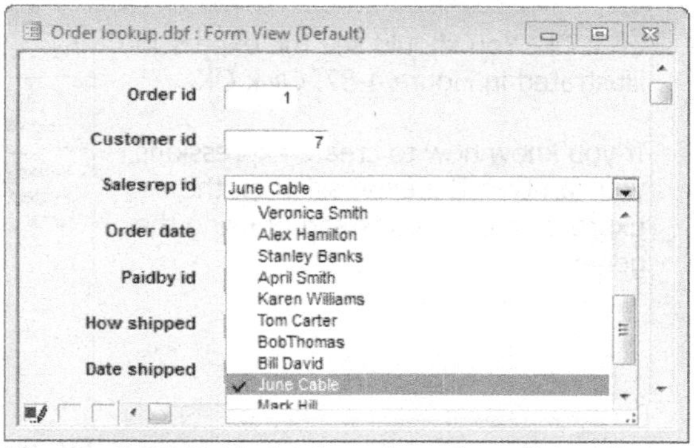

Figure 4-35 Table Lookup drop-down list options

Exercise 4.8: Create A Lookup Popup Dialog Box

In this exercise you will create a lookup popup dialog box for the Customer ID field in the Orders table. Like Exercise 4.7, the values will come from a table in a different database. The reason is because the application that you are creating currently does not have any data. You will also create a popup dialog box for the Product ID field in the Order Detail table on your own.

1. Open the Field Rules dialog box for the Orders table, then select the Customer ID field.

2. On the Lookups tab, open the Lookup styles drop-down list and select Table lookup.

3. Click the button at the end of the Table field and select <More Files ...>. In the CBC APP Data folder, double-click on the Customers.dbf file.

4. Click the button at the end of the Linking field. You should see the Expression Builder. Click the Insert button, then click the Insert button on the Select Field dialog box. Click OK to close the Expression Builder.

Create The Sort Order

In the previous exercise no sort order was selected and the values in the drop-down list appeared in the order that they are in, in the table. In this part of the exercise you will create a sort order of last name, then first name.

1. Click the button at the end of the Display Order field, then click the **CREATE ORDER USING GENIE BUTTON.**

2. On the **ORDER BUILDER**, open the Sort by drop-down list and select Last Name.

3. Open the next drop-down list and select First Name.

   You should have the options shown in Figure 4-36.

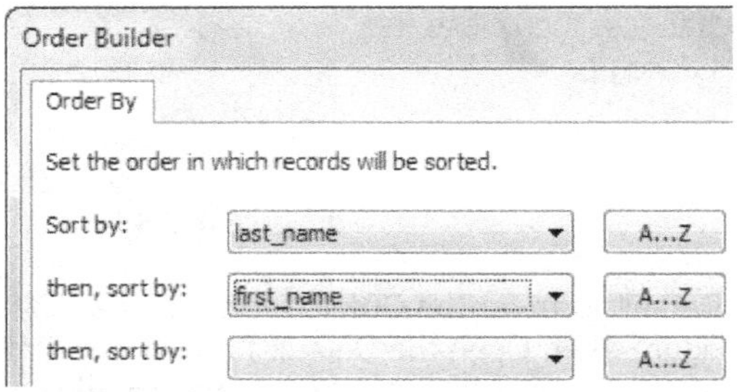

Figure 4-36 Order Builder options

4. Click OK. You should see the expression illustrated in Figure 4-37. Click OK.

   If you know how to create expressions, you can type the expression on the Expression Builder instead of using the genie.

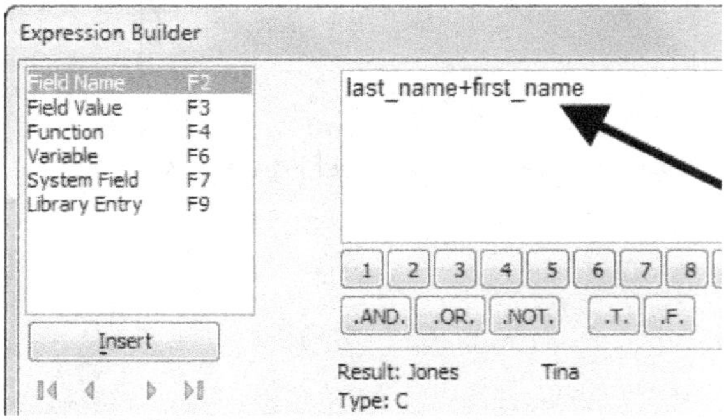

Figure 4-37 Expression illustrated

Select The Lookup And Fill Fields

As in the previous exercise you will display one field on the form and fill a different field with a value from the lookup table.

1. Open the Source drop-down list and select the Customer ID field.

2. Open the Fill drop-down list and select the Customer ID field, then change the Display to No.

3. On the next row, open the Source drop-down list and select the Last Name field, then change the Display to Yes.

4. Repeat step 3 to add the following fields: First Name, Address and City.

   You should have the options shown in Figure 4-38.

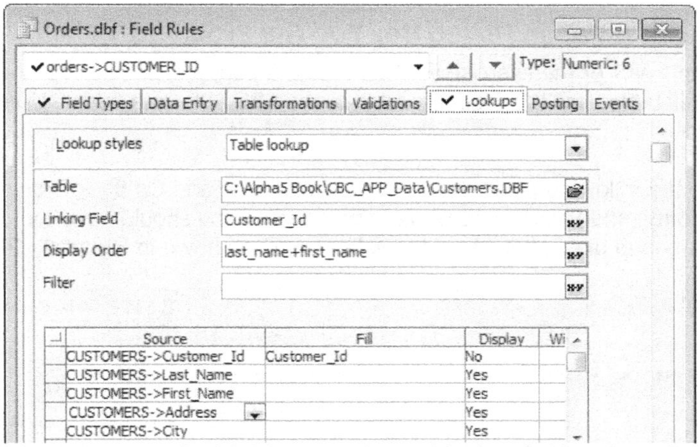

Figure 4-38 Linked field, sort order and lookup fields selected

Create The Popup Dialog Box

1. Open the Auto popup drop-down list and select **POPUP ON ENTRANCE**.

2. Open the Browse layout to display drop-down list and select Default browse.

3. Open the Position drop-down list and select **CUSTOM**.

4. Change the Custom Width to `6.00`, then change the Custom Height to `5.00`.

   Figure 4-39 shows the options that you should have selected.

   Save the changes.

   The reason that I set the column width and height is to keep the dialog box from taking up the entire screen.

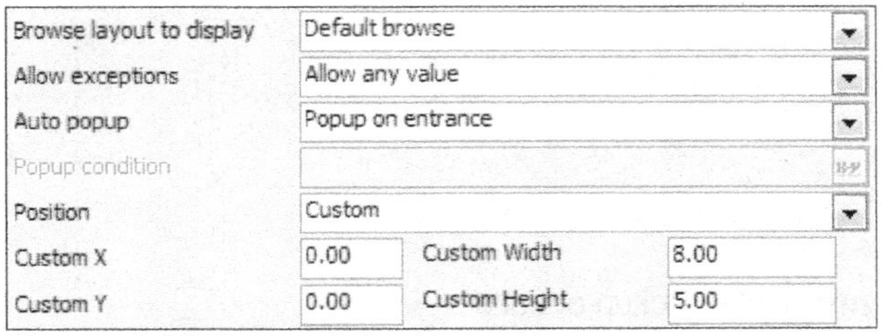

Figure 4-39 Popup dialog box options

5. Open the default form for the Orders table, then click in the Customer ID field.

   You should see the popup dialog box shown in Figure 4-40.

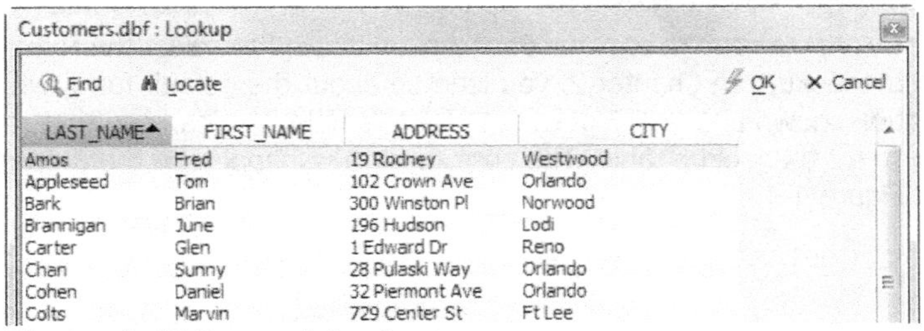

Figure 4-40 Popup dialog box

The columns can be resized by moving the vertical line between the column headings, like you do in a spreadsheet.

Create A Popup Dialog Box For The Product ID Field

In this part of the exercise you will create a popup dialog box for the Product ID field in the Order Detail table. Use the Products table in the CBC APP Data folder. Use the Item ID field as the linking field.

Use the following fields: Item ID, Product Name and On Back Order. Select the **USER CAN ADD RECORDS** and **USER CAN EDIT RECORDS** options. You should have the options shown in Figure 4-41. The popup dialog box should look like the one shown in Figure 4-42.

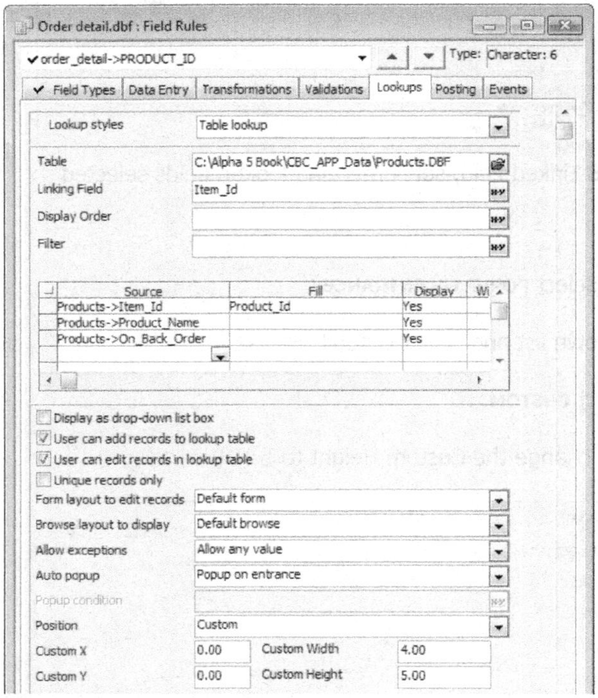

Figure 4-41 Lookup options

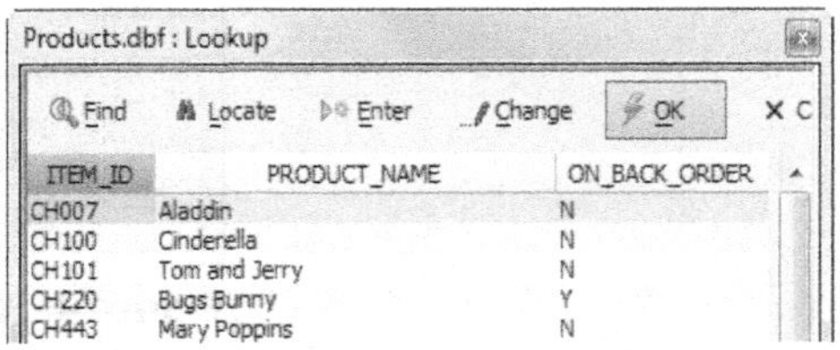

Figure 4-42 Product ID popup dialog box

Lookup Layout Options

The **FORM LAYOUT TO EDIT RECORDS** option is used to select the form that will be used to edit records in the lookup. In Chapter 2, you learned about the default form, which you see displayed in the option shown above in Figure 4-41 for this field. You can use that form or you can create a custom form for the lookup table. The custom form will appear in the drop-down list for the fields, as shown in Figure 4-43.

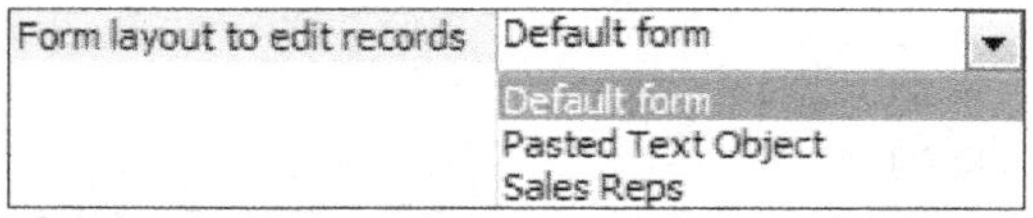

Figure 4-43 Form layout to edit records drop-down lists options

The **BROWSE LAYOUT TO DISPLAY** option is used to select a browse that will be used to display the lookup data. You can set the default browse or select a custom one from the drop-down list.
I created two custom browses, but neither would display in the drop-down list.

Exercise 4.9: Add More Field Rules

At a minimum, the field rules in Table 4-5 need to be created. You should create them before going to the next chapter.

Table	Field	Rule
Contact Type	Contact ID	Always Required
Contact Type	Contact Date	Always Required
Contacts	Last Name	Always Required
Order Detail	Order ID	Always Required
Orders	Order ID	Auto increment, Always Required
Orders	Customer ID	Always Required
Orders	SalesRep ID	Always Required
Paid By	Paid By ID	Auto increment, Always Required
Paid By	Paid By	Always Required
Products	Product ID	Auto increment, Always Required
Products	Product Name	Always Required
Sales Reps	Sales Rep ID	Auto increment, Always Required
Sales Reps	Rep First Name	Always Required
Sales Reps	Rep Last Name	Always Required

Table 4-5 Field rules that need to be created

Field Rules For Memo Fields
Memo fields do not have field rules. You can use the following options on the Field Rules dialog box for memo fields.

① The Default Descriptive name and Field Description fields on the Field Types tab can be used.
② A Lookup field can be created to fill in a memo field.

USING THE APPEND GENIE AND APPEND BUILDER

In this chapter you will learn how to create append operations using the Append Genie and Append Builder tools. This will let you add data to the application that you are creating in this book. You will also learn about the following:

☑ Master and Transaction tables
☑ Mapping fields
☑ Append operations
☑ Duplicating a table

CHAPTER 5

Overview

If you haven't noticed, the tables that you have created, do not have any data. I thought about having you type in the data, but came to the conclusion that doing so would make you mad, so I decided to kill the following three birds with one stone, as they say. Yes, I said three <smile>.

① You will learn how to use the **APPEND OPERATION** to add data to the tables that you have created.
② In addition to using the Append Genie, you will also learn how to append data using the Append Builder.
③ This will be a good test of how well you created the tables and field rules in the previous chapters.

Yes, this chapter may be out of order in terms of learning Alpha Five, but I figured that was better then typing in data <smile>. Plus, when you extracted the files in the zip file, you had to have seen the CBC APP Data folder, that you used in the previous chapter. I suspect that you were curious to know what the tables would be used for. Primarily, they will be used to add data to the tables in the application that you are creating.

How To Start A New Operation
There are several ways to open the Create New Operation dialog box (shown later in Figure 5-2), as explained below.

① Right-click on the table that you want to create the operation for and select Create Operation.
② On the Operations tab, right-click on a blank space and select New Operation.
③ On the Operations tab, right-click on an existing operation and select New <type> Operation. (1)
④ With an existing operation selected, open the **APPEND MENU** and select New <type> Operation. (1)
⑤ On the Operations tab with no operation selected, open the Operation menu and select New Operation, as shown in Figure 5-1.

(1) The "type" doesn't matter on the menu because you can select the type of operation that you want to create on the Create New Operation dialog box.

What Happens During The Append Process?

There are three main tasks that happen during the append process, as explained below.

① The master database file is locked. When a database file is locked, no one else should use it.
② Some or all of the records in the transaction file are added (copied) to the master file.
③ If needed, indexes are updated.

Operation Menu

The menu shown in Figure 5-1 is available when the Operations tab on the Control Panel is selected. The options are also available on the shortcut menu when you right-click on a blank space on the Operations tab.

The **NEW OPERATION** option opens the Create New Operation dialog box, shown later in Figure 5-2.

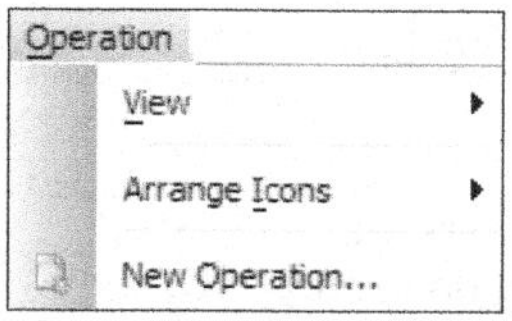

Figure 5-1 Operation and shortcut menu

> **Location Of The Data To Append**
> All of the tables that will be used to append data to the tables in your database are in this folder. C:\Alpha 5 Book\CBC_APP_Data

Exercise 5.1: Use The Append Genie To Add Records To The Contact Type Table

In this exercise you will create an append operation using the Append Genie, which will add records to the Contact Type table.

1. Open the CBC APP database if it is not already open, then click on the Operations tab.

2. Right-click in the window and select **NEW OPERATION.**

   You will see the dialog box shown in Figure 5-2.

   As luck would have it, you want to append records to the Contact Type table. Both options are already selected, as shown in the figure.

   The options in the Step 1 list on the left side of the dialog box are the types of operations that you can create. When you select an option in this list, you will see a brief description of how the operation will manipulate the data, as illustrated in the figure.

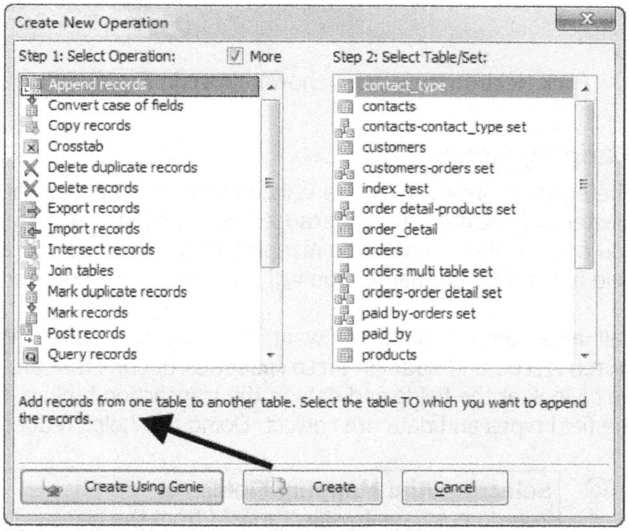

Figure 5-2 Create New Operation dialog box

The **CREATE USING GENIE BUTTON** opens the corresponding genie for the type of operation that you selected.

The **CREATE BUTTON** opens the Append Builder, which is used to create the operation on your own.

What Are Master And Transaction Tables?

The next screen on the genie explains in greater detail what the Append operation does. It also explains that the **MASTER TABLE** is the table that records will be added to and that the **TRANSACTION TABLE** contains the records that will be added.

3. Click the **CREATE USING GENIE** button.

4. Click Next. On the Transaction Table screen, click the button at the end of the Transaction table field and select <More Files ...>.

5. Navigate to, then open the CBC APP Data folder.

   Double-click on the Contact Type.dbf file. This is the table that will be used as the transaction table.

   You should see the path for the transaction table shown in Figure 5-3. Click Next.

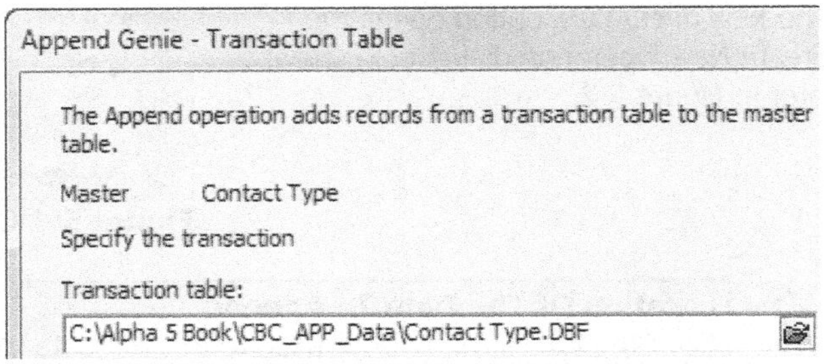

Figure 5-3 Transaction Table genie screen

On the screen shown in Figure 5-4, you have to select whether or not the fields in the transaction table, have the same name as the fields in the master table that they will be added to. When in doubt, select No.

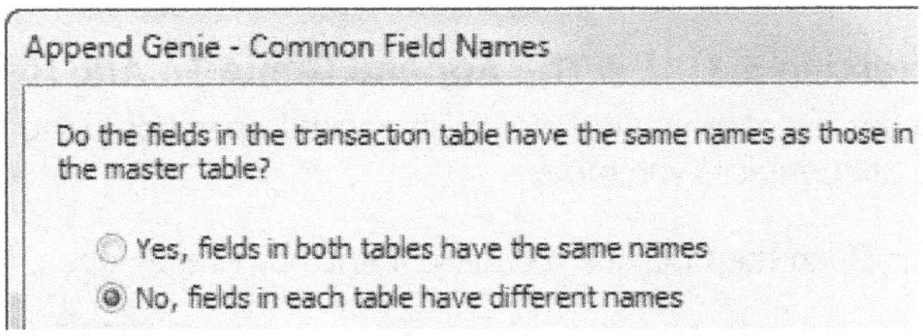

Figure 5-4 Common Field Names genie screen

6. Click Next on the screen shown above in Figure 5-4.

Mapping Fields

There may be fields in the transaction table that appear not to have a corresponding field in the master table. Often, this is because the same data has different field names. When this is the case, you can do what is known as mapping fields. This lets you append data to a field, even though the field has a different name. You will see how this works later in Figure 5-5.

Call me a control freak if you want, but I prefer to select the fields myself, instead of using the **MATCH FIELDS** and **SUGGEST FIELD MAPPINGS** options that are on the Match Field Names genie screen. I also look at the fields and data in the transaction table before I append data, to make sure that the field types and data are correct. Doing this helps reduce appending data to the wrong field.

> **Selecting And Mapping Fields**
> You do not have to select a field from the transaction table for each field in the master table, as shown in Figure 5-5. There may be fields in the transaction table that do not have a matching (corresponding) field in the master table. That is okay, unless you need to append the data. If that is the case, close the Append Genie, add the field to the master table, then start the Append Genie again.

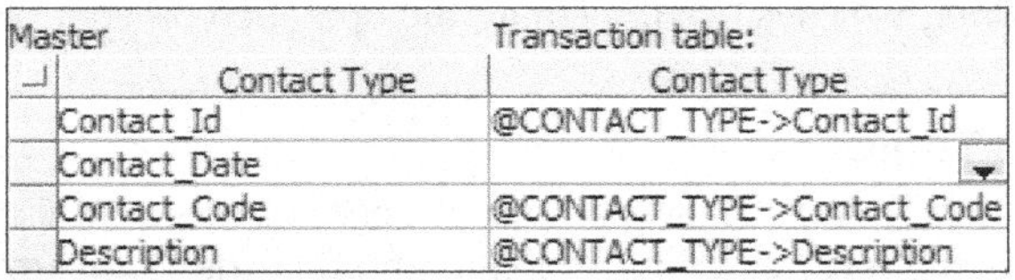

Figure 5-5 Master table field without a transaction table field

7. In the Transaction table column, open the first drop-down list and select the Contact ID field.

8. Select the fields in the Transaction table for the other three fields.

   You should have the options shown in Figure 5-6.

   Click Next.

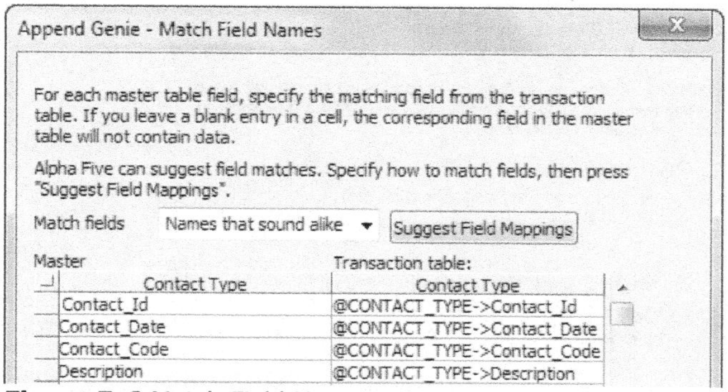

Figure 5-6 Match Field Names genie screen

Using Expressions

When you select a field in the transaction table, you will see the option illustrated in Figure 5-7. Selecting this option opens the Expression Builder. This is used to create a formula to manipulate the data in the transaction table, so that it can be mapped to a field in the master table.

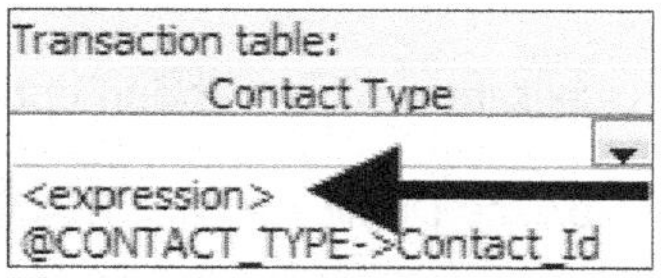

Figure 5-7 Expression option illustrated

For example, if the master table stores the first and last name in one field and the first and last name is stored in two fields in the transaction table, you would create a formula in the Expression Builder to combine the data in the two name fields.

Appending Data Conditionally

There may be times when you do not need to append all of the data in a specific field in the transaction table. When that is the case, create an expression to exclude the data that you do not want to append. For example, if there is a sales rep that you do not want to append, create an expression to exclude the sales rep.

Checking For Duplicate Records

The **DUPLICATE RECORD ACTION** screen shown in Figure 5-8 is used to select how duplicate records should be handled. Clicking the **ADVANCED OPTIONS FOR DUPLICATE RECORD CHECKING BUTTON** opens the dialog box shown on the right of the figure.

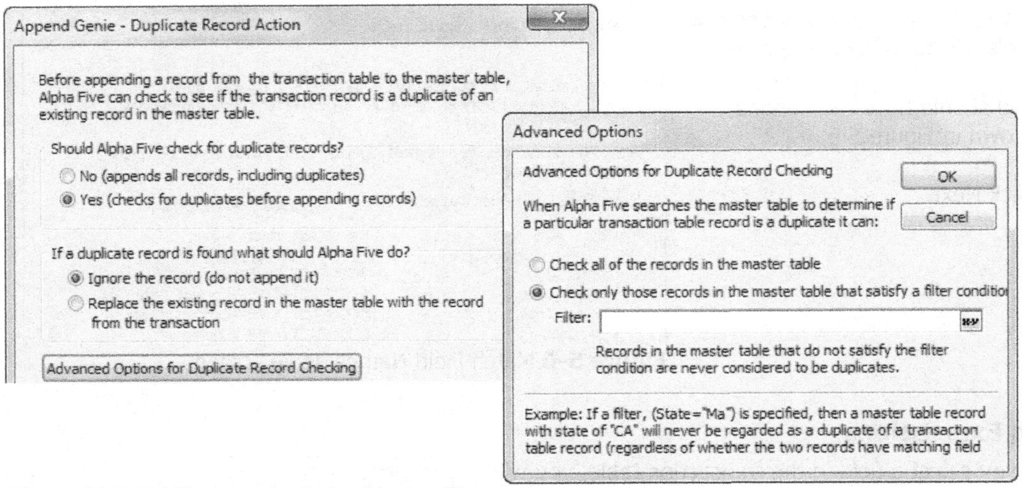
Append Genie - Duplicate Record Action
Before appending a record from the transaction table to the master table, Alpha Five can check to see if the transaction record is a duplicate of an existing record in the master table.
Should Alpha Five check for duplicate records?
No (appends all records, including duplicates)
Yes (checks for duplicates before appending records)
If a duplicate record is found what should Alpha Five do?
Ignore the record (do not append it)
Replace the existing record in the master table with the record from the transaction
Advanced Options for Duplicate Record Checking
Advanced Options
Advanced Options for Duplicate Record Checking
OK
Cancel
When Alpha Five searches the master table to determine if a particular transaction table record is a duplicate it can:
Check all of the records in the master table
Check only those records in the master table that satisfy a filter conditio
Filter:
Records in the master table that do not satisfy the filter condition are never considered to be duplicates.
Example: If a filter, (State="Ma") is specified, then a master table record with state of "CA" will never be regarded as a duplicate of a transaction table record (regardless of whether the two records have matching field

Figure 5-8 Duplicate record checking options

9. Select No on the Duplicate Record Action screen, then click Next.

The options shown in Figure 5-9 are used to select specific records to append. For all of the exercises in this chapter, you should append all records.

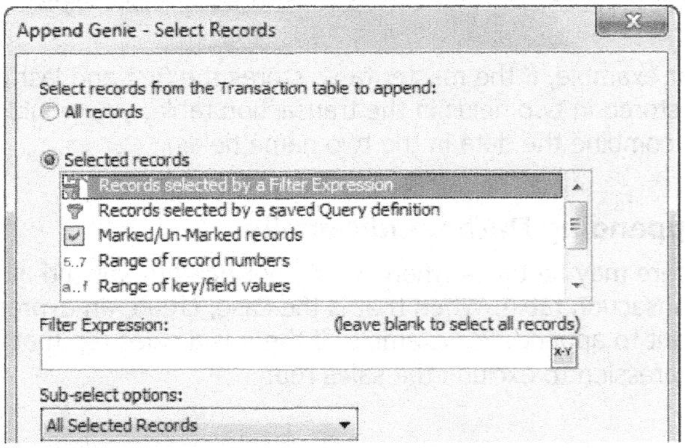
Append Genie - Select Records
Select records from the Transaction table to append:
All records
Selected records
Records selected by a Filter Expression
Records selected by a saved Query definition
Marked/Un-Marked records
Range of record numbers
Range of key/field values
Filter Expression:
(leave blank to select all records)
Sub-select options:
All Selected Records

Figure 5-9 Select Records genie screen

10. Select the **ALL RECORDS** option, then click Next.

11. Select No on the screen shown in Figure 5-10, then click Next.

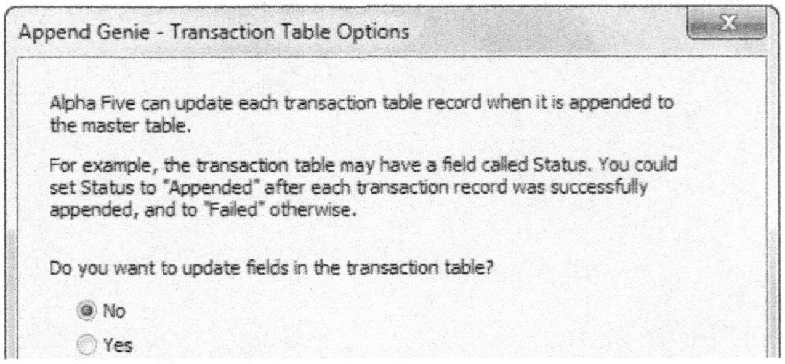
Append Genie - Transaction Table Options
Alpha Five can update each transaction table record when it is appended to the master table.
For example, the transaction table may have a field called Status. You could set Status to "Appended" after each transaction record was successfully appended, and to "Failed" otherwise.
Do you want to update fields in the transaction table?
No
Yes

Figure 5-10 Transaction Table Options genie screen

Save The Append Operation

As shown by the option selected in Figure 5-11, you can save the append operations that you create. If you think that you will have the need to run the operation again, you should save it.

The **DON'T RUN** option opens the Append Builder, shown later in Figure 5-21. You can save the append operation from that window also.

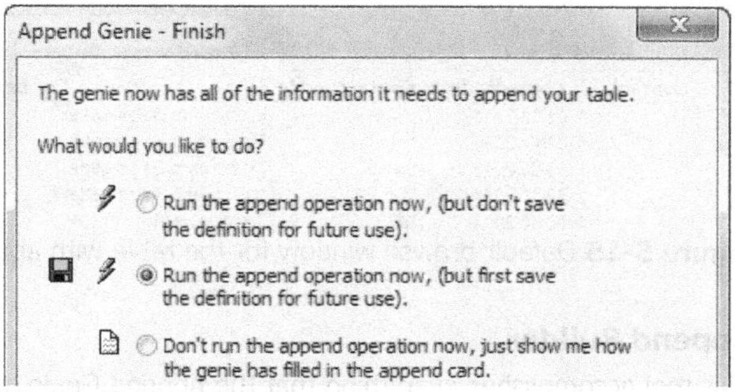
Append Genie - Finish
The genie now has all of the information it needs to append your table.
What would you like to do?
Run the append operation now, (but don't save the definition for future use).
Run the append operation now, (but first save the definition for future use).
Don't run the append operation now, just show me how the genie has filled in the append card.

Figure 5-11 Finish genie screen

12. Accept the default option shown above in Figure 5-11 to save the operation, then run the append operation.

    Click Finish.

    Type `app_contact_type` in the Name field shown in Figure 5-12, then click OK.

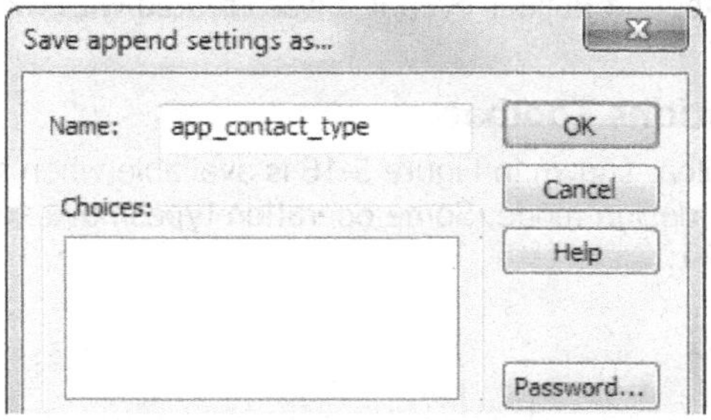
Save append settings as...
Name:
app_contact_type
OK
Cancel
Choices:
Help
Password...

Figure 5-12 Save append settings as dialog box

> **Operation File Names**
> Yes, I know that each type of operation has it's own symbol on the Operations tab on the Control Panel, but I am not about to memorize the symbols. Instead, I use a prefix. For append operations, I use the prefix **APP**. Also, if I use the same prefix for all append operations, they will automatically be listed together in alphabetical order on the Operations tab. See, there is a method to the madness <smile>.

Run The Append Operation

13. You should see the message shown in Figure 5-13.

    The message lets you know how many records will be appended.

    Click OK.

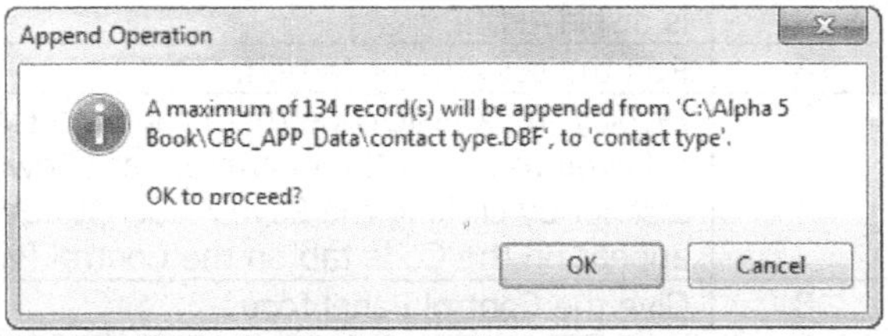
Append Operation
A maximum of 134 record(s) will be appended from 'C:\Alpha 5 Book\CBC_APP_Data\contact type.DBF', to 'contact type'.
OK to proceed?
OK
Cancel

Figure 5-13 Append Operation message

When the append operation is complete, you will see the message shown in Figure 5-14. This message lets you know how many records were appended.

Clicking the **VIEW RESULT BUTTON** displays the default browse window for the table, shown in Figure 5-15. This will let you view the data that was appended.

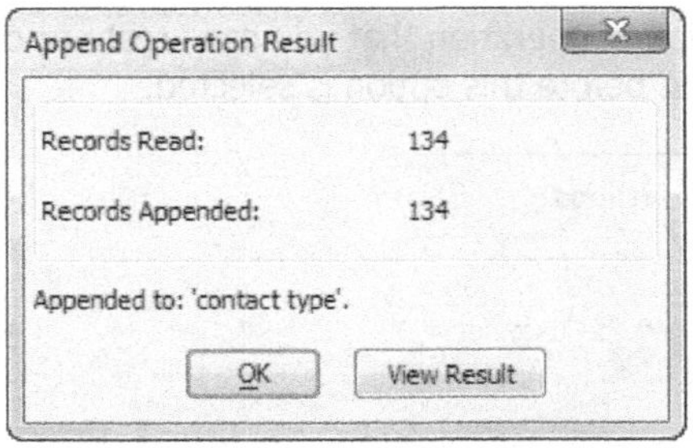
Append Operation Result
Records Read:
134
Records Appended:
134
Appended to: 'contact type'.
OK
View Result

Figure 5-14 Append Operation Result dialog box

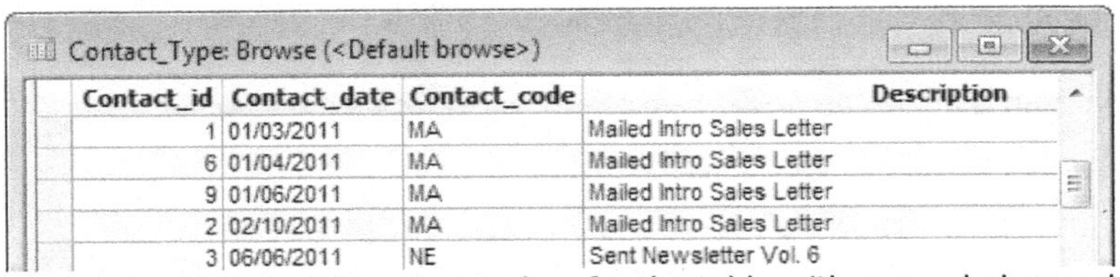

Contact_id	Contact_date	Contact_code	Description
1	01/03/2011	MA	Mailed Intro Sales Letter
6	01/04/2011	MA	Mailed Intro Sales Letter
9	01/06/2011	MA	Mailed Intro Sales Letter
2	02/10/2011	MA	Mailed Intro Sales Letter
3	06/06/2011	NE	Sent Newsletter Vol. 6

Figure 5-15 Default browse window for the table with appended records

Append Builder

This tool accomplishes everything that the Append Genie does. The difference is that you are not prompted to select options. If you save an append operation and need to open it later, it will open in the Append Builder even if it was created with the Append Genie.

Operations Toolbar

The toolbar shown in Figure 5-16 is available when an operation is being created or the operation is open in design mode. Some operation types have additional buttons. The options are explained in Table 5-1.

Figure 5-16 Operations toolbar

Button	Is Used To . . .
1	Save the selected operation.
2	Save the selected operation with a different name.
3	Create a new operation. (2)
4	Open an operation. A dialog box similar to the one shown in Figure 5-17 is displayed. (2)
5	Select records for the operation. A dialog box similar to the one shown in Figure 5-18 is displayed.
6	Run the selected operation.
7	Display the Xbasic code that is automatically generated from the options that you selected to create the operation, as shown in Figure 5-19. This code can be saved as a script by clicking the Save As Script button. If you save the code as a script, it will appear on the Code tab on the Control Panel.
8	Give the Control Panel focus.

Table 5-1 Operations toolbar buttons explained

(2) The type of operation that you can create or open, depends on the type of operation that is selected before this option is selected.

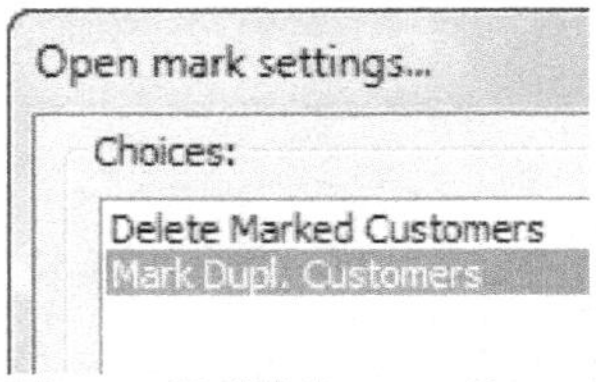

Figure 5-17 Open <Operation Type> dialog box

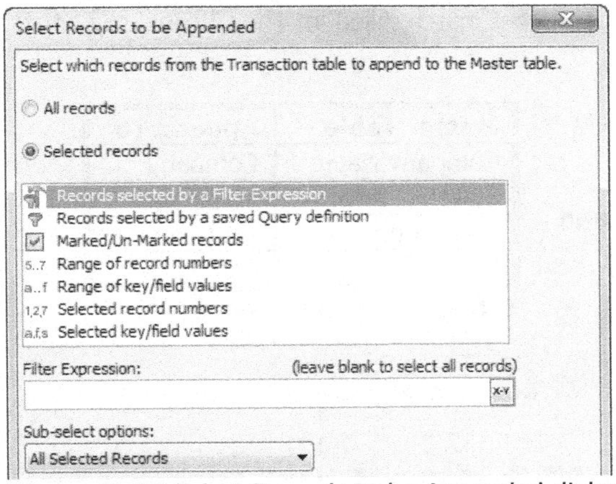

Figure 5-18 Select Records to be Appended dialog box

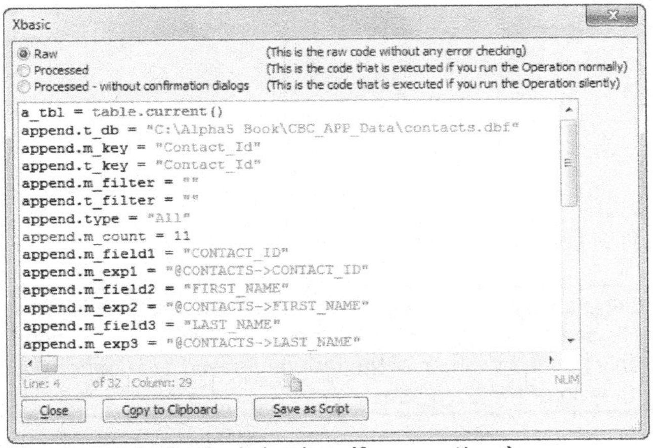

Figure 5-19 Xbasic dialog box (for operations)

Operation Type Menu

Each type of operation (mark, update, append, etc.) has a menu with the same name. The menu has the same options as the Operations shortcut menu. [See Chapter 2, Operations Shortcut Menu]

Exercise 5.2: Use The Append Builder To Add Records To The Contacts Table

Using the Append Builder will give you the opportunity to see if you like using it better then the Append Genie.

1. On the Control Panel, right-click on the Contacts table and select **CREATE OPERATION.**

2. On the Create New Operation dialog box, click the **CREATE** button.

3. Click the button at the end of the Transaction field and select <More Files ...>, then double-click on the Contacts.dbf file in the CBC App Data folder.

As you can see, fields with the same name were automatically matched. In this exercise, the master contacts table has additional fields that need to be matched. Maybe I want too much, but I would like to have all of the fields in the master table automatically displayed in the same order that they are in, in the table, with fields from the transaction table that match, filled in. Then I could see what fields are left to match.

4. Make the dialog box longer, then add the fields in Table 5-2.

   When finished, you should have the options shown in Figure 5-20.

Master Table	Append To
Company Name	Company
State Province	State
Postal Code	Zip Code
Note	Comments

Table 5-2 Fields to map

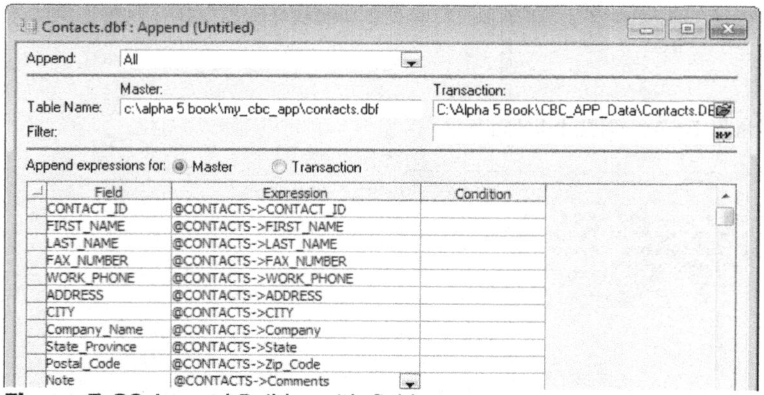

Figure 5-20 Append Builder with fields to append selected

The **ALL** append type does not require a **LINKING KEY FIELD** for each table, so the field is not displayed when the All append type is selected. The Linking key fields, shown for illustration purposes only, in Figure 5-21, are only needed if either of the Unique append type options are selected in the Append field at the top of the dialog box.

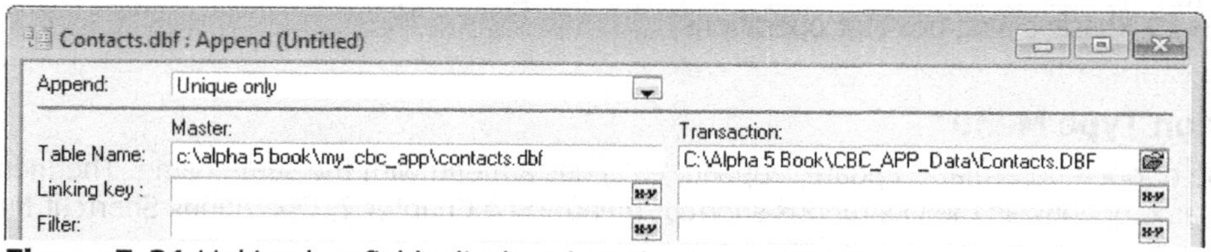

Figure 5-21 Linking key fields displayed on the Append Builder

5. Click the Save button on the toolbar. Type `app_contacts` in the Name field, then click OK.

Run The Append Operation

1. Click the Run button on the toolbar, then click OK to append the records.

2. Close the Append Builder.

Exercise 5.3: Create The Remaining Append Operations

The previous exercises in this chapter showed you how to use the Append Genie and the Append Builder. In this exercise you will create and run the remaining append operations on your own to add data to the tables.

Append all records from the transaction table. Field names that do not match exactly are listed for each table. There are fields in the transaction tables that will not be mapped to a field in the CBC APP application. Save each append operation as app_table name.

Create The Order Detail Table Append Operation

1. Use the Order Detail transaction table.
2. Map the Product ID field in the master table to the Item ID field in the transaction table. 271 records should be appended.

Create The Orders Table Append Operation

1. Use the Order Header transaction table.
2. Map the fields in Table 5-3.

   136 records should be appended.

Master Table Field	Maps To Transaction Table Field
Salesrep ID	Rep ID
Paidby ID	Paid By ID
Shipvia ID	Ship Via

Table 5-3 Orders table fields to map

Create The Paid By Table Append Operation

1. Use the Paid By transaction table. 4 records should be appended.

Create The Products Table Append Operation

1. Use the Products transaction table.
2. Map the Product ID field in the master table to the Item ID field in the transaction table. 25 records should be appended.

Create The Sales Reps Table Append Operation

1. Use the Sales Reps transaction table.
2. Map the Sales Rep ID field in the master table to the Rep ID field in the transaction table. 10 records should be appended.

Exercise 5.4: Duplicate A Table

I guess by now you are wondering why the application that you are creating does not have a table for customers. The reason that it has not been created until now is because I wanted to show you how to duplicate a table. The Contacts table has the same fields that the Customers table needs. The Contacts table also has the field rules and data that the Customers table needs. Are you really surprised? <smile> In this exercise you will learn how to duplicate a table.

1. Right-click on the Contacts table ⇒ Utilities ⇒ Duplicate.

2. Check all four options on the dialog box, then type `Customers` in the **NEW TABLE NAME** field shown in Figure 5-22.

   The button illustrated in the figure opens the Xbasic Code dialog box.

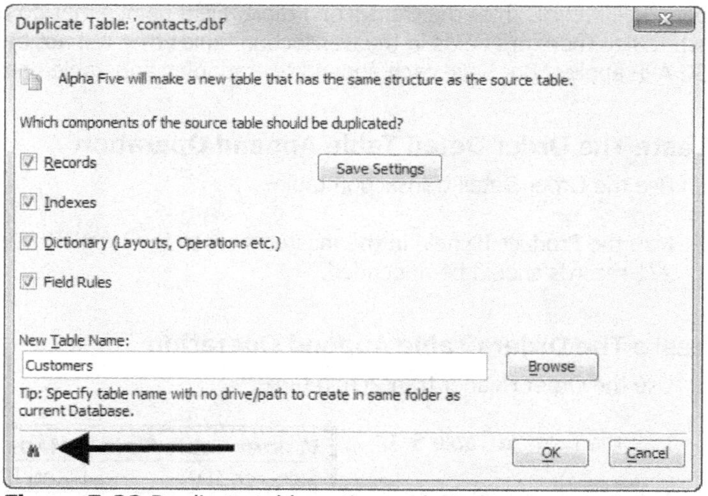
Duplicate Table: 'contacts.dbf'
Alpha Five will make a new table that has the same structure as the source table.
Which components of the source table should be duplicated?
Records
Save Settings
Indexes
Dictionary (Layouts, Operations etc.)
Field Rules
New Table Name:
Customers
Browse
Tip: Specify table name with no drive/path to create in same folder as current Database.
OK
Cancel

Figure 5-22 Duplicate table options selected

3. Click the Save Settings button. You will not see any changes. Click OK.

4. You will see a message saying that the table was duplicated. Click Yes to view the table. You will see that the Customers table has data. If you view the field rules for the Customers table, you will see that it also has field rules.

5. Rename the following fields in the Customers table, then save the changes. Sadly, doing this loses the field rules.
   Contact ID to `Customer ID`
   State Province to `State`
   Postal Code to `Zip Code`

6. Add the field rules in Exercise 4.1 Create An Auto Increment Field to the Customers table.

USING THE SET EDITOR

After completing the exercises in this chapter you will be able to create sets by learning about the following:

- ☑ Relational databases
- ☑ Types of relationships
- ☑ How linking works
- ☑ Creating one-to-one linked table sets
- ☑ Creating one-to-many linked table sets
- ☑ Create sets with more than two tables
- ☑ Add and drop tables and sets

Overview

Now that all of the tables have been created and the field rules for the tables have been set up, you are ready to create the sets. If you do not define the sets properly, you will have more problems than you can handle when you use them as the basis for a form, report or browse. To create sets properly, you need to understand some key terms, including relationships.

The three types of relationships are explained later in this chapter. Even if you do not use relationships in the applications that you create, it is good to understand the concept, as it will help you develop applications in general and design better table structures, because you will have a better understanding of how data in one table relates to data in another table.

In this chapter you will learn about primary key fields, relational databases, their attributes and sets. Earlier in this book I stated that there are terminology differences between Alpha Five and many other relational database management systems. I know that many people that are learning Alpha Five, have a background that includes developing applications in Access, FoxPro, FileMaker Pro and SQL. In order to be able to understand the Alpha Five terminology that will be covered in this chapter, I will include how Alpha Five uses the same concept that other databases use.

What Is Normalization?

Normalization is the process of determining the structure of the data. This means looking at all of the fields in all of the tables to ensure that the same data is not in several tables, unless it is an ID field. You also have to make sure that the fields in a table are in the right table. Once you gain more experience, you will be able to do this before you create any tables.

Relational Databases

In Chapter 3, I wrote a little about linking tables. The reason that tables can be linked is because there is a relationship between them, thus the term "Relational Databases". Yes, this is a complicated topic and there are a lot of books on the concepts associated with relational databases and how to create them, so I won't bore you with the details, but please hear me out and don't skip this section. If you have never created a database before using this book, or have very little experience creating tables, the next few sections in this chapter will be your crash course in databases, relationships and sets. You will learn how all of the components fit together.

Figures 6-1 and 6-2 show the layout of two tables.

Orders			
Order ID	Order Date	Order Amount	Cust ID
1000	1/2/2005	$263.99	48
1001	1/2/2005	$322.45	57
1002	1/3/2005	$196.00	3
1003	1/4/2005	$124.99	48

Table Name
Field Names
Records

Figure 6-1 Orders table layout

Orders Detail		
Order ID	Product ID	Quantity
1000	43	4
1000	76	2
1001	76	3
1001	10	2
1003	10	1
1004	25	3

Table Name
Field Names
Records

Figure 6-2 Orders Detail table layout

Primary Key Fields

In Chapter 3 you created primary keys in some of the tables that you created. The primary keys are the **ID FIELDS**. You will see these two terms (Primary key and ID fields) used interchangeably. I prefer to use the term ID field because primary key fields usually have "ID" as part of the field name.

> ID is short for identification. It is jargon that the programming community uses to reference a field that can be used to link the data in one table to the data in another table.

All of the tables in the CBC APP database have at least one ID field. The reason ID fields are used is because by design they provide a way for each record in the table to have a unique way to be identified.

I have taught several database classes and almost without fail, this topic causes a lot of confusion. For some reason, people want to create primary key fields on string (what Alpha Five calls character fields). Please don't do that. It can cause you problems, especially if the field is not set to not allow duplicate values. Yes, I know that this contradicts what I said in Chapter 3. I know that people will continue to create ID fields that have non-numeric data, until database structures are changed to no longer allow it, so I added a few character fields as ID fields in the application that you are creating in this book to show how character ID fields should be created if you insist on using them.

If you needed to create a report that showed all of the orders and what items were on each order, you would need a way to link the Orders and Orders Detail tables, shown above in Figures 6-1 and 6-2. Think of "linking" as having the ability to combine two or more tables "virtually" and being able to display the result of this "virtual linking" on a computer screen or on a report.

In Figures 6-1 and 6-2 above, the common ID field is the Order ID field. If you look at the data in the Orders Detail table, you will see that some records have the same Order ID number. That's okay. This means that some customers placed orders with more than one item. Each record in the Orders Detail table represents one item that a customer ordered. If you were to "virtually" join the data in the tables shown in Figures 6-1 and 6-2 above, it would look like the table shown in Figure 6-3.

Orders				Orders Detail		
Order ID	Order Date	Order Amount	Cust ID	Order ID	Product ID	Quantity
1000	1/2/2005	$263.99	48	1000	43	4
1000	1/2/2005	$263.99	48	1000	76	2
1001	1/2/2005	$322.45	57	1001	76	3
1001	1/2/2005	$322.45	57	1001	10	2
1002	1/3/2005	$196.00	3			
1003	1/4/2005	$124.99	48	1003	10	1
				1004	25	3

Figure 6-3 Virtually joined tables

This "virtual" join is what happens when tables are **LINKED**. If all of the data in the tables in Figures 6-1 and 6-2 shown earlier was stored in one table instead of two, at the very minimum, the Order Date and Order Amount fields would be repeated for every record that is in the Orders Detail table. Repetition of data is why this information is stored in two tables instead of one. It is poor table design to have the same information (other than fields that are used to join tables) stored in more than one table.

> Usually if you see a record in the Orders Detail table, like Order ID 1004 shown above in Figure 6-3, or any child table that is in a parent-child relationship, there is a problem with the data in at least one of the tables. This happens because **REFERENTIAL INTEGRITY** was not enforced between the tables. All of the records in the child table should have at least one matching record in the parent table. Parent tables are used to get data from a child table.

How Do Relationships Work?

A relationship works by matching fields from tables. Often the "related" fields have the same name in both tables. For example, the relationship between the Order Header and Order Detail tables is based on the Order ID field. This is the field that both tables have in common.

Types Of Relationships

The Employee list report shown in Figure 6-4 requires two tables. These tables are linked by a common field, the Employee ID field. This field is what connects (joins) data from both tables. Doing this allows data from both tables to be used in the same report.

The Employee ID field in the Employee table is how the matching record (known as a **ONE-TO-ONE RELATIONSHIP**) or records (known as a **ONE-TO-MANY RELATIONSHIP**) in the Employee Addresses table are found. These are the two most common types of relationships.

Figure 6-4 Employee list report

A **ONE-TO-ONE RELATIONSHIP** means that there is only one matching record in the child table for each parent record. In the order scenario discussed earlier, if you also need to display the customer that placed the order, the link that would be created between the Orders table and the Customer table would be a one-to-one relationship because each order can only have one customer.

A **ONE-TO-MANY RELATIONSHIP** means that there can be two or more matching records in the child table for the parent record. This is the most popular type of relationship. In the order scenario, the link that would be created between the Orders table and the Orders Detail table would be a one-to-many relationship because each order can have more than one item.

Another example of this would be a table that stores the titles of all the books that Capri Book Company sells and another table that stores the publisher of each book. At first you may think that the publisher information should be stored in the same table as the books. Each publisher publishes many books (hopefully), but each book only has one publisher. In this example, the publisher table would be the "one" side of the equation and the table with all of the books would be the "many" side of the equation.

The **MANY-TO-MANY RELATIONSHIP** is the third type of relationship. It is not used as much as the other two types of relationships. This type of relationship has records in both tables that are related to more than one record in the other table. An example is authors and books. An author can write more than one book and one book can be written by more than one author. In Alpha Five, this type of relationship can be created when the primary table can have one-to-many relationships with two other tables.

Alpha Five Does Not Fully Support Many-To-Many Relationships
While Alpha Five allows many-to-many relationships to be created, they cannot be used with forms or browses. You can write code in Xbasic to read from and write to a set that is based on a many-to-many relationship.

My 2 Cents On Understanding The Types Of Relationships
If you are struggling trying to understand what type of relationship to use for a particular group of tables, the key is to understand the data in the tables. The more familiar you are with the data, the easier it will be to figure out which type of relationship needs to be created during the design phase. If you miss any relationships during the design phase, you should be able to catch them during the development or prototype phase.

One-To-One Link Variations

Prior to using Alpha Five, all of the database development software that I have used treated one-to-one relationships as discussed in the previous section.

Alpha Five has what it calls **VARIATIONS** of one-to-one links. These variations are used when there are no matching records or when there are multiple matching records. To me, that seems to defeat the purpose of what a one-to-one relationship is suppose to do; which is find the one matching record in the child table. On the other hand, maybe there is something about these variations that I do not understand. Be that as it may, the variations are explained below.

① If the **FIRST MATCH** option is selected, the first matching record found in the child table will be linked to, even if there are more matching records.
② If the **CLOSEST MATCH** option is selected, the closest matching record in the child table will be linked to, if no exact matches are found.
③ If the **LAST MATCH** option is selected, only the last matching record found in the child table will be selected.

From these three options, in my opinion, only the First Match option should be used because there should only be one matching record in the child table for a one-to-one relationship. If there is more than one match, there is a problem. This is one of the reasons to create ID fields.

The Closest Match option seems scary to me. If the Order table is the parent table and the Customer table is the child table, if the Customer table does not have the Customer ID field that the Order table has, a completely different customer will be displayed with the order and no one would know.

The Last Match option is also problematic to me, because it indicates that there is probably more than one matching record in the child table, which should not be, in a one-to-one relationship.

How Linking Works

More than likely, some forms and most reports that you create will require data from more than one table. Basic reports like a Product List report will only use one table, so there is no linking involved. For reports that require two or more tables, the tables need to be linked. In Alpha Five, this linking is stored in what is called a **SET**.

The best way to understand the basic concept of linking tables is to look at the records or a portion of the records in the tables that need to be linked. When you create a form or report that is based on data that you are not familiar with, you should take the time to look at the data in the tables.

Figures 6-5 and 6-6 show the records in an Employee and Employee Addresses table. The field that these tables have in common is the Employee ID field.

Employee

Employee ID	Supervisor ID	Last Name	First Name	Position	Birth Date	Hire Date
1	5	Davolio	Nancy	Sales Representative	12/8/1972	3/29/1991
2		Fuller	Andrew	Vice President, Sales	2/19/1969	7/12/1991
3	5	Leverling	Janet	Sales Representative	8/30/1971	2/27/1991
4	5	Peacock	Margaret	Sales Representative	9/19/1973	3/30/1992
5	2	Buchanan	Steven	Sales Manager	3/4/1975	9/13/1992
6	5	Suyama	Michael	Sales Representative	7/2/1963	9/13/1992
7	5	King	Robert	Sales Representative	5/29/1972	11/29/1992
8	5	Callahan	Laura	Inside Sales Coordin	1/9/1974	1/30/1993
9	5	Dodsworth	Anne	Sales Representative	1/27/1976	10/12/1993
10	2	Hellstern	Albert	Business Manager	3/13/1968	3/1/1993
11	10	Smith	Tim	Mail Clerk	6/6/1973	1/15/1993
12	10	Patterson	Caroline	Receptionist	9/11/1979	5/15/1993
13	2	Brid	Justin	Marketing Director	10/8/1977	1/1/1994
14	13	Martin	Xavier	Marketing Associate	11/30/1975	1/15/1994
15	13	Pereira	Laurent	Advertising Specialis	12/9/1970	2/1/1994
0	0					

Record: 15 of 15 No Filter Search

Figure 6-5 Employee table data

Employee Addresses

Employee ID	Address1	Address2	City	Region	Country	Postal Code
1	507 - 20th Ave. E.		Port Moody	BC	Canada	V3D 4F6
2	908 W. Capital Way	Suite 100	Coquitlam	BC	Canada	V3H4J7
3	722 Moss Bay Blvd.		Vancouver	BC	Canada	V6M 8S9
4	4110 Old Redmond Rd.		Richmond	BC	Canada	V5S 6H7
5	14 Garrett Hill		London		UK	SW1 8JR
6	Coventry House		London		UK	EC2 7JR
7	Edgeham Hollow	Apt #243	London		UK	RG1 9SP
8	4726 - 11th Ave. N.E.		New Westminster	BC	Canada	V7J 5G5
9	7 Houndstooth Rd.		Nottingham		UK	WG2 7LT
10	13920 S.E. 40th Street		Burnaby	BC	Canada	V2C 8H3
11	30301 - 166th Ave. N.E.	Apt #3D	North Vancouver	BC	Canada	V3K 2G9
12	16 Maple Lane		West Vancouver	BC	Canada	V3L 5S3
13	2 impasse du Soleil		Haguenau	Bas-Rhin	France	67500
14	9 place de la Liberté		Schiltigheim	Bas-Rhin	France	67300
15	7 rue Nationale		Strasbourg	Bas-Rhin	France	67000
0						

Record: 15 of 15 No Filter Search

Figure 6-6 Employee Addresses table data

Depending on the table structure, tables can have more than one field that they can be linked by. An example of this would be the Orders Detail table. This table has an ID field that can be used to link it to the Orders table. There is a Product ID field in the Orders Detail table that is used to retrieve the Product Name from another table (the Product table) to print on the report, instead of printing the Product ID number. Displaying the product name on the report is more meaningful than displaying the Product ID field, which usually contains a (sequential) number. If you are asking why the Product Name field is not stored in the Orders Detail table, there are two reasons that come to mind.

① The ID field takes up less space than the Product Name field, thereby keeping the size of the Orders Detail table smaller.

② If a Product Name has to be changed for any reason, it only has to be changed once in the Product table. Every place that the Product Name field is used on any form or report would automatically be updated with the revised product name. If the product name was stored in the Orders Detail table, every record in the Orders Detail table that had that product name would have to be changed, as well as, any other table that stored the product name in a field. That would be a lot of extra work.

For the most part, Alpha Five will use a set like a table. In addition to creating layouts, operations can be saved for a set. When entering data into a form that is based on a set, the data entered is automatically placed in the correct table.

Requirements To Link Tables

The requirements to link tables are explained below.

① The fields that will be used to create a link must have the same field type and length. The fields do not have to have the same name. If these requirements are not met, you will see error messages when you try to view data from the set in a form or browse.
② Links can be created on multiple fields.
③ Fields that will be used to link tables cannot be calculated fields.
④ Expressions can be used to create links. The length of the fields used in the expression must be the same length as the field that the expression is linking to.

How Sets Are Created

The first step in creating a set is determining which table is the main table, which Alpha Five calls the **PRIMARY TABLE**. In the discussion of orders in this chapter, the Orders table would be the primary table. The Orders Detail table would be linked to the Orders table. Alpha Five would call the Orders Detail table a **CHILD TABLE**. The Customer table would also be a child table in this scenario. Alpha Five refers to tables that are linked to child tables as **GRANDCHILD TABLES**. In this example, the Products table would be a grandchild table because it would be linked to the Orders Details table, which is a child table.

What Is The Set Editor?

The Set Editor shown in Figure 6-7, is a visual tool that is used to link tables together to create a set. In the Set Editor, a **ONE-TO-ONE RELATIONSHIP** is indicated by a single line between the parent and child tables shown later in Figure 6-18. A **ONE-TO-MANY RELATIONSHIP** is indicated by a double line between the parent and child tables shown later in Figure 6-21. Now that you have a brief introduction of what goes into creating a set, it's time to create some sets.

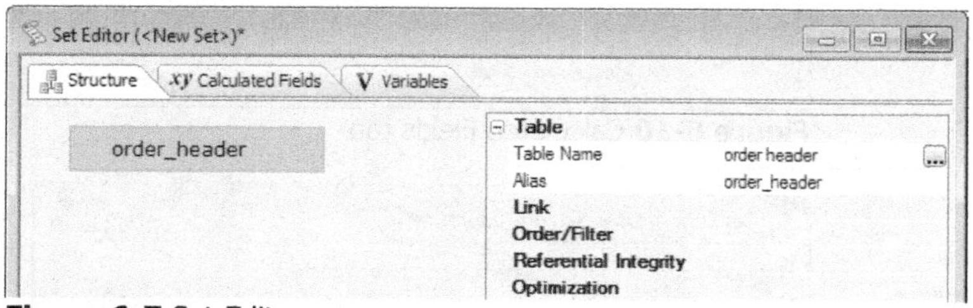

Figure 6-7 Set Editor

Set Editor Toolbar

When the Set Editor is open, the options on the toolbar shown in Figure 6-8 are available. Table 6-1 explains the buttons on the toolbar that are specific to sets.

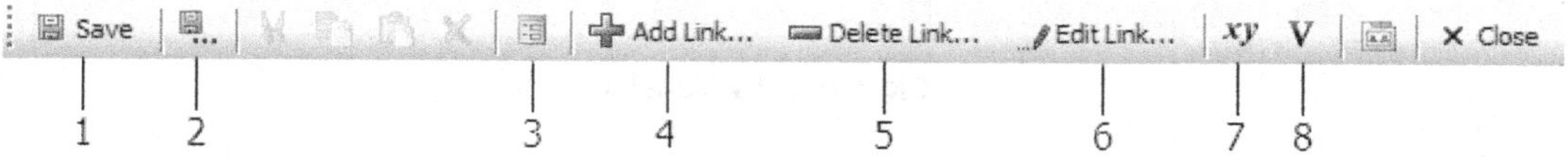

Figure 6-8 Set Editor toolbar

Button	Is Used To . .
1	Save the current set.
2	Save the current set with a different file name.
3	View the current set on a form, as shown in Figure 6-9. Being able to view the data on a form will aid in letting you know if the relationship was created correctly.
4	Add a link to the table that is selected on the Structure tab. The selected table has a blue background.
5	Delete the link for the table that is selected. There is no undo option. If you delete a link by mistake, close the Set Editor. When prompted to save the changes, click No, then reopen the Set Editor.
6	Display the Structure tab on the Set Editor.
7	Display the **CALCULATED FIELDS TAB** shown in Figure 6-10, on the Set Editor. The options on this tab are used to create calculated fields that will be used as a field to link on. (1)
8	Display the **VARIABLES TAB** shown in Figure 6-11, on the Set Editor. The options on this tab used to define global and session variables that will be used as a field to link on. (1)

Table 6-1 Set Editor toolbar buttons explained

(1) [See Chapter 3, Table 3-4]

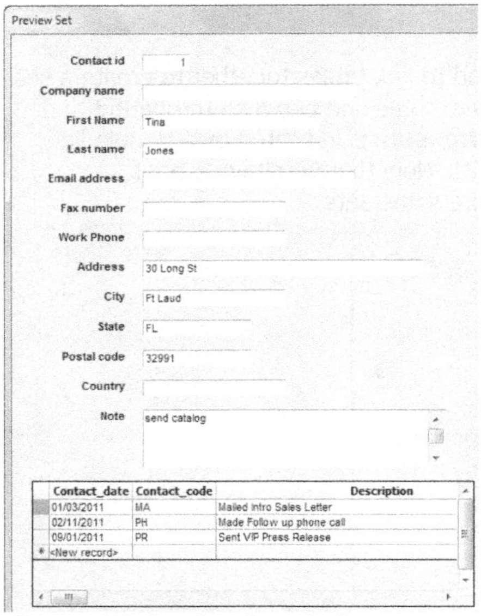

Figure 6-9 Preview Set window

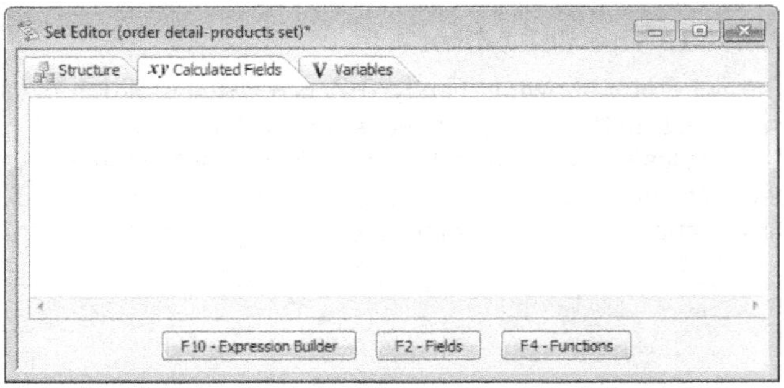

Figure 6-10 Calculated Fields tab

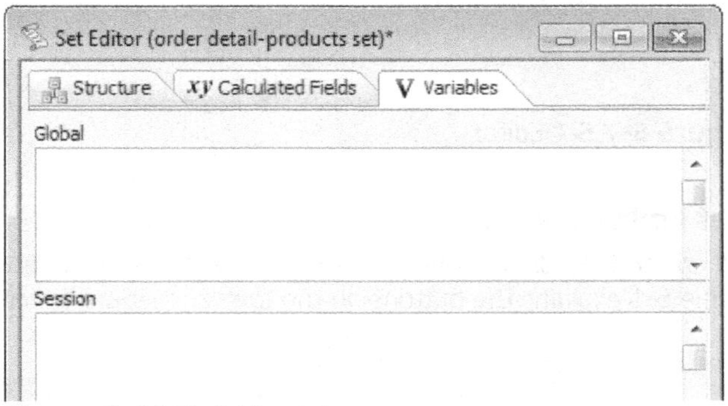

Figure 6-11 Variables tab

Set Menu

Like the other tools in Alpha Five, sets and the Set Editor have their own menu.

Figure 6-12 shows the menu when a set is selected on the Tables/Sets tab. This is also the menu displayed when a set is right-clicked on.

The menu shown in Figure 6-13 is available when the Set Editor is open.

The majority of options were explained earlier in Table 6-1.

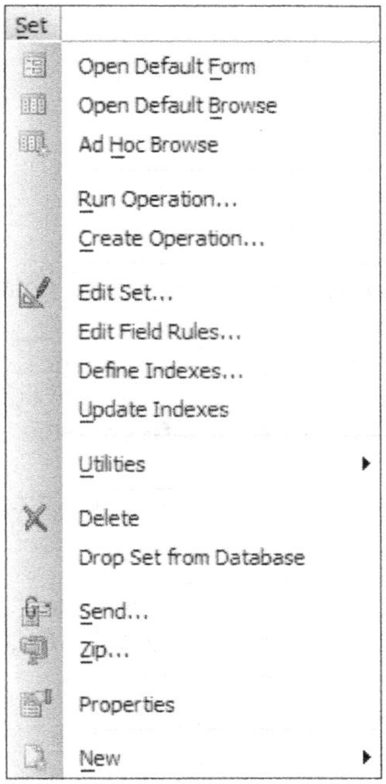

Figure 6-12 Set menu when the Set Editor is not open

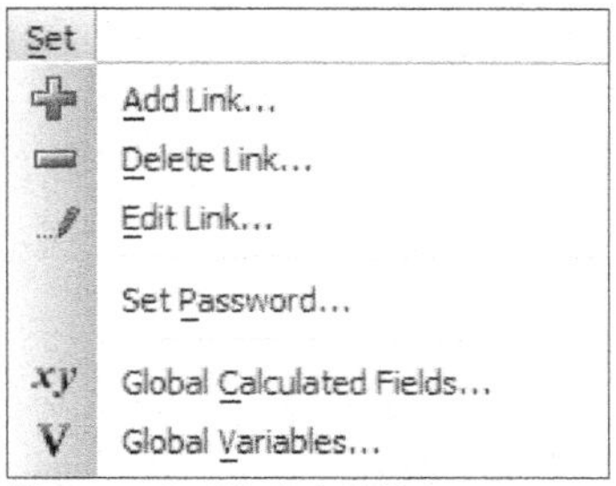

Figure 6-13 Set Editor menu

> The **SET PASSWORD** option on the menu shown above in Figure 6-13 opens the dialog box shown in Figure 6-14. I don't think that this is working properly because you cannot set up a password from the dialog box shown in the figure. That or the option on the menu has the wrong name.

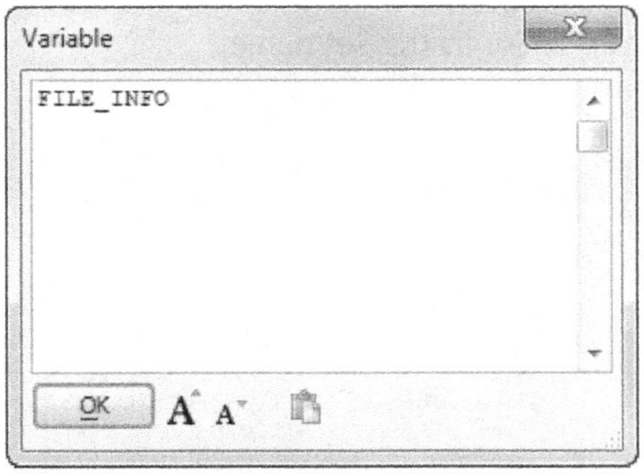

Figure 6-14 Variable dialog box (for sets)

Exercise 6.1: Create The One-To-One Order Detail - Product Set

In this exercise you will create a set based on a one-to-one relationship between the Order Detail and Products table. This set will allow the products name to be viewed for each item ordered, in addition to the Product ID field, which is not very helpful to the people using the application.

1. On the Tables/Sets tab, right-click on an empty space and select New Set.

2. On the dialog box shown in Figure 6-15, select the Order Detail table, then click OK.

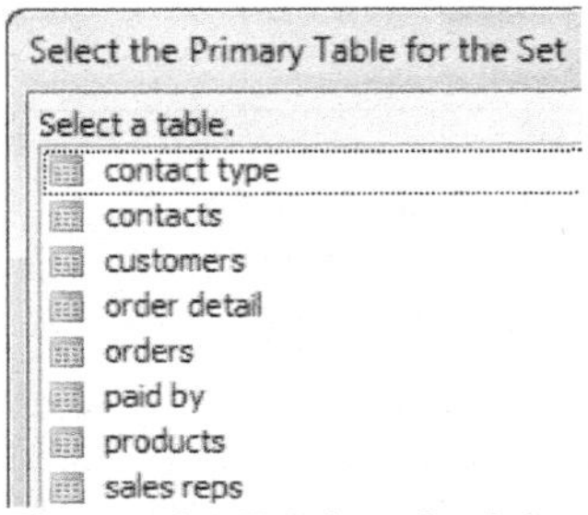

Figure 6-15 Select the Primary Table for the Set dialog box

3. Click on the right side of the Order Detail table to display the shortcut menu shown in Figure 6-16, then select **ADD NEW CHILD**.

Figure 6-16 Table shortcut menu

4. On the Add Relation dialog box, open the **TABLE TO LINK** field drop-down list and select the Products table.

5. Open the first Parent field drop-down list and select the Product ID field. The same field should now be in the first Child field, as shown in Figure 6-17. Click OK.

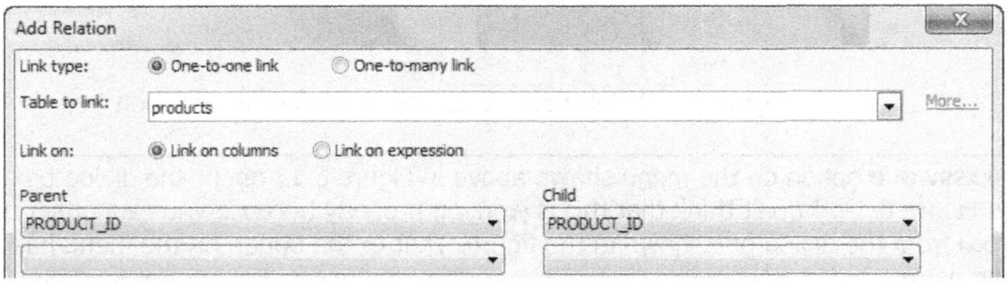

Figure 6-17 Order Detail and Products tables link options

6. Click the Save button. Type `Order Detail-Products set` as the set name, then click OK.

Figure 6-18 shows the Set Editor with the link.

The options on the Structure tab are used to create and edit sets.

On the right side of the dialog box are options to customize the relationship.

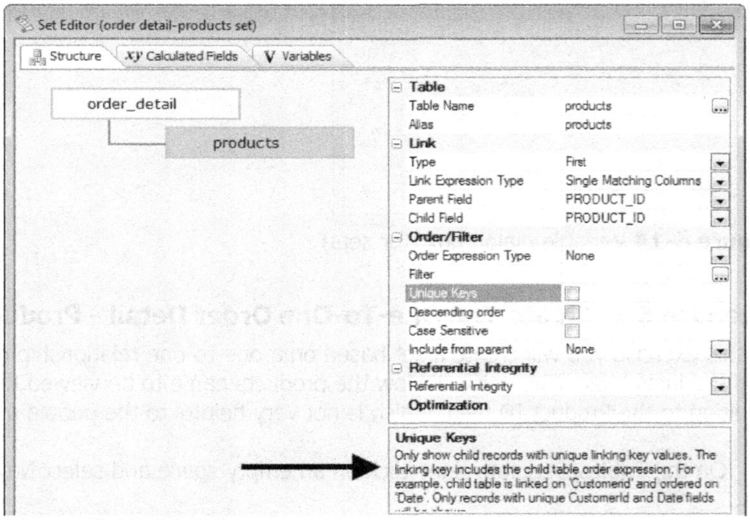

Figure 6-18 Set Editor

Structure Tab Options

In addition to the Calculated Fields and Variables tab options, there are a lot of options on the right side of the Structure tab that can be used to customize the set. If you click on an option in the left column, a description of the option is displayed, as illustrated at the bottom of the figure.
The options are for the table that is selected on the left. The options are explained below.

Table Section

The options in this section are used to modify the selected tables attributes.

① **TABLE NAME** Is used to select a different table. Changing the table after a set is created, changes the set. Clicking the button at the end of the field opens the **SELECT TABLE DIALOG BOX**, to select a different table. It looks similar to the dialog box shown earlier in Figure 6-15.

② **ALIAS** Is used to create or change the alias name of the table. This option is used to reference a table by a different name. This is useful if you need to use the same table in a set, more than once.

Link Section

The options in this section are used to customize the link for the selected table.

① **TYPE** Is used to select one of the following types of relationship links: First (the default), Last, Closest and Many. The first three were explained earlier in this chapter in the One-To-One Link Variations section. The **MANY** option is a one-to-many relationship.

② **LINKS EXPRESSION TYPE** Is used to select the number of columns of data that will be used to create the link between the tables. **SINGLE MATCHING COLUMNS** is the default. It is used when only one column of data is needed to create the link. Select the **MULTIPLE MATCHING COLUMNS** option when two or more columns are needed to create the link. Select the **EXPRESSION** option when fields in the table need to be manipulated or combined to create a field to link on.

③ **PARENT FIELD** Is used to select or change the field in the parent table that will be used to create a link to a child table. (2)

④ **CHILD FIELD** Is used to select or change the field in the child table that will be used to create a link to a parent table. (2)

(2) The drop-down list contains all of the fields in the table.

Order/Filter Section

> **Filters Created In Sets**
> If you create a filter in the Set Editor, it will automatically be applied to all layouts that are created based on the set. This may not be what you want. Therefore, it is best to create filters on the form or report that requires it.

The options in this section are used to control how the child records are displayed.

① **ORDER EXPRESSION TYPE** Is used to select how the records in the child table will be sorted. Selecting any option other then "None" will display the **CHILD ORDER** field, illustrated in Figure 6-19, so that you can create an expression.

② **FILTER** Is used to create a condition that will filter out child records. This option is often used to exclude child records that have duplicate values in the field being linked on.

③ **UNIQUE KEYS** If checked, only one record per value in the linked field will be displayed. Selecting this option for a one-to-one relationship can increase performance because fewer records have to be read.

④ **DESCENDING ORDER** If checked, the child records will be sorted in descending order.

⑤ **CASE SENSITIVE** If the records in the child table are sorted, check this option if the sort expression is case sensitive.

⑥ **INCLUDE FROM PARENT** Is used to select whether or not records from the parent table should be displayed if there is no matching record in the child table. I prefer to display all of the records from the parent table, if for no other reason then to see that something is wrong with the data. The options are explained below.

- ☑ **NONE** Is the default. This option will always include the parent record even if no matching child records are found.
- ☑ **MATCH** Only include the parent record if a matching child record is found.
- ☑ **NO MATCH** Only include the parent record if there is no matching child record. This option in my opinion, is useful on a report that is being used to clean up data. Records that appear on this type of report indicate a problem with the data.

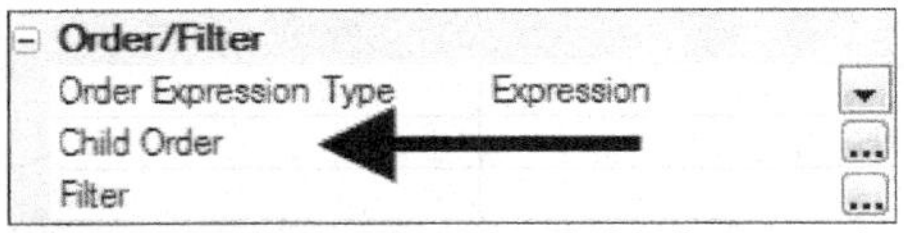

Figure 6-19 Child Order field illustrated

> **Unique Keys Option**
> This option should not be used for one-to-many relationships because the goal is to link all records with the same value in the field being linked on.

Understanding Referential Integrity

In the application that you are creating in this book, you would not want the names and addresses of people in the Customers table that were not customers. You also want to be able to see customers and their orders on one screen. Alpha Five accomplishes both of these tasks through sets.

In order to make these features work, you would have to create a link between the Customers table and the Order Header table. You want to ensure that you do not get one customers order mixed up with another customers order. You also want to ensure that you can enter an unlimited number of orders for each customer.

A relationship where one record (in this example, the one record is in the Customers table) can be linked to many records (in this example, the Order Header table) is a "one-to-many" relationship. The "one" side is the Customers table and the "many" side is the Order Header table.

Ensuring that a record exists in the table on the "one" side (the Customers table) before any records can be entered on the "many" side (the Order Header table) is known as **REFERENTIAL INTEGRITY.**

Using referential integrity is optional. It helps to keep the data consistent because it does not let child records get unlinked from its parent record. Exercise 6.2 and 6.3 create one-to-many sets without enabling referential integrity. In Exercise 6.4 you will learn how to enable referential integrity. If the set will only be used for reports, referential integrity is not needed because data is not changed when a report is run. Alpha Five provides two variations of referential integrity: Cascade changes/Deletes and Prevent changes, as explained below.

Cascade Changes/Deletes

To explain this referential integrity concept, use the Publisher table as the parent table and the Books table as the child table. If you enable the cascade option, any time that you change the primary key in the parent table, (the Publisher table) Alpha Five will automatically change the primary key to the new value for all child records in the other (the Books table) related table(s). The value in the linking field in the child table cannot be changed manually.

For example, if you change the Publisher ID in the Publishers table, the Publisher ID in the Book table is updated automatically for each book that is published by that publisher.

> Cascade changes and deletes are done behind the scene. Alpha Five does not tell you when it is changing records in other tables.

The cascade delete portion of the option works like this. If a record is deleted in the parent table, all of the related records in the child table(s) are marked for deletion. For example, if you delete a Publisher ID from the Publisher table, all the books published by that publisher in the Books table will be marked for deletion.

Prevent Changes

If this option is selected, the linking fields in the parent or child tables cannot be changed.

Exercise 6.2: Create The One-To-Many Products - Order Detail Set

In this exercise you will create a set based on a one-to-many relationship between the Products and Order Detail tables.

1. Create a new set and select the Products table.
2. Click the Add Link button on the toolbar.
3. Select the **ONE-TO-MANY LINK** option, then open the Table to link field drop-down list and select the Order Detail table.
4. Open the Parent field drop-down list and select the Product ID field. You should have the options shown in Figure 6-20. Click OK.

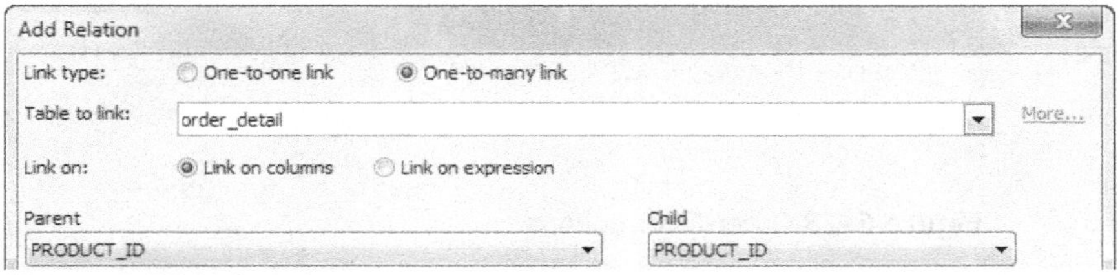

Figure 6-20 Link options

The **MORE . . . LINK** in the upper right corner on the Add Relation dialog box opens the **PICK A DATABASE DIALOG BOX**, which is used to select a table in a different database to use to create a relationship to.

5. Save the set as `Products-Order Detail set.`

As shown in Figure 6-21, there is a double line between the tables. This visual lets you know that this is a one-to-many link.

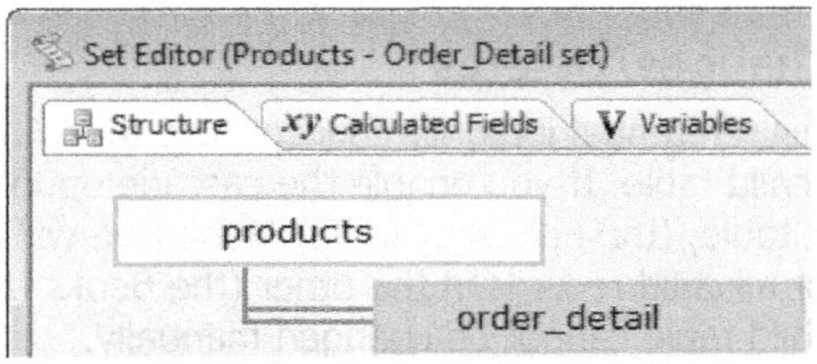

Figure 6-21 Products-Order Detail set

Sort The Child Records

In this part of the exercise you will sort the child records on the Product ID field.

1. Open the Order Expression Type field drop-down list on the Set Editor and select **SINGLE COLUMN**.
2. Open the Child Order field drop-down list and select Product ID. You should have the options shown in Figure 6-22.

   Save the changes.

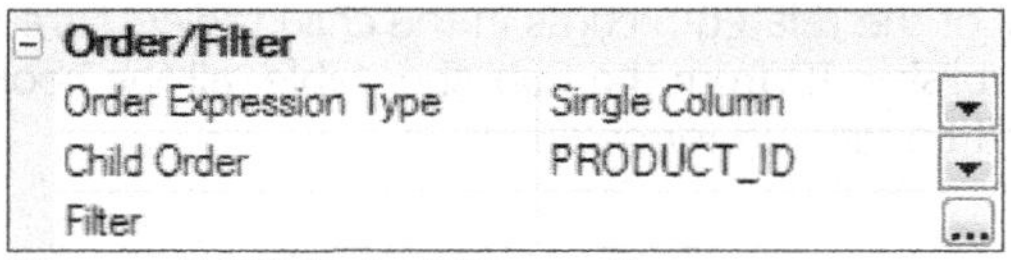

Figure 6-22 Order/Filter options

Exercise 6.3: Create The One-To-Many Customers - Orders Set

1. Create a new set and select the Customers table. Click the Add Link button on the toolbar, then select the **ONE-TO-MANY LINK** option.
2. Open the Table to link field drop-down list and select the Orders table.
   Open the Parent field drop-down list and select the Customer ID field, then click OK.
3. Open the Order Expression Type field drop-down list and select **SINGLE COLUMN**.
   Open the Child Order field drop-down list and select Customer ID.
4. You should have the options shown in Figure 6-23.

   Save the set as `Customers-Orders set`.

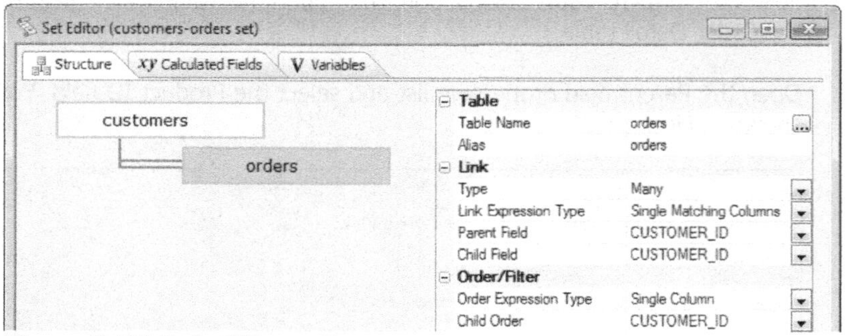

Figure 6-23 Order/Filter options

Exercise 6.4: Create The Orders - Order Detail Set With Referential Integrity

This set needs referential integrity enabled so that if a record is deleted in the Orders table, the items on the order are deleted from the Order Detail table. In the real world, orders are not deleted from the database, they are marked as cancelled. It is only stated here to illustrate the referential integrity concept.

1. Create a new set and select the Orders table. Click the Add Link button, then select the **ONE-TO-MANY LINK** option.

2. Open the Table to link field drop-down list and select the Order Detail table. Open the Parent field drop-down list and select the Order ID field, then click OK.

3. Open the Order Expression Type field drop-down list and select **SINGLE COLUMN**. Open the Child Order field drop-down list and select Order ID.

4. Open the **REFERENTIAL INTEGRITY** drop-down list and select Cascade Changes/Deletes.

5. Save the set as `Orders-Order Detail set.`

   You should have the options shown in Figure 6-24.

   The thick line indicates that the cascade changes/ deletes referential integrity option has been applied.

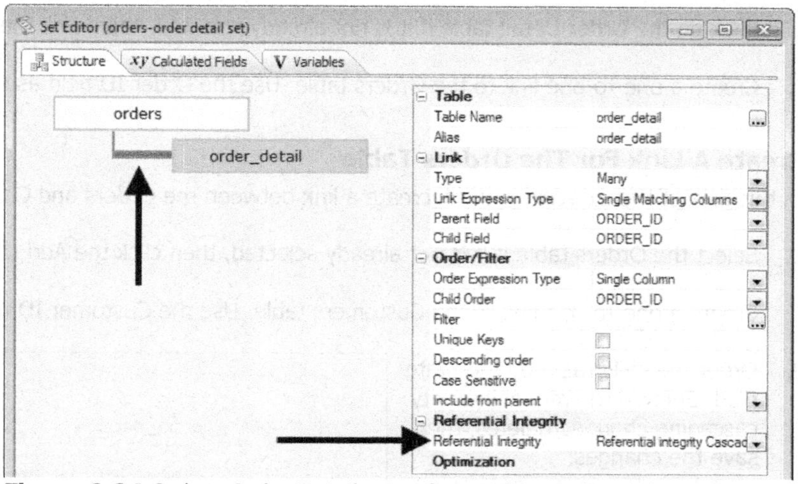

Figure 6-24 Orders-Order Detail set referential integrity options

Exercise 6.5: Create Sets On Your Own

In this exercise you will create two sets on your own.

1. Create a one-to-many set named `Contacts-Contact Type set`, for the Contacts and Contact Type tables.

2. Link on the Contact ID field. Sort the child table on the Contact Date field and enforce cascading referential integrity.

3. Create a one-to-many set named `Orders-Paid By set`, for the Orders and Paid By tables.

4. Link on the Paid By ID field. Sort the child table on the Paid By ID field and enforce cascading referential integrity.

Exercise 6.6: Create A Product Set With More Than Two Tables

So far in this chapter all of the sets that you have created only used two tables. In this exercise you will create a set that uses four tables. This set will let you view products by name, each order that has a specific product and the customer that ordered it.

1. Create a new set using the Products table as the primary table.

2. Add a one-to-many link to the Order Detail table. Use the Product ID field as the link for both tables.

3. Order the child table by the Product ID field.

4. Save the set as `Products multi table set.`

Create A Link For The Child Table

In this part of the exercise you will create a link between the Order Detail table and the Orders table.

1. Click on the Order Detail table if it is not already selected, then click the Add Link button.

2. Create a one-to-one link to the Orders table. Use the Order ID field as the link field.

Create A Link For The Orders Table

In this part of the exercise you will create a link between the Orders and Customers tables.

1. Select the Orders table if it is not already selected, then click the Add Link button.

2. Create a one-to-one link to the Customers table. Use the Customer ID field as the link field.

3. Order the child table by the State field. Enforce referential integrity cascading changes/deletes, then save the changes.

   The structure of the set should look like the one shown in Figure 6-25.

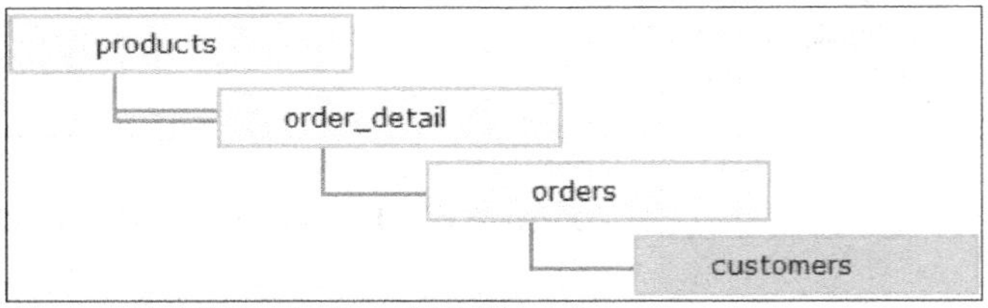

Figure 6-25 Product multi table set

> **Referential Integrity And Linked Tables**
> If the Link Expression Type selected is Expression, the order of the fields in the expression must match the order of fields in the tables for referential integrity to work. For example, if the fields used to create the expression are Order ID and Customer ID, that is the order that the ID fields must be in, in the table.

View The Properties Of A Set

You have created several sets in this chapter. Alpha Five provides a way for you to view a lot of information about a set. (Similar information is available just for tables.) Having this information may be helpful if you encounter a problem down the road or if you want to see key information about the set quickly.

1. On the Tables/Sets tab, right-click on the Order Detail-Products set and select Properties.

2. Click on the Products table. You will see the options shown in Figure 6-26.

   The arrow style to the left of the selected table indicates the type of relationship between the tables.

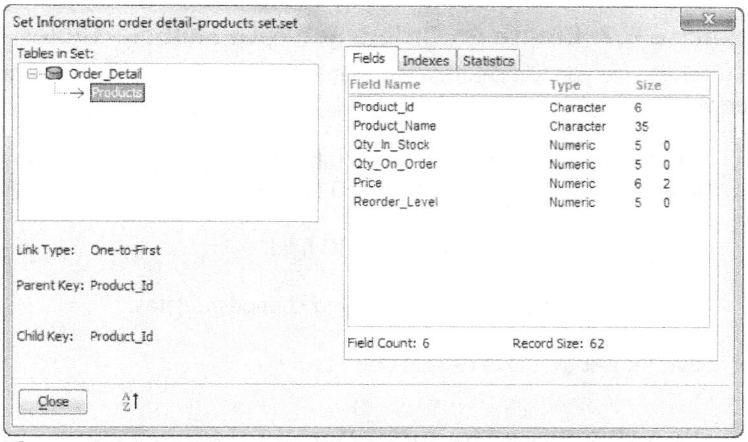

Figure 6-26 Set Information Fields tab information

Figure 6-27 shows the index information for the set.

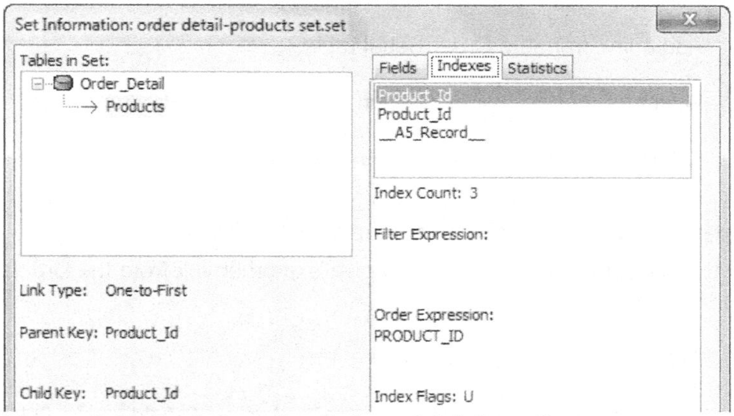

Figure 6-27 Set Information Indexes tab information

Figure 6-28 shows some statistics for the set, like how many records are in the table.

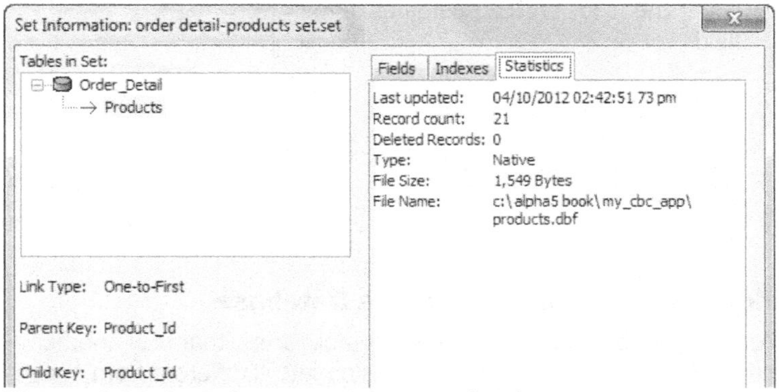

Figure 6-28 Set Information Statistics tab information

It would be nice to be able to drag and drop to change the order of the tables if you needed to change a link in the set.

Exercise 6.7: Create An Orders Set With Multiple Tables

In this exercise you will create a set that lets you view the data in several tables from the orders perspective.

1. Create a new set using the Orders table as the primary table. Add a one-to-many link to the Order Detail table. Use the Order ID field as the link for both tables.

2. Order the child table by the Order ID field.

3. Enforce referential integrity cascading changes/deletes.

4. Save the set as `Orders multi table set.`

Create A Link From The Order Detail Table

In this part of the exercise you will create a link from the Order Detail table.

1. Add a link from the Order Detail table.

2. Select the one-to-one link option, then select the Products table.

3. Select the Product ID field as the link field.

Create Another Link From The Orders Table

In this part of the exercise you will create another link from the Orders table to the Customers table. This will be a one-to-one link.

1. Add a link to the Orders table.

2. Select the Customers table. Use the Customer ID field as the link field.

3. Order the fields on the Customer Name field.

   Save the changes.

   The structure should look like the one shown in Figure 6-29.

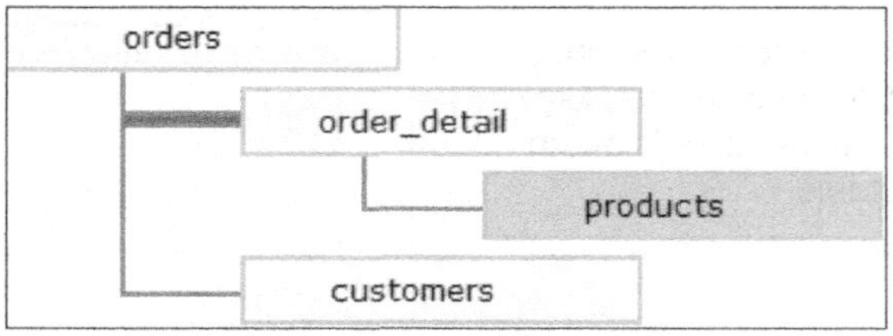

Figure 6-29 Orders multi table set

Adding Tables And Sets To The Database

There may be times when you need a table or set that is in another database. If so, you can add it to the current database. Adding tables or sets is different from appending data to a table like you learned in the previous chapter. The difference is that adding a table or set is creating a link to data in the other database, while appending data places a copy of data from one source into a table in an Alpha Five database.

Exercise 6.8: Add A Table Or Set To The Database

In this exercise you will learn how to add a set and table from the CBC Data database to the current database.

1. On the Tables/Sets tab, right-click on a blank space and select **ADD TABLE/SET**.

2. Click on the button at the end of the **LOOKIN** field at the top of the dialog box. Navigate to your folder, then open the CBC APP Data folder.

3. Double-click on the Order set to add or drop.set file. As shown in Figure 6-30, in the Selected Tables/Sets list on the right, you will see the set from the CBC APP Data database that will be added to the current database.

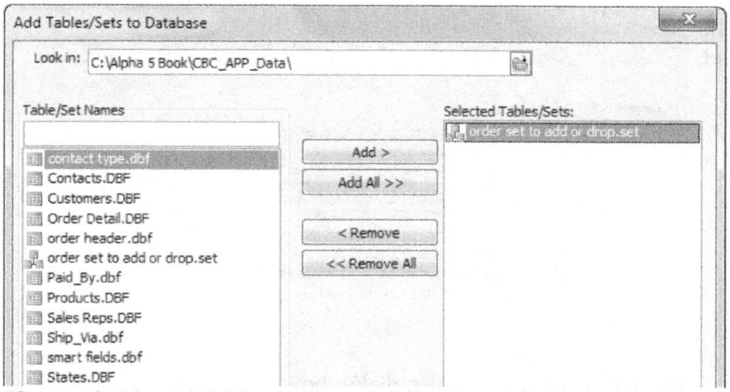
Add Tables/Sets to Database
Look in: C:\Alpha 5 Book\CBC_APP_Data\
Table/Set Names
Selected Tables/Sets:
order set to add or drop.set
contact type.dbf
Contacts.DBF
Customers.DBF
Order Detail.DBF
order header.dbf
order set to add or drop.set
Paid_By.dbf
Products.DBF
Sales Reps.DBF
Ship_Via.dbf
smart fields.dbf
States.DBF
Add >
Add All >>
< Remove
<< Remove All

Figure 6-30 Add Tables/Sets to Database dialog box

4. Click on the Ship Via table in the list on the left, then click the Add button.

5. Click OK. The dialog box shown in Figure 6-31 appears to let you know that the tables or sets that you are adding are not in the same folder as the current database.

   Click OK. You will see the table and set that you added on the Tables/Sets tab.

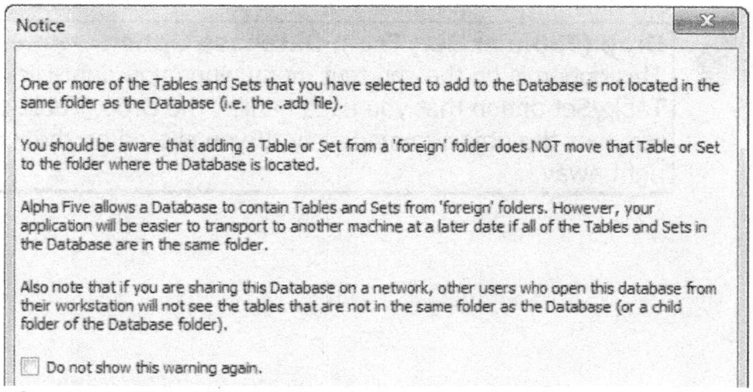
Notice
One or more of the Tables and Sets that you have selected to add to the Database is not located in the same folder as the Database (i.e. the .adb file).
You should be aware that adding a Table or Set from a 'foreign' folder does NOT move that Table or Set to the folder where the Database is located.
Alpha Five allows a Database to contain Tables and Sets from 'foreign' folders. However, your application will be easier to transport to another machine at a later date if all of the Tables and Sets in the Database are in the same folder.
Also note that if you are sharing this Database on a network, other users who open this database from their workstation will not see the tables that are not in the same folder as the Database (or a child folder of the Database folder).
Do not show this warning again.

Figure 6-31 Add Table/Set Notice dialog box

Notice that the path in the Full Name column is different. The path is where the physical table or set is. This is what the message in Figure 6-31 is letting you know.

> **Modifying A Set**
> You will probably have the need to modify a set. When that is the case, make sure that all of the layouts that use any table in the set are closed. If a table is open when you try to modify a set, the set cannot be modified, only viewed.

Dropping Tables And Sets From A Database

This feature works the opposite of adding tables and sets covered in the previous exercise. The reason that you would drop a table or set from a database is because you no longer need to use it in the database. Dropping a table or set does not delete it. It just removes the table or set from the Control Panel.

Exercise 6.9: Drop A Set From The Database

In this exercise you will learn how to drop the set that you added in the previous exercise.

1. On the Tables/Sets tab, right-click on a blank space and select Drop Table/Set. The Drop Tables dialog box has a tab for tables and one for sets.
2. On the Sets tab, click on the Order set to add or drop set, as shown in Figure 6-32, then click OK.

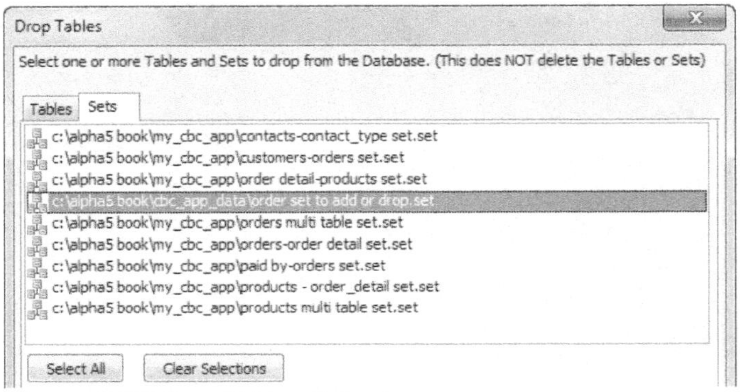

Figure 6-32 Drop Tables dialog box

3. When prompted to drop a table or set from the database, click Yes. The set has been removed from the Control Panel.

> **Drop (Table or Set) From Database Option**
> This option is on the shortcut menu when you right-click on an object. Unlike the Drop Table/Set option that you used earlier, the Drop (Table or Set) from database option removes the object immediately. If you clicked on the wrong object, you may not notice right away.

GETTING STARTED WITH THE LAYOUT EDITOR

In this chapter you will learn about the following features of the layout editor that are used with forms, browses, reports, letters and mailing labels.

- ☑ Layout workspace
- ☑ Layout menu and toolbar options
- ☑ Floating toolbars
- ☑ Properties panel
- ☑ Drag Drop List panel
- ☑ Toolbox panel
- ☑ Selecting fields and objects
- ☑ Using the grid
- ☑ Adding fields to the layout
- ☑ Aligning objects
- ☑ Add a password to a layout

CHAPTER 7

Overview

Now that you have created the database, tables, sets and field rules for the application, as well as, appended data to the tables, there needs to be a way to view and edit the current data, add new data and run reports. Yes, Alpha Five automatically creates a default form and browse for each table and set in the database, but your expectations are higher. While default objects are good for a quick view of the data, applications usually need items that are a bit more sophisticated.

The tool in Alpha Five that is used to create forms, browses, letters, labels and reports is the **LAYOUT EDITOR**. This editor is used to create what Alpha Five calls layouts. Actually, each layout type (form, browse, letter, label and report) has it's own editor, but a large percent of the options are the same for all of the layout types.

Unlike the other chapters, this one does not have any exercises. That is done on purpose because the goal of this chapter is to cover the options on the Layout Editor that you will use on a regular basis. If you have used the Layout Editor before and are comfortable with it, meaning you know how to use it to create a form or report, you can browse through this chapter. If you have not used the Layout Editor before, you should treat this chapter like every other chapter and take the time to get to know your way around the Layout Editor. That way, in the chapters that you learn how to create forms, etc., you will only have to focus on creating it and not fumbling around looking for options or figure out what the options do.

How To Follow Along

As stated earlier, this chapter does not have exercises. If you want to follow along in this chapter, follow the steps below to open the Form layout editor.

1. On the Forms tab, click the New button on the Control Panel.

2. Select the Customers table, then click Finish. You should see a basic form in the editor. As topics are discussed, you can try them out on this form.

Control Panel Layout Menu

When you click on one of the layout tabs (forms, reports, etc.) you will see the menu shown in Figure 7-1, if no layout is selected on the tab.

The options on the layout menu are available for all layout types. They are explained in Table 7-1.

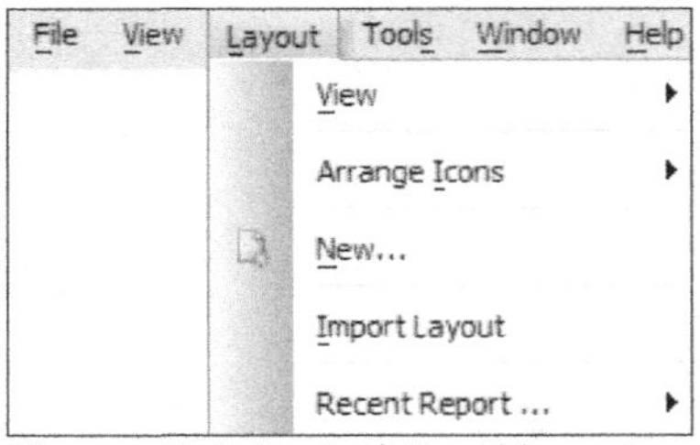

Figure 7-1 Control Panel layout menu

Option	Is Used To . . .
View	Select how the objects on the tab are displayed. [See Chapter 2, Table 2-8, Buttons 5, 6, 7 and 8]
Arrange Icons	Select the sort order of objects on the tab.
New	Create a new layout using a genie. The genie that opens depends on the layout tab that is selected.
Import Layout	Add a layout to the database that is not in the database that is open.

Table 7-1 Control Panel layout menu options explained

Option	Is Used To . . .
Recent <Layout Type>	Select a layout that you recently opened.

Table 7-1 Control Panel layout menu options explained (Continued)

Layout Editor Workspace

In Chapter 2 you learned about the Alpha Five workspace. Figure 7-2 shows the layout editor workspace. The options are explained below.

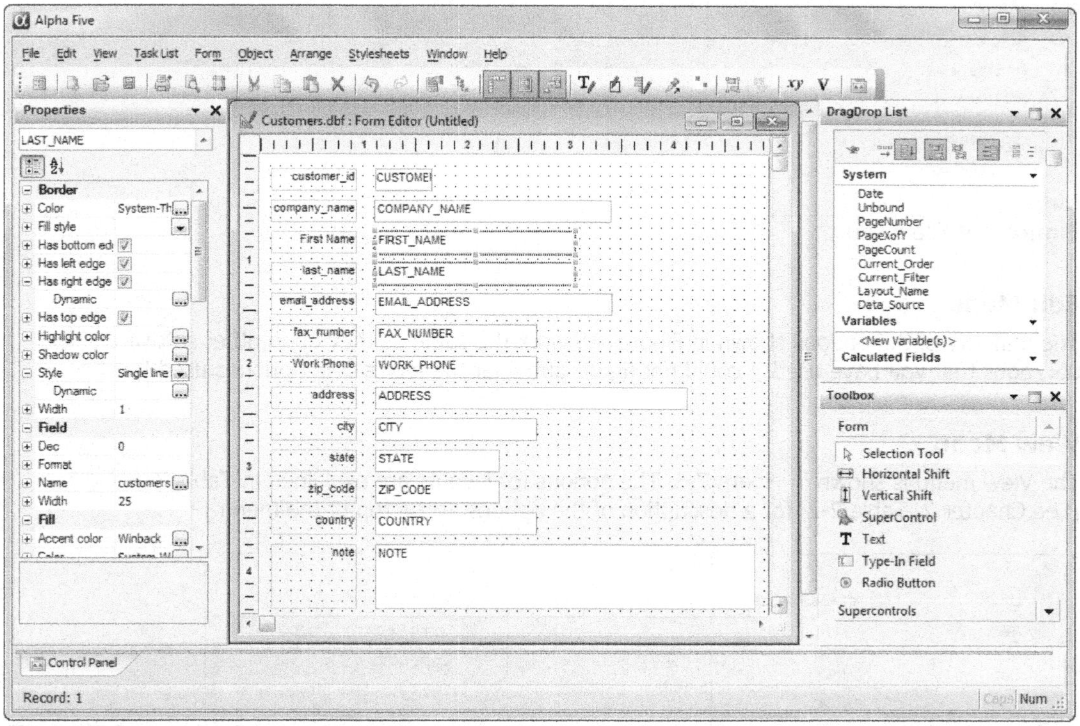

Figure 7-2 Layout Editor workspace

Layout Editor Menu

You will see the menu shown in Figure 7-3 when a layout is open. This figure shows the menu when a form is open. The majority of these options are available for forms, browses, reports, letters and labels. The menu options for layouts are explained in Tables 7-2 to 7-5.

Figure 7-3 Layout Editor menu

File Menu

This menu is shown in Figure 7-4. The options provide the same functionality as they do in other software packages that you have used.

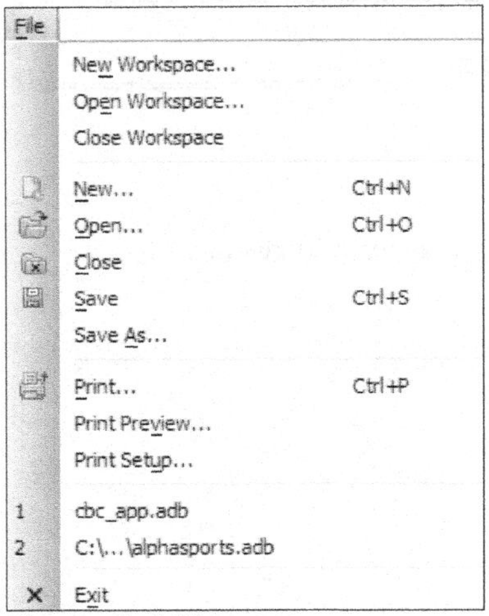

Figure 7-4 File menu

Edit Menu

The majority of the options shown in Figure 7-5 work the same as they do in other software packages that you have used. I could not figure out what the **PASTE LINK** option is used for.

View Menu

The View menu is shown in Figure 7-6. The options for layouts are explained in Table 7-2. [See Chapter 2, Table 2-2, for a description of the options at the top of the menu.]

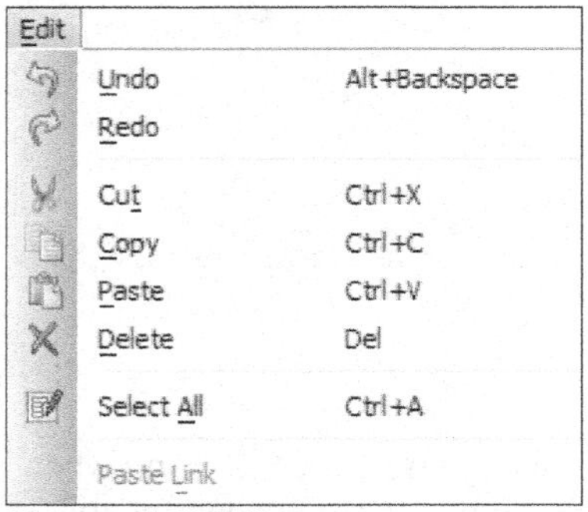

Figure 7-5 Edit menu

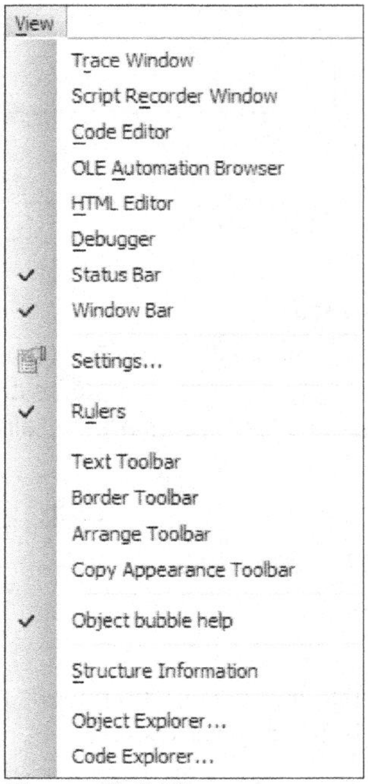

Figure 7-6 View menu

Option	Is Used To . . .
Rulers	Display or hide the rulers on the layout window.
Text Toolbar	Display or hide the toolbar shown in later in Figure 7-64. The options are used to modify the text of the selected object.
Border Toolbar	Display or hide the toolbar shown in later in Figure 7-65. The options are used to modify the borders of the selected object.
Arrange Toolbar	Display or hide the toolbar shown in later in Figure 7-66. The options are used to modify the alignment of the selected object.
Copy Appearance Toolbar	Display or hide the toolbar shown in later in Figure 7-67. The options are used to copy and paste formatting properties.
Object Bubble Help	Display or hide the popup help window for the object that the mouse is hovered over, as illustrated in Figure 7-7.
Structure Information	Display information about the table or set that the layout is based on. Chapter 3, Figure 3-14, shows the dialog box that is displayed when the form is based on a table. Chapter 6, Figure 6-26, shows the dialog box that is displayed when the form is based on a set.
Object Explorer	Open the dialog box shown in Figure 7-8. It is used to view all of the properties of all of the objects on the layout. This dialog box is often used to find an objects name that will be used in a script.
Code Explorer	Open the dialog box shown in Figure 7-9. It is used to view or edit the code for events on the form. The event code can also be exported to a text file.

Table 7-2 View menu options explained

Figure 7-7 Object Bubble Help illustrated

The **ROLL-UP BUTTON** shrinks the dialog box to the size of a button. This is useful if you want to keep the dialog box open while you are working, but want to keep it out of the way.

The **RECORDER BUTTON** opens the **XBASIC RECORDER DIALOG BOX**. It is used to create a script using relative or explicit syntax for an object on the form.

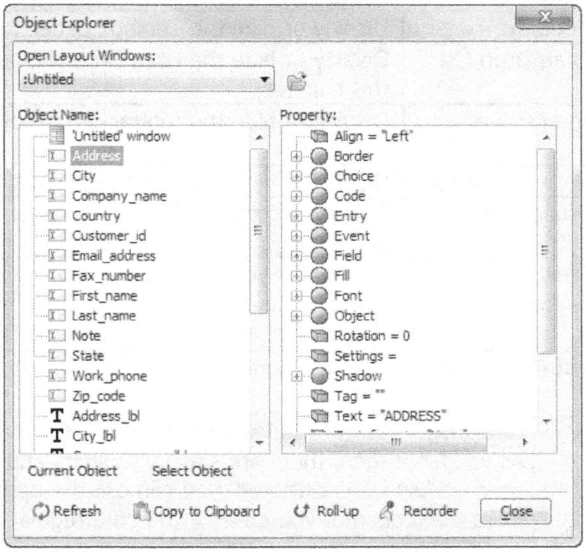

Figure 7-8 Object Explorer dialog box

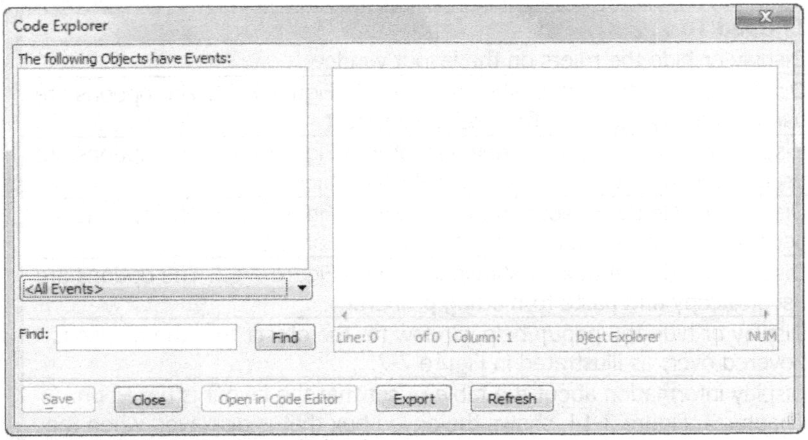

Figure 7-9 Code Explorer dialog box

Task List Menu

The Task List menu is shown in Figure 7-10. These tools are used when designing a form. The options are explained in Table 7-3.

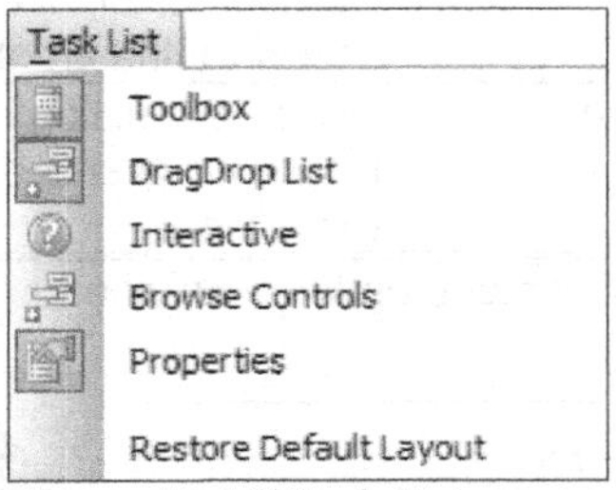

Figure 7-10 Task List menu

Option	Is Used To . . .
Toolbox	Display or hide the Toolbox panel. [See Toolbox Panel, later in this chapter]
Drag Drop List	Display or hide the Drag Drop List panel. [See Drag Drop List Panel, later in this chapter]
Interactive	Display or hide the Interactive panel. [See Interactive Panel, later in this chapter]
Browse Controls	Display or hide the Browse Controls panel.
Properties	Display or hide the Properties panel. [See Properties Panel, later in this chapter]
Restore Default Layout	Have the layout workspace look like it did when Alpha Five was first installed, if you made changes to the workspace. For example, the Toolbox and Drag Drop List panels are placed on the right side of the workspace.

Table 7-3 Task List menu options explained

Keeping Your Workspace From Being Cluttered
As you have seen, there are several toolbars and panels that you can open. If you find that your workspace is cluttered, you can use the options on the View and Task List menus to close the tools that you aren't using on a regular basis.

Object Menu

The Object menu is shown in Figure 7-11. The options are explained in Table 7-4.

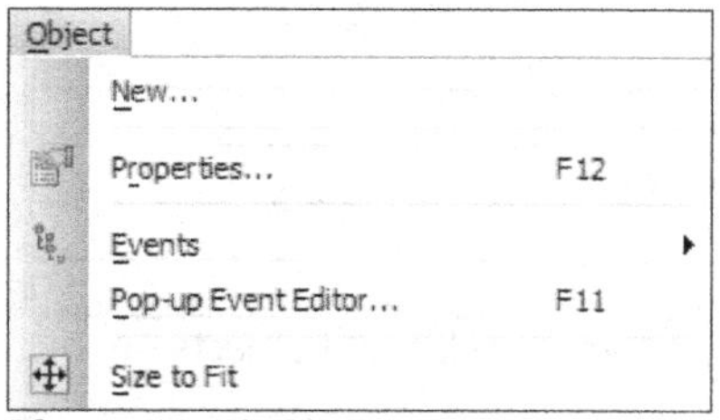

Figure 7-11 Object menu

Option	Is Used To . . .
New	Create a new object by selecting one from the dialog box shown in Figure 7-12.
Properties	Open the Properties dialog box. The dialog box that opens depends on the object that is selected.
Events	Create an event for the selected object. Events are pre-written actions that are available for certain objects or components.
Pop-up Event Editor	Open the Events for dialog box shown later in Figure 7-18.
Size to Fit	Automatically resize the selected object to fit the size of the contents that will be displayed in it.

Table 7-4 Object menu options explained

The object types that appear in the list depend on the layout type that you are creating.

Compare this figure to Chapter 13, Figure 13-12, which is the same dialog box for reports. Some options are the same and others are different.

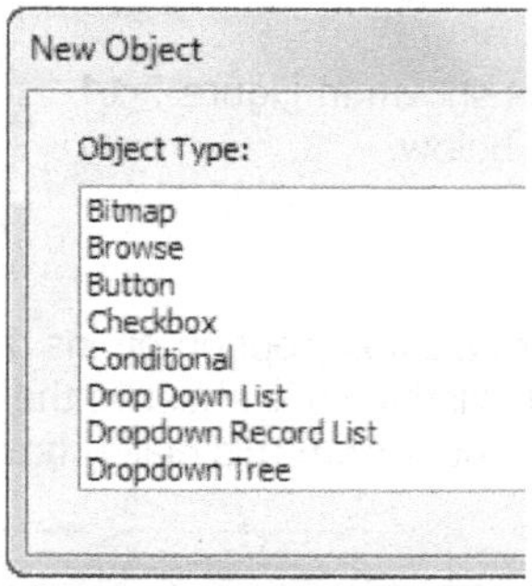

Figure 7-12 New Object dialog box (layouts)

Arrange Menu

The Arrange menu is shown in Figure 7-13. The options are explained in Table 7-5.

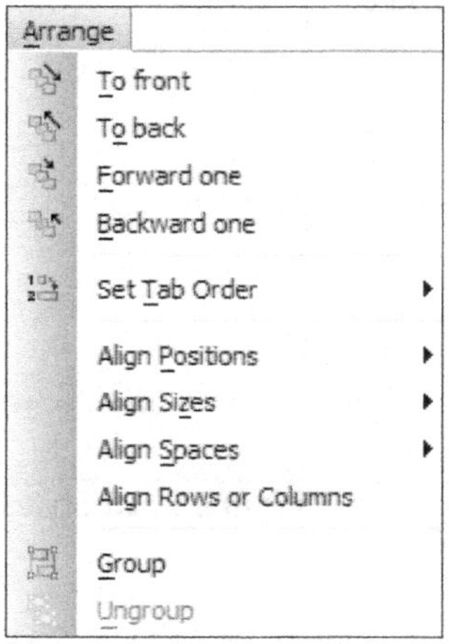

Figure 7-13 Arrange menu

Option	Is Used To . . .
To front	Move the selected object to the top layer.
To back	Move the selected object to the last layer.
Forward one	Move the selected object up one layer.
Backward one	Move the selected object down one layer.
Set Tab Order	Select the order that the cursor moves between fields and objects on the layout.
Align Positions	Align the selected objects on the same side of the object. (1)
Align Sizes	Make the selected objects the same size. (1)
Align Spaces	Place the same amount of space between the selected objects. (1)
Align Rows or Columns	Display the message shown later in Figure 7-63. This message tells you to use the options on the rulers to align objects. (1)
Group	Join the selected objects, so that they will function as one object. This option is enabled when two or more objects are selected.
Ungroup	Remove the selected objects from the group, so that they can function individually. This option is enabled when a group object is selected.

Table 7-5 Arrange menu options explained

(1) The alignment is based on the first object selected.

Stylesheets Menu

The Stylesheets menu is shown in Figure 7-14. The option is explained below.

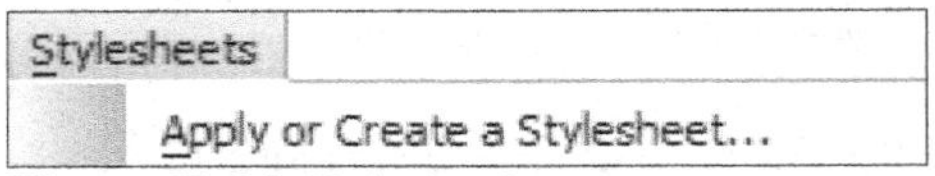

Figure 7-14 Stylesheets menu

The **APPLY OR CREATE A STYLESHEET** option opens the dialog box shown in Figure 7-15. This dialog box is used to apply an existing style sheet to the layout. You can also create a new style sheet, import or export a style sheet from this dialog box.

If checked, the **SHOW LEGACY STYLESHEETS** option will display style sheets from previous versions of Alpha Five, which you can also use.

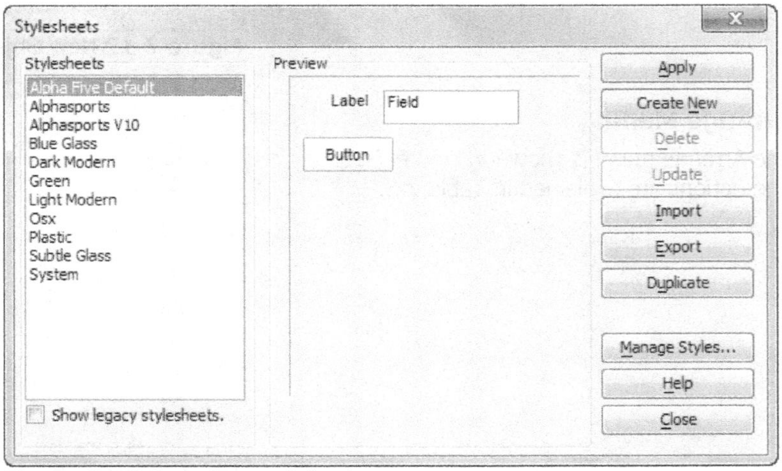

Figure 7-15 Stylesheets dialog box

Apply A Stylesheet To Selected Objects
In addition to being able to apply a style sheet to a form, it can also be applied to individual objects on the form. To apply a style sheet to objects, select the objects on the form, then open the Stylesheets dialog box. Select the stylesheet that has the formatting that you want to use, then click the Apply button. You will see the message shown in Figure 7-16. Click the **SELECTED OBJECT(S) BUTTON**, then click Close. The formatting from the stylesheet will be applied to the objects that you selected.

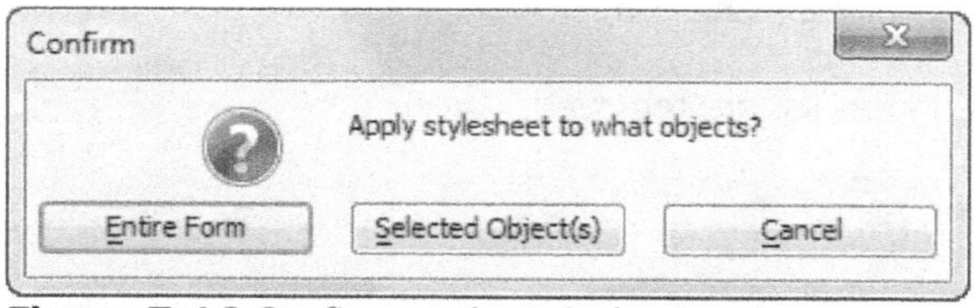

Figure 7-16 Confirm apply stylesheet message

Layout Editor Toolbar

The toolbar is shown in Figure 7-17. The buttons specifically for layouts are explained in Table 7-6. The toolbar has three more buttons on the right then what is displayed, but they are not specific to layouts. This is the toolbar that you will see when you are creating or editing a form. It is shown here because the majority of options are also used by other layouts.

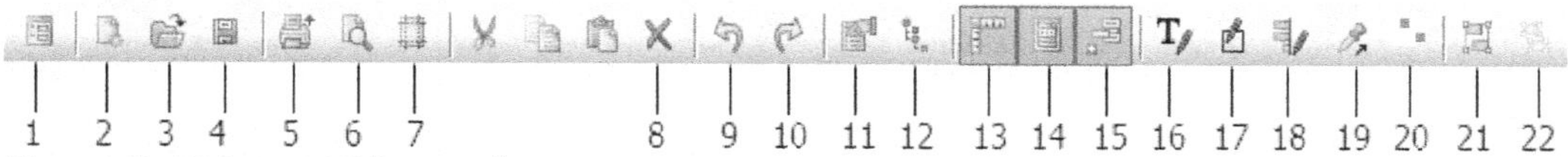

Figure 7-17 Layout Editor toolbar

Button	Is Used To . .
1	Display the layout (form, report etc.) in preview mode with data or in design mode.
2	Create a new layout without using a genie.
3	Open an existing layout.
4	Save the current layout.
5	Print the current layout.
6	Preview the form.
7	Open the Print Setup dialog box, to select options to print the layout.
8	Delete the selected object(s) from the layout.
9	Undo an action. Click this button for each action that you want to undo. (2)
10	Redo an action. Click this button for each action that you want to reapply. (2)
11	Open the Properties dialog box. The dialog box that opens depends on the object that was selected prior to selecting this option. For example, if a field on a form is selected, the Field Properties dialog box opens.
12	Open the dialog box shown in Figure 7-18. The options on the dialog box are used to create an event for the selected object on the form.
13	Display or hide the rulers.
14	Display or hide the Toolbox.
15	Display or hide the Drag Drop List.
16	Display or hide the Text toolbar, shown later in Figure 7-64.

Table 7-6 Layout Editor toolbar buttons explained

Button	Is Used To . .
17	Display or hide the Border toolbar, shown later in Figure 7-65.
18	Display or hide the Arrange toolbar, shown later in Figure 7-66.
19	Display or hide the Copy Format toolbar, shown later in Figure 7-67.
20	Display or hide the Anchor toolbar, shown later in Figure 7-68.
21	Group objects. [See Table 7-5]
22	Ungroup objects. [See Table 7-5]

Table 7-6 Layout Editor toolbar buttons explained (Continued)

(2) When the record is saved, the actions in this list are removed.

Double-clicking on a field on a form also opens this dialog box.

This dialog box is used to create an action for the selected object. An action will remind you of a macro in Excel. The action can be created as an Action script or in Xbasic.

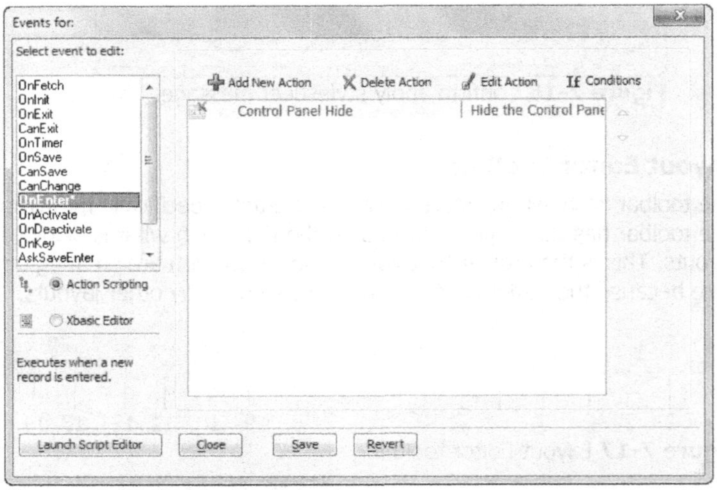

Figure 7-18 Events for dialog box

Design Window

This is the window in the middle of the workspace. It is where you create and edit the layout. As shown earlier in Figure 7-2, a form is being created. This is the space where you add fields, objects and controls. The options on the menu and toolbar covered earlier in this chapter are used when the design window is open.

Panels

By default, three panels are displayed when the layout workspace is opened: Properties, Drag Drop List and Toolbox. These panels (or **TASK PANES,** as they are sometimes called) contain options to customize the layout.

By default, the Properties panel is displayed as a button, as illustrated in Figure 7-19. To display it as shown earlier in Figure 7-2, click on the button.

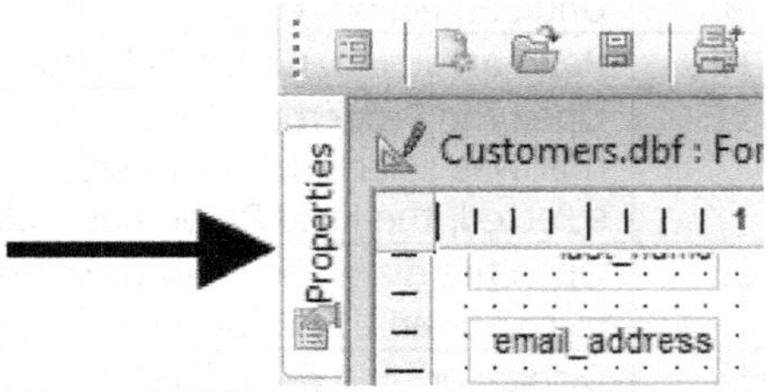

Figure 7-19 Properties panel minimized

For the most part, these panels work the same way. They can be **DOCKED** (how they are by default) or **UNDOCKED** (also known as a **FREE-FLOATING PANEL**) like the floating toolbars covered later in this chapter. They can be docked on the right or left side of the workspace. The panels are explained below.

Panel Shortcut Menu

By now it should not be a surprise that the panels have their own shortcut menu, as shown in Figure 7-20. The options are explained in Table 7-7.

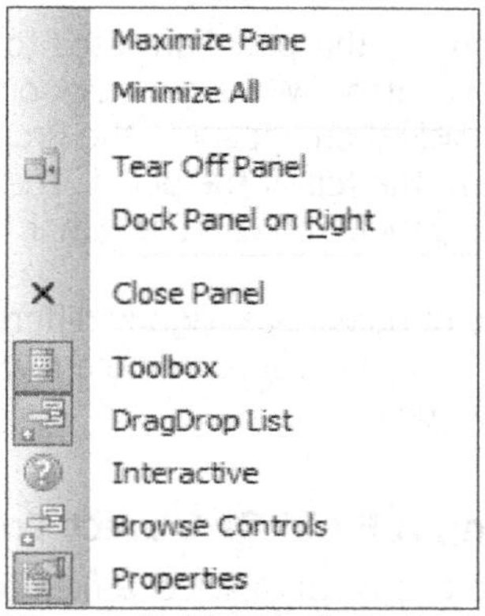

Figure 7-20 Panel shortcut menu

> The Panel shortcut menu options are also available by clicking on the down arrow button across from the name of the panel.

Option	Is Used To . . .
Maximize Pane	Make the panel longer.
Minimize All	Minimize the panel(s) that are docked on the same side of the workspace. If this option is selected on either panel shown earlier on the right side of Figure 7-2, both panels will be minimized, as shown in Figure 7-21.
Tear Off Panel	Undock the panel so that it is free-floating and can be moved.
Dock Panel on Right	Dock the panel on the right side of the workspace if the panel is currently on the left side of the workspace. If the panel is currently on the right side of the workspace, this menu option will be **DOCK PANEL ON LEFT**.
Close Panel	Close the selected panel.
Toolbox	Display or hide the Toolbox panel.
Drag Drop List	Display or hide the Drag Drop List panel.
Interactive	Display or hide the Interactive panel.
Browse Controls	Display or hide the Browse Controls panel, which is used to add interactive functionality like links and buttons, to cells in a browse.
Properties	Display or hide the Properties panel.

Table 7-7 Panel shortcut menu options explained

> **Double-Click Panel Tips**
>
> ① Double-clicking on the Drag Drop List or Toolbox panels Title bar will minimize both panels, as shown on the left in Figure 7-21.
>
> ② Double-clicking on the Properties panel Title bar, minimizes it, as shown earlier in Figure 7-19.

Figure 7-21 Multiple panels minimized

Properties Panel

The options on this panel are used to manage the functionality of the selected object on the layout, or the layout itself. When you click on an object in the design window, the properties for the object that you clicked on appear in the Properties panel. The name of the selected object is in the drop-down list at the top of the panel. The Object Property dialog boxes have the same options as the Properties panel. You can use either tool to change most of the properties.

Each type of object has slightly different properties on this panel. For example, a field has border, field and fill properties to name a few, while a fields label (I call it the field header) does not have field properties.

Selecting A Field Or Object To Change Properties

There are two ways to select a field or object, as explained below.

① Click on the field or object in the editor. This may be the easiest way.

② Click the arrow illustrated in Figure 7-22, to display a list of all of the objects on the layout, as shown in Figure 7-23.

_LBL at the end of a field on the Properties Panel indicates a fields label is selected, as shown in Figure 7-22.

It may be me, but sometimes the drop-down list doesn't close after I select an option.

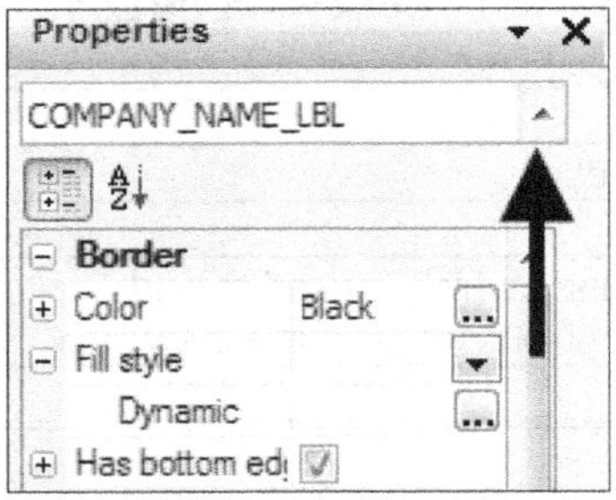

Figure 7-22 Extension for a fields label in the Properties panel

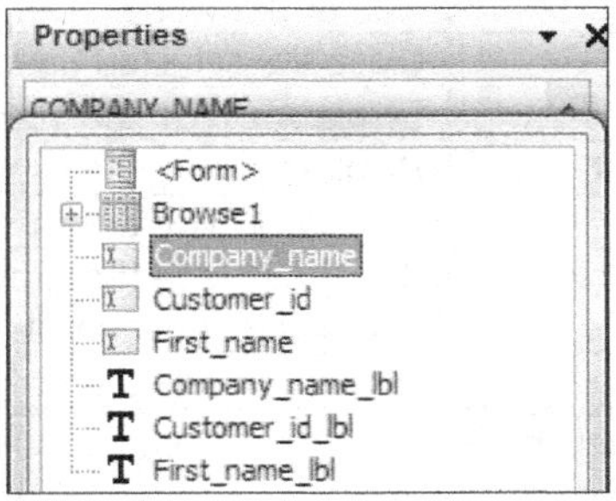

Figure 7-23 List of objects on the layout

This button sorts the options on the panel in alphabetical order, as shown in Figure 7-24.

It may be me, but I find the sort option (for the Properties panel) confusing because I do not know what part of the field or object the option is for.

For example, looking at the two Color options shown at the bottom of Figure 7-24, do you know what part of the object each color option will change? I rest my case.

Figure 7-24 Property options sorted in alphabetical order

 This button means that the property has a dialog box with more options.

 This button indicates that there is a drop-down list of options for the property.

Dynamic Property Option

Clicking on the plus sign + in front of a property will display the dynamic property for the object. The button at the end of the **DYNAMIC** property opens the Expression Builder to create a formula for the object. The dynamic property can also be used to display the data in a field. For example, on the Customer Information form in the Alpha Sports database, there is a text field that displays the customers name. This is helpful because it makes it easier to know which customer record is being displayed. You will learn how to do this in Chapter 11, Exercise 11.3.

As you will learn, you may not always need to apply the formatting that you create to every record. There are formatting techniques that apply the formatting only if a condition is met. This is known as **CONDITIONAL FORMATTING**. Examples of conditional formatting include the following:

① Highlighting records when the data in one field is greater than a constant value.
② Highlighting records with a specific color that have data missing in a field.
③ Check the value or length of a field and apply different formatting, depending on the value or length of the field.
④ Print a background color on every other detail record on the report.
⑤ Formatting one field with a border based on the value in another field.

> Many of the options on the Properties panel are also on the Object ⇒ Properties dialog box, but the Properties panel may be easier to use because it is already visible on the workspace and displays all of its options. Some options like the **SMART FIELD** and **FLY-OVER EFFECTS** options are only on the Object Properties (Setup tab) dialog box.

1. Select a field on the form, then scroll down the options on the Properties panel to see what options are available.

2. Select a label, then view the options on the Properties panel.

> **Changing Properties For More Than One Object At The Same Time**
> If you need to change the same property for multiple objects, select all of the objects, group them, then change the properties.

Using The Color Picker

Clicking on the ellipsis button next to a color option in the Properties panel opens the dialog box shown in Figure 7-25.

The options are used to select a system color or create a custom color.

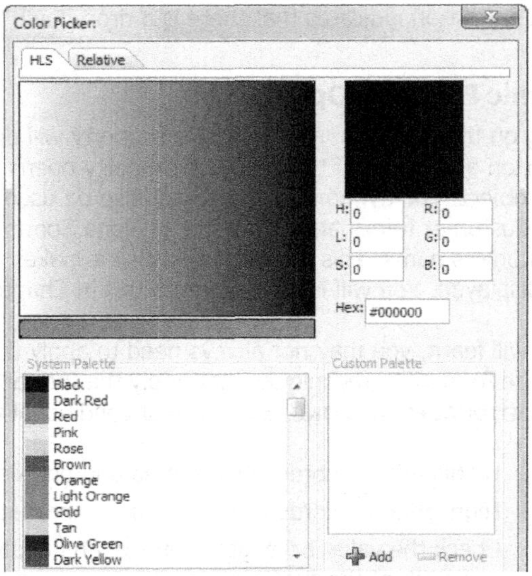

Figure 7-25 Color Picker dialog box

Properties Panel Misc Options

The options in this section of the Properties panel may be the ones that you use the most. As shown in Figure 7-26, the following options are available:

DISABLE SPELLCHECK Turns off spell check on a field by field basis. The spell check option is also on the Object Properties dialog box.

ENABLED If checked, the data in the field can be changed in the layout, as long as the Read only option is not checked. (3)

NAME Is used to change the display name of the field or object.

READ ONLY Prevents the data in the field from being changed. (3)

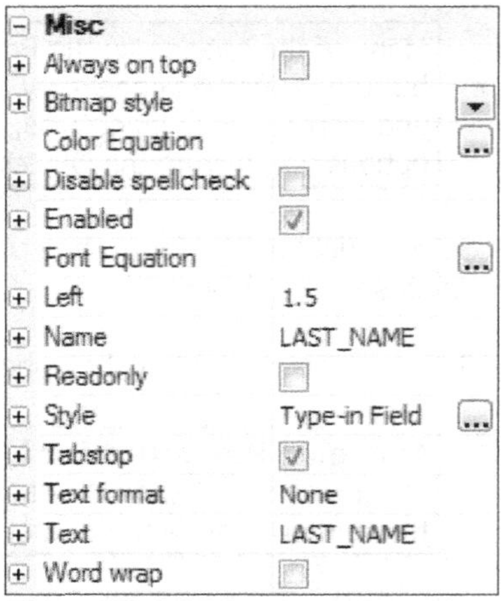

Figure 7-26 Misc property options

STYLE Changes the type of field. [See Chapter 11, What Is A Smart Field?]

TAB STOP If checked, the field will not be skipped when the Tab key is pressed to go from field to field on the layout. If the Enabled option is not checked or the Read only option is checked, the data in the field cannot be changed, even with the Tab Stop option enabled. (3)

(3) Pay attention to these three options because selecting certain combinations will prevent data from being entered into a field, which may not be what you want.

Rename An Object

By default, Alpha Five creates default names for all objects. The default name for each object is displayed at the top of the Properties panel in the drop-down list, as shown in Figure 7-27.

Field names are used for fields, which you probably would not have the need to rename. If you add a Line object (from the New Object dialog box shown earlier in Figure 7-12) to a layout, the default name that Alpha Five creates is shown at the top of Figure 7-27. To rename the object, type in the new name in the Name field shown earlier in Figure 7-26.

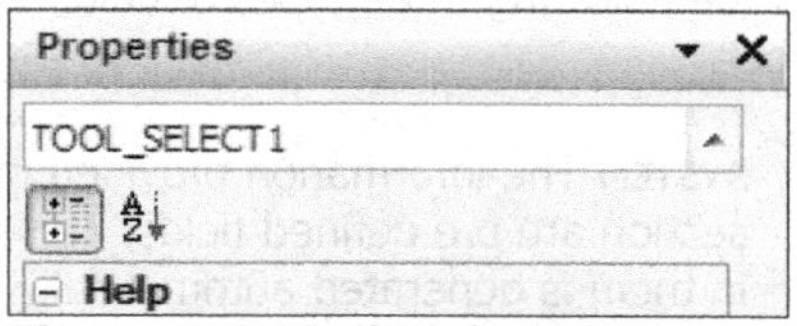

Figure 7-27 Default line object name

Layout Properties On The Properties Panel

So far, all of the discussions about the Properties panel have been about objects on a layout. As shown earlier at the top of Figure 7-23, the Properties Panel also contains options for the layout, in this case a form. If you select the layout option in the drop-down list, you will see the properties for the layout type.

Figure 7-28 shows the properties for a report.

Figure 7-29 shows the properties for a form.

These options are also on the Properties dialog box for the layout. Objects on the layout also have a Properties dialog box.

The properties for the layout are covered in the chapter that the layout type is covered in.

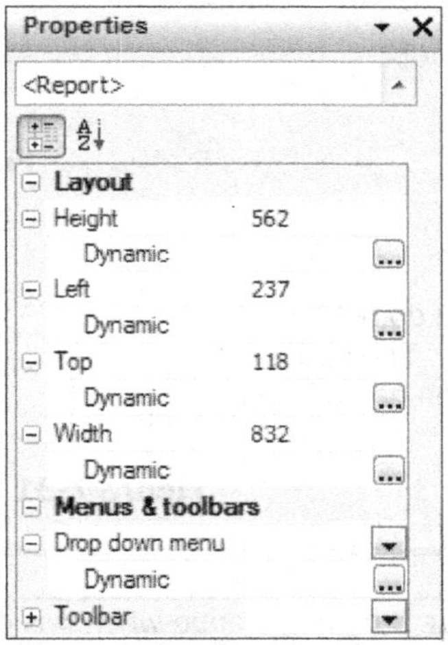

Figure 7-28 Report properties

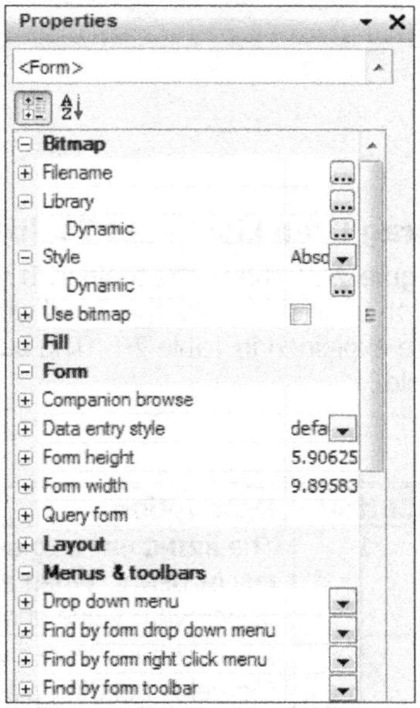

Figure 7-29 Form properties

Drag Drop List Panel

In addition to being able to add fields from the table(s) that the layout is attached to, the panel shown in Figure 7-30 is used to add the following three types of fields explained below, to the layout.

① **SYSTEM** The information provided in the fields in this section are pre defined fields. This means that the data in them is generated automatically.
② **VARIABLES** Are fields that you create to temporarily store data.
③ **CALCULATED FIELDS** Are fields that you create to compute a value.

To add a field in this panel to the layout, click on it, then drag the mouse pointer to the layout. Fields in this panel that have been added to the layout have a check mark. The arrow at the beginning of a section is used to display or hide the section.

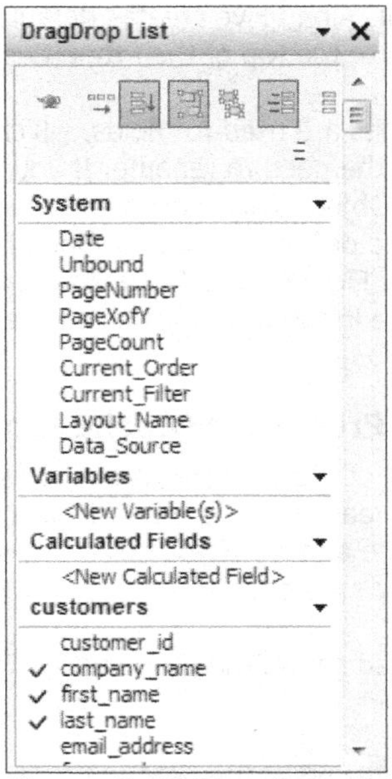

Figure 7-30 Drag Drop List panel

Drag Drop List Panel Toolbar

Figure 7-31 shows the toolbar. If you do not see all of the buttons, make the panel wider. The options are explained in Table 7-8. The button name is in bold.

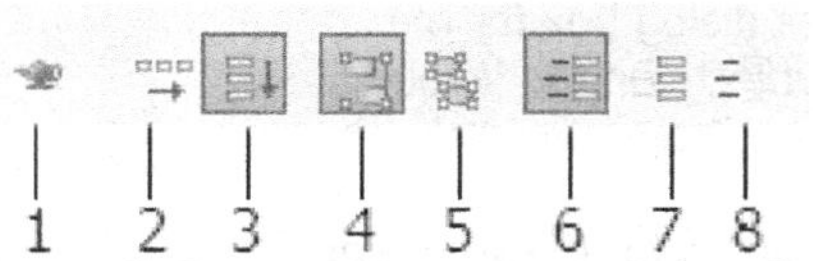

Figure 7-31 Drag Drop List panel toolbar

Button	Description
1	The **BRING UP FIELD GENIE** button is orange when it is enabled. It enables the **DROP FIELDS GENIE**. When a field is dragged to the layout, this genie will appear to let you select what value should be displayed in the field.
2	Select the **CONTROLS ACROSS** option before dragging a field to the layout if you want the fields heading placed above the field, as shown on the left of Figure 7-32.
3	Select the **CONTROLS DOWN** option before dragging a field to the layout if you want the fields heading placed to the left of the field, as shown on the right of Figure 7-32.
4	If the **GROUP CONTROLS** option is selected and more than one field is added to the layout at the same time, the fields will automatically be placed in a group.
5	If the **DON'T GROUP CONTROLS** option is selected and more than one field is added to the layout at the same time, the fields will not be placed in a group.
6	If the **FIELDS WITH TITLES** option is selected, the field and title will be added to the layout.
7	If the **FIELDS ONLY** option is selected, only the field will be added to the layout.
8	If the **TITLES ONLY** option is selected, only the title will be added to the layout.

Table 7-8 Drag Drop List panel toolbar buttons explained

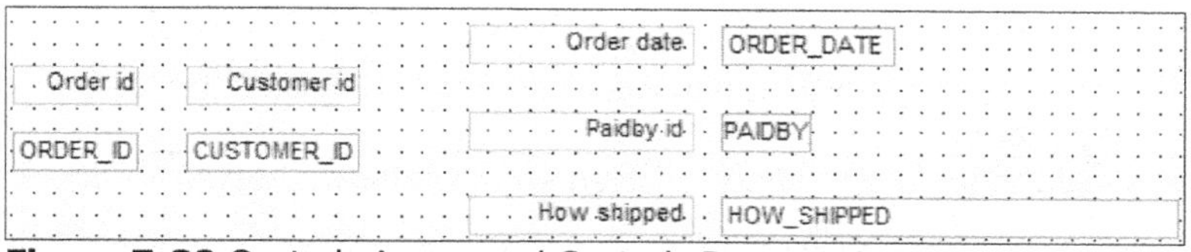

Figure 7-32 Controls Across and Controls Down options

Drag Drop List Panel Shortcut Menu

This panel has two shortcut menus, one for fields that have already been added to the layout, as shown in Figure 7-33 and one for fields that have not been added to the layout, as shown in Figure 7-34.

Figure 7-35 shows the shortcut menu for a field that has been added to the layout twice and deleted from the layout at least once.

Once the form is saved, the second occurrence of the **SELECT** and **EXTEND SELECT** options on the shortcut menu shown in Figure 7-33 go away. The options on these three shortcut menus are explained in Table 7-9.

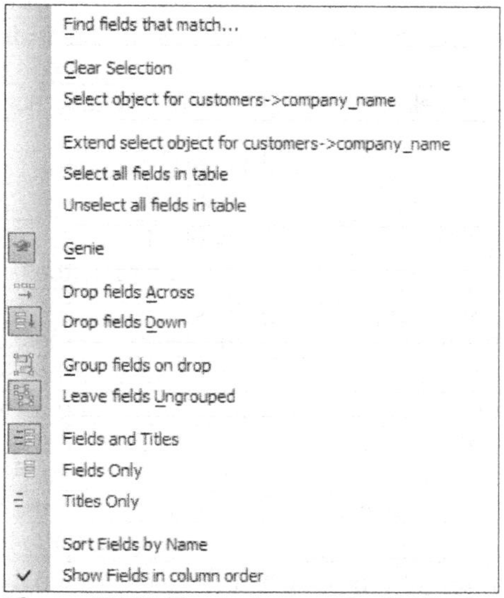

Figure 7-33 Shortcut menu for fields already on the layout

Figure 7-34 Shortcut menu for fields not on the layout

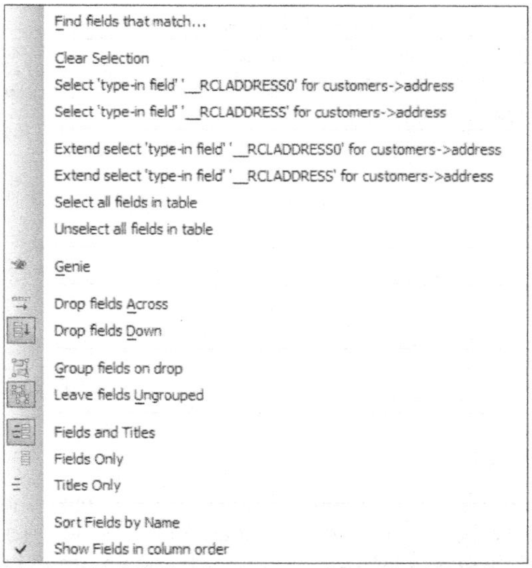

Figure 7-35 Shortcut menu for a field that has been added to the layout twice

Option	Is Used To . . .
Find fields that match	Open the dialog box shown in Figure 7-36 to find fields that match the pattern that you select.
Clear Selection	Is used to remove the prior selected search patterns created on the Find Fields dialog box.
Select object for <field name>	Select an object on the layout and remove the selection from other objects on the layout. (4)
Extend select object for <field name>	Select an object on the layout and leave the other objects that are selected on the layout. (4)
Select all fields in table	Select all of the fields in the table in the Drag Drop List panel. This will let you add all of the fields to the layout at the same time.
Unselect all fields in table	Remove the selection from all fields in the table in the Drag Drop List panel.
Genie	Enable/disable the Drop Fields Genie.
Drop fields Across	Enable/disable the Controls Across option.
Drop fields Down	Enable/disable the Controls Down option.
Group fields on drop	Enable/disable the Group Controls option.
Leave fields Ungrouped	Enable/disable the Don't group controls option.
Fields and Titles	Enable/disable the Fields with Titles option.
Fields Only	Enable/disable the Fields Only option.
Titles Only	Enable/disable the Titles Only option.
Sort Fields by Name	Sort the fields in the table in the Drag Drop List panel in alphabetical order.
Show Fields in column order	Sort the fields in the table in the Drag Drop List panel in the order that they are in the table.

Table 7-9 Drag Drop List panel shortcut menu options explained

(4) This option is only available for a field already on the layout.

This dialog box is especially helpful when using a set that has a lot of tables. It will keep you from having to scroll down the long list of tables and fields to find the field that you are looking for.

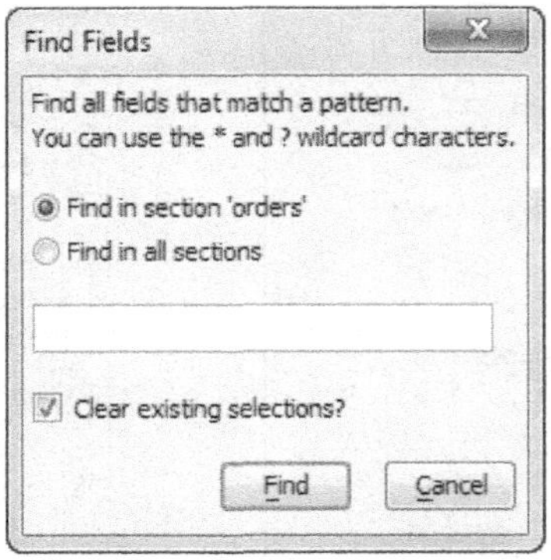

Figure 7-36 Find Fields dialog box

Toolbox Panel

The options on the panel shown in Figure 7-37 will make the layout interactive. This panel has two sections: The Form section and the Supercontrol section. To see all of the options in the Form section, scroll down the list by clicking on the down arrow button on the Supercontrols button.
To use a control, click on it in the Toolbox, then draw a box on the layout. From there a genie will walk you through setting up the control.

The **SUPERCONTROLS** shown in Figure 7-38 add more interactive functionality to the form then the options in the form section. In previous versions of Alpha Five, you had to spend additional money for these Supercontrols. Starting in Alpha Five version 11, the Supercontrols from version 10 are included as part of the software for no additional cost.

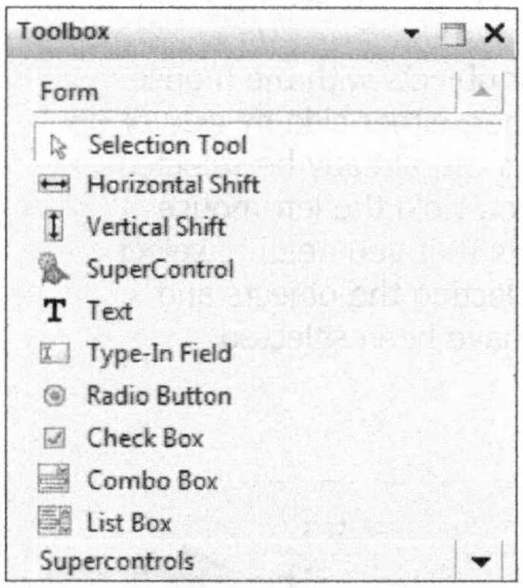

Figure 7-37 Toolbox panel

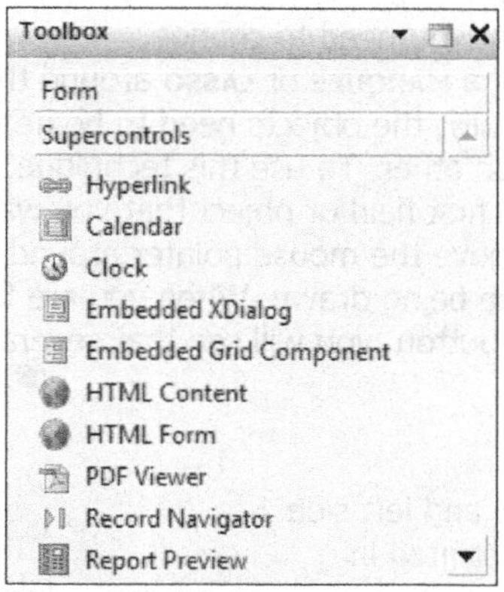

Figure 7-38 Supercontrols

Interactive Panel

The panel shown in Figure 7-39 is used to type in Xbasic statements, that you want to see the result of immediately. Usually, this is done for testing purposes.

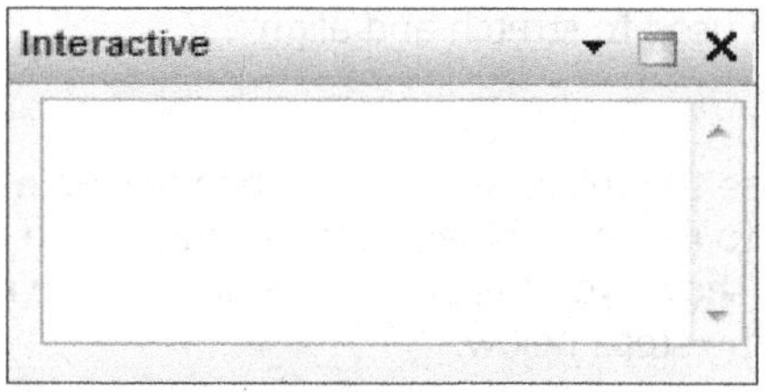

Figure 7-39 Interactive panel

Selecting Fields And Objects

A lot of the editing that you will do requires fields and other objects to be selected. Often, you will have the need to apply the same changes to several fields or objects.

To select a single field or object, click on it with the left mouse button.

When an object is selected you will see a frame around it, as illustrated in Figure 7-40. You will see squares on the frame.

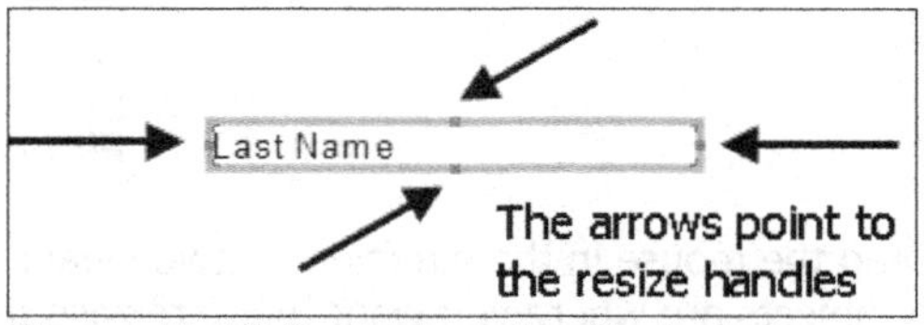

Figure 7-40 Resize handles illustrated

These squares are called **RESIZE HANDLES**. They are used to change the size of the object to make it wider, longer, shorter or smaller. You will learn how to resize objects later in this chapter.

> When I use the word "field", I am referring to a field in a table or a calculated field that you create. "Objects" refer to items like the field heading, a text object or an image.

Selecting Multiple Fields And Objects

There are two ways to select the fields or objects that you need, as explained below.

① Click on one field or object. Press and hold down the **SHIFT** key, then click on the other fields or objects that you need to change.

② Draw what is called a **MARQUEE** or **LASSO** around the fields or objects with the mouse. To do this successfully, the objects need to be near each other, either side by side or up and down from each other. To use this technique, no objects can already be selected. Click outside of the first field or object that you want to select. Hold the left mouse button down and move the mouse pointer around the objects that you need to select. You will see a frame being drawn. When you are finished selecting the objects and release the mouse button, you will see that several objects have been selected.

Rulers

The rulers are across the top and left side of the design window, as illustrated in Figure 7-41.

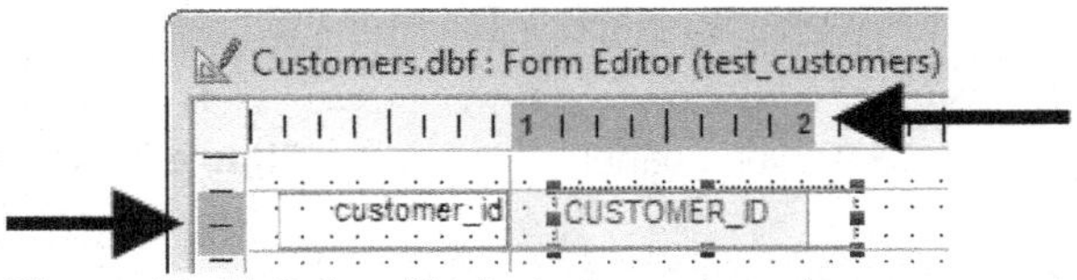

Figure 7-41 Rulers illustrated

Believe it or not, the rulers have shortcut menus. The options on the shortcut menus are used to stretch and align objects.

You can use the rulers as a guide when adding a field or object to the layout. You can also use the rulers to resize an object. When you select a field, then move or resize it, the ruler will display a bar that shows you the size of the object. The rulers can be used to move fields or objects, by following the steps below.

1. Click on the ruler over the fields or objects that you want to move.

   The fields or objects that will be moved will automatically be selected, as shown in Figure 7-42.

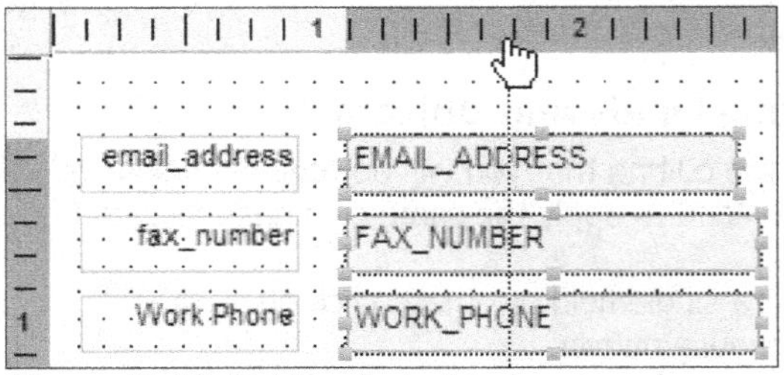

Figure 7-42 Fields selected to be moved

2. Drag the mouse in the direction that you want to move the fields or objects. When the fields or objects are where you want them, release the mouse button.

Vertical Ruler Shortcut Menu

Figure 7-43 shows the shortcut menu. The options are explained in Table 7-10.

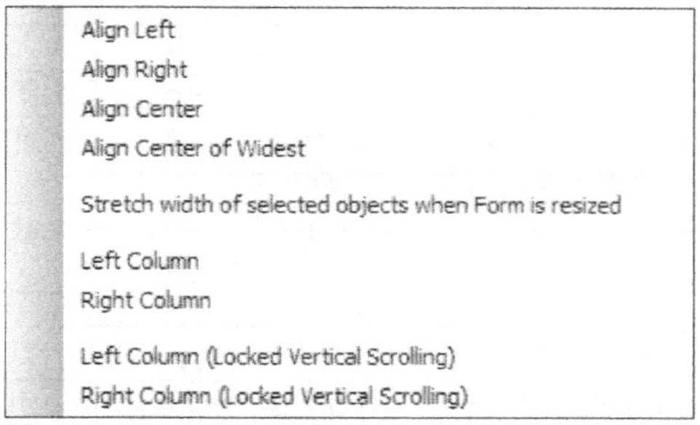

Figure 7-43 Vertical ruler shortcut menu

Option	Description
Align Left	[See Table 7-13]
Align Right	[See Table 7-13]
Align Center	Aligns on the center of the object.
Align Center of Widest	Center aligns the selected objects based on the widest object that is selected.
Stretch width of selected objects when Form is resized	Allows the object to be resized vertically if the form is resized.
Left Column	Is used to create a column on the left side of the form. (5)
Right Column	Is used to create a column on the right side of the form. (5)
Left Column (Locked Vertical Scrolling)	Forces the left column section to be visible when you scroll up and down.
Right Column (Locked Vertical Scrolling)	Forces the right column section to be visible when you scroll up and down.

Table 7-10 Vertical ruler shortcut menu options explained

(5) The "column" created by this option is not visible on the form. It acts like the freeze pane option in Excel. This section (column) of the form will stay visible when you scroll right or left, but not when you scroll up and down, unless the corresponding locked vertical scrolling option is selected.

Horizontal Ruler Shortcut Menu

Figure 7-44 shows the shortcut menu. The options are explained in Table 7-11.

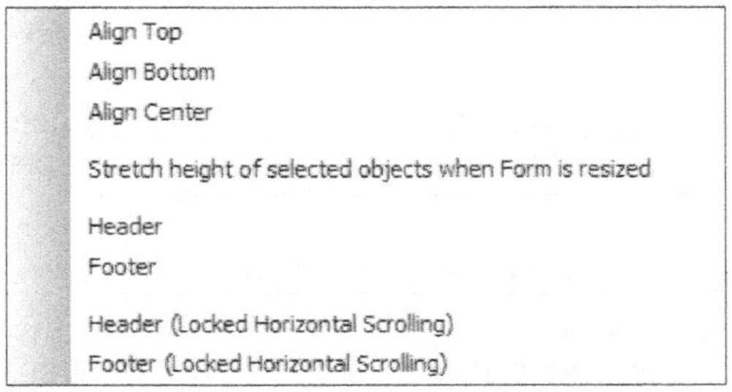

Figure 7-44 Horizontal ruler shortcut menu

Option	Description
Align Top	[See Table 7-13]
Align Bottom	[See Table 7-13]
Align Center	Aligns on the center of the object.
Stretch height of selected objects when Form is resized	Allows the object to be resized horizontally if the form is resized.
Header	Is used to select a section at the top of the form that you want to stay visible. (6)
Footer	Is used to select a section at the bottom of the form that you want to stay visible. (6)
Header (Locked Horizontal Scrolling)	Forces the header section to be visible when you scroll left or right.
Footer (Locked Horizontal Scrolling)	Forces the footer section to be visible when you scroll left or right.

Table 7-11 Horizontal ruler shortcut menu options explained

(6) This section of the form will stay visible when you scroll up and down, but not when you scroll left and right unless the corresponding locked horizontal scrolling option is selected.

Using The Grid

This option is available for all layouts except the Browse layout. By default, in the background of the layout, you will see a grid that has dots. That is because the **DISPLAY GRID** option is enabled. These dots can be used to align objects. Displaying or using the grid is optional. The dialog box shown in Figure 7-45 has options that let you enable or disable the grid.

The **SNAP TO GRID** option causes objects to automatically align to the closest set of dots on the grid. The option for this dialog box is on the menu of the type of editor that you have open.

For example, when the Form Editor is open, this option is on the Form menu.

If the Report Editor is open, the **GRID** option is on the Report menu.

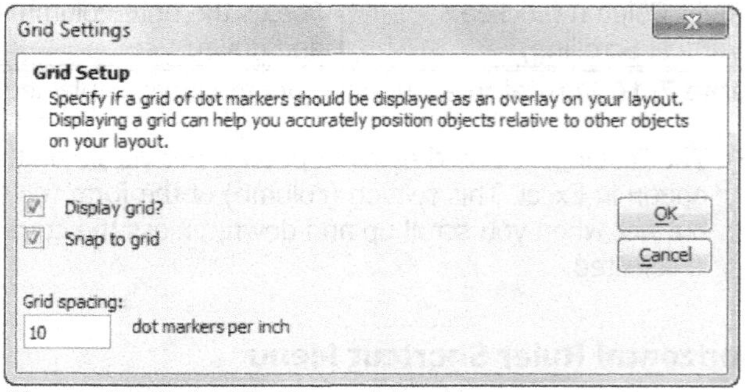
Grid Settings
Grid Setup
Specify if a grid of dot markers should be displayed as an overlay on your layout. Displaying a grid can help you accurately position objects relative to other objects on your layout.
Display grid?
Snap to grid
OK
Cancel
Grid spacing:
10
dot markers per inch

Figure 7-45 Grid Settings dialog box

The **GRID SPACING** option is used to select how many dots will appear on the background in an inch. The default is 10. A larger number displays more dots per inch.

Adding Fields And Objects To The Layout

I think that the fastest way to add a field or object to the layout is to use the Drag Drop List panel. Click on the object that you want to add to the layout in the panel, then drag it to where you want it on the layout. You can add more than one object in the Drag Drop List panel at the same time, but using ① above in the Selecting Multiple Fields And Objects section.

If you want to add several fields that are next to each other in the Drag Drop List panel, click on the first field. Press and hold down the **SHIFT** key, then click on the last field that you want to add, as shown in Figure 7-46. Once selected, drag the fields to the layout.

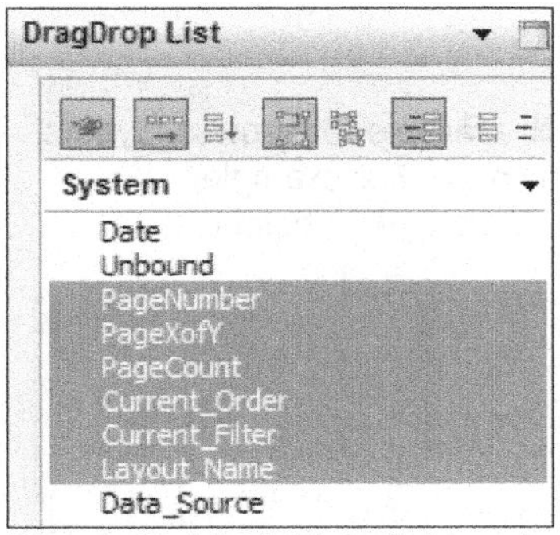

Figure 7-46 Multiple fields selected to be added to the layout at the same time

Cut, Copy And Paste Options

These three features in Alpha Five work just like they do in word processing software. The keyboard shortcuts in Table 7-12 are another way to use these options. These options are also on the Edit menu and toolbar.

Shortcut	Is Used To . . .
Ctrl + X	Cut the selected object.
Ctrl + C	Copy the selected object.
Ctrl + V	Paste the selected object.

Table 7-12 Keyboard shortcuts

Using The Undo And Redo Options

There will be times when you do something on a layout that you do not want. When that is the case, click the Undo button on the toolbar. Each time that you click the Undo button, another action will be undone. The Redo option works the opposite. It will re-add an action that was previously undone.

Moving And Resizing Objects

Probably as often as you add objects to the layout, you will have the need to move or resize them. To **MOVE AN OBJECT**, click on it, then drag the object to its new location.

To **RESIZE AN OBJECT**, click on it. Place the mouse pointer on the appropriate resize handle, as shown earlier in Figure 7-40. Drag the resize handle in the direction that you need. You will see the color on the ruler change above the field. This may make it easier to see the size that you are adjusting the object to.

Nudging Objects

So far in this chapter you have learned how to move and resize objects using the mouse. You can also move and resize objects using the keyboard. This is helpful if you use a laptop and do not use a mouse. Using the keyboard to move or resize objects is known as **NUDGING AN OBJECT**.

How To Move An Object By Nudging It

1. Without using the mouse, click on the object that you want to move.

2. Use one of the four arrow keys on the keyboard to move the object in the direction that you need to reposition it.

Dynamic Guidelines

Like the grid covered earlier in this chapter, dynamic guidelines are not available for browse layouts. This option is available from the Layout menu in the layout editor workspace. For example, Form ⇒ Dynamic Guidelines or Letter ⇒ Dynamic Guidelines, opens the dialog box below.

Figure 7-47 shows the options. By default, the **USE DYNAMIC GUIDELINES** option is enabled.

The **SNAP TO ADJACENT OBJECTS** option is used to select how close the selected object has to be to another object before it is automatically aligned with it.

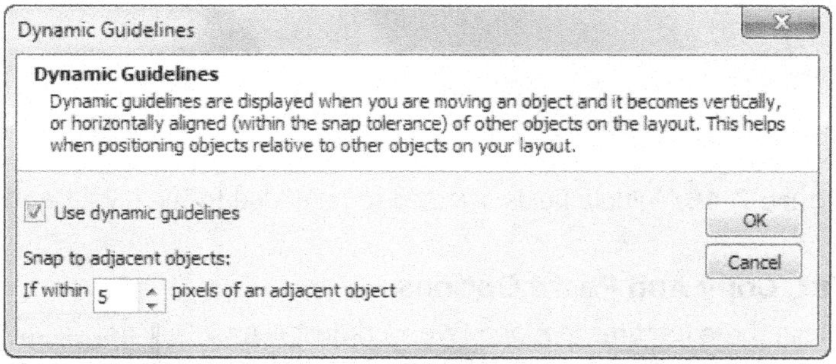

Figure 7-47 Dynamic Guidelines dialog box

The guidelines are used to help align the selected object(s) with other objects on the layout. When this feature is enabled and you select an object to align, you will see blue lines in the direction that you are moving the object. The blue lines let you know if the selected object is lined up with other objects on the layout. And yes, the guidelines work without the rulers enabled.

Figure 7-48 shows two fields being moved vertically. Figure 7-49 shows the guidelines when a field is being moved horizontally to the right. Compare these figures to the one shown earlier in Figure 7-42, which did not have the guidelines feature enabled.

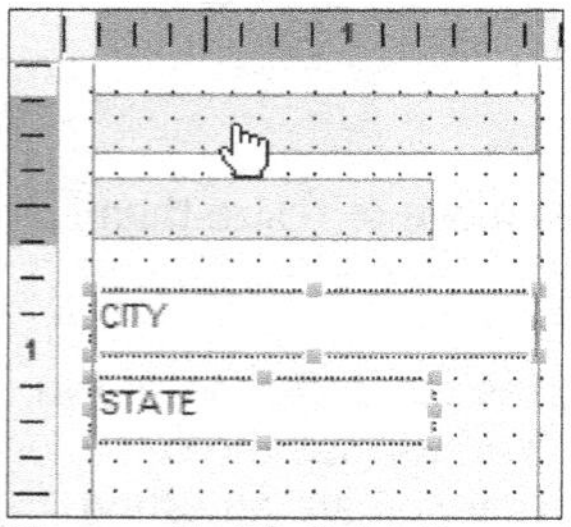

Figure 7-48 Guidelines when a field is moved vertically

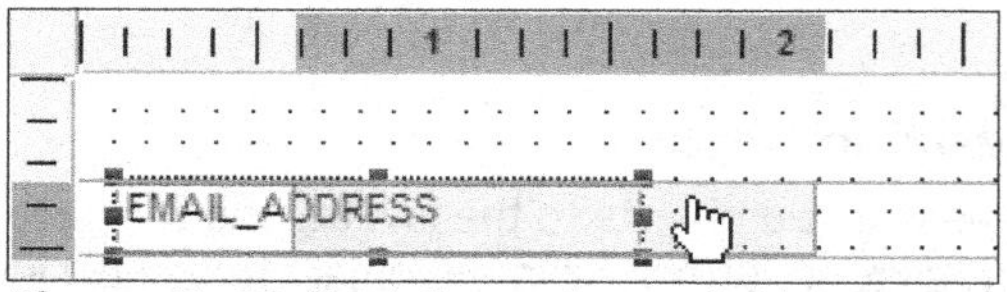

Figure 7-49 Guidelines when a field is moved horizontally

Aligning Objects

The align options are very helpful in making your layouts look as professional as possible. As you read earlier in Table 7-5, there are four ways to align objects from the Arrange menu. Each of the alignment options are explained below.

> **How The Align Options Work**
> The most important thing to remember about using the align options is that the object that you click on first is the object that the other objects that you select will be aligned to.

Align Positions Options

In addition to moving objects, you will have the need to have multiple objects line up.

The **ALIGN POSITION** options, shown in Figure 7-50 are used to line up several objects at the same time. The options are explained in Table 7-13.

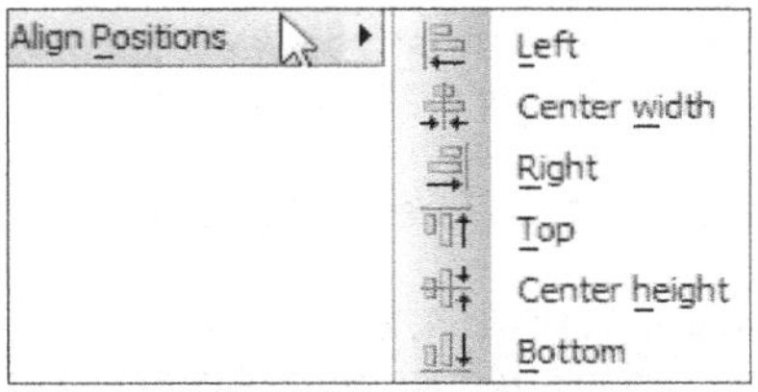

Figure 7-50 Align Positions options

Align Option	How It Aligns . . .
Left	On the left side of the object.
Center Width	Horizontally, so that the objects are centered.
Right	On the right side of the object.
Top	On the top edge of the object.
Center Height	Vertically, so that the objects are centered.
Bottom	On the bottom edge of the object.

Table 7-13 Align Positions options explained

To align objects, follow the steps below.

1. Select the object that you want the other objects that you select aligned to, then select the other objects that you want aligned.

2. Arrange ⇒ Align Positions ⇒ Select the align option that you need.

As shown in Figure 7-51, the field and heading are not lined up. After selecting both objects and selecting the Align positions left option, the field and heading look like the ones shown in Figure 7-52.

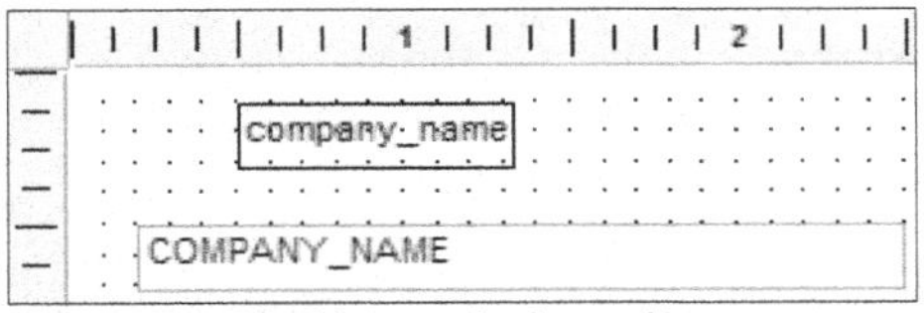

Figure 7-51 Objects before alignment

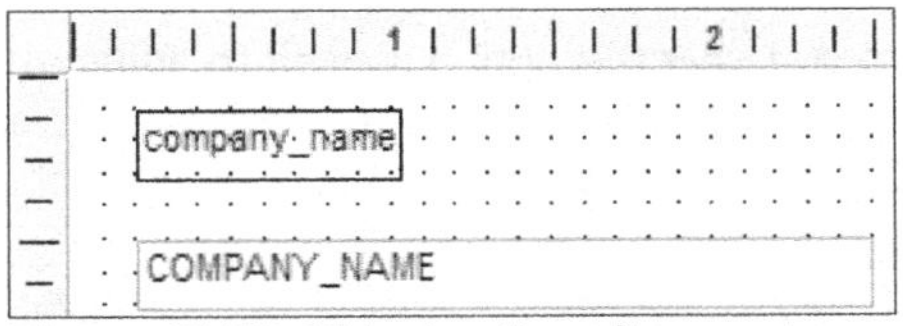

Figure 7-52 Objects after alignment

Align Sizes Options

The **ALIGN SIZES** options shown in Figure 7-53 are used to make the selected objects the same size. The options are explained in Table 7-14.

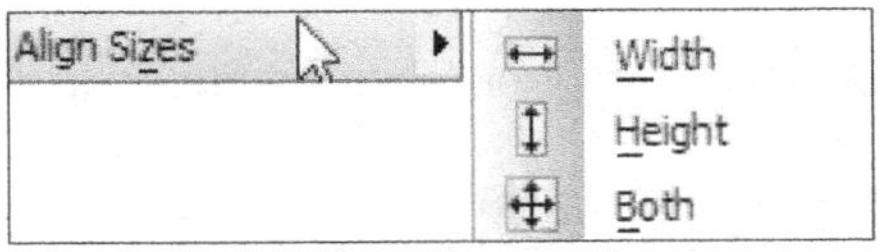

Figure 7-53 Align Sizes options

Option	Makes The Selected Objects The Same . . .
Width	Width.
Height	Height.
Both	Width and height.

Table 7-14 Align Sizes options explained

To make objects the same size, follow the steps below.

1. Select the object that you want the other objects that you select to be the size of, then select the other objects that you want resized.

2. Arrange ⇒ Align Sizes ⇒ Select the sizing option that you need.

As shown in Figure 7-54, the fields are not the same size. After selecting the objects and selecting the Align sizes width option, the fields are the same width as shown in Figure 7-55.

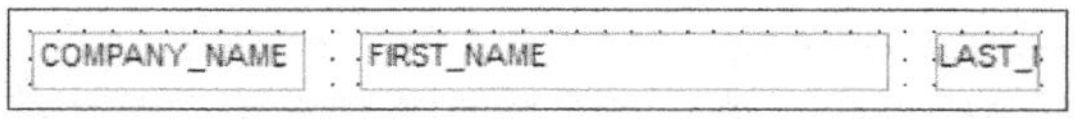

Figure 7-54 Fields before being resized

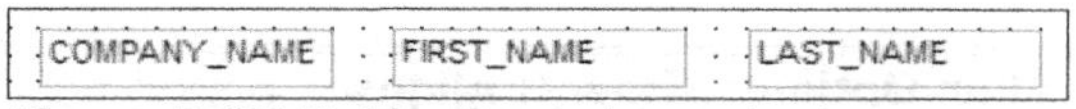

Figure 7-55 Fields after being resized

Align Spaces Options

In addition to aligning objects on a specific side, there are options that can be used to adjust the amount of space between objects.

The **ALIGN SPACES** options shown in Figure 7-56 are used to put the same amount of space between the selected objects. These options are also on the **ARRANGE TOOLBAR**. They are named **HORIZONTAL SPACING** and **VERTICAL SPACING** on the toolbar. The options are explained below.

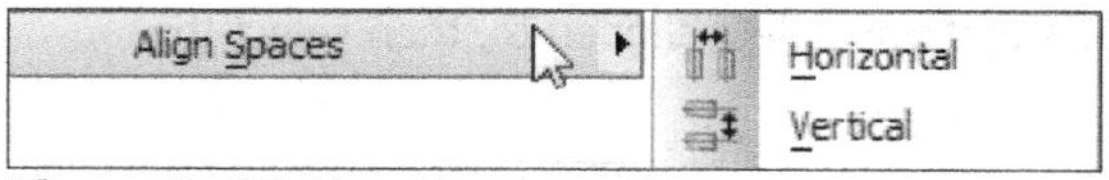

Figure 7-56 Align Spaces options

Three or more objects have to be selected to use this option. The key to using the space options successfully is to move the first two objects that you select to the position that you want the other objects to emulate.

The **HORIZONTAL SPACING** option is used to adjust the space between objects in the same row. This option takes the fields shown in Figure 7-57 and changes the horizontal spacing to what is shown in Figure 7-58. There is an equal amount of space horizontally between the fields.

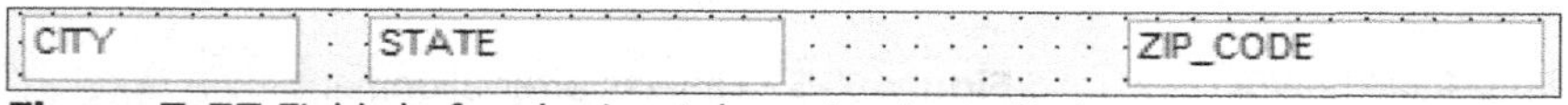

Figure 7-57 Fields before horizontal spacing is applied

Figure 7-58 Fields after horizontal spacing is applied

The **VERTICAL SPACING** option is used to adjust the space between objects in the same column. This option takes the fields shown in Figure 7-59 and changes the vertical spacing to what is shown in Figure 7-60. There is an equal amount of space vertically between the fields.

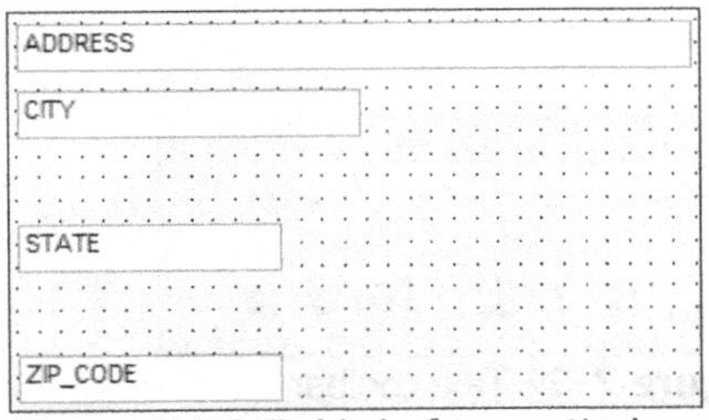

Figure 7-59 Fields before vertical spacing is applied

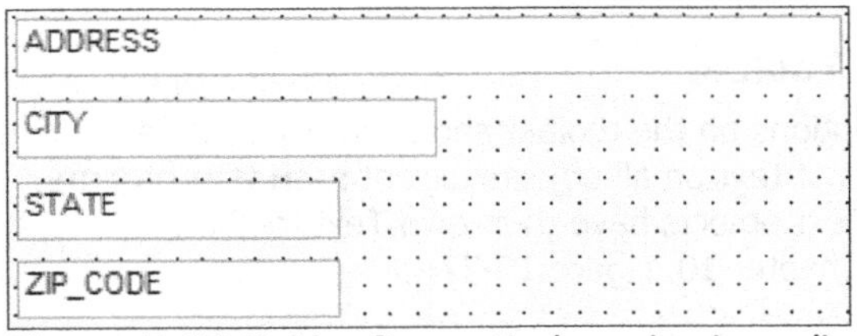

Figure 7-60 Fields after vertical spacing is applied

To apply the same amount of space between objects, follow the steps below.

1. Select the objects that you want to change the spacing between.
2. Arrange ⇒ Align Spaces ⇒ Select the spacing option that you need.

As shown in Figure 7-61, the fields do not have the same amount of space between them. After selecting the objects and then selecting the Align Spaces Horizontal option, the fields have the same amount of space between them as shown in Figure 7-62.

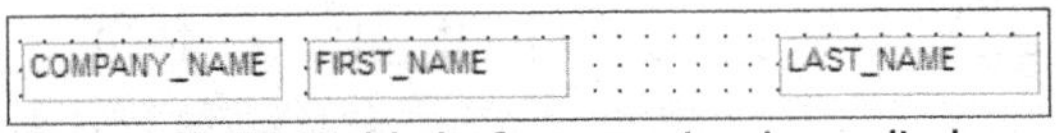

Figure 7-61 Fields before spacing is applied

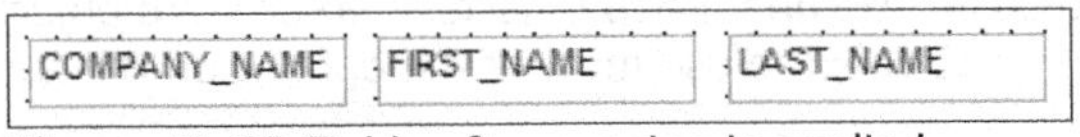

Figure 7-62 Fields after spacing is applied

Aligning Rows And Columns

Like the other align options, this option is on the Arrange menu.

When you select it, you will see the dialog box shown in Figure 7-63.

This message is telling you how to use the align rows and columns options that are on the shortcut menus on the rulers.

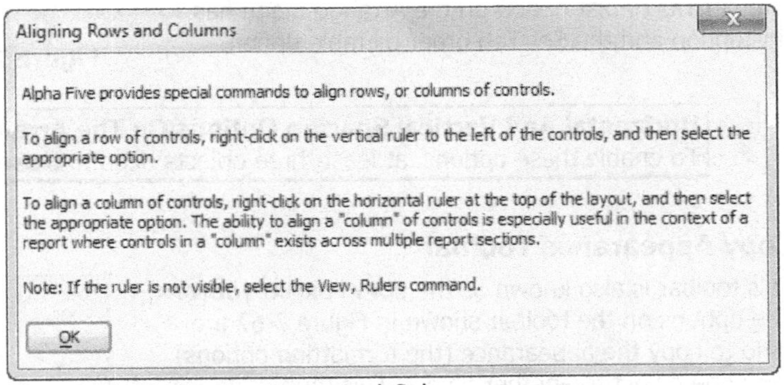

Figure 7-63 Aligning Rows And Columns message

Floating Toolbars

There are several toolbars (available from the View menu) that can be used to modify the selected objects on the layout. Each toolbar has the formatting options that you will probably use the most. Many of the options will remind you of options in word processing software. The toolbars are shown in Figures 7-64 to 7-68.

The Text and Border floating toolbars do not support objects that are grouped. Some of the options on the Arrange toolbar are supported.

Text Toolbar

The options on the toolbar shown in Figure 7-64 are used to format text on all objects except **RICH TEXT OBJECTS.** Rich Text objects have their own Text toolbar.
[See Chapter 10, Figure 10-32]

Figure 7-64 Text toolbar

Border Toolbar

The options on the toolbar shown in Figure 7-65 are used to add or modify a border around the selected object(s).

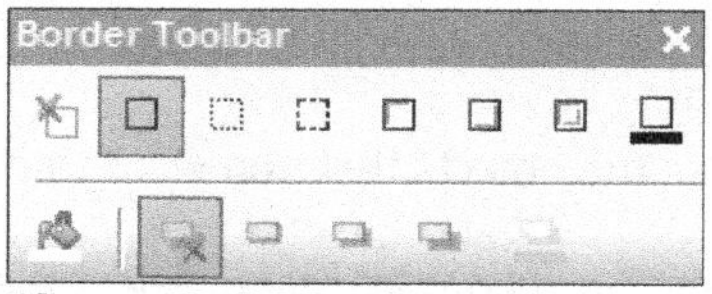

Figure 7-65 Border toolbar

Arrange Toolbar

The options on the toolbar shown in Figure 7-66 are used to align, size and group objects. Two or more objects need to be selected to use most of the options on this toolbar.

The **TAB ORDER BUTTON**, illustrated in the figure uses the **BY EXAMPLE TAB ORDER** option.

The **SET TAB ORDER** option on the Arrange menu has this option and the Set Tab order by table option.

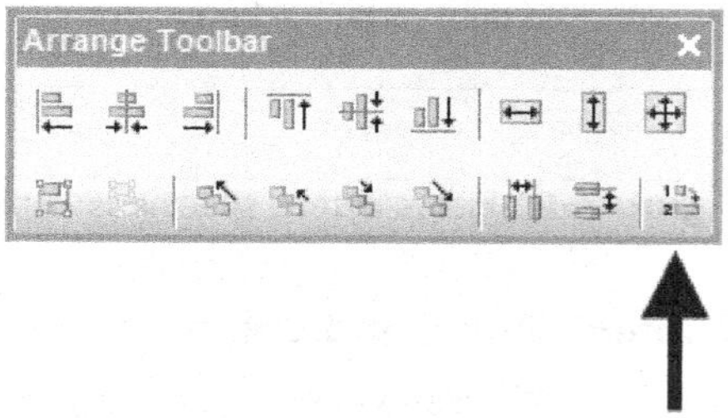

Figure 7-66 Arrange toolbar

> **Horizontal And Vertical Spacing Options On The Arrange Toolbar**
> To enable these options, at least three objects need to be selected.

Copy Appearance Toolbar

This toolbar is also known as the **COPY FORMAT TOOLBAR.** The options on the toolbar shown in Figure 7-67 are used to copy the appearance (the formatting options) from one object to another object. This formatting can also be copied to all objects that are the same data type.

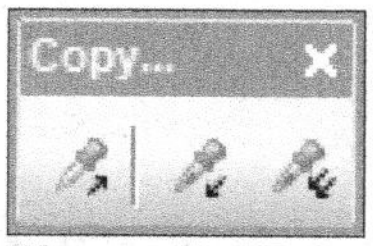

Figure 7-67 Copy Appearance toolbar

Anchor Toolbar

The options on the toolbar shown in Figure 7-68 are used to make sure that forms will work with any screen resolution, even if the user resizes the form.

These options will allow the fields to stretch horizontally. The options cannot be used with objects that are grouped. If may be me, but the options on this toolbar are not intuitive.

The **QUICK SELECT BUTTON** (in each corner on the figure) when clicked, enables the appropriate anchor options.

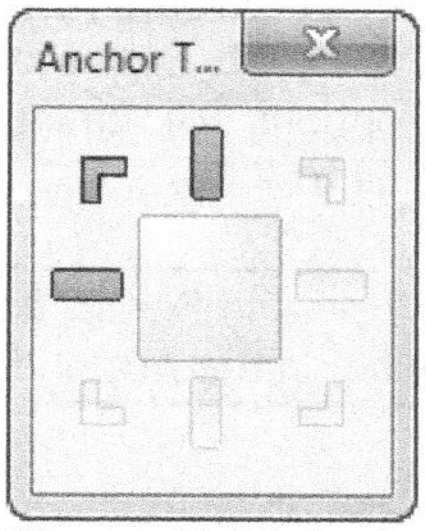

Figure 7-68 Anchor toolbar

For example, if you click on the top left button, the Anchor to top and Anchor to left buttons are automatically selected, as shown in the figure.

How To Remove An Anchor

To remove an anchor, click on the field, open the Anchor toolbar, then click on the bar that corresponds to the anchor that you want to remove. In Figure 7-68 above, there are two bars (one on the left and one on the top).

How To Dock Floating Toolbars

These toolbars can be **FREE FLOATING** or they can be docked to one side of the workspace or up near the menu. To dock a toolbar, click on its Title bar, then drag the toolbar to the side of the workspace that you want to dock the toolbar.

If you want the toolbar docked below the menu, drag it there, then release the mouse button, as illustrated in Figure 7-69.

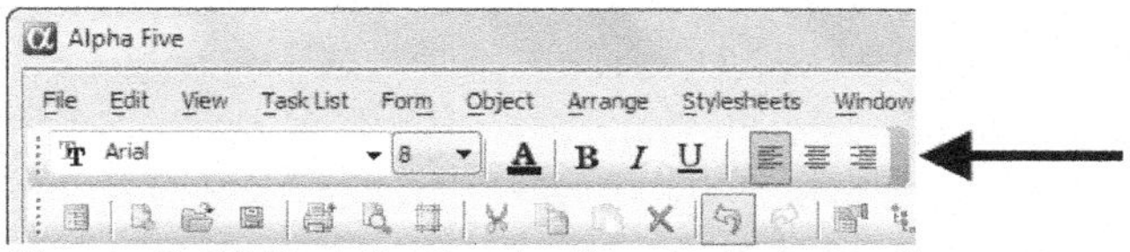

Figure 7-69 Text floating toolbar docked near the menu

How To Undock Floating Toolbars

Click on the dotted lines on the left side of the floating toolbar and drag the toolbar towards the center of the workspace, then release the mouse button.

Adding A Password To A Layout

This feature is helpful if you only want certain users to be able to modify a layout. If a layout has a password, it can't be opened in design mode without entering a password. To password protect a layout, follow the steps below.

1. Open the layout, then File ⇒ Save As.
2. Type in a new name for the layout if you want, then click the Password button.
3. On the dialog box shown in Figure 7-70 type an alphanumeric password up to eight characters, then click OK.

Figure 7-70 Define Password dialog box

4. You will be prompted to enter the password again. Do so, then click OK twice to close both dialog boxes.

[illegible]

How To Rename An Account

[illegible]

How To Sort Existing Transactions

[illegible] that you want to [illegible]

[illegible]

How To Create A Tracking Tag

[illegible]

Adding A Password To An Account

[illegible]

CREATING FORMS

In this chapter you will learn how to:

- ☑ Create forms using the Form Genie
- ☑ Use the Drag Drop List panel to add fields from tables to a form
- ☑ Use the options on the Form Properties and Field Properties dialog boxes to customize forms

CHAPTER 8

Overview

So far, you have created the tables to store the data in, created field rules for tables and created sets. You have not created forms to enter data into the tables. In Chapter 7 you viewed a browse, but as you saw, it was not very appealing to the eye. This chapter will teach you how to create forms.

Forms allow you to enter, display, browse, change or print data. Fields and titles (headings) on a form are called **CONTROLS**. Controls are objects that are used to display data or perform actions.

Like creating tables, creating forms also has a genie. Using the Form Genie can be a real time saver. Although forms created with a genie may not give you exactly what you are looking for, they can give you a great head start.

The forms that you are going to create in this chapter will be used for what I call maintenance forms. Maintenance forms are forms for tables that are used to help maintain and validate data in the other tables during data entry. The following tables are the maintenance tables in this application: Contact Type, Products, Paid By and Sales Reps.

There are literally hundreds if not thousands of options available to create forms. This chapter covers some of the basic form options and Chapters 10 and 11 cover more form options.

Using The Form Genie

Believe it or not, all forms are started by using this genie. It provides the options shown in Figure 8-1 as the starting point. The options are explained below.

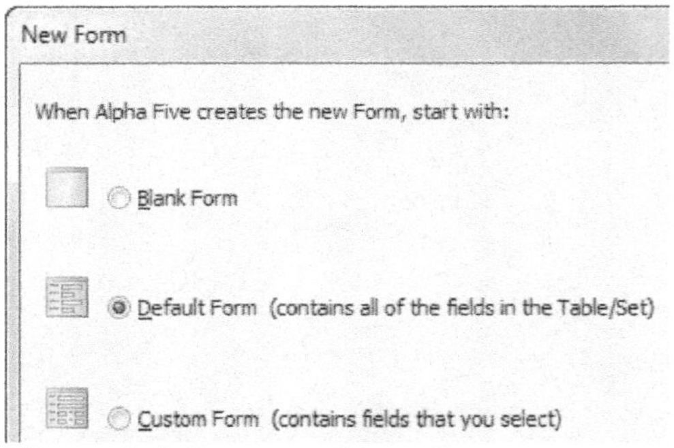

Figure 8-1 Form creation options

① **BLANK FORM** Select this option if you want to add fields to the form on your own. You can apply a style sheet to the form using this option.

② **DEFAULT FORM** As its name suggests, this is the option that is automatically selected when you open the Form Genie. In addition to being able to apply a style sheet, all of the fields in the table or set are automatically added to the form. This option does not allow you to select the fields for the form, but when the form is in the design view, you can delete the fields that are not needed.

③ **CUSTOM FORM** Select this option if you want to select the fields that will appear on the form. This option is also used to create a single column, multi-column or tabbed form.

How To Open The Form Genie

There are several ways to open the Form Genie, as explained below.

① On the Control Panel's Form tab, click the New button.

② On the Forms tab, right-click on an empty space and select New.

③ On the Forms tab, right-click on any form and select New Form. It doesn't matter which form you right-click on because you have to select the table or set on the genie.
④ Form ⇒ New Form.

Exercise 8.1: Create The Contact Type Form

In this exercise you will create a basic form.

1. On the Control Panel's Forms tab, click the New button.

2. On the dialog box shown in Figure 8-2, select the Contact Type table, then click Next.

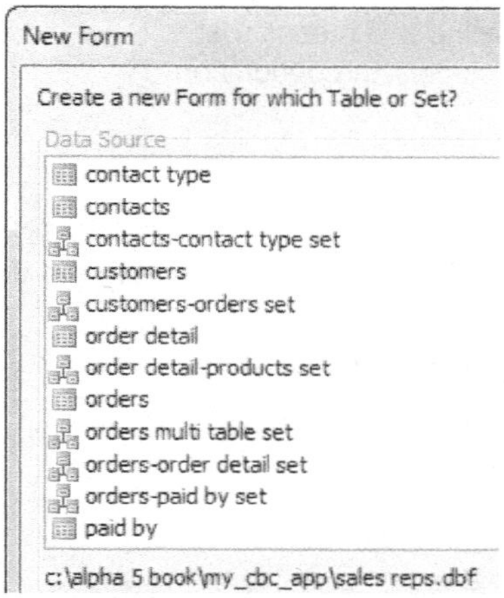

Figure 8-2 New Form (genie) dialog box

3. Accept the Default form option on the screen shown earlier in Figure 8-1, then click Next.

4. The screen shown in Figure 8-3 is used to select a style sheet, including **LEGACY STYLE SHEETS.**

   Select the legacy option, scroll down the list and select the Gray Lines style sheet, then click Next.

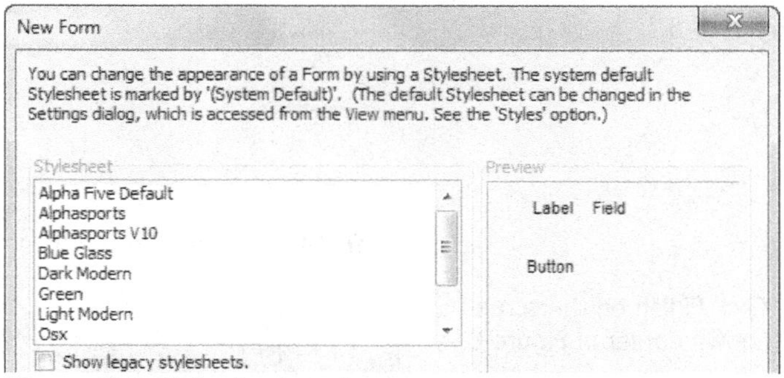

Figure 8-3 Style sheet genie screen

Selecting A Different Default Style Sheet
More than likely, the majority, if not all of the forms for an application will use the same style sheet. If that is the case, especially if you use a legacy style sheet, it should be selected as the default. If you want to select a different default style sheet, change the default style sheet on the Settings dialog box.

The options shown on Figure 8-4 are used to select the **HORIZONTAL** and **VERTICAL SPACING** between fields.

When you finish creating this form, you can decide if the default spacing options will meet the needs of the applications that you will create on your own.

If they don't, you can change them on this screen or you can select the default spacing that you need on the Settings dialog box. Doing this means that you will not have to change the spacing options on every form that you create.

Figure 8-4 Field spacing and XBasic screen

Viewing The XBasic Code For A Form

The code for the form is created from the options that you selected on the Form Genie.

If you have the need to view the code, click the **SHOW XBASIC** button, shown above in Figure 8-4.

You will see the window shown in Figure 8-5.

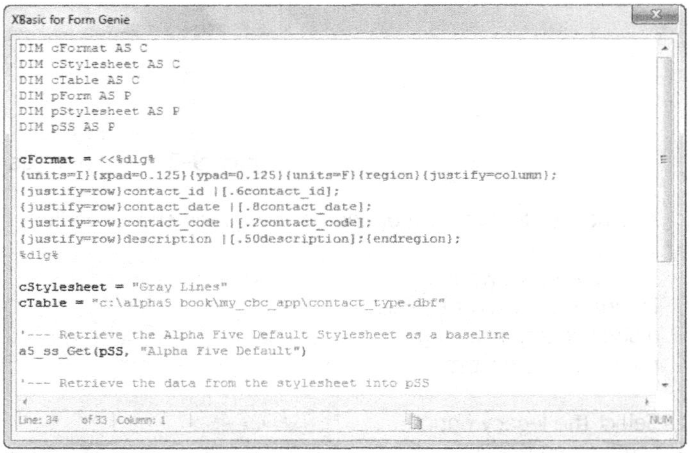

Figure 8-5 XBasic for Form Genie

5. Click Finish on the screen shown earlier in Figure 8-4.

   Your form should look like the one shown in Figure 8-6.

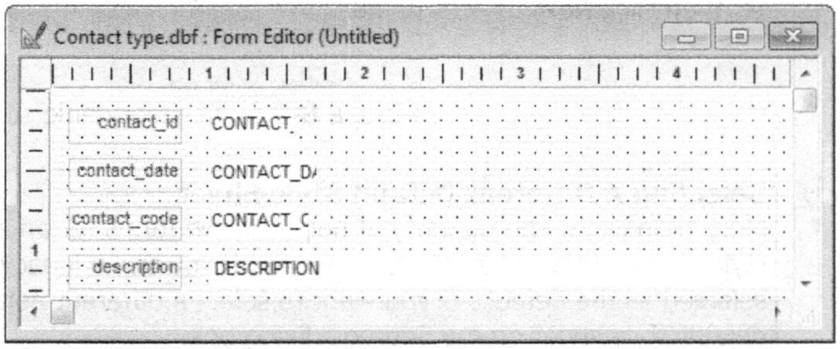

Figure 8-6 Contact Type form

6. Click the Save button on the toolbar. In the Name field on the Save Form As dialog box type `Contact Type`, then click OK. Now that you have created your first form, it is time to learn about the editor features for forms.

Forms Workspace

In Chapter 7 you learned about the layout workspace, which covered features that most of the layout types have. This section covers the options and features that are specific to forms.

Form Workspace Menu

Figure 8-7 shows the Form menu that is available when a form is opened in design mode.

The options on the Form menu are explained in Table 8-1. The other menu options and toolbar options were explained earlier in Chapter 7.

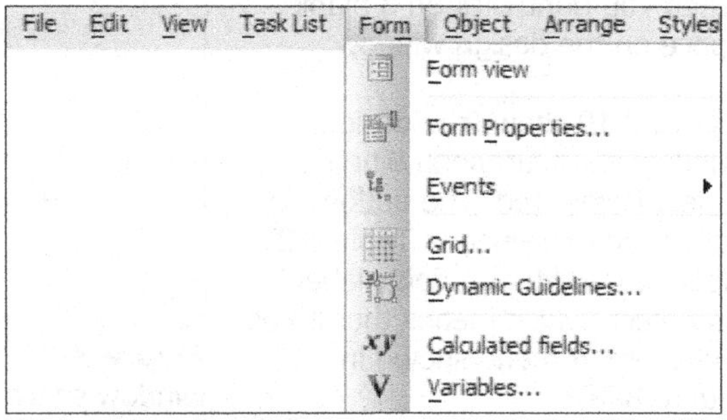

Figure 8-7 Form workspace menu

Option	Description
Form view	Displays the form as it will appear to the user.
Form Properties	Opens the Form Properties dialog box, which is covered later in this chapter.
Events	[See Chapter 7, Table 7-4]
Grid	[See Chapter 7, Using The Grid]
Dynamic Guidelines	[See Chapter 7, Dynamic Guidelines]
Calculated fields	[See Chapter 3, Table 3-4, Button 7]
Variables	Opens the **DEFINE NEW VARIABLES DIALOG BOX** shown in Figure 8-8. It has the same functionality as the **VARIABLE DEFINITION DIALOG BOX**, even though they look different. [See Chapter 3, Table 3-4, Button 8].

Table 8-1 Form workspace menu options explained

Define New Variables Dialog Box
When I click the **DEFINE FIELD RULES** button on this dialog box, the dialog box closes. I don't think that is what should happen.

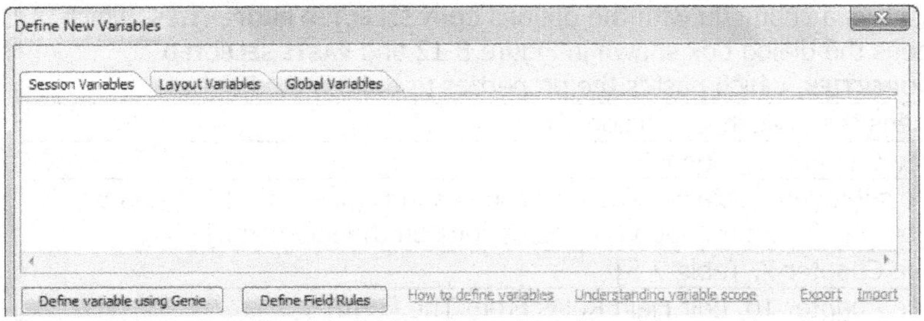

Figure 8-8 Define New Variables dialog box (for a form or browse)

Form Design Window Shortcut Menu

The design window has two variations of its shortcut menu. The shortcut menu shown in Figure 8-9 displays the options when you right-click on a blank space on the design window.

Figure 8-10 shows the design window shortcut menu when an object is selected. The options for forms are explained in Table 8-2. Keep in mind that a fields label is an object, which means that it has the shortcut menu shown in Figure 8-10.

Figure 8-9 Form design window shortcut menu

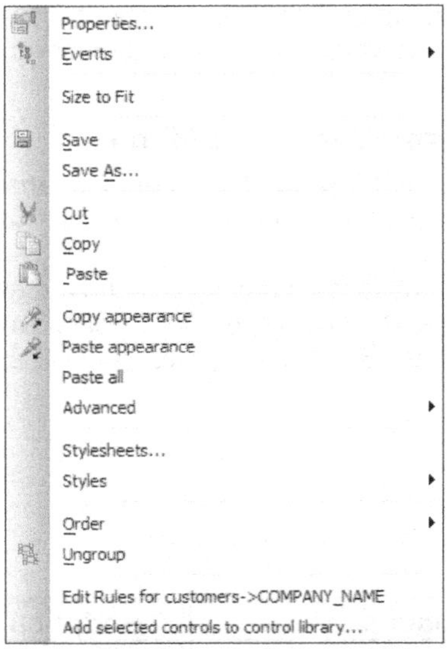

Figure 8-10 Form design window shortcut menu when an object is selected

Option	Description
Properties	Opens the Form Properties dialog box, which is covered later in this chapter.
Events	[See Chapter 7, Table 7-4]
Size to Fit	[See Chapter 7, Table 7-4]
Copy Appearance	Copies all of the property formatting of the selected object to the object(s) that are the same type. (1)
Paste Appearance	Pastes all of the copied appearances to the other object(s) that are the same type. (1)
Paste all	Opens the dialog box shown in Figure 8-11. It is used to paste the copied appearance formatting options to all of the objects of the same type. (1)
Advanced	Displays a submenu with the options **COPY SELECTED PROPERTIES**, which opens the dialog box shown in Figure 8-12 and **PASTE SELECTED PROPERTIES**, which pastes the properties to the selected objects.
Stylesheets	Opens the Stylesheets dialog box.
Styles	[See Chapter 11, Styles]
Order	The submenu displays the options shown in Figure 8-15. [See Chapter 7, Table 7-5 for a description of the options on the submenu.]
Ungroup	[See Chapter 7, Table 7-5]
Edit Rules for <field name>	[See Chapter 10, Edit Field Rules From The Form]

Table 8-2 Form design window shortcut menu options explained

Option	Description
Add selected controls to control library	Is used to add objects on the form (or report) to the Control Library (part of the Toolbox). The reason to do this is because you may have the need to use the objects on another form. For example, you need to have the Product name field formatted a specific way. After you have the field formatted the way you need it, select this option. Then when you work on another form, you can add the field to the new form by selecting it in the Toolbox.

Table 8-2 Form design window shortcut menu options explained (Continued)

(1) You can accomplish the same task by selecting all of the objects that you want to apply the appearance properties to and then selecting the options on the Properties Panel or floating toolbars. This option is only available after the Copy Appearance option has been selected for a field.

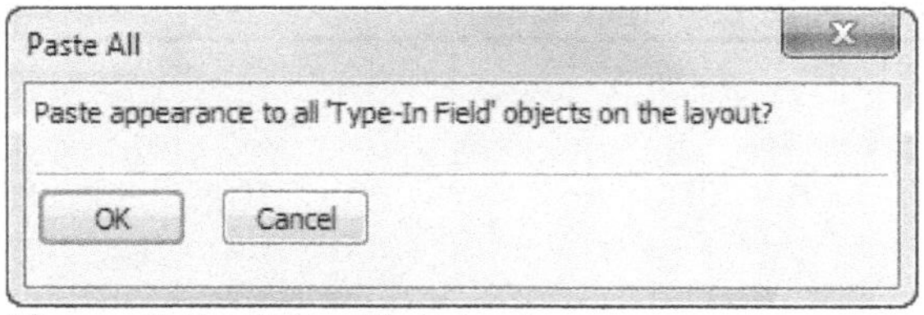

Figure 8-11 Paste All dialog box

How To Copy Selected Properties

The options shown in Figure 8-12 are used to select the formatting properties that you want to copy to other objects. This option is different from the Copy Appearance option, which copies all of the formatting, because you can select specific formatting properties to copy.

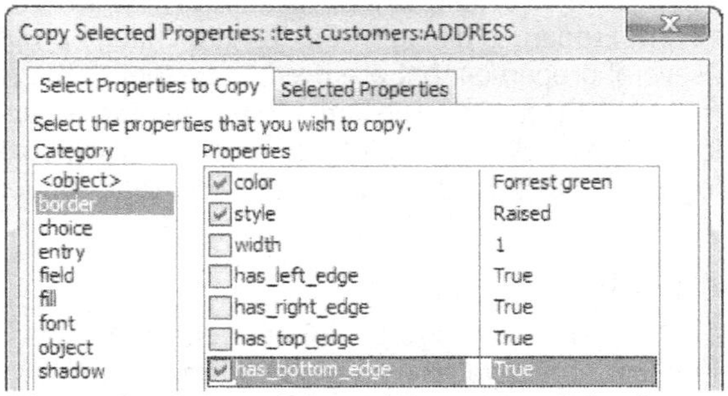

Figure 8-12 Copy Selected Properties dialog box

Click on each option in the Category list to see the properties that can be copied.

Check the options in the Properties list that you want to copy.

Once you have selected the properties, click on the **SELECTED PROPERTIES** tab shown in Figure 8-13. This tab lists the options that you selected to copy.

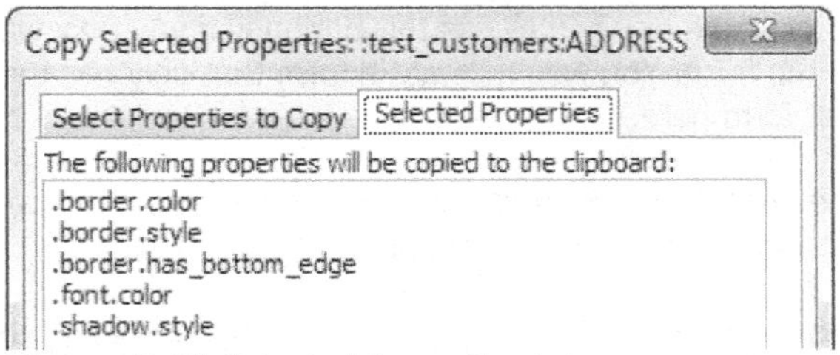

Figure 8-13 Selected Properties tab

If you change your mind about a property and want to remove it, clear the check mark on the Select Properties to Copy tab. If the property does not have a check mark, check it, then clear it. Look on the Selected Properties tab to make sure the property has been removed. When you have the properties that you want to copy, click the Copy button.

Check Marks On The Copy Selected Properties Dialog Box Disappear
Once you check an option, it is added to the Selected Properties tab. When you come back to a category, you may not see the check marks that you added earlier. It's okay, I guess that is the way it is suppose to work. I would rather the check marks stayed, unless I remove them.

Select the objects on the form that you want to copy the properties to, then right-click on a selected object ⇒ Advanced ⇒ Paste selected properties, as shown in Figure 8-14.

The properties will be pasted to the selected objects.

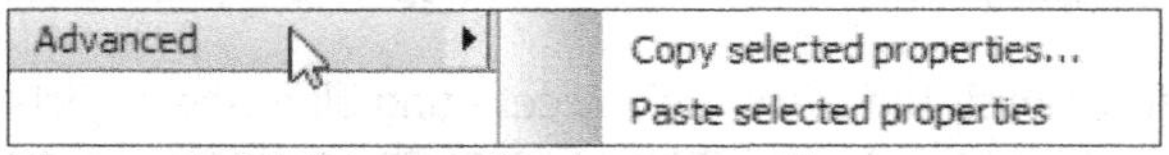

Figure 8-14 Advanced submenu options

The objects that you copy to do not have to be the same type. As long as the object has the properties that you are copying, the options will be pasted to it.

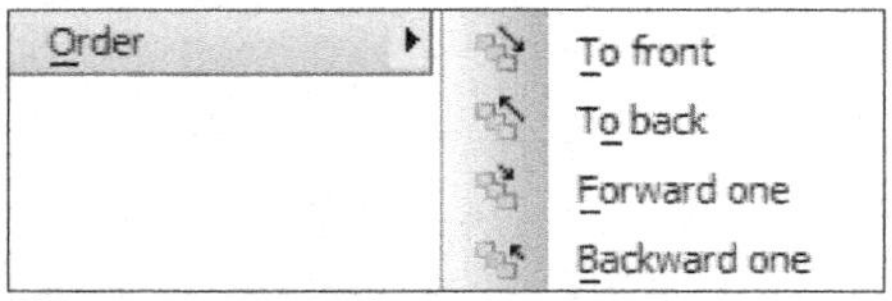

Figure 8-15 Order submenu options

Form Properties Dialog Box (Non Tabbed Form)

The Form Properties dialog box is used to change properties for the form. Each tab on the dialog box has several properties that are used to customize the form that is currently open. In Chapter 7 you learned that these properties are also on the Properties panel. Keep in mind that the Form Properties dialog box, as well as, other object property dialog boxes like the Field Properties and Text Properties dialog boxes have options like bubble help, that are not on the Properties panel.

Form Tab

The options shown in Figure 8-16 are general options that are used to control how the form opens and the data that is displayed on the form.

The **QUERY FORM** option is used to select the form to use when the Query By Form option is selected. An example of when to use this option is if you only want to allow the user to search on certain fields on the form. You would create a form that only has the fields that you want to search on and select that form here.

The **COMPANION BROWSE** option is used to select the browse that will be used to display the data in the form when the **F8** key is pressed.

The drop-down list for both of these options displays the layouts that were created from the same data source as the form.

Filter/Order Tab

The options shown in Figure 8-17 are used to create a filter or order expression that will select and sort the records that will be displayed on the form.

If the **USE THE LAST RUN QUERY** option is selected, the other options on the tab are not available.

The **TABLE** option displays the table that the form is bound to. If the form was created based on a set, the primary table from the set is displayed.

Clicking the button at the end of the **FILTER EXPRESSION FIELD** opens the Filter Builder, which is used to create criteria to select the records that will be displayed on the form.

Clicking the button at the end of the **ORDER EXPRESSION FIELD** opens the Order Builder, which is used to select the sort order of the records displayed on the form. You will learn how to use both of these options, later in this book.

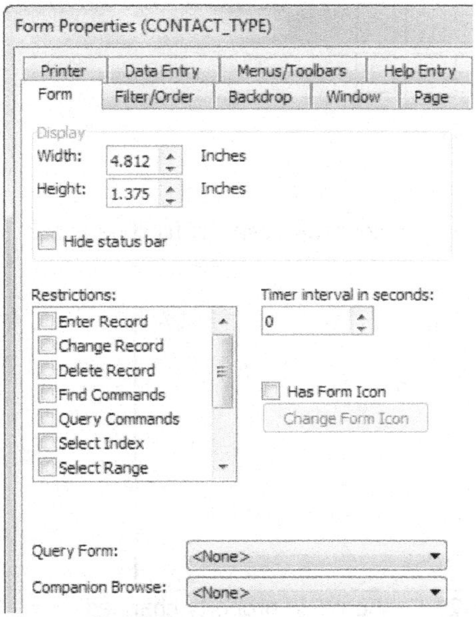

Figure 8-16 Form tab

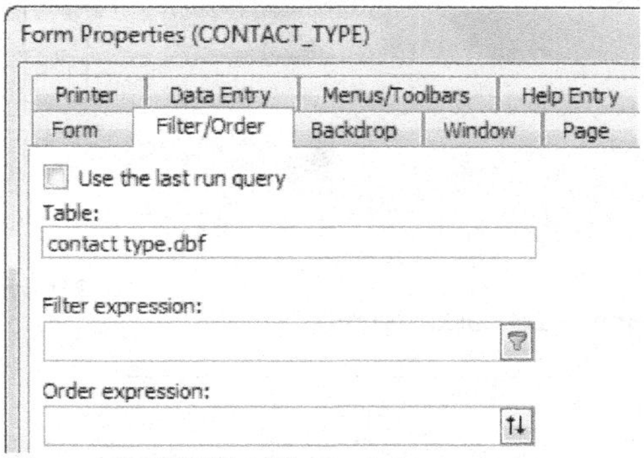

Figure 8-17 Filter/Order tab

Backdrop Tab

The options shown in Figure 8-18 are used to select the background options for the form. In addition to selecting a color and fill style, an image can be used as the background.

Figure 8-19 shows the Fill Style options for the Gradient Horizontal capsule option. This option is on the Properties panel, but you may find it easier to use the Form Properties dialog box because you can see what the options that you selected will look like before they are applied to the form.

Window Tab

The options shown in Figure 8-20 are used to select where the form will be positioned on the screen, the width and height of the form and the Windows options that the form will have. You can resize the form in design mode to set the size options on this tab.

The **CAPTION FIELD** is used to enter what you want displayed on the Title bar of the form. The default caption is the forms file name. Figure 8-21 shows the form that you created in Exercise 8.1, with the Caption field value changed to My Contacts.

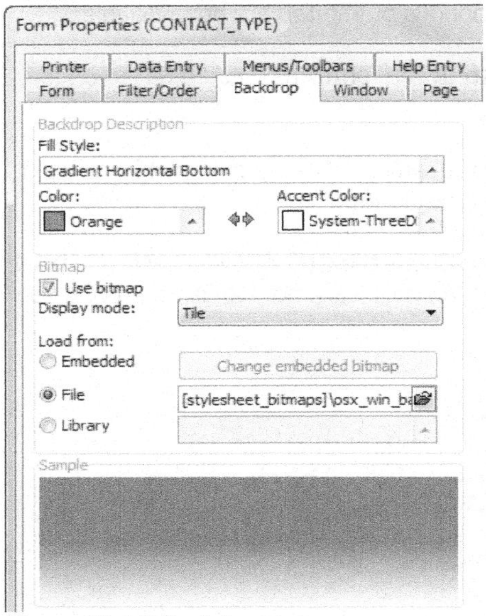

Figure 8-18 Backdrop tab

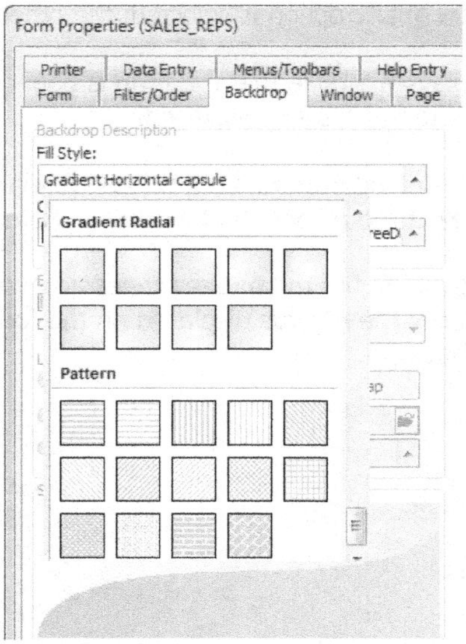

Figure 8-19 Gradient Horizontal capsule fill style option

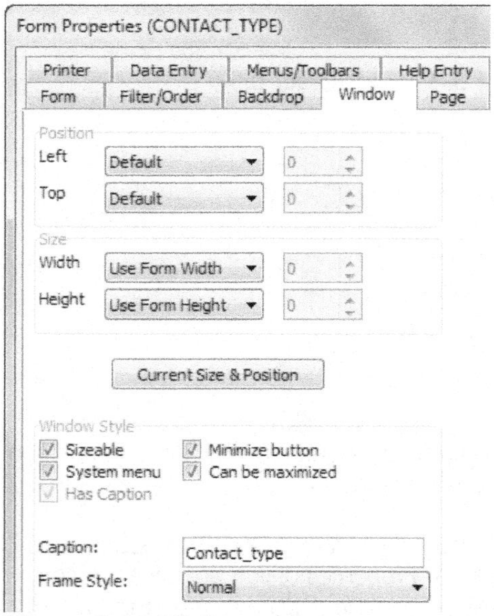

Figure 8-20 Window tab

Figure 8-21 Caption field property changed

Page Tab

The options shown in Figure 8-22 are used to select the layout for the page, if the form will be printed.

Printer Tab

The options shown in Figure 8-23 are used to select the printer options if the form will be printed. The Properties button will open a dialog box that has additional options for the printer that you select.

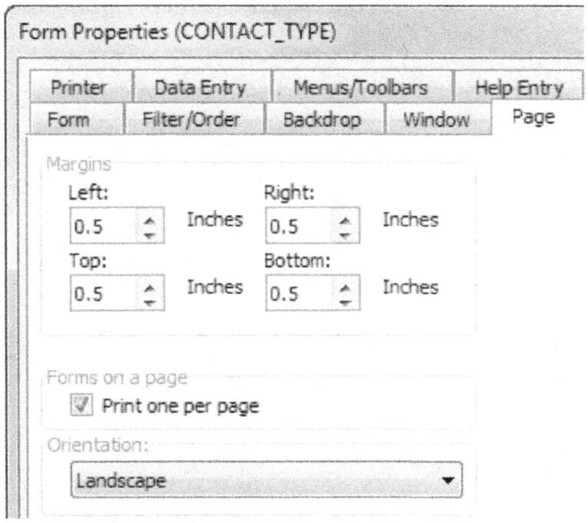

Figure 8-22 Page tab

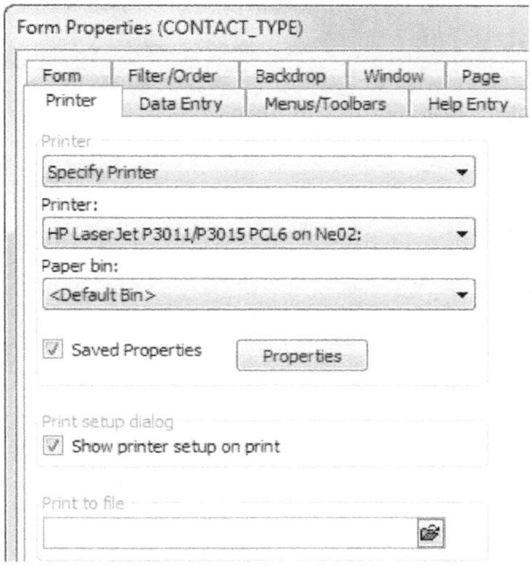

Figure 8-23 Printer tab

Data Entry Tab

The options shown in Figure 8-24 are used to override the default data entry option set on the Settings dialog box.

Menus/Toolbars Tab

The options shown in Figure 8-25 are used to select what menu (including right-click menus) and toolbar options the form will have, if any. You can also create custom menus and toolbars.

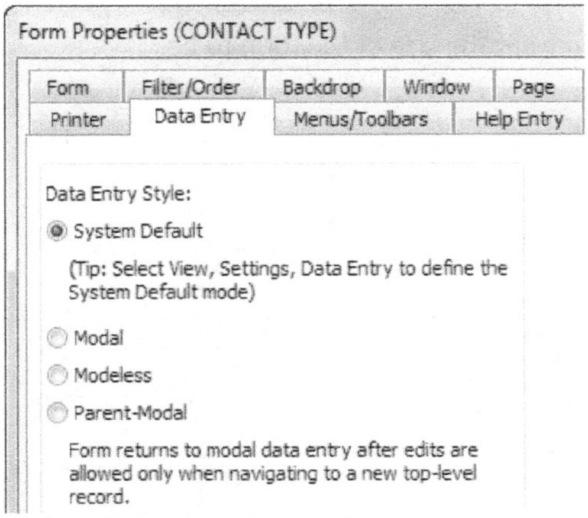

Figure 8-24 Data Entry tab

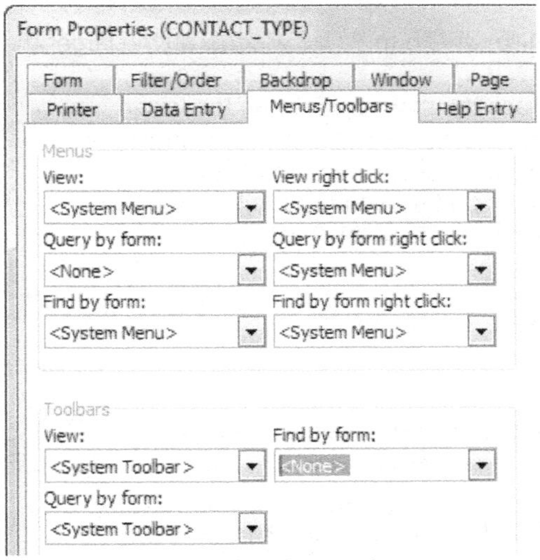

Figure 8-25 Menu/Toolbars tab

Help Entry Tab

The options shown in Figure 8-26 are used to add a custom help file to the form.

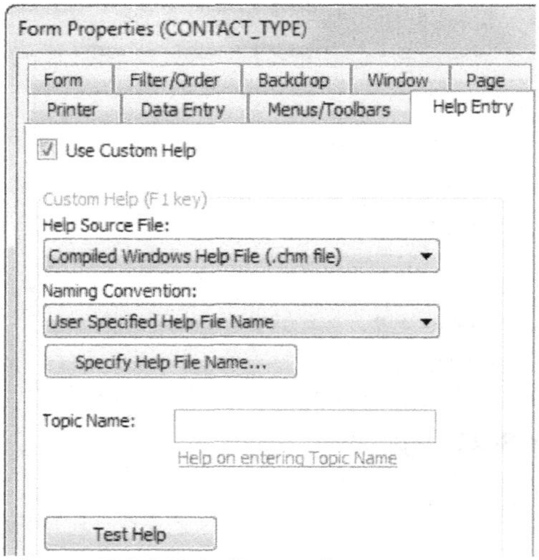

Figure 8-26 Help Entry tab

Exercise 8.2: Resizing A Form

The default size of a form is determined by the fields and objects on the form. The form that you created in Exercise 8.1 only has four fields, so the form is not very large. The form would look better if it was resized. As you learned in the previous section, there are options on the Form Properties dialog box that can be used to change the size of a form. The other option is to resize the form manually, which in my opinion is much easier. Follow the steps below to resize the Contact Type form.

1. Make the Form Editor window a little larger than you want the size of the form to be.
2. Place the mouse pointer in the lower right corner of the form, as illustrated in Figure 8-27, then drag the mouse down and to the right until the form is the size that you want it to be.

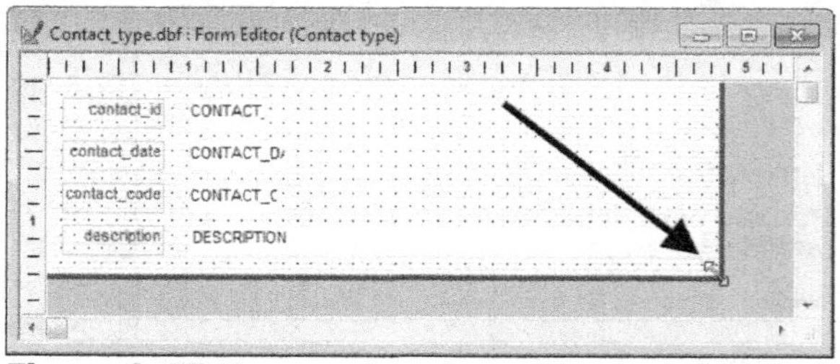

Figure 8-27 Mouse pointer in position to resize the form

3. Select all of the fields on the form and move them down.

   Your form should look like the one shown in Figure 8-28.

   Save the changes.

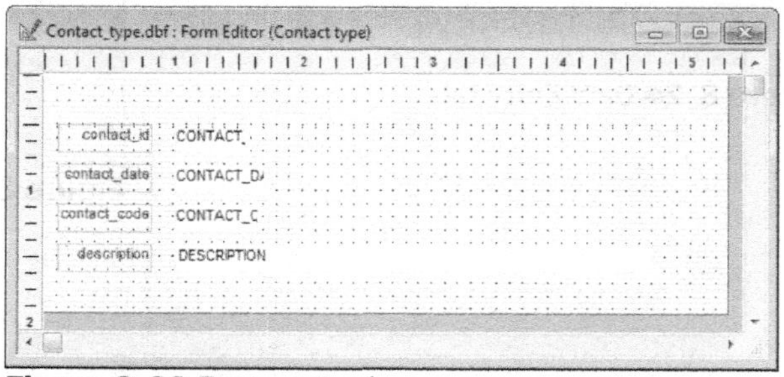

Figure 8-28 Form resized

Object Properties Dialog Box

The options on this dialog box are similar to the ones on the Form Properties dialog box that you learned about earlier in this chapter. The difference between these dialog boxes is that each type of object on the form has its own Object Properties dialog box.

Figure 8-29 shows the Object Properties dialog box for a line object.
Figure 8-30 shows the Object Properties dialog box for the Record Navigator Supercontrol.
Notice the name on the Title bar on these dialog boxes.

The Object Properties dialog box that you will probably use the most is the one for fields, so it is covered below.

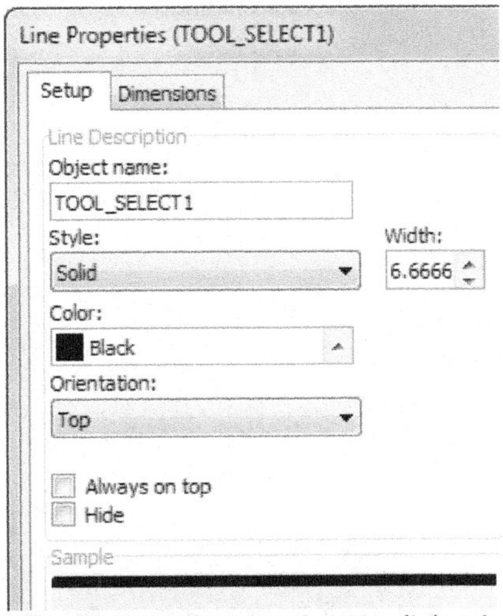

Figure 8-29 Line Properties dialog box

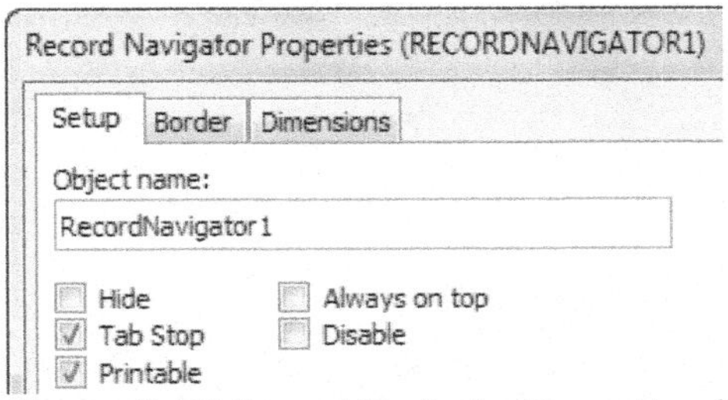

Figure 8-30 Record Navigator Properties dialog box

Field Properties Dialog Box

As indicated by the name of the dialog box, it is for fields from a table. To open this dialog box, right-click on a field on the form and select Properties. This dialog box has options like setting up the right-click menu, that cannot be set up any place else. All objects on a form do not use this dialog box. Instead, they use the Text Properties dialog box covered, which is later in this chapter.

Setup Tab

The options shown in Figure 8-31 are used to select general options for the field.

The **COLOR** and **FONT EQUATION** options are explained in Chapter 9.

The **READ ONLY** option prevents the user from modifying the data in the field.

The **TAB STOP** option allows the user to use the Tab key to move from field to field on the form.

ALWAYS ON TOP Prevents any other field or object from overlapping or covering the field.

ALWAYS MODELESS Keeps the field in data entry mode, regardless of the form settings.

DISABLE Does not allow the field to be used when the form is previewed.

DON'T SPELL CHECK Does not allow the data in the field to be spell checked.

USER-DEFINED SMART FIELD [See Chapter 11, What Is A Smart Field?]

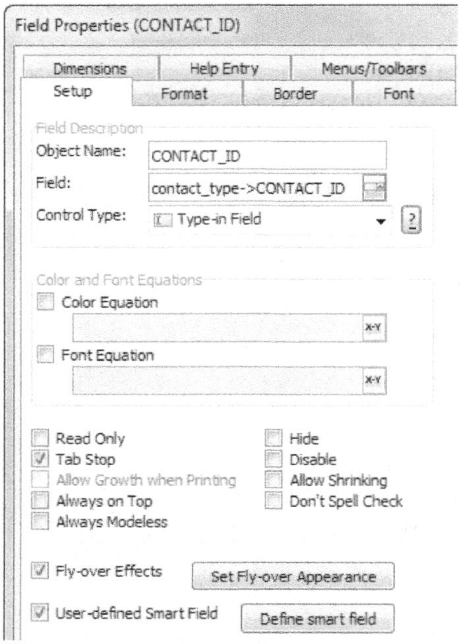

Figure 8-31 Setup tab

Format Tab

The options shown in Figure 8-32 are used to select how the object is aligned and whether or not it is rotated. The **FORMAT STYLE** drop-down list displays different options for formatting the object. The options in the drop-down list change, depending on the field type of the object that is selected.

Figure 8-33 shows some of the format options for a numeric field.
Figure 8-34 shows some of the format options for a date field.
Figure 8-35 shows the format options for a character field.

Ellipsis Option

The **ELLIPSES** option at the bottom of the tab is only available for text fields. Use this option for a field on a form or a cell in a browse when all of the data in a field cannot be displayed in the allocated amount of space. This option lets the user know that there is more data in the field then what is displayed. The options are explained below.

① **NONE** This is the default option. An ellipsis will not be displayed.

② **END ELLIPSIS** The ellipsis will be displayed at the end of the text.

③ **PATH ELLIPSIS** This option will display the path to a file with the ellipsis. This option is best suited for fields that contain a link to a file.

④ **WORD ELLIPSIS** For the most part, this option will display the ellipsis at the end of a full word, where the End Ellipsis option does not.

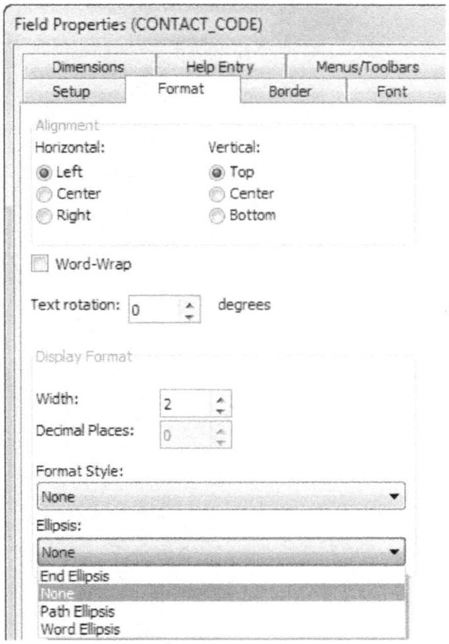

Figure 8-32 Format tab

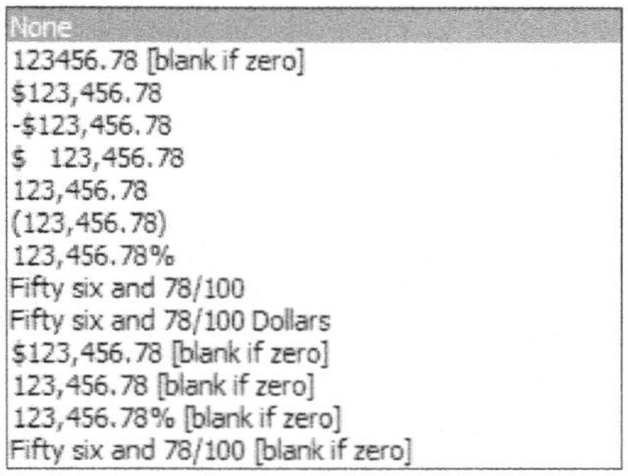

Figure 8-33 Format style options for a numeric field

Figure 8-34 Format style options for a date field

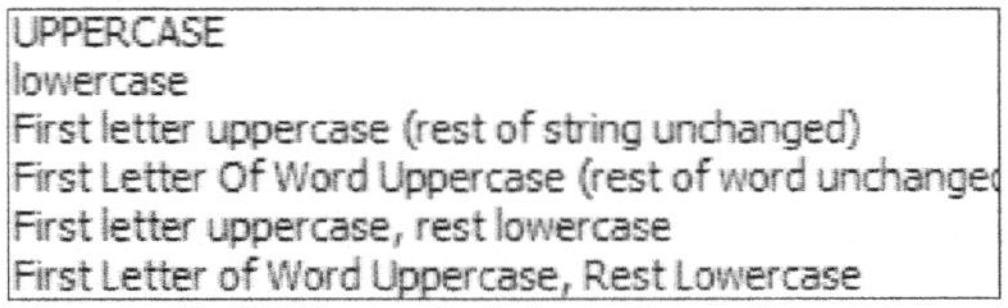

Figure 8-35 Format style options for a character field

Border Tab

The options shown in Figure 8-36 are used to select whether or not the object will have a border and what the border should look like.

The **USE SYSTEM THEME** option disables the other options on the tab so that the border cannot be changed.

Font Tab

The options shown in Figure 8-37 are used to select the font, font size and attributes for the object. They work the same as they do in word processing software.

Dimensions Tab

The options shown in Figure 8-38 are used to select the position, size and whether or not the object will be anchored. These are the same **ANCHOR** options that are on the Anchor toolbar that you learned about in Chapter 7.

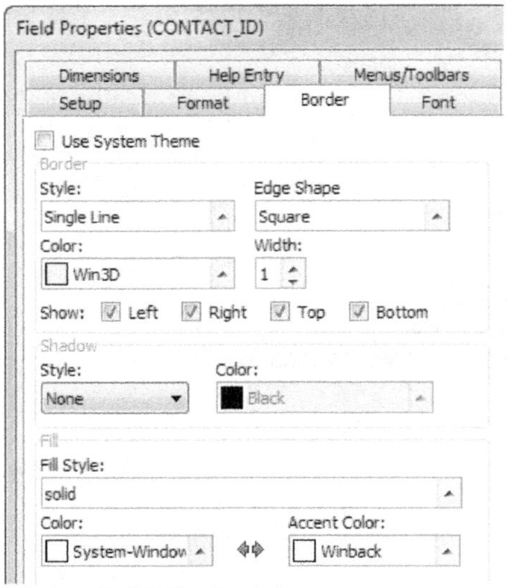

Figure 8-36 Border tab

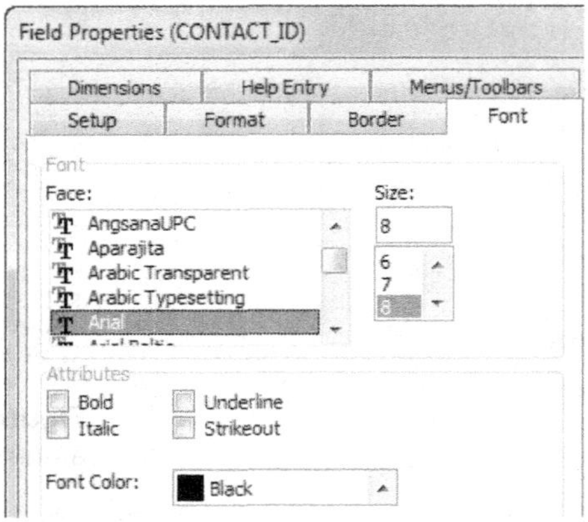

Figure 8-37 Font tab

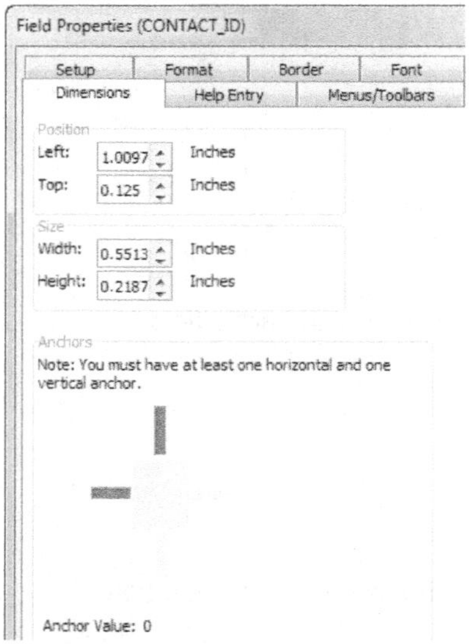

Figure 8-38 Dimensions tab

Help Entry Tab

The options shown in Figure 8-39 are used to create a custom help file for the object.

BUBBLE HELP (TEXT) is the option to use when you want the help message to popup when the mouse pointer is over the object.

Menus/Toolbars Tab

The options shown in Figure 8-40 are used to select a right-click menu for the object.

The **SET ALL FIELDS** button is used to add the selected right-click menu to all fields on the form.

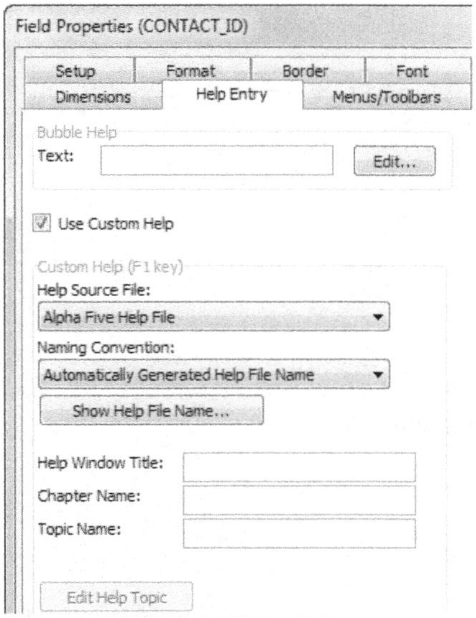

Figure 8-39 Help Entry tab

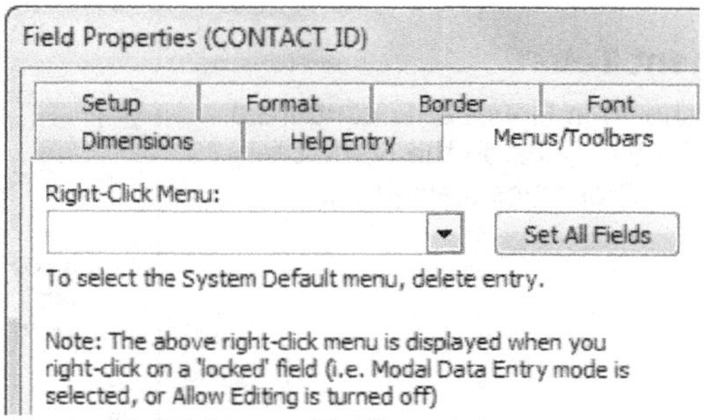

Figure 8-40 Menus/Toolbars tab

Text Properties Dialog Box

Not all objects on a form have field properties. Some objects like calculated fields have text properties instead. The differences are on the Setup tab. The Alignment tab replaces the Format tab on the Field Properties dialog box. These tabs are explained below.

Setup Tab

Figure 8-41 shows the setup options for a text object.

PRINTABLE TEXT By default, this option is selected. Clear this option if you do not want the object to print. You will probably use this more for reports then forms.

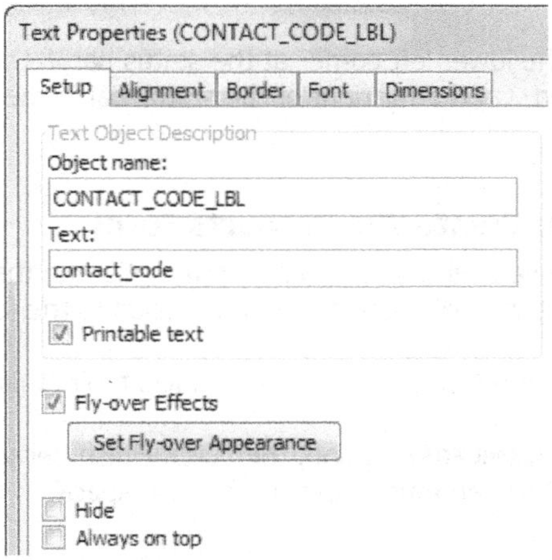

Figure 8-41 Setup tab

Alignment Tab

The tab shown in Figure 8-42 contains a subset of the options on the Format tab on the Field Properties dialog box.

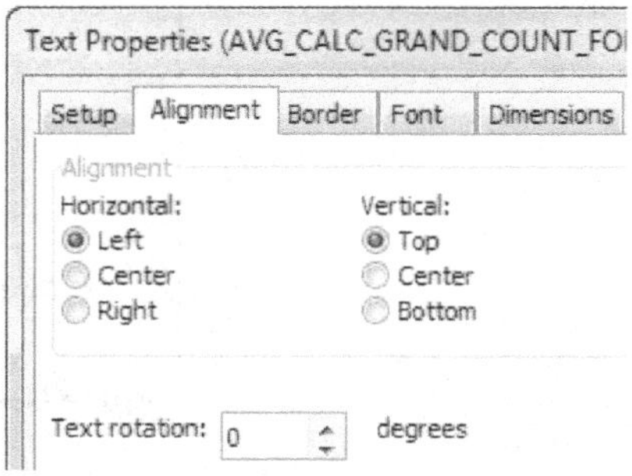

Figure 8-42 Alignment tab

Preview The Form

To view the form as it will be seen when used, click the Form View button on the toolbar.

The Contact Type form, should look like the one shown in Figure 8-43. Yes, the form is kind of bland looking, but trust me, when you are doing a lot of data entry, you really do not want a lot of distractions on the form.

The Form view menu and toolbar are covered in Chapter 17.

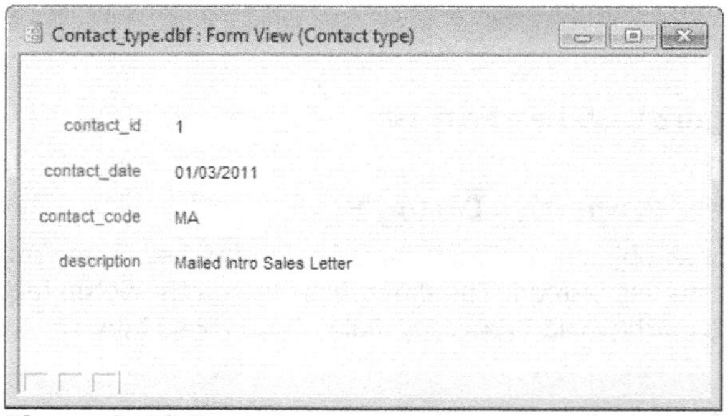

Figure 8-43 Form view

If you look in the lower left corner at the status bar in the workspace, you will see the record number that is displayed. On the far right of the status bar is the name of the table (or set) that the form is based on.

Exercise 8.3: Create The Products Form

In this exercise you will use the Blank Form option on the Form Genie to create the Products form. This means that you will manually add the fields to the form.

1. Open the Form Genie. Select the Products table, then click Next.

2. Select the **BLANK FORM** option, then click Finish because this form does not need a style sheet. You should see an empty form in the workspace.

Using The Drag Drop List Panel To Add Fields To The Form

In this part of the exercise you will add the fields to the form manually. As you learned in Chapter 7, there are two ways to add fields to the form using this panel; with or without using the Drop Fields Genie.

1. Make sure that the following buttons on the Drag Drop List toolbar are not enabled: Bring up field genie and Group controls. The Controls Across button should be enabled.

2. Scroll down to the list of fields until you see the fields for the Products table. Drag the Product ID field to the upper left corner of the form.

3. Place the Product Name field next to the Product ID field.

4. Select the remaining fields in the Drag Drop List, then add them to the form next to the Product Name field.

5. Make the form wider, then align the fields if necessary. Save the form as `Products`.

Using The Drop Fields Genie

In this part of the exercise you will use the Field Genie to add a field to the form. As you will see, when you add a field to the form with the genie, there are options to determine whether the field will display the actual value from the table or a calculated value.

1. Click the following buttons on the Drag Drop List toolbar: Bring up field genie and Controls Down.

2. Add the Qty on order field to the form below the Qty on order field that is already on the form.

   Yes, I know that this field is already on the form, but this copy of the field will be used to display a total of the quantity of all products that are on order. You should see the dialog box shown in Figure 8-44. The options are explained in Table 8-3.

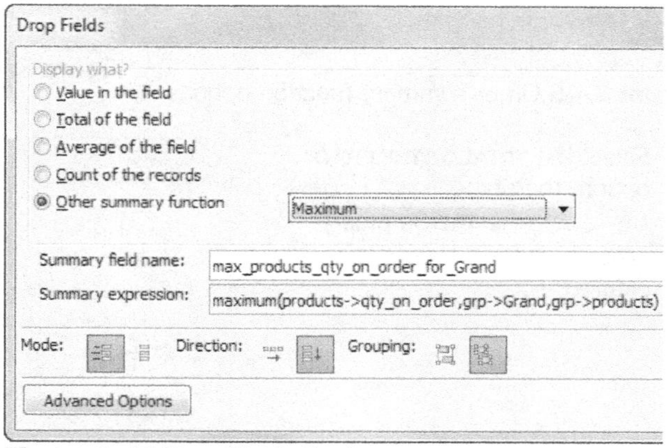

Figure 8-44 Drop Fields Genie

Option	This Option Displays The . . .
Value in the field	Value stored in the table for the field.
Total of the field	Total amount of values in the selected field for all records in the table. (2)
Average of the field	Average amount of values in the selected field for all records in the table. (2)
Count of the records	Total number of records in the table. (2)
Other summary function	Options shown in Figure 8-45, which you can select to create a calculated field. (2)
Summary field name	Name of the field that you are creating. You can change the name to something meaningful.
Summary expression	Code for the expression based on the options selected on this dialog box.
Mode	Label for the Summary field on the form, like the field title options on the Drag Drop List panel do.

Table 8-3 Drop Fields dialog box options explained

Option	This Option Displays The . . .
Direction	How the Summary field and label will be displayed on the form like the Controls across and down options on the Drag Drop List panel do.
Grouping	Summary field and label as a group, like the group options on the Drag Drop List panel do.
Advanced Options button	Dialog box shown in Figure 8-46. It is used to select how you want the summary value calculated.

Table 8-3 Drop Fields dialog box options explained (Continued)

(2) The corresponding expression is shown in the **SUMMARY EXPRESSION** field, shown above in Figure 8-44.

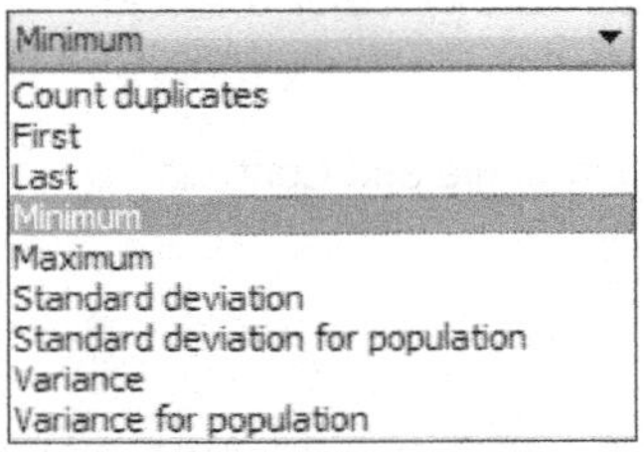

Figure 8-45 Other summary function options

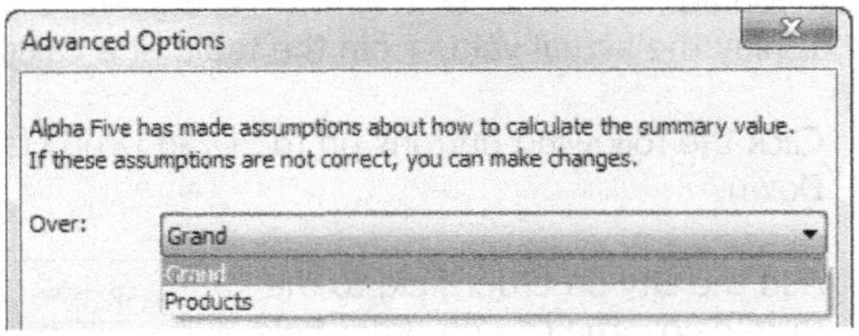

Figure 8-46 Advanced Options dialog box

3. Select the **TOTAL OF THE FIELD** option, then type `Total qty on order` in the Summary field name field, shown in Figure 8-47.

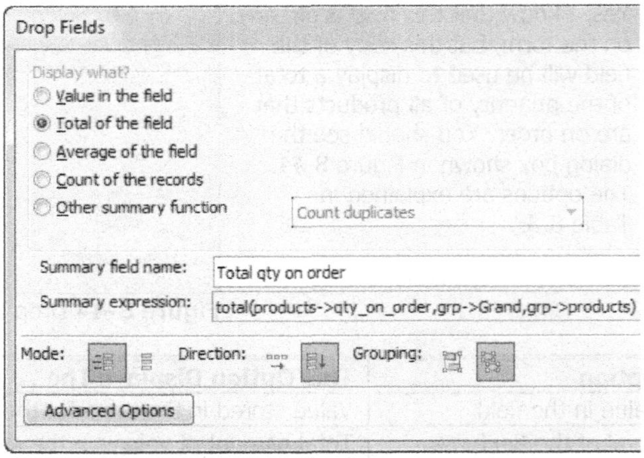

Figure 8-47 Summary field information

4. Click OK. Align the summary field with the Qty on order field.

5. Save the changes, then view the form.

   The form should look like the one shown in Figure 8-48.

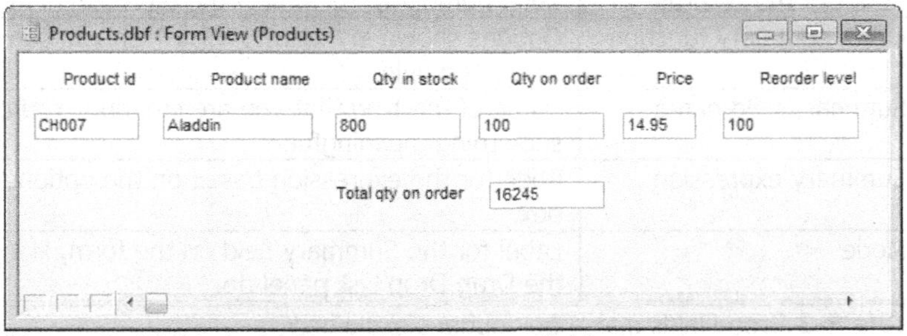

Figure 8-48 Products form with summary field

Format A Field

The Total qty on order field would look better if the value displayed a dollar sign and comma.

1. Display the Products form in design view, then click on the Total qty on order field.

2. Open the Field Properties dialog box, then click on the Format tab.

   Open the Format Style drop-down list and select the option illustrated in Figure 8-49.

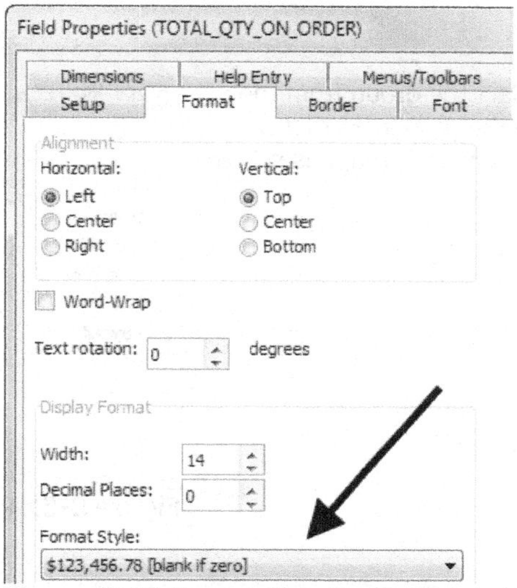

Figure 8-49 Format Style for the Total qty on order field illustrated

3. Save the changes.

   The field should have the formatting shown in Figure 8-50.

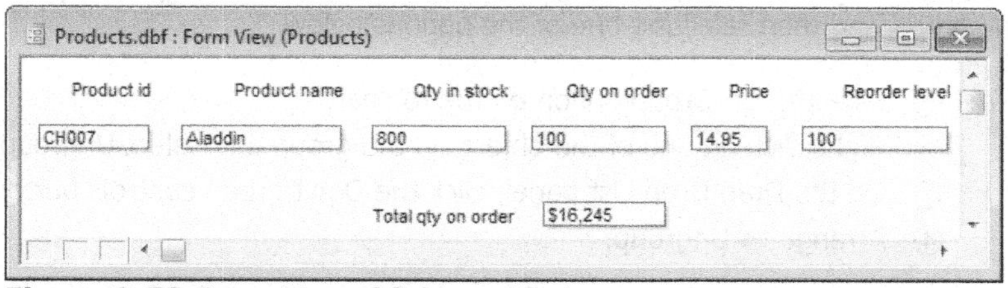

Figure 8-50 Formatting of field modified

How To Apply A Style To The Form

In Exercise 8.1 you added a style to the form when you used the Form Genie. If you do not add a style to the form when you are using the genie, you can still add a style by following the steps below. For now, you can just read how to apply a style.

1. Stylesheets ⇒ Apply or Create a Stylesheet.

2. Select a style that you like on the Stylesheets dialog box, then click Apply and close the dialog box. Save the changes.

Grouping Objects

This feature is used to be able to perform the same action for two or more objects without having to select each object individually. Actions include resizing, moving and formatting. When you need to group objects, follow the steps below.

1. Select all of the objects on the form that you want to group together.

2. Select one of the options below.

   ① Click the Group button on the toolbar.
   ② Right-click on one of the selected objects and select Group.
   ③ On the Drag Drop List panel, click the Group controls button.
   ④ Arrange ⇒ Group.

On the Properties panel, select the group from the drop-down list. You will see the properties that are available for all of the objects in the group, as shown in Figure 8-51.

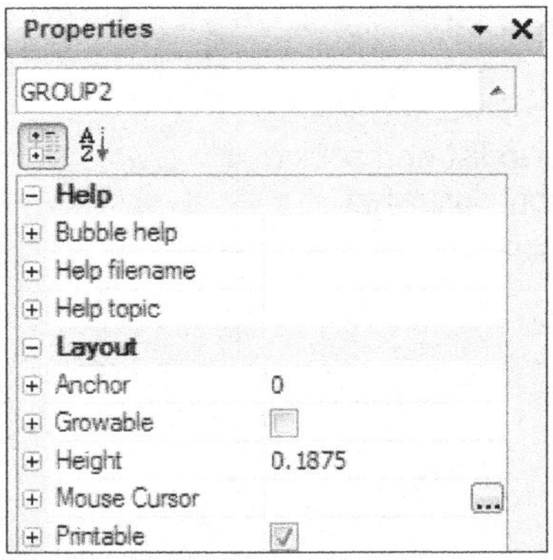

Figure 8-51 Properties for a group

Removing A Group

If you no longer need objects in a group, you can remove the group by clicking on an object in the group and then selecting one of the options below.

① Click the Un-Group option on the toolbar.
② Right-click on one of the objects in the group and select Ungroup.
③ On the Drag Drop List panel, click the Don't group controls button.
④ Arrange ⇒ Ungroup.

Modifying An Object That Is Grouped

Yes, most of the time you will want to apply the same change to all objects in the group. An example of when you may want to only modify some objects in a group is if there are different types of objects (like fields, lines and labels) in the group. The steps below shown you how to modify one object in the group.

1. Click once on the object in the group that you want to modify. (All of the objects in the group are selected).

2. Click again on the object that you want to modify. You will see black squares around the object.

3. Make the changes that you need, then save the changes.

> If you double-click on a grouped object, you will see a message that lets you know that the object does not have any events. This happens because double-clicking on an object is used to open the **EVENTS FOR DIALOG BOX**.

Exercise 8.4: Create The Paid By Form

In this exercise you will learn how to use the custom option on the Form Genie to create a form.

1. Open the Form Genie. Select the Paid By table, then click Next.

2. Select the **CUSTOM FORM** option, then click Next.

Custom Form Layout Options

The options shown in Figure 8-52 are used to select the layout style, number of columns and fields for the form.

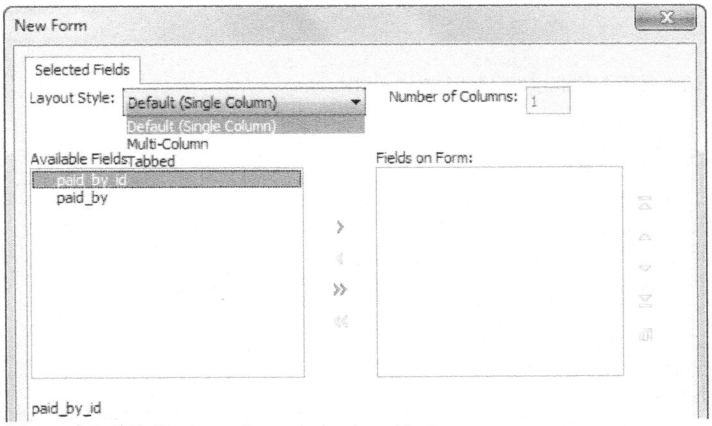

Figure 8-52 Custom form layout options

Selected Fields Tab Options

The layout styles are explained below.

① **DEFAULT (SINGLE COLUMN)** As the name indicates, the fields will be placed in a single column.

② **MULTI-COLUMN** Is used to place the fields in more than one column. This option enables the **NUMBER OF COLUMNS** option. Type in the number of columns that you need. Figure 8-53 shows how the **FIELDS IN COLUMN** option changes. Select the column that you want to add fields to in the drop-down list, then add fields to the column.

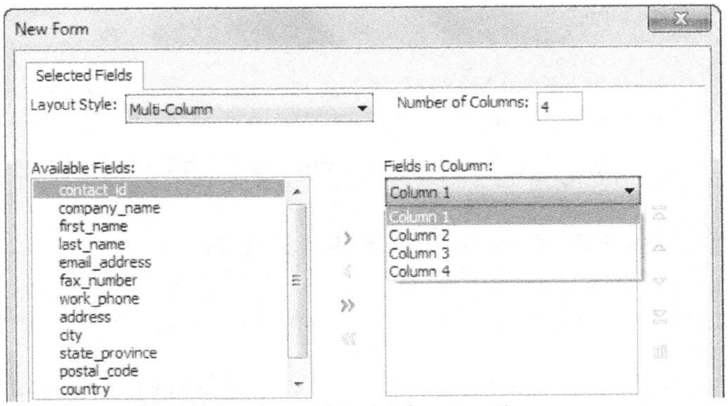

Figure 8-53 Multi-column layout form options

③ **TABBED** The options shown in Figure 8-54 are used to create a form that has tabs. Each tab has different data. Like the Multi-Column layout style, the Tabbed layout style can use more than one column and you select the fields for each column on the tab. The **<ABOVE THE TAB CONTROL>** option places the fields above the tabs on the form. The **<BELOW THE TAB CONTROL>** option places the fields below the tabs on the form.

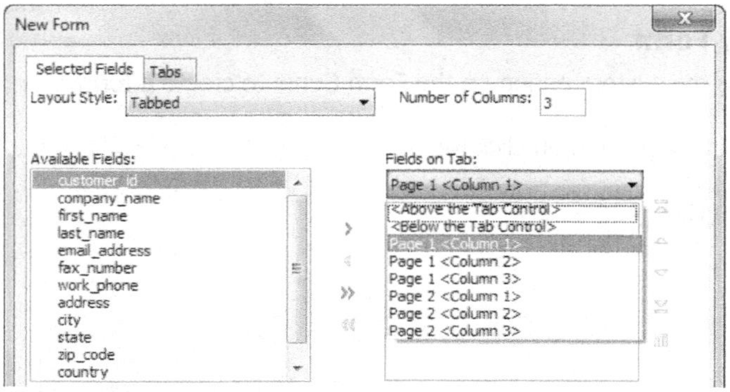

Figure 8-54 Selected Fields tab options

Tabs Tab Options

The options shown in Figure 8-55 are used to give the tabs a name and to change the order of the tabs, if necessary.

To change the tab name, click on the tab in the list on the left. Type in the new name in the Tab Name field, then click the Change button.

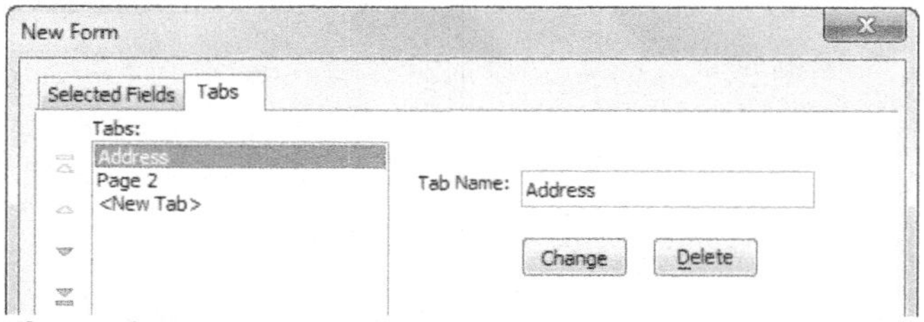

Figure 8-55 Tabs tab options

Add The Fields To The Form

1. Select the Multi-Column layout style, then type `2` in the Number of Columns field.
2. Add the Paid By ID field to Column 1, then add the Paid By field to Column 2.
3. Click Finish.

   The form should look like the one shown in Figure 8-56.

   Save the form as `Paid By`.

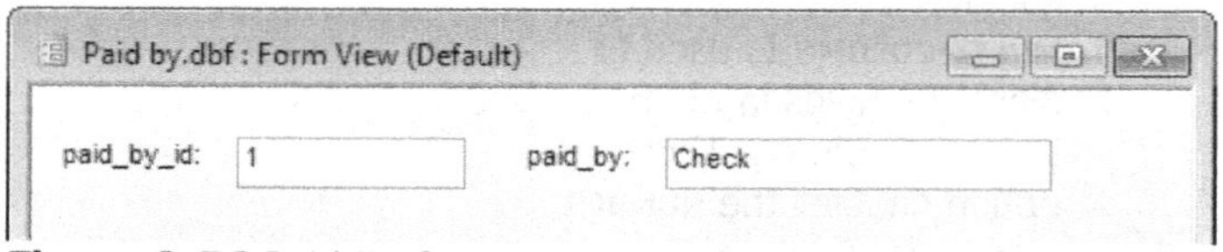

Figure 8-56 Paid By form

Exercise 8.5: Create The Sales Rep Form

You have created forms using each of the Form genie options. In this exercise you will create a form for the Sales Rep table, using the Form genie option of your choice.

1. Create a form that includes all of the fields in the Sales Reps table.
2. Your form should look like the one shown in Figure 8-57.

   Save the form as `Sales Reps`.

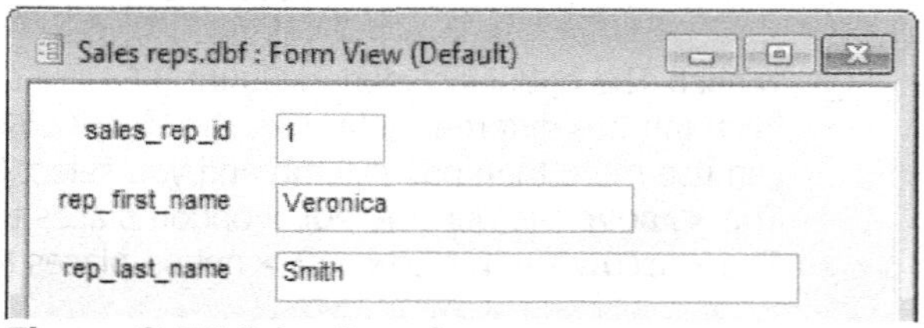

Figure 8-57 Sales Reps form

Using The Properties Panel

In Chapter 4 you learned how to change the title of a field when it is displayed on a layout. If you did not change it on the Field Rules dialog box or know that you want the field title to appear one way on a form and another way on a report, you can change the title on the Fields Property panel.

> **Opening Forms**
> Unless instructed otherwise, forms (browses and reports for that matter) should be opened in design mode.

Exercise 8.6: Change The Headings Of A Field

As shown above in Figure 8-57, the fields headings are long and do not make the form look as professional as it could. Using shorter headings without the underscore character would make the form look better.

1. If necessary, open the Sales Reps form, then click on the Sales Rep ID heading (aka label). At the top of the Properties panel you should see **SALES_REP_ID_LBL**.

2. Scroll to the bottom of the Properties panel, then click in the **TEXT** field.

3. Delete the text that is in the field, then type `Sales Rep Nbr`.

> **Changing Text Objects**
> You can also double-click in a text object on the form and type in the new text.

4. Change the other two headings on the form to `First Name` and `Last Name`, as shown in Figure 8-58.

   Save the changes.

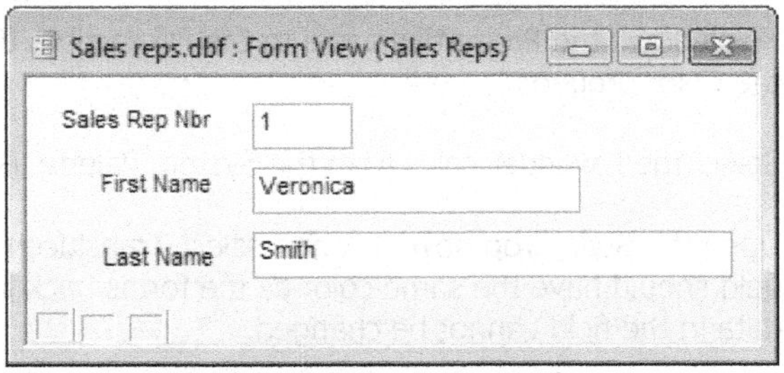

Figure 8-58 Field headings changed

Exercise 8.7: Add A Gradient Background Color To A Form

Earlier in this chapter you applied a style sheet to a form, which changed the appearance of the form. The background can also contain a color. In this exercise you will add the background manually, instead of using a style sheet.

1. Open the Sales Reps form.

2. In the Fill section of the Properties panel, click the ellipsis button at the end of the Color field.

3. On the **COLOR PICKER DIALOG BOX**, select the Lavender color from the **SYSTEM PALETTE LIST**. (Yes, the word Lavender is misspelled.) Click OK. You can also create a custom color.

4. In the Fill section of the Properties panel, open the Style drop-down list and select **GRADIENT HORIZONTAL CAPSULE**.

5. Save the changes.

   Your form should look like the one shown in Figure 8-59.

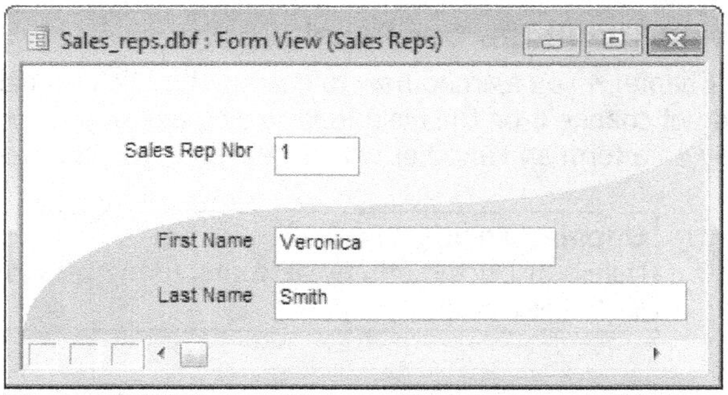

Figure 8-59 Form with a gradient background color

Using The Backdrop Tab Options
You can also use the Form Properties dialog box to add a background color to a form.

Using The Fill Color Properties

Just like you can add a background color to a form, you can add a background color to a field, by using the options in the Fill section on the Properties panel. Usually, the ID field on a form cannot be changed. You could change the background color to let the user know that they cannot change the information in the field.

Exercise 8.8: Add A Fill Color To A Field

1. Open the Sales Rep form, then click on the Sales Rep ID field.

2. Scroll down the Properties panel to the Fill section, then click the ellipsis button at the end of the Color property.

3. Select the Lavender color from the System Palette list, then click OK.

4. Open the Style drop-down list and select Translucent 10%. Save the changes. The Sales Rep ID field should have the same color as the forms background. This should indicate to users that the data in the field cannot be changed.

CREATE A CUSTOM BROWSE

In this chapter you will learn about the following:

- ☑ The Browse Genie
- ☑ Stand-alone browse
- ☑ Embedded browse
- ☑ Browse workspace

CHAPTER 9

Overview

A browse displays records in a layout that has rows and columns, like a spreadsheet. A browse is a type of form because in addition to viewing data, you can add, edit and delete data in a browse, just like you can in a form. In some cases, it can be more efficient to add, edit and delete data in a browse because you can see a lot of records on the screen at one time.

When you learned how to create tables, you saw that a default browse was automatically created. The default browse is good if you just want to quickly view all of the data in a table. In this chapter you will learn how to create browses and customize them.

Browse Types

There are two types of browses that you can create, as explained below. The biggest design difference between the browse types is that the stand-alone browse type does not have a Properties panel.

① **STAND ALONE BROWSE** This browse type looks like the default browse that you have already seen. It has its own file name.
② **EMBEDDED BROWSE** This browse type is added to a form. The browse is stored in the form and does not have its own file name.

Differences Between Forms And Browses

Below are the differences that I have noticed between forms and browses. A browse does not have the following:

① The **DRAG DROP LIST** panel.
② A **TOOLBOX PANEL**. Instead it has the Browse Controls panel.
③ The **ARRANGE** and **ANCHOR FLOATING TOOLBARS**.
④ An **OBJECT MENU**. The Properties, Events and Pop-up Event Editor options that are usually on the Object menu are on the Browse menu.

How To Open The Browse Genie

Like forms, there is a genie to create a stand alone browse. There are several ways to open this genie, as explained below.

① On the Control Panel's Browse tab, click the New button.
② On the Browses tab, right-click on an empty space and select New.
③ On the Browses tab, right-click on any browse and select New Browse. It doesn't matter which browse you right-click on because you have to select the table or set on the genie to create the new browse.
④ Open the Browse menu and select New Browse.

Exercise 9.1: Create A Products Browse

In this exercise you will create a stand alone browse for the Products table.

1. On the Browses tab on the Control Panel, click the New button.

2. Select the Products table on the screen shown in Figure 9-1, then click Next.

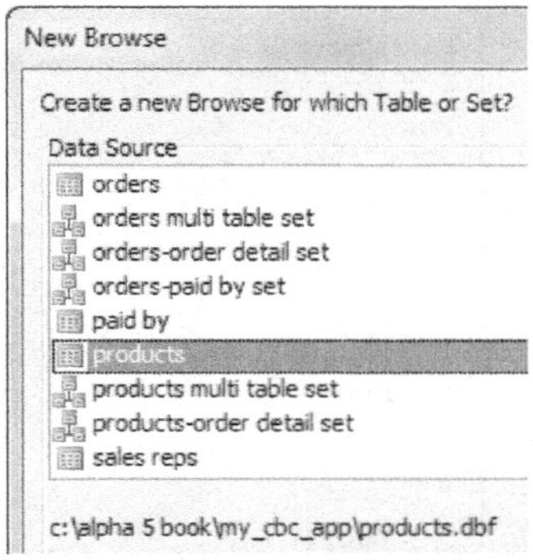

Figure 9-1 Browse Genie table screen

3. On the screen shown in Figure 9-2, add all of the fields except the Product ID field, then click Next.

   The buttons to the right of the Fields in Browse list are used to change the order of how the fields will appear in the browse, from left to right.

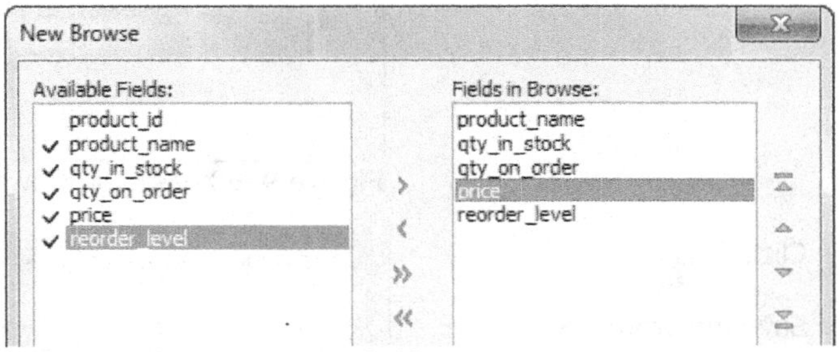

Figure 9-2 Browse genie field screen

Add A Style Sheet To The Browse

The screen shown in Figure 9-3 is used to select a style sheet to apply to the browse.

By default, the legacy style sheets are displayed.

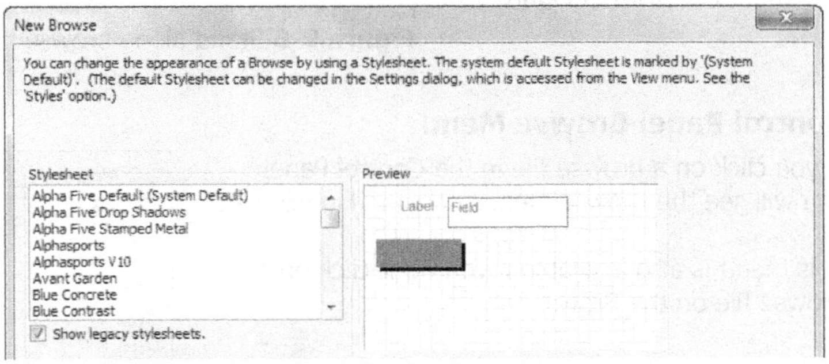

Figure 9-3 Browse genie style sheet screen

4. Select the Square But Hip style sheet, then click Next.

View The Xbasic Code For the Browse

If you click the **SHOW XBASIC** button shown in Figure 9-4, you will see the code for the browse that you are creating, as shown in Figure 9-5.

Figure 9-4 Browse genie Xbasic screen

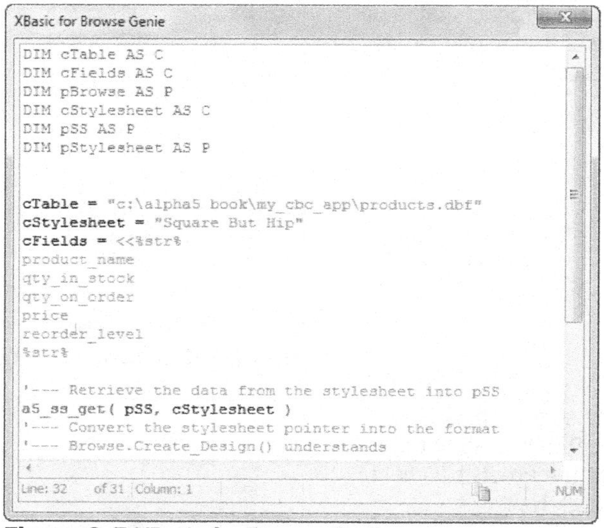

Figure 9-5 XBasic for Browse Genie

5. Click Finish.

   Save the browse as `Products.`

   Your browse should look like the one shown in Figure 9-6.

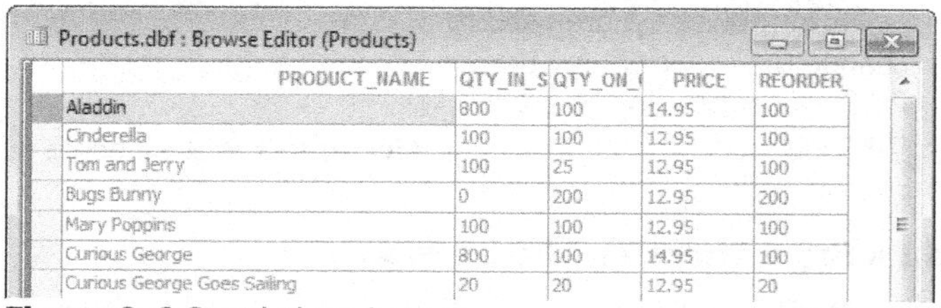

Figure 9-6 Stand alone browse

Control Panel Browse Menu

If you click on a browse file in the Control Panel you will see the Browse menu shown in Figure 9-7.

This menu is also available if you right-click on a browse file on the Browse tab.

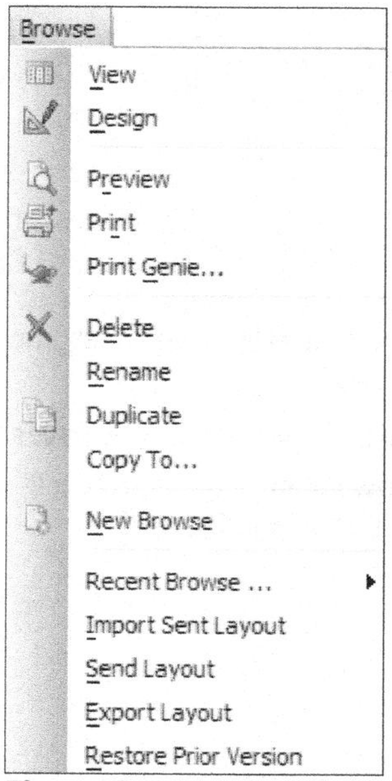

Figure 9-7 Browse menu

Browse Workspace

In Chapter 7 you learned about the layout workspace, which covered features that most of the layout types have. This section covers the options and features that are specific to a browse, when opened in design mode.

Task List Menu

Figure 9-8 shows the menu.

The **FIELDS** option displays the Fields panel, which has the same functionality that the Drag Drop List panel has for forms.

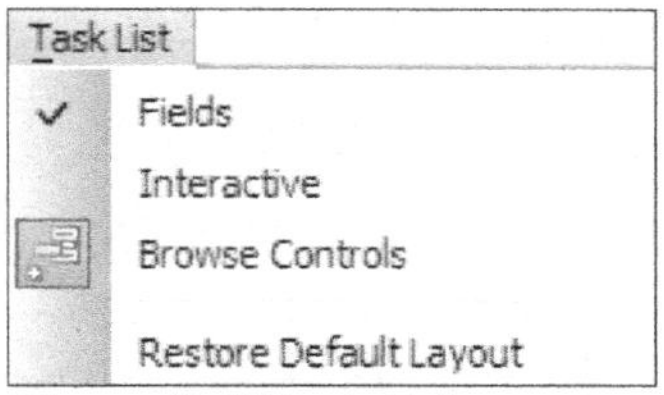

Figure 9-8 Task List menu

> **Restore Default Layout Option**
> When I select this option on the Task List menu, only the Fields panel is displayed. I thought that the Browse Controls panel would also be displayed, if it wasn't already visible.

Browse Menu (Design View)

Figure 9-9 shows the menu. The options on the Browse menu are explained in Table 9-1.

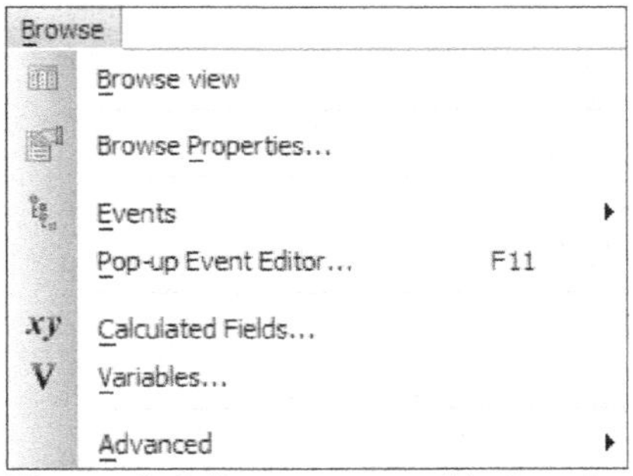

Figure 9-9 Browse menu (design view)

Option	Description
Browse view	Displays the browse as it will appear to the user.
Browse Properties	Opens the Browse Properties dialog box, which is covered later in this chapter.
Events	[See Chapter 7, Table 7-4]
Pop-up Event Editor	[See Chapter 7, Table 7-4]
Calculated Fields	[See Chapter 3, Table 3-4]
Variables	Opens the **DEFINE NEW VARIABLES DIALOG BOX**. It has the same functionality as the **VARIABLE DEFINITION DIALOG BOX**.

Table 9-1 Browse menu (design view) options explained

Option	Description
Advanced	Opens a submenu that has the following options: The **SHOW XML DEFINITION** option opens the dialog box shown in Figure 9-10, which displays the XML code for the browse. The **CREATE XDIALOG WITH EMBEDDED BROWSE** option opens the dialog box shown in Figure 9-11, which is used to create a sample XBasic script that will display an Xdialog that uses the current browse layout.

Table 9-1 Browse menu (design view) options explained (Continued)

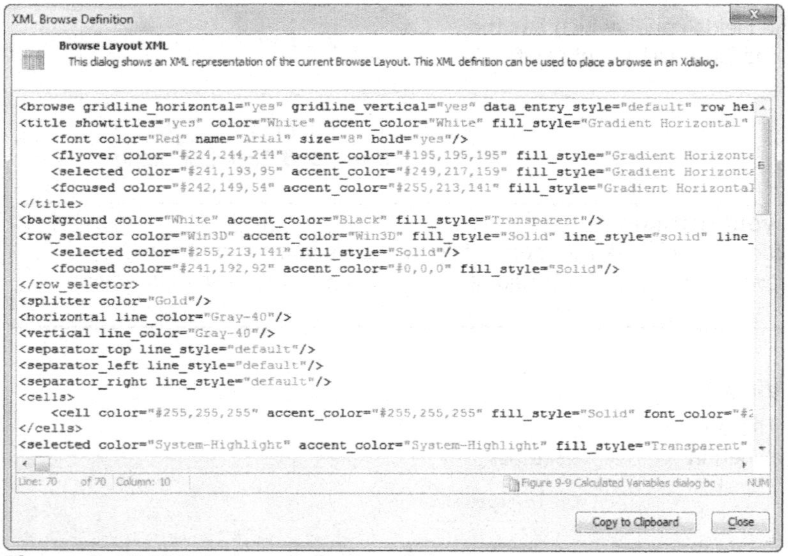
XML Browse Definition
Browse Layout XML
This dialog shows an XML representation of the current Browse Layout. This XML definition can be used to place a browse in an Xdialog.
Copy to Clipboard
Close

Figure 9-10 XML Browse Definition dialog box

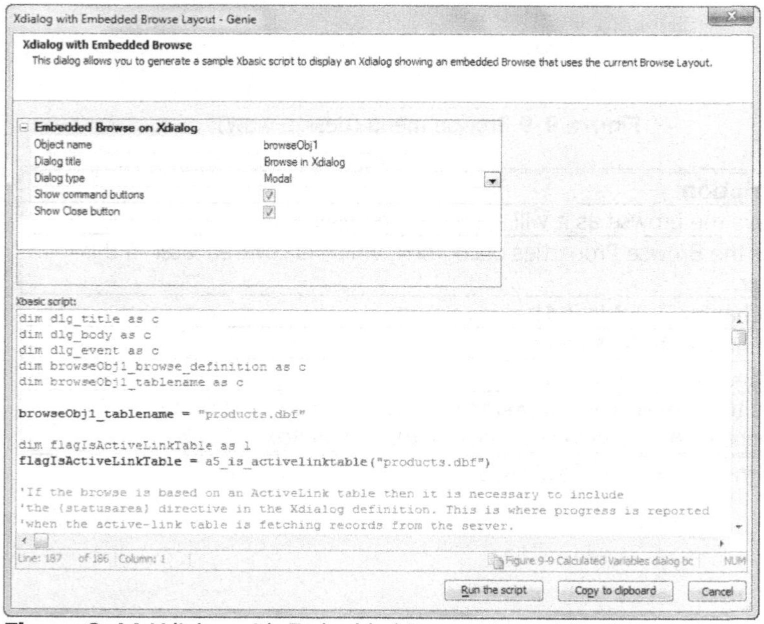
Xdialog with Embedded Browse Layout - Genie
Xdialog with Embedded Browse
This dialog allows you to generate a sample Xbasic script to display an Xdialog showing an embedded Browse that uses the current Browse Layout.
Embedded Browse on Xdialog
Object name
browseObj1
Dialog title
Browse in Xdialog
Dialog type
Modal
Show command buttons
Show Close button
Xbasic script:
Run the script
Copy to clipboard
Cancel

Figure 9-11 Xdialog with Embedded Browse Layout Genie

Column Menu

Figure 9-12 shows the menu. The options are explained in Table 9-2.

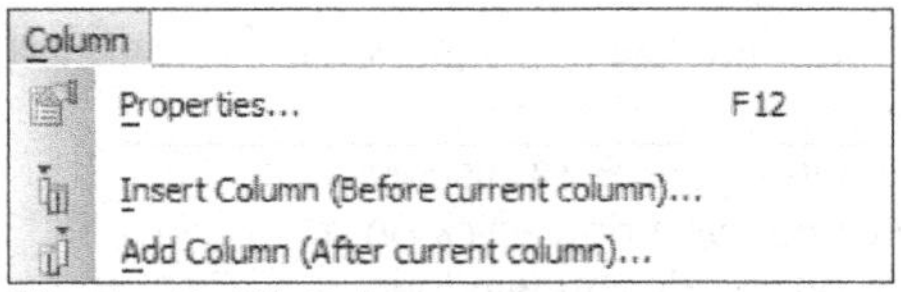

Figure 9-12 Column menu

Option	Description
Properties	Opens the Columns Properties dialog box, which is covered later in this chapter.
Insert Column (Before current column)	[See Insert And Add Columns, later in this chapter]
Add Column (After current column)	[See Insert And Add Columns, later in this chapter]

Table 9-2 Column menu options explained

> **Floating Toolbars**
> A Browse only has the following toolbars on the View menu in the workspace: Text, Border and Copy Appearance.

Design Mode Toolbar

The toolbar shown in Figure 9-13 is available when a browse is opened in design mode. The options specifically for a browse are explained in Table 9-3.

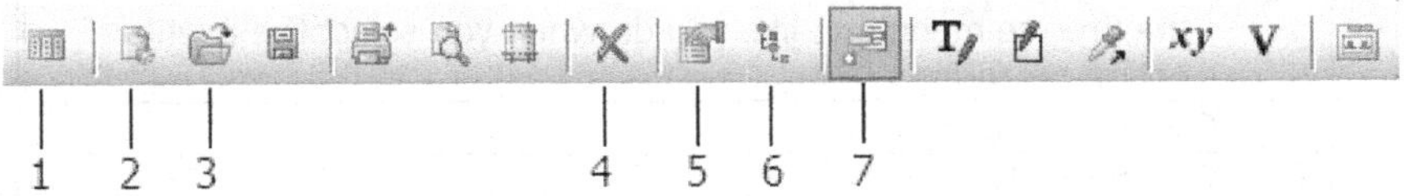

Figure 9-13 Design mode toolbar

Button	Is Used To . . .
1	Toggle between design mode and browse view.
2	I believe that this button is suppose to open a new browse window. When I click on the button, the browse that I have open goes blank. I don't think that this is suppose to happen because the toolbar is only available when there is a browse window displayed, meaning there is no other way to access the toolbar.
3	Open an existing browse.
4	Delete the selected column.
5	Open the Column Properties dialog box.
6	Open the Events for dialog box.
7	Display or hide the Fields panel, even though the button says Drag Drop List.

Table 9-3 Design mode toolbar buttons explained

Browse Design Window Shortcut Menu

The design window has two variations of its shortcut menu. The shortcut menu shown in Figure 9-14 displays the options when you right-click on a blank space on the design window.

Figure 9-15 shows the design window shortcut menu when you right-click on a column heading on a browse. The options for a browse are explained in Table 9-4.

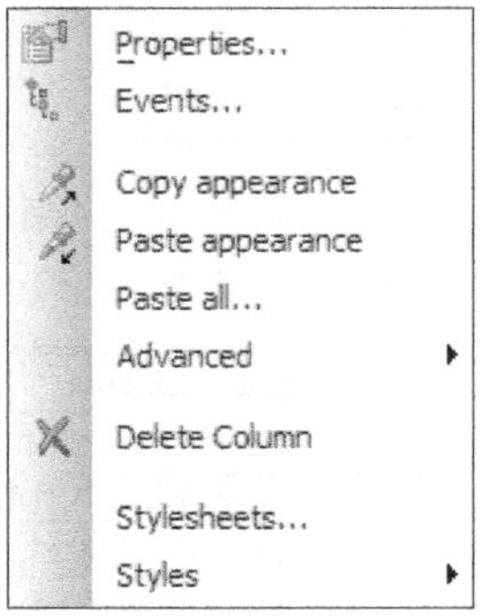

Figure 9-14 Design window shortcut menu

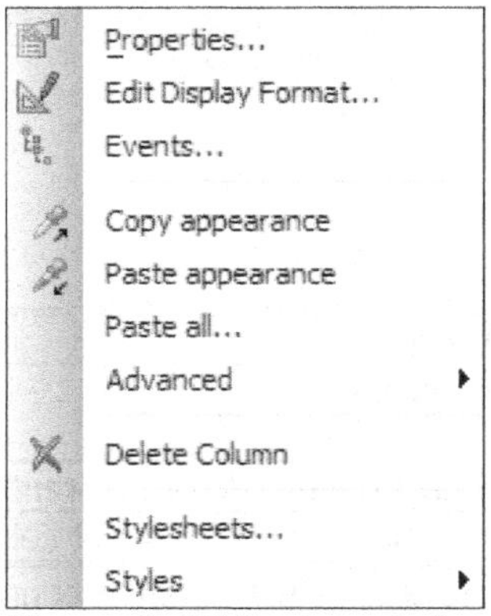

Figure 9-15 Design window shortcut menu when a browse column heading is selected

Option	Description
Properties	Opens the Column Properties dialog box.
Edit Display Format	Opens the dialog box shown in Figure 9-16. The options are used to select how the content in cells is displayed.
Events	Opens the Code Editor window. I was expecting to see the Events for dialog box, like you do when you select the Events option on the Browse menu and like you do when you select the Events option for forms.
Copy Appearance	[See Chapter 8, Table 8-2]
Paste Appearance	[See Chapter 8, Table 8-2]
Paste all	[See Chapter 8, Table 8-2]
Advanced	[See Chapter 8, Table 8-2]
Delete Column	Deletes the selected column.
Stylesheets	[See Chapter 7, Stylesheets Menu]
Styles	Opens the dialog box shown in Figure 9-17. It is used to create a new style, apply an existing style or update an existing style. A column must be selected prior to selecting this option.

Table 9-4 Design window shortcut menu options explained

Browse Properties Dialog Box

The Browse Properties dialog box is used to change properties for the browse. Each tab has several properties that are used to customize the browse. The Help button on the Browse Properties dialog box provides a brief explanation of the options.

Browse Tab

The options shown in Figure 9-18 are used to change the appearance or color of different parts of the browse. Later in this chapter you will learn how to use many of the options on this tab.

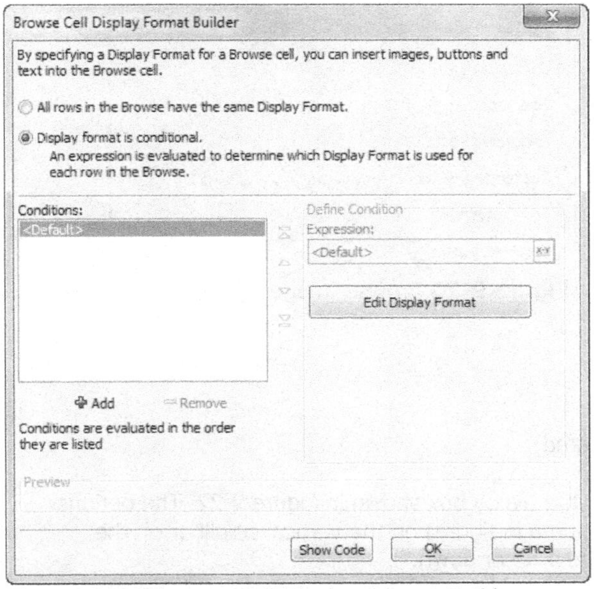

Figure 9-16 Browse Cell Display Format Builder

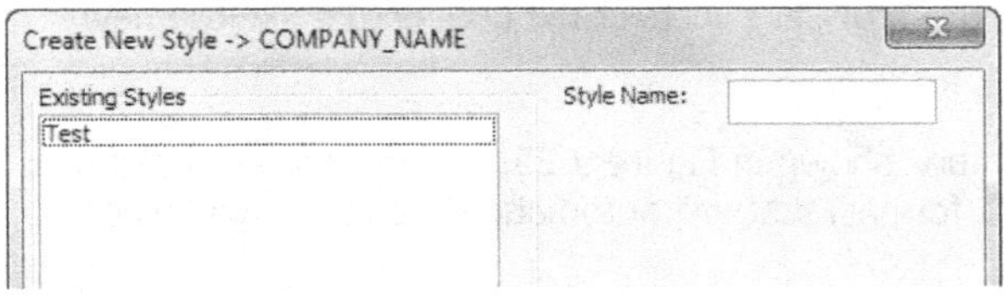

Figure 9-17 Create New Style dialog box

The **LINE STYLE PROPERTIES BUTTON** opens the dialog box shown in Figure 9-19. The options are used to change the style and color of the lines in the grid.

The **BROWSE IMAGE PROPERTIES BUTTON** opens the dialog box shown in Figure 9-20. The options are used to add icons to the browse to indicate the features shown. To add an image, click on the arrow at the end of the field to open the **INSERT IMAGE DIALOG BOX.**

Based on the option selected in Figure 9-20, when a column is sorted in descending order, a lightning bolt icon will be displayed in the column header, as illustrated in Figure 9-21.

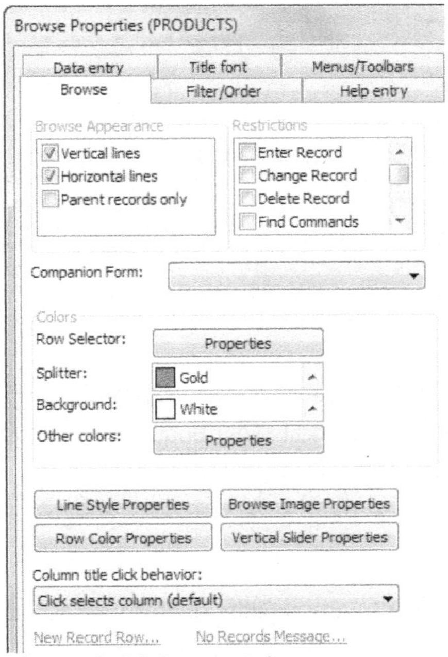

Figure 9-18 Browse tab

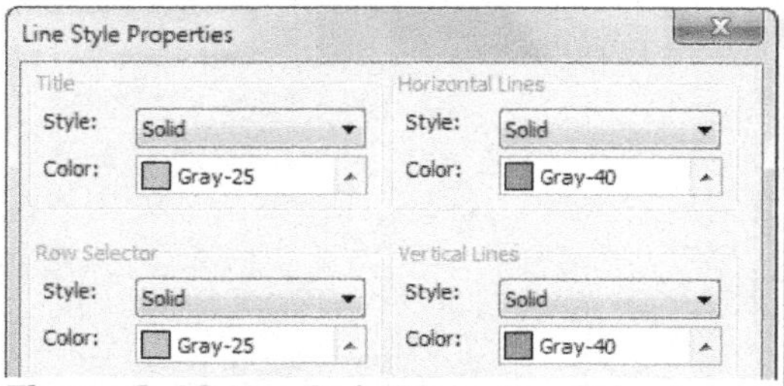

Figure 9-19 Line Style Properties dialog box

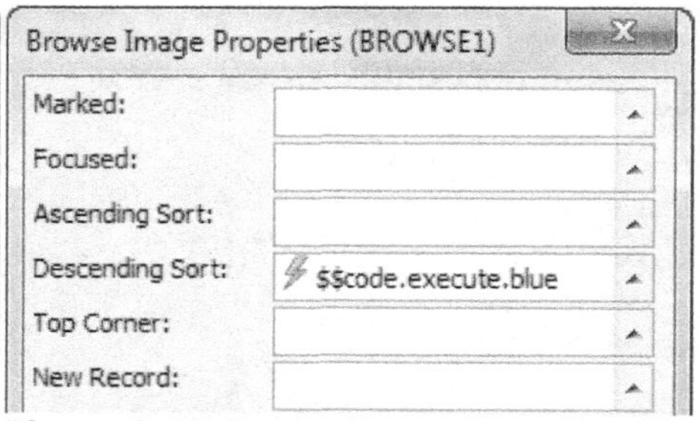

Figure 9-20 Browse Image Properties dialog box

Figure 9-21 Column header with image illustrated

The **VERTICAL SLIDER PROPERTIES BUTTON** opens the dialog box shown in Figure 9-22. The options are used to display a message (See example column in figure) on the vertical scrollbar on the browse, as shown in Figure 9-23, when you slide it up or down.

The **NEW RECORD ROW LINK** opens the dialog box shown in Figure 9-24. The options are used to change how a row for a new record appears in the browse. I suspect the goal is to make the new record row stand out on the browse.

The **NO RECORDS MESSAGE LINK** opens the dialog box shown in Figure 9-25. The options are used to create a custom message (in plain text or HTML format) that will automatically be displayed when a query does not find any matching records.

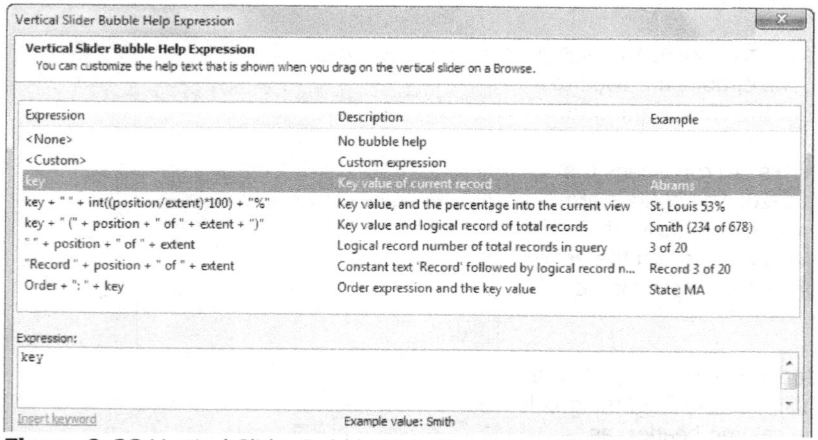

Figure 9-22 Vertical Slider Bubble Help Expression dialog box

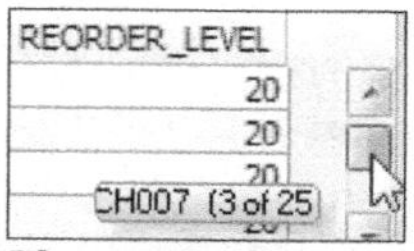

Figure 9-23 Vertical Slider bubble help applied to the scroll bar

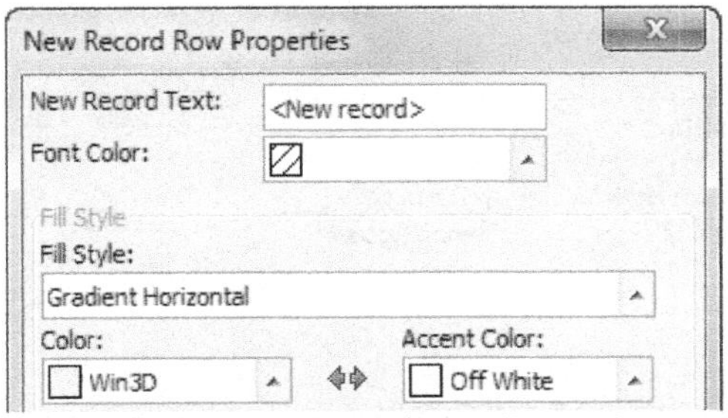

Figure 9-24 New Record Row Properties dialog box

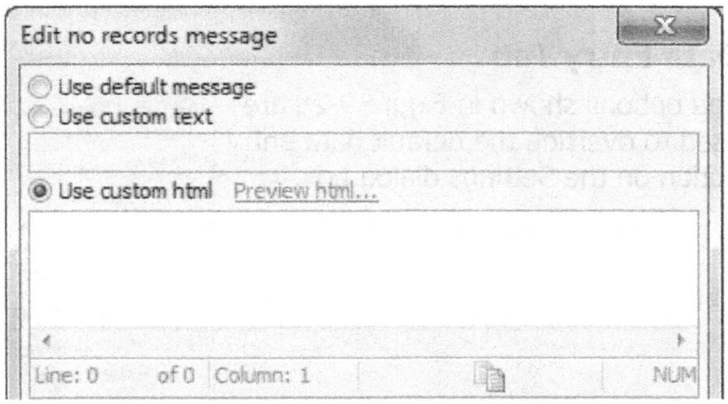

Figure 9-25 Edit no records message dialog box

Filter/Order Tab

The options shown in Figure 9-26 are used to create a filter or order expression to exclude records in the table or set from being displayed on the browse.

If the **USE THE LAST RUN QUERY** option is selected, the other options are removed from the tab.

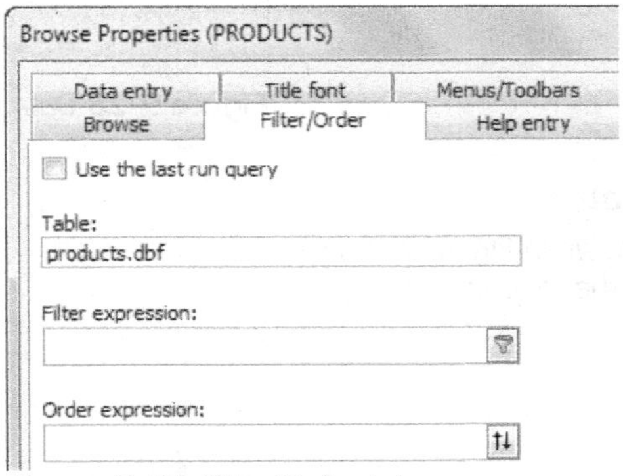

Figure 9-26 Filter/Order tab

Help Entry Tab

The options shown in Figure 9-27 are used to add a custom help file to the browse.

The **USE CUSTOM HELP** option enables the other options on the tab so that one of the following types of help files can be selected to use with the browse.

① Alpha Five help file.

② **.HLP FILE** (Standard Windows help file)

③ **.CHM FILE** (Compiled Windows help file)

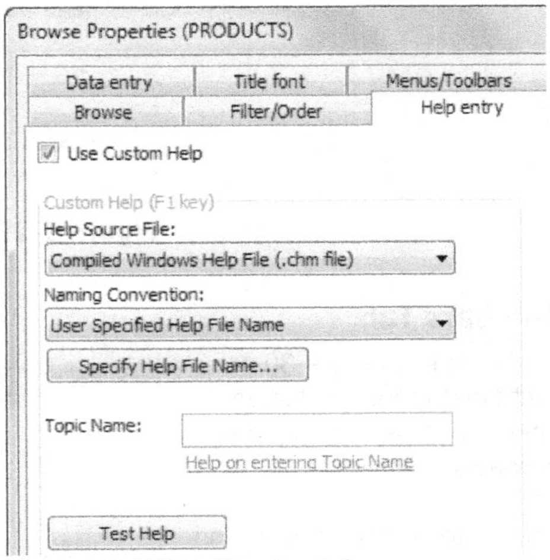

Figure 9-27 Help entry tab

Data Entry Tab

The options shown in Figure 9-28 are used to override the default data entry option on the Settings dialog box.

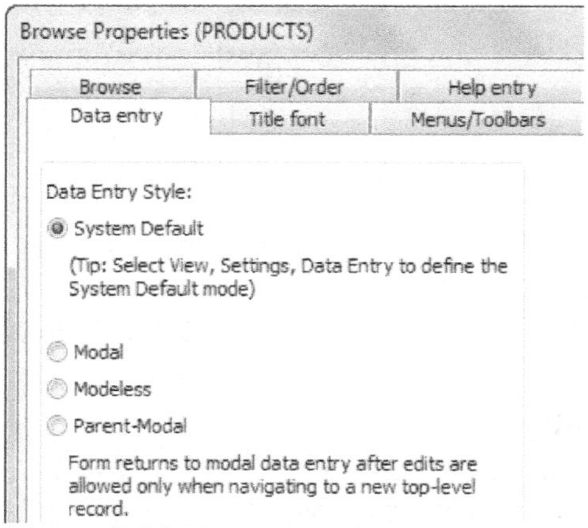

Figure 9-28 Data entry tab

Title Font Tab

The options shown in Figure 9-29 are used to select the font and its characteristics.

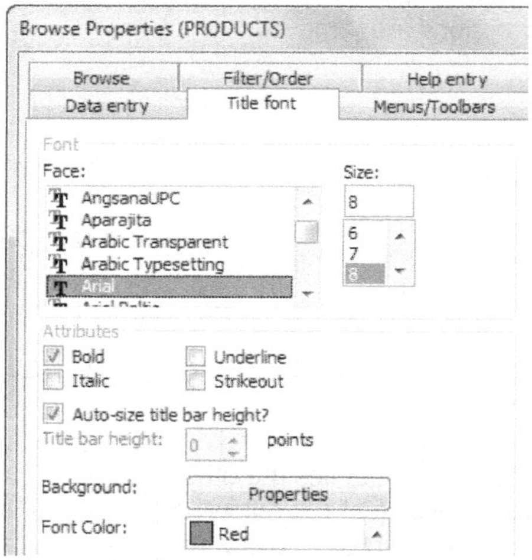

Figure 9-29 Title Font tab

Menus/Toolbars Tab

The options shown in Figure 9-30 are used to select what menu (including right-click menus) and toolbar options the form will have, if any.

You can also create custom menus and toolbars for the browse.

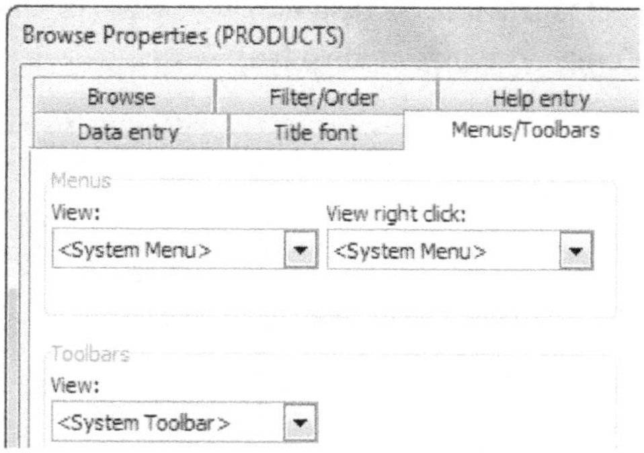

Figure 9-30 Menus/Toolbars tab

Column Properties Dialog Box

To open this dialog box, right-click on a cell on the browse and select Properties. This dialog box has options like setting up the right-click menu, that cannot be set up any place else. This dialog box can also be opened when a cell is selected and you press the **F12** key. I am not sure why this dialog box is only named Column Properties when some of the options on it are for cells.

Setup Tab

The options shown in Figure 9-31 are used to select general options for the cells in a column.

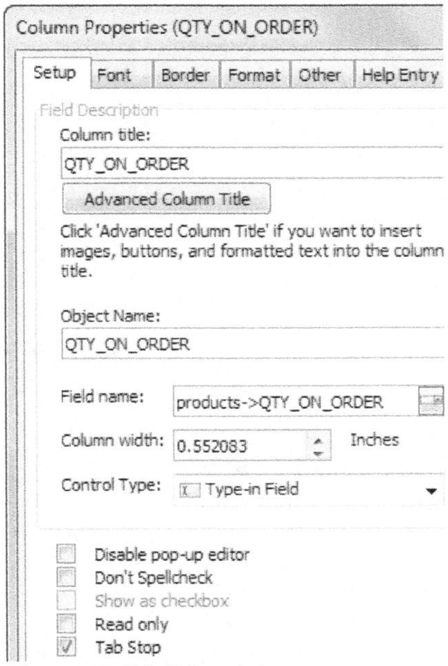

Figure 9-31 Setup tab

Font Tab

The options shown in Figure 9-32 are used to select the font, font size and attributes for the cells in a column. They work the same as they do in word processing software.

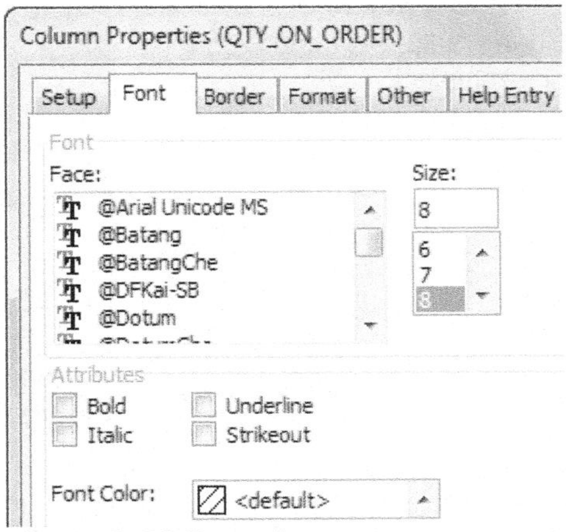

Figure 9-32 Font tab

Border Tab

The options shown in Figure 9-33 are used to select whether or not the cells will have a border and what the border should look like.

Figure 9-33 Border tab

Format Tab

The options shown in Figure 9-34 are used to select how the data in a column is aligned and whether or not it is rotated.

The **FORMAT STYLE** drop-down list displays different options for formatting the column.

The options in the drop-down list change, depending on the type of data that is in the column.

[See Chapter 8, Figures 8-33, 8-34 and 8-35 for format style option examples]

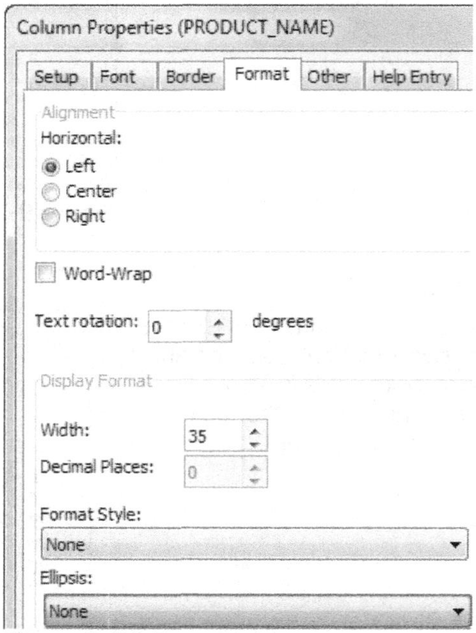

Figure 9-34 Format tab

Other Tab

The options shown in Figure 9-35 are used to create conditional formatting expressions to select when specific colors will be applied to fonts and the background of cells in the browse.

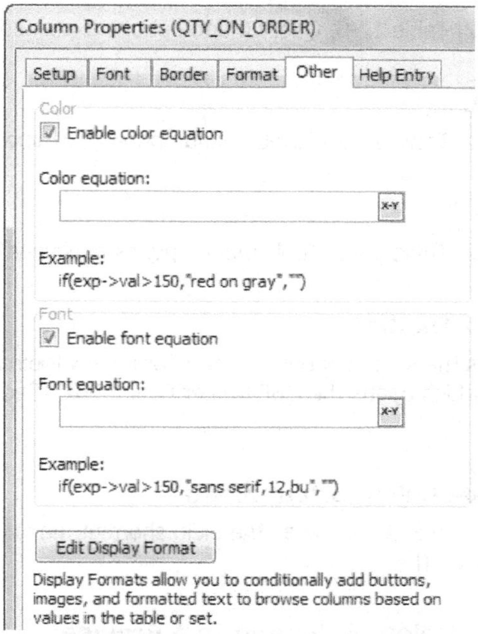

Figure 9-35 Other tab

Help Entry Tab

The options shown in Figure 9-36 are used to create a custom help file for the cells in a column.

BUBBLE HELP is the option to use when you want the help message to popup when the mouse pointer is over a cell.

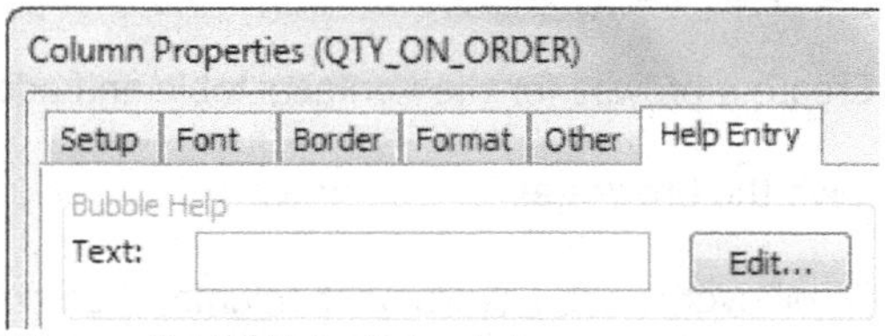

Figure 9-36 Help Entry tab

Viewing A Browse

Viewing a browse is similar to viewing a form. The majority of menu and toolbar options are the same. The differences are explained below.

Browse Menu

The **FORM VIEW** option displays the data currently shown in the browse, in a form.

[See Chapter 12, Table 12-3, Form menu options explained]

Records Menu

[See Chapter 12, Table 12-4, Records menu options explained]

Find Menu

[See Chapter 12, Table 12-5, Find menu options explained]

Query Menu

[See Chapter 12, Table 12-6, Query menu options explained]

Scripts Menu

[See Chapter 12, Table 12-8, Scripts menu options explained]

Tools Menu

[See Chapter 12, Table 12-9, Tools menu options explained]

Browse View Toolbar

This toolbar has the same options that the Form view toolbar has except for Button 15 (on the Form view toolbar), which opens the QBF Helper Dialog box. [See Chapter 12, Figure 12-24, Form view toolbar]

Preview Mode Cell Shortcut Menu

This shortcut menu is the same as the Field shortcut menu. [See Chapter 12, Preview Mode Form Field Shortcut Menu]

Exercise 9.2: Delete A Column In A Browse

In this exercise you will create a browse and then delete a column from the browse. Deleting a column from a browse is similar to deleting a column from a spreadsheet. The difference is that when a column is deleted from a browse, the data is not deleted from a table.

1. Create a browse for the Contacts table and add all of the fields.

2. Save the browse as `Contacts`.

3. Scroll over to the Fax Number column, then right-click on the column heading. Select **DELETE COLUMN**, then save the changes. If you closed the browse and opened the Contacts table, you would see that the Fax Number field and data are still in the table.

Exercise 9.3: Change The Date Format Of A Column In A Browse

In this exercise you will learn how to change the date format. Changing the date format on the browse does not change the format of the data in the table.

1. Create a browse for the Orders table and add all of the fields.

2. Save the browse as `Order header info`.

3. Right-click on the Order Date column and select Properties.

4. On the Format tab, open the Format Style drop-down list and select the first December 31, 1998 option, then click OK.

5. Save the changes. The Order Date column should look like the one shown in Figure 9-37.

ORDER_DATE
February 1, 2011
February 1, 2011
February 1, 2011
February 1, 2011
February 2, 2011

Figure 9-37 Date format changed

Exercise 9.4: Duplicating A Browse

You may have the need to have a copy of a browse. For example, in one part of the application the browse may need to be read-only and in another part, the data in the browse needs to have the ability to be changed.

1. Open the Contacts browse.

2. File ⇒ Save As. Type `Contacts read only` as the file name.

> **Duplicating A Browse**
> The shortcut menu has a duplicate option, which can be used to create a copy of the browse.

Exercise 9.5: Make A Browse Read Only

If you are like me, when you think of a form as being read only, you think that not being able to change the data makes the form read only. In Alpha Five, not only is that true, but to set a browse to read only, the design of the browse also be set to read only. At first that may not sound problematic until you realize that if the design has to be set to read only, you can't open the browse to edit it. The only work around that I can think of is to make a copy of the browse without the Open/Edit layout restriction option selected. Then, you can change that copy of the form and save it as the version of the browse that is restricted.

1. Open the Contacts read only browse.

2. Browse ⇒ Browse Properties. On the Browse tab in the **RESTRICTIONS LIST**, check the following options: Enter Record, Change Record, Delete Record, Move Columns, Delete Columns, Open/Edit Layout.

3. Click OK, then save the changes. When you view the browse, you will see that you cannot add or edit the data or modify the layout.

Changing The Column Size In A Stand Alone Browse

Changing the column size in a stand alone browse works the same way that it does in a spreadsheet. Place the mouse pointer on the vertical bar after the column that you want to resize, then move the mouse pointer in the direction that you want to resize the column. When you have resized the columns, save the changes.

Exercise 9.6: Adding Color To The Browse

There are a lot of options to add color to a browse. The Browse Properties dialog box has color options. In this exercise you will learn about these options.

How To Change The Row Selector Properties

1. Open the Contacts browse, then open the Browse Properties dialog box.

2. On the Browse tab, click the Row Selector Properties button.

Row Selector Properties

The options on this dialog box are used to change various color options for rows in the browse.

The options are used to change the color of the first column in the browse (the column before the data illustrated in Figure 9-38).

The options in the Color list are explained below.

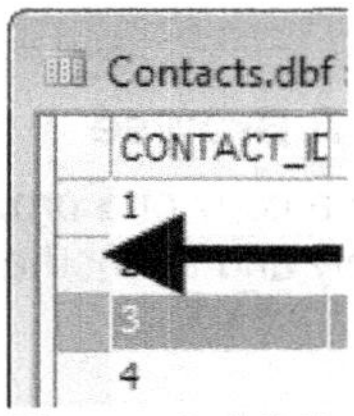

Figure 9-38 Row Selector column illustrated

① **ROW SELECTOR** The options shown in Figure 9-39 are used to change the row colors. This option changes the background color of the first column for the rows that are not selected. The default color is light gray.

② **SELECTED** The options shown in Figure 9-40 are used when more than one row is selected. This option is used to select the color for the rows that are selected that do not have focus. The default color is light orange.

③ **FOCUSED** The options shown in Figure 9-41 are used to select the color for the row that has focus.

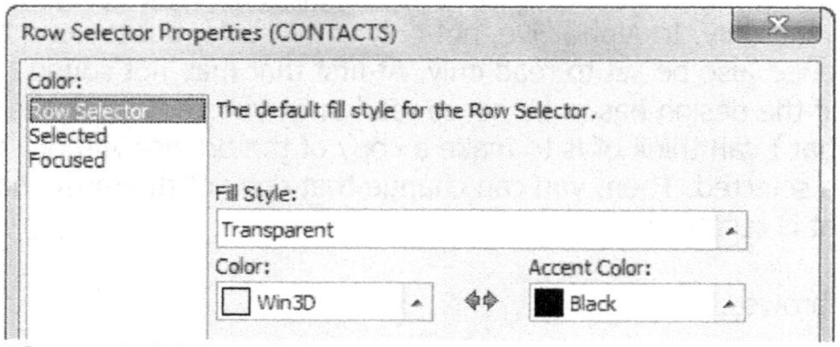

Figure 9-39 Row Selector options

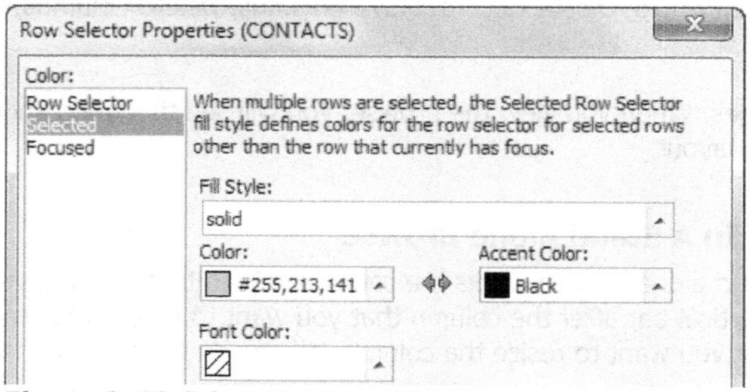

Figure 9-40 Selected color options

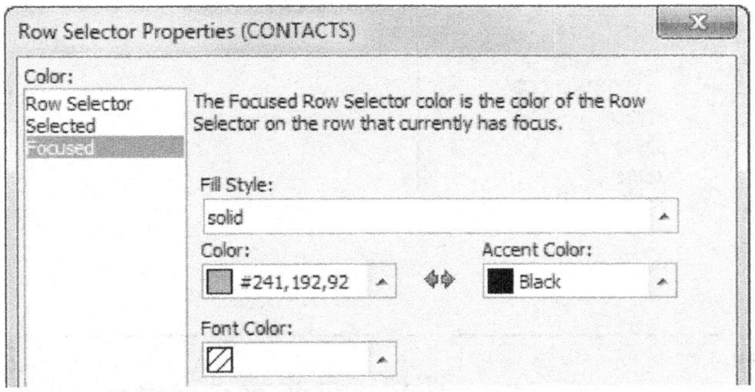

Figure 9-41 Focused color options

3. Change the Row Selector Fill Style option to the first option in the Pattern section. On the System tab, change the **ACCENT COLOR** to Light Yellow.

4. Change the Selected color to Dark blue.

5. Change the Focused color to Sky Blue, then click OK twice to close both dialog boxes.

6. Test the color changes by selecting several rows, then save the changes.

What Is The Splitter Bar?

The splitter feature will remind you of the freeze pane option in Excel. This tool is available in all browses. The **SPLITTER BAR** is to the left of the Row Selector column. You can select which columns will always be displayed in the browse no matter how far to the right you scroll. The problem in my opinion, is that because the default color for the splitter bar is light gray, you can't see it. In this part of the exercise you will learn how to use the splitter bar and how to change it's color.

1. On the Browse Properties dialog box, Browse tab, open the **SPLITTER DROP-DOWN LIST** and select the Orange color on the System tab.

2. Click OK. You should now see the splitter bar illustrated in Figure 9-42.

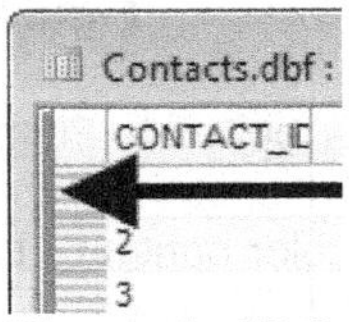

Figure 9-42 Splitter bar illustrated

3. Click on the Splitter bar and drag it to the right, to the First Name column, as illustrated in Figure 9-43, then release the mouse button. Now, when you scroll to the right, the Contact ID and Company Name columns will still be displayed on the browse, as shown in Figure 9-44.

Figure 9-43 Splitter bar moved

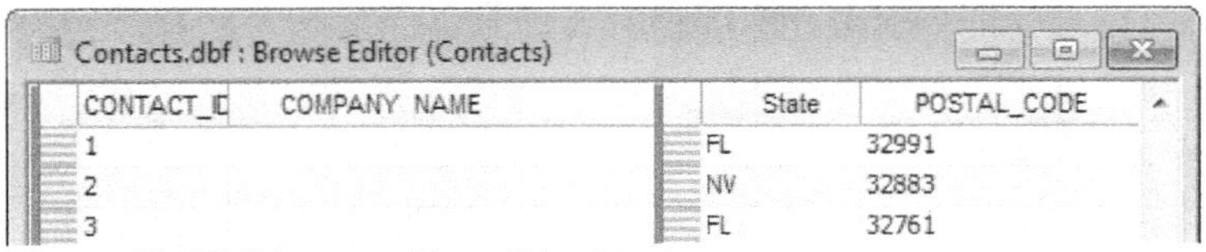

Figure 9-44 Browse with splitter bar in use

4. Save the changes.

> **How To Remove The Splitter Bar**
> To remove the splitter bar, click on it, then drag it all the way to the left, as illustrated earlier in Figure 9-42.

Change The Color Of The Selected Row Or Column

The default color for selected rows and columns is blue. You can have selected rows one color and selected columns a different color. The **OTHER COLORS PROPERTIES BUTTON** is used to change these and other colors on the browse, as you will learn in this part of the exercise.

1. On the Browse Properties dialog box, Browse tab, click the Other Colors Properties button.

2. On the dialog box shown in Figure 9-45 change the Selected color option to Light Yellow, then change the Focused color to Dark Rose.

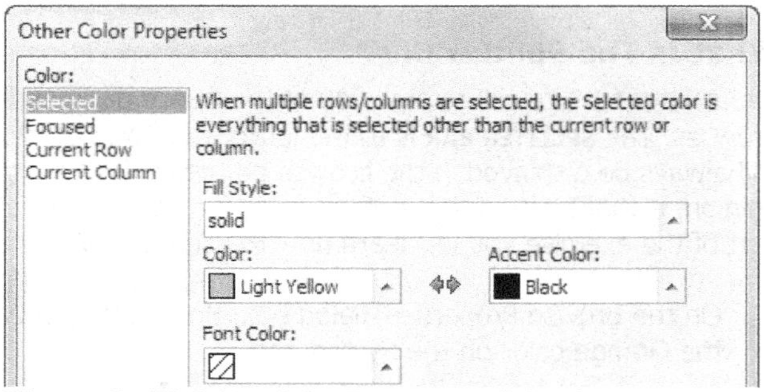

Figure 9-45 Other Color Properties dialog box

3. Change the Current Row color option to Plum.

4. Change the Current Column color option to Lavender.

5. Click OK twice to close both dialog boxes. Save the changes. Test the current row and column options by selecting a row, then select a column.

Change The Row Background Color

By default, the background color of every other row is a different color. This style is sometimes referred to as green bar, because at one point there was computer paper that came pre-printed with light green bars on it to make the report easier to read. You can create the same effect in a browse by selecting the row background color(s) that you want, as you will see in this part of the exercise.

1. Open the Browse Properties dialog box. On the Browse tab, click the **ROW COLOR PROPERTIES BUTTON**.

2. Select the Row Color 2 option, then check the Enabled option. Change the color to Pale Blue.

3. The **NUMBER OF ROWS** option shown in Figure 9-46 is used to select how many consecutive rows you want to have this color.

   Change the option to 2.

   Save the changes.

   The browse should look like the one shown in Figure 9-47.

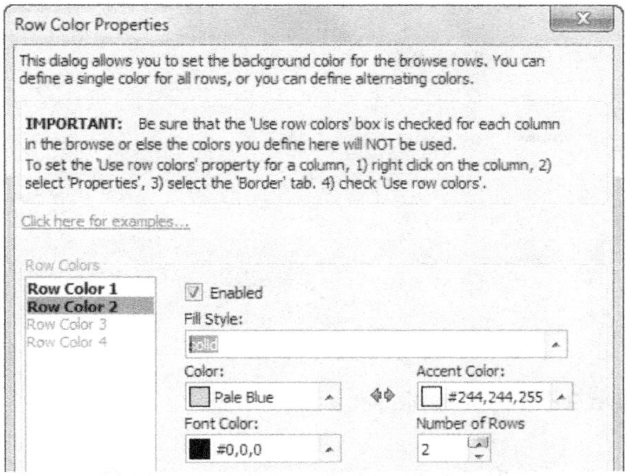

Figure 9-46 Row Color Properties dialog box

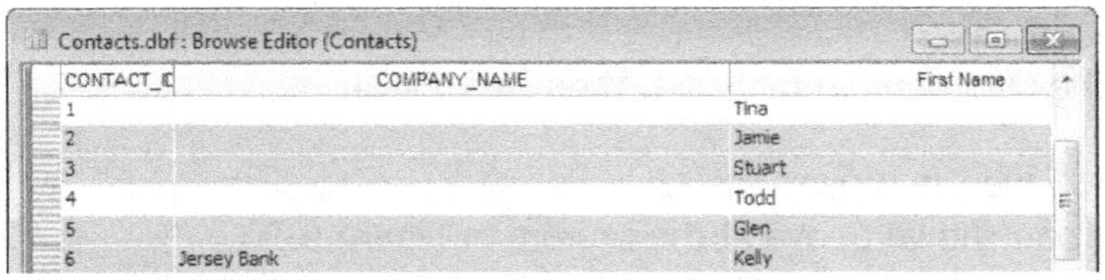

Figure 9-47 Browse with alternating background color

How To Use The Memo Editor

You may have seen a button at the end of a memo field. This button opens the Memo Editor which is used to enter data into a memo field, instead of typing in the memo field cell in the browse. This is especially helpful if a lot of information has to be entered into a memo field. By design, memo fields are usually displayed as the last column in a browse, which makes the button easier to see.

If a memo field is not displayed as the last column, when the cursor is in the memo field, the button is still displayed, but it appears at the beginning of the field to the right, as illustrated in Figure 9-48. When you click the button, the dialog box shown in Figure 9-49 is displayed. Once the content is entered, click the Save button on the Memo Editor dialog box. If the memo field has a lot of text, this dialog box can also be used to read the information in the field.

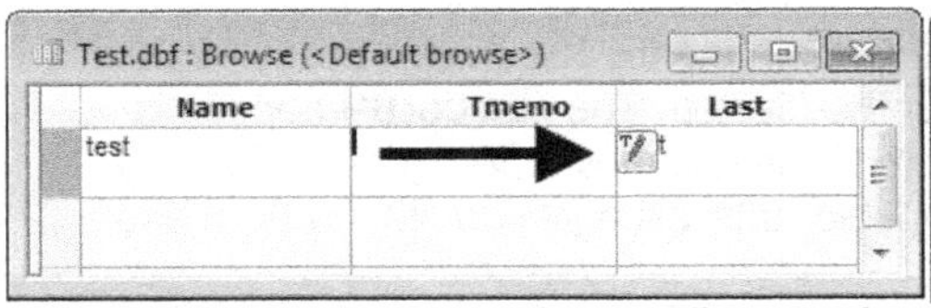

Figure 9-48 Memo Editor button illustrated

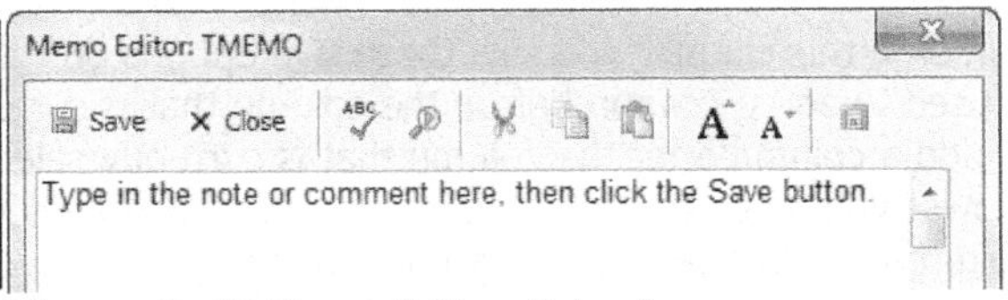

Figure 9-49 Memo Editor dialog box

Designing A Browse For A Set

By default, a browse that is based on a set will display all virtual records. For example, in Chapter 6 you created the Orders multi table set with one-to-many links, shown at the top of Figure 9-50. On the bottom of the figure is the browse with all of the data from the set. As you can see, data from the Orders table (the parent table) is repeated for each record in the order Detail table (the child table). This may not be what you want displayed in the browse. You may only want to have the parent records. You will learn how to do this in the next exercise.

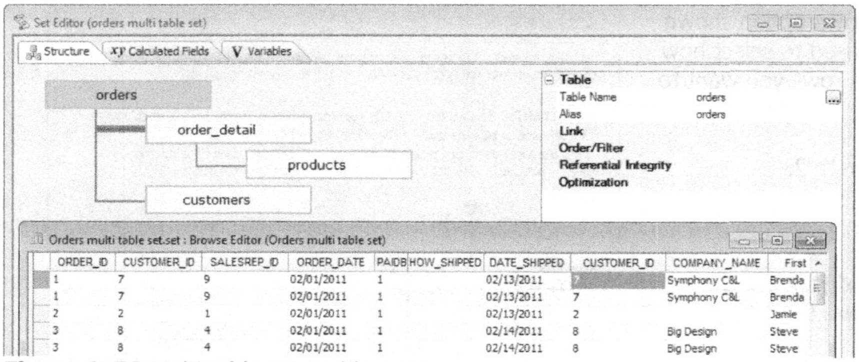

Figure 9-50 Multi table set and browse

Exercise 9.7: Create A Browse For A Set

In this exercise you will create the browse shown above in Figure 9-50.

1. Open the Browse Genie. Select the Orders multi table set, then click Finish.

2. Make the larger columns smaller. Save the browse as `Orders multi table set.` Your browse should look like the one shown above at the bottom of Figure 9-50.

3. Open the Browse Properties dialog box. On the Browse tab in the Browse Appearance section, check the **PARENT RECORDS ONLY** option. Save the changes. The browse should look like the one shown in Figure 9-51. Compare the Order ID's to those shown above in Figure 9-50. You will not see duplicate Order ID numbers.

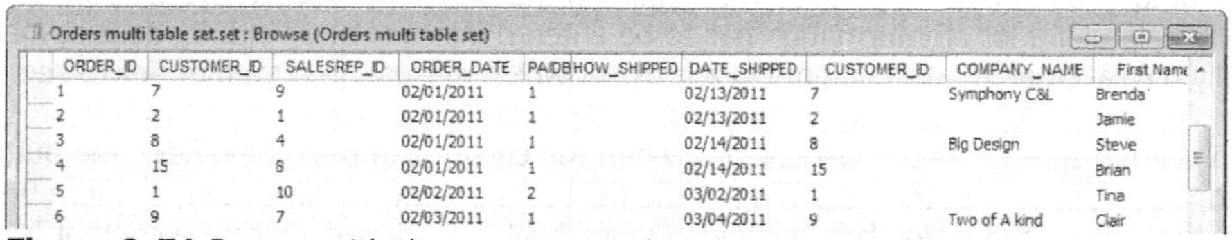

Figure 9-51 Browse with the parent records only option enabled

Insert And Add Columns

Earlier in this chapter you saw these two options on the Column menu. The **INSERT COLUMN** option is used to add a column before the column that is currently selected. The **ADD COLUMN** option is used to add a column after the column that is currently selected. The columns that can be added to a browse can come from the table, a system field or a variable. Interestingly enough, you can add a field that is already on the form or browse.

Exercise 9.8: Adding Columns To A Browse

In this exercise you will add a field from a table and a system field to a browse.

Insert A Column

1. Save the Products browse as `Products & more columns.`

2. Click on the Product Name column, then Column ⇒ Insert Column.

   The dialog box shown in Figure 9-52 is used to select the field to add to the browse.

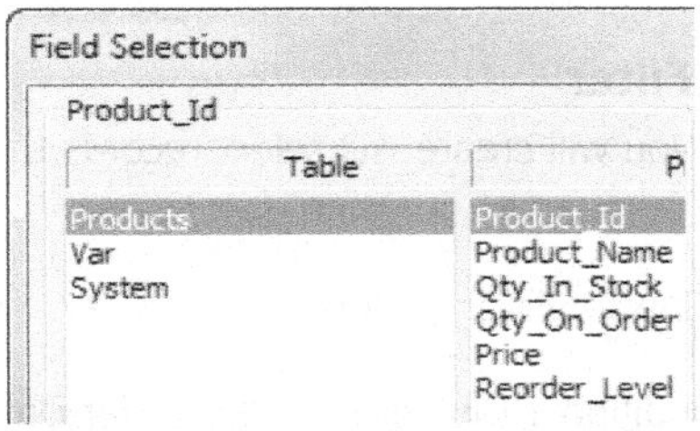

Figure 9-52 Field Selection dialog box

3. As luck would have it, the field that will be added is the field that is selected. Click OK. The Product ID field should be the first column in the browse. Save the changes.

Add A Column

1. Click on the Reorder column in the browse.
2. Column ⇒ Add Column. Select the System table on the Field Selection dialog box, then select the Date field.
3. Click OK. You should see the Date column at the end of the browse. Save the changes.

Ad Hoc Browse

Chapter 2 briefly discussed this option. This tool is used to create a form or browse and create a filter for the records that will be displayed on the form or browse. The only downside is that the filter can't be changed after the browse is saved.

Exercise 9.9: Create An Ad Hoc Browse With A Filter

In this exercise you will create an Ad Hoc Browse using the Orders table. The filter that you will create will display orders in a specific date range.

Create The Browse

1. On the Tables/Sets tab, right-click on the Orders table, then select **AD HOC BROWSE**.
2. Add the following fields to the Selected Fields list: Order ID, Customer ID, Order Date, How Shipped and Date Shipped, as shown in Figure 9-53.

Ad-Hoc Browse Dialog Box

The options at the bottom of the dialog box shown in Figure 9-53 are used to select the layout type, create a filter and select the order criteria.

The **LAYOUT TYPE** options are used to select a form or browse for the layout.

The **SPECIFY FILTER** button is used to create a filter to select the records that will be displayed. You can also select the order that the records will appear in the form or browse.

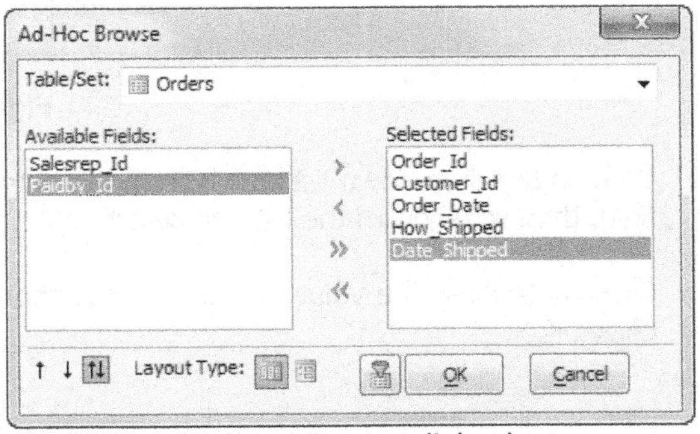

Figure 9-53 Ad-Hoc Browse dialog box

Create The Filter

The filter that you will create will select records that have an order date between 2/16/2011 and 7/1/2011.

1. Click the Specify Filter button.

2. On the Condition 1 tab, click on the Order Date field in the first list, then select the **IS BETWEEN OPERATOR** in the second list. Wouldn't it be helpful if the list of operators were in alphabetical order?

3. Click on the first blank drop-down list. On the Value dialog box, click on the drop-down list for the first value field.

4. Scroll down the list on the dialog box shown in Figure 9-54 and select 2/16/2011, then click the **INSERT** button.

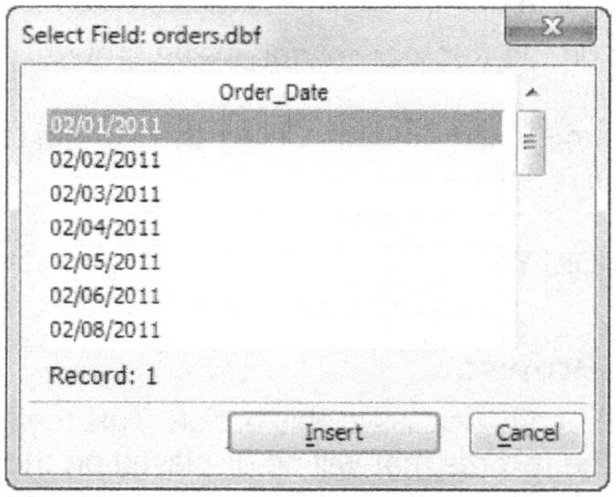

Figure 9-54 Select Field dialog box

5. The date should be in the first Value field shown in Figure 9-55.

   Click OK.

   The options on this dialog box are used to select the data (the value) for the filter.

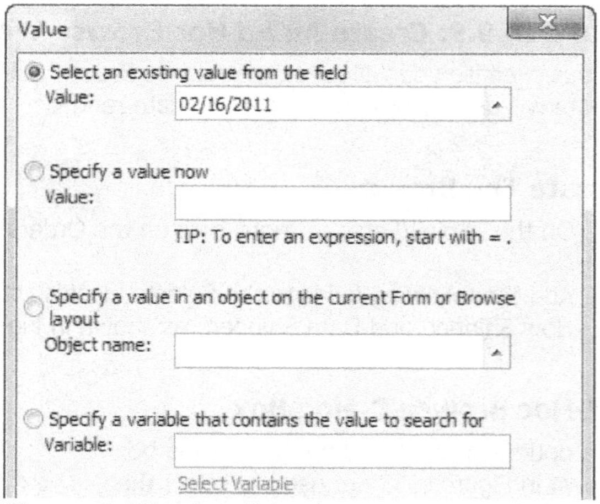

Figure 9-55 Value dialog box

6. Click on the drop-down list across from the date. Click on the drop-down list for the first Value field, then scroll down the list and select 7/1/2011, then click the Insert button.

7. Click OK to close the Value dialog box. You should have the options shown in Figure 9-56. Click OK.

Filter/Order Builder

If you need another condition, click the **ADD CONDITION** button.

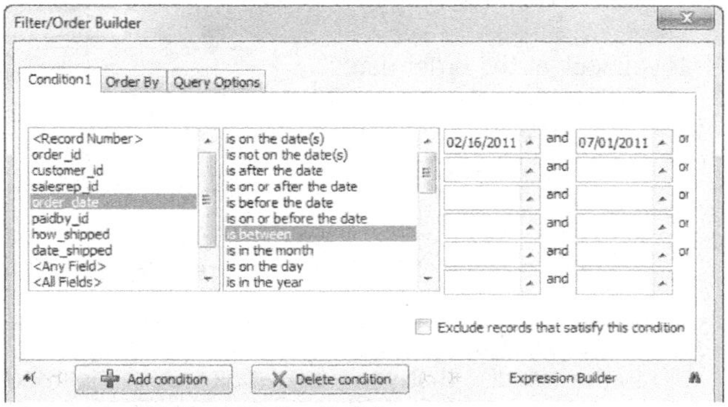

Figure 9-56 Filter/Order Builder

> **Filter/Order Builder**
> Before closing this dialog box make sure that you have all of the filter criteria that you need, unless you want to use the Expression Builder. If you discover after you have closed the dialog box that you need to make a change and the Ad-Hoc Browse dialog box shown earlier in Figure 9-53 is open, click the Specify Filter button. The Filter/Order Builder will not open. Instead, you will see the dialog box shown in Figure 9-57. You can make changes on this dialog box.

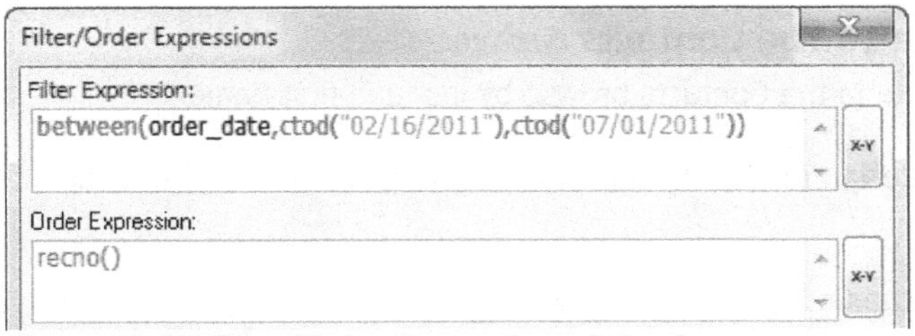

Figure 9-57 Filter/Order Expressions dialog box

The options shown in Figure 9-58 are used to select the sort options.

The options shown in Figure 9-59 are used to create a query to select the records. The Sub-select options are used to select the **Top N** or **Bottom N** records for the query.

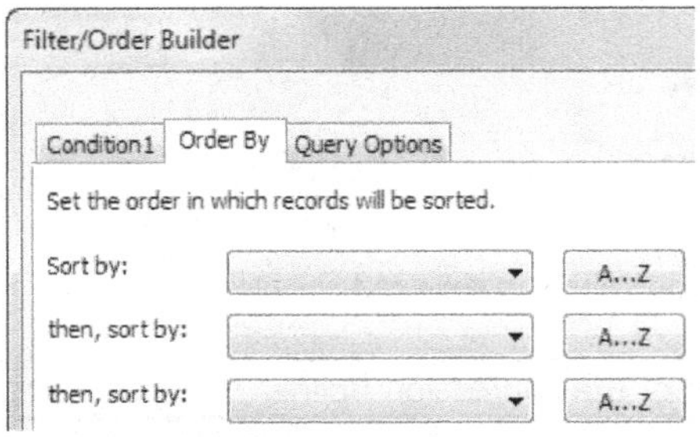

Figure 9-58 Order By tab

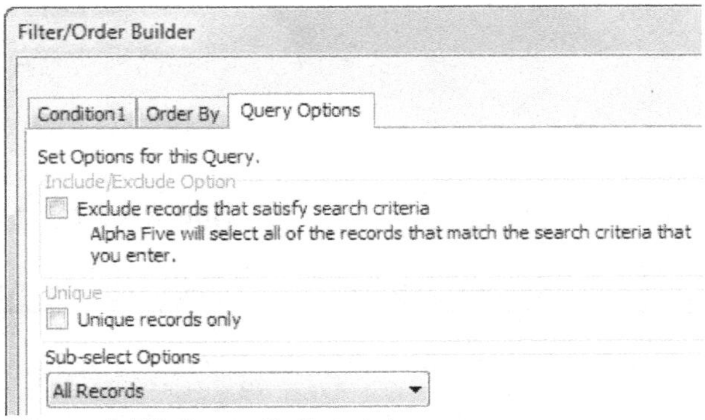

Figure 9-59 Query Options tab

8. Click OK to close the Ad-Hoc Browse dialog box. Save the browse as `Ad hoc browse filter`. The browse should look like the one shown in Figure 9-60.

If you look at the order dates, they will all be between 2/6/2011 and 7/1/2011.

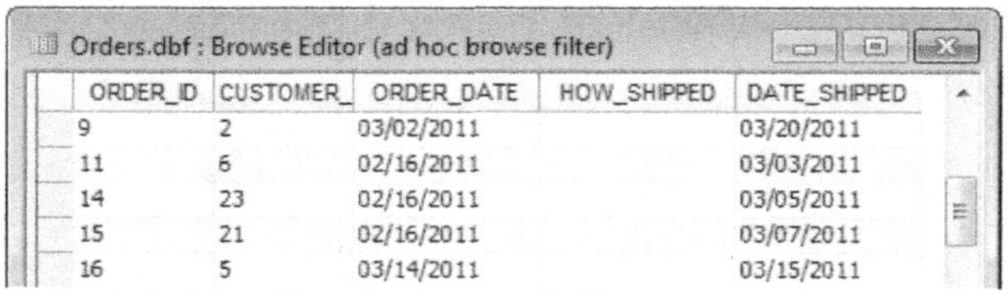

Figure 9-60 Ad hoc browse with filter

> **Order By Tab**
> In the exercise that you just completed, you learned about the Filter/Order Builder. The **ORDER BY TAB**, shown earlier in Figure 9-58, can also be accessed from the Filter/Order tab on the Browse Properties dialog box, shown earlier in Figure 9-26 by clicking the button at the end of the Order Expression field. This tab can also be accessed from the Browse view toolbar by clicking the **QUERY GENIE BUTTON**. The difference between the Filter/Order Builder and the Query Genie is that the Query Genie also has options to run a query.

Sorting Records

> Alpha Five refers to sorting records as **ORDERING RECORDS**.

Exercise 9.10: Sort The Data In The Contacts Browse

In this exercise you will sort the data in the Contacts browse by last and first name.

1. Open the Contacts browse in design mode. Open the Browse Properties dialog box, then click on the Filter/Order tab.

2. Click the button at the end of the Order Expression field.

3. Open the Sort by drop-down list and select the Last Name field.

4. Open the first **THEN, SORT BY** drop-down list and select the First Name field shown in Figure 9-61.

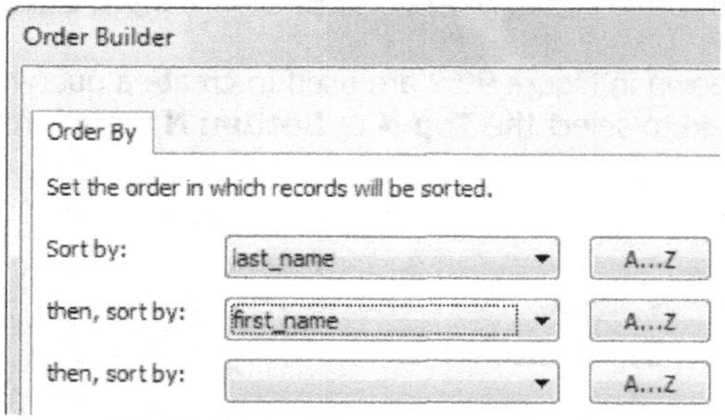

Figure 9-61 Sort order options selected

> The Order Builder shown above in Figure 9-61 is part of the Expression Builder.

5. Click OK twice to close both dialog boxes, then save the changes. View the browse.

As shown in Figure 9-62, the records in the browse are in alphabetical order by last name, then first name.

If you scroll down to the last name Riker, you will see an example of this.

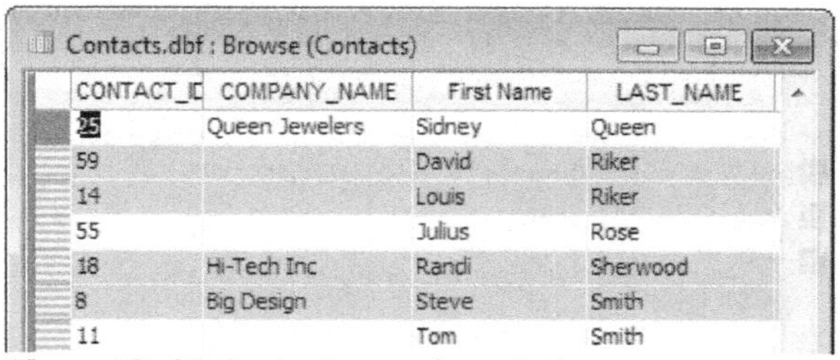

Figure 9-62 Contact records sorted

Conditional Color Formatting

Alpha Five provides the functionality to have color applied to font and cell background colors based on conditions that you select. The two genies explained below are used to create conditional color formatting.

① The **COLOR EQUATION GENIE** is used to create conditional formatting to change the color of text or the background color of an object.
② The **FONT EQUATION GENIE** is used to create conditional formatting to change the font color and other font attributes.

Exercise 9.11: Apply Conditional Formatting To Change The Background And Font Color

In this exercise you will change the background color and font of the Qty In Stock field based on the value in the field. If the value is less than 300, the background color will be changed to lavender and the font will be changed to bold.

Create An Expression To Conditionally Change The Background Color

1. Open the Products browse, then click in the Qty In Stock column.

2. Open the Column Properties dialog box, then click on the Other tab.

3. Check the **ENABLE COLOR EQUATION** option, then click the button at the end of the Color equation field.

4. On the first row, change the Background Color to Lavender.

5. In the Expression field type `Qty_In_Stock <300`. You should have the options shown in Figure 9-63. Click OK. The two buttons at the bottom of the dialog box are explained below.

   ① **VIEW EXPRESSION** (The binoculars) Opens the dialog box shown in Figure 9-64, which is used to view the expression.
   ② **SWITCH FROM GENIE TO EXPRESSION BUILDER MODE** Opens the Expression Builder.

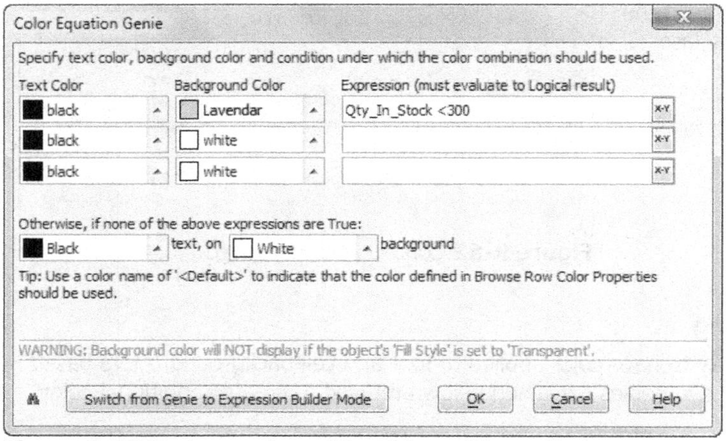
Color Equation Genie
Specify text color, background color and condition under which the color combination should be used.
Text Color
Background Color
Expression (must evaluate to Logical result)
black
Lavendar
Qty_In_Stock <300
black
white
black
white
Otherwise, if none of the above expressions are True:
Black
text, on
White
background
Tip: Use a color name of '<Default>' to indicate that the color defined in Browse Row Color Properties should be used.
WARNING: Background color will NOT display if the object's 'Fill Style' is set to 'Transparent'.
Switch from Genie to Expression Builder Mode
OK
Cancel
Help

Figure 9-63 Background conditional formatting options

Expression
case(Qty_In_Stock<300,"black on Lavendar",.T.,"Black on White")
OK

Figure 9-64 Expression dialog box

Create An Expression To Conditionally Change The Font Color

1. Check the **ENABLE FONT EQUATION** option, then click the button at the end of the Font equation field.

2. Check the B option on the first row.

   In the Expression field, type `Qty_In_Stock <300`, as shown in Figure 9-65.

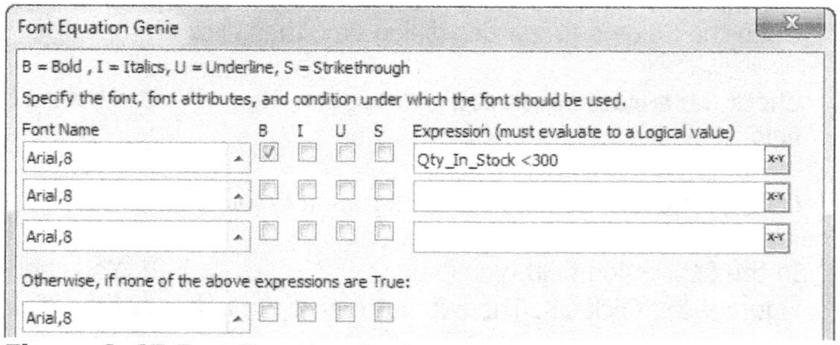
Font Equation Genie
B = Bold , I = Italics, U = Underline, S = Strikethrough
Specify the font, font attributes, and condition under which the font should be used.
Font Name
B I U S
Expression (must evaluate to a Logical value)
Arial,8
Qty_In_Stock <300
Arial,8
Arial,8
Otherwise, if none of the above expressions are True:
Arial,8

Figure 9-65 Font Equation Genie options

3. Click OK. The Other tab should have the options shown in Figure 9-66. Click OK. The **EDIT DISPLAY FORMAT BUTTON** opens the **BROWSE CELL DISPLAY FORMAT BUILDER.**

4. Save the changes, then preview the browse, which should look like the one shown in Figure 9-67.

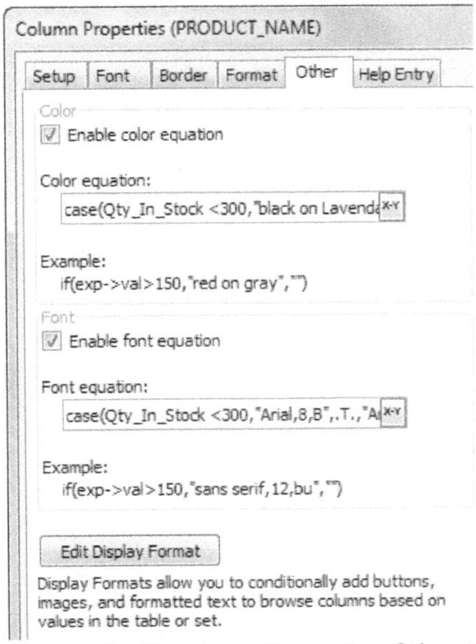

Figure 9-66 Column Properties Other tab options

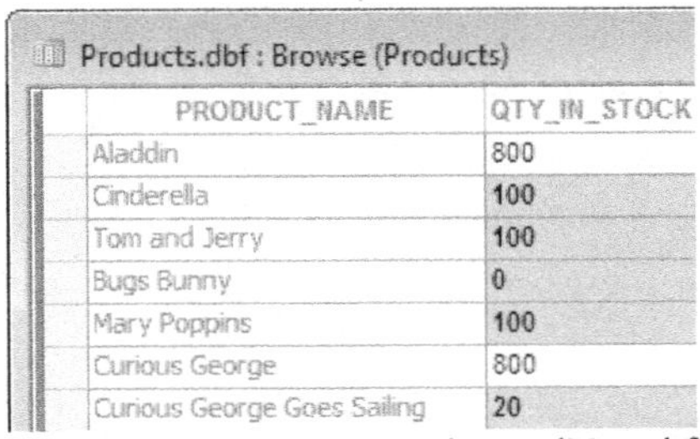

Figure 9-67 Browse with conditional formatting applied to the Qty In Stock field

Bubble Help Messages

This feature is helpful if you think that the person using the browse may not know what data should be entered in a field. You can add what Alpha Five calls **BUBBLE HELP**. This is the same as a **TOOL TIP** that many other software packages use.

Exercise 9.12: Add Bubble Help To A Column

In this exercise you will learn how to create a bubble help message for a column.

1. Open the Orders multi table set browse.

2. Click on the Work Phone column. Open the Column Properties dialog box, then click on the **HELP ENTRY TAB.**

Bubble Help Dialog Box

If you do not need to format the Bubble help message, you can type the message in the Text field on the Column Properties dialog box Help Entry tab. If you want to format the text, click the Edit button. The formatting options are explained below.

① **NO FORMATTING** The options show in Figure 9-68 are available. You can select how long the cursor has to be in the field before the help message will be displayed.
② **SIMPLE FORMATTING** Figure 9-69 shows the formatting options that can be added to the help message.
③ **USE HTML** Figure 9-70 shows the options that are available to create a help message in HTML format.

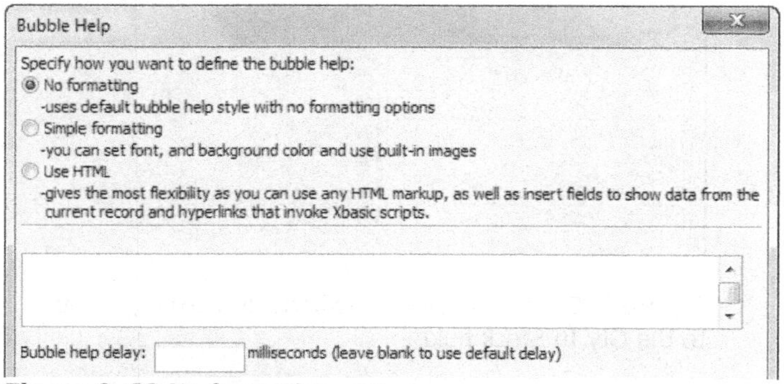

Figure 9-68 No formatting options

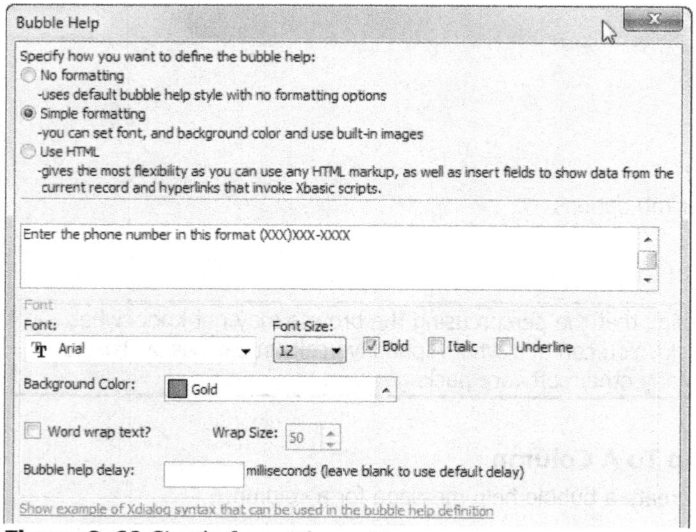

Figure 9-69 Simple formatting options

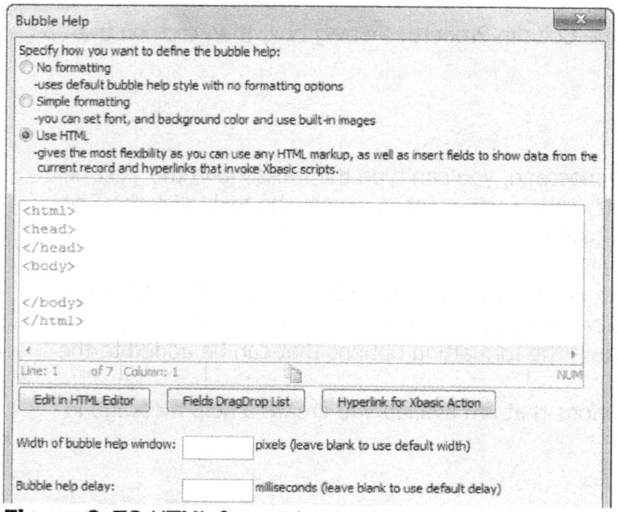

Figure 9-70 HTML formatting options

1. Select the Simple formatting option, then type
   `Enter the phone number in this format \(XXX)XXX-XXXX.`
2. Select the Font size 12 and the Bold option.
3. Change the background color to Gold, as shown earlier in Figure 9-69, then click OK twice to close both dialog boxes.
4. Save the changes. Preview the browse. When you hold the mouse pointer over the Work Phone column or click in the column, you will see the message shown in Figure 9-71.

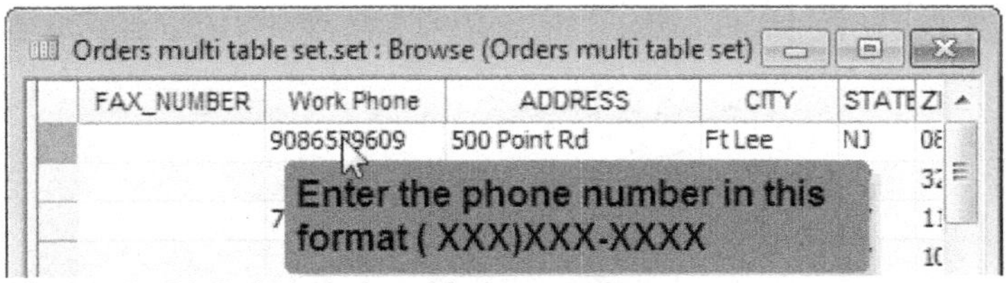

Figure 9-71 Bubble help added to a column

ENHANCING FORMS PART 1

In this chapter you will learn techniques including the following, that will help make forms look professional.

- ☑ Use the Form Genie to create a form that has an embedded browse
- ☑ Add system fields
- ☑ Add an embedded browse to a form
- ☑ How to make forms read only
- ☑ Create a form that has non scrollable regions
- ☑ Using Rich Text Objects

CHAPTER 10

Overview

In Chapter 8, you learned the basics of creating forms. In this chapter, you will learn how to use more features to enhance the appearance and functionality of forms. In Exercise 10.7 you will learn an easy way to create a basic form without using the Form Genie.

Exercise 10.1: Add A System Field To A Form

In this exercise you will add the system date field, which displays today's date, to a form and make the field read only.

1. Open the Contact Type form.

2. From the Drag Drop List panel, add the Date field in the System section to the top of the form, above and to the right of the Contact ID field.

3. Open the Field Properties dialog box for the Date field.

   On the Setup tab, check the **READ ONLY** option, then clear the Tab Stop option shown in Figure 10-1.

   Click OK.

   Clearing the Tab Stop option alone is not enough to keep the data in a field from being changed because the user could click in the field and change the data.

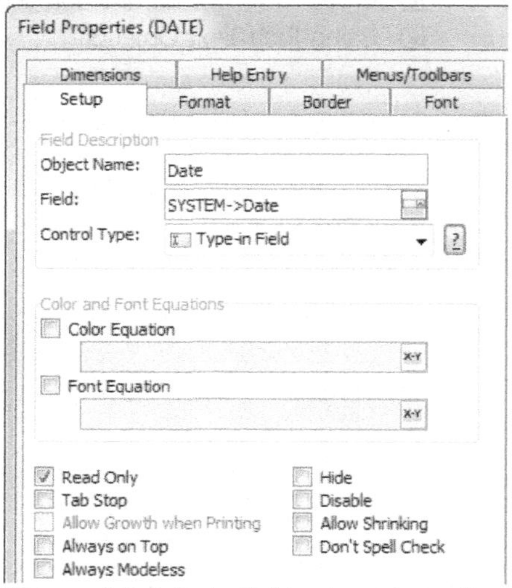

Figure 10-1 Date field setup properties

4. Delete the heading for the date field.

   Save the changes.

   When previewed, the form should look like the one shown in Figure 10-2.

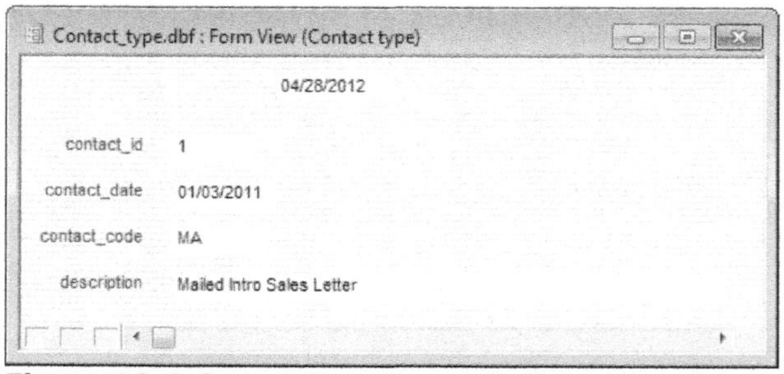

Figure 10-2 Contact Type form with the system date field

Exercise 10.2: Create A Form With An Embedded Browse

In Chapter 8, you learned that you could create a form that is based on a set. In this exercise you will use the Form Genie to create a form that displays customers and their orders. You will also learn how to embed a browse in a form using a genie and how to make the entire form read-only.

1. Open the Form Genie and select the Customers-orders set, then click Next.

2. Select the Custom Form option, then click Next.

3. Add the following fields to the form: Company Name, First Name, Last Name, Address, City, State, Zip Code and Note.

4. Click on the **<BROWSE ORDERS>** option at the bottom of the Available Fields list and add it to the Fields on Form list, as shown in Figure 10-3.

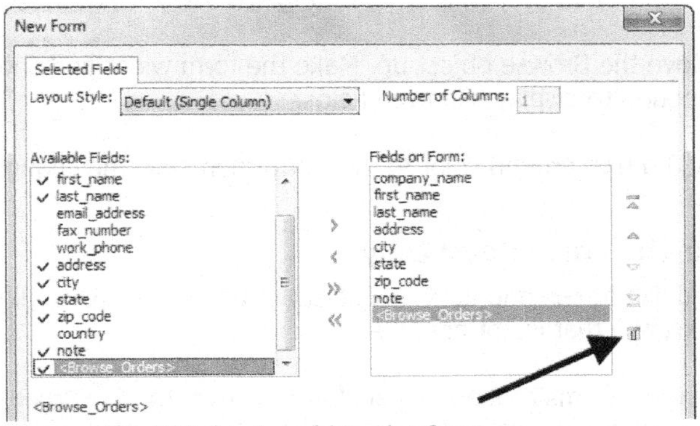

Figure 10-3 Fields to add to the form

Select The Fields For The Browse

By default, all fields in the child table will be added to the browse. The **CHOOSE COLUMNS** button, illustrated above in Figure 10-3, is used to select the fields and the order that they will appear in from left to right in the browse.

1. Click the Choose Columns button.

2. Remove the Customer ID and ShipVia ID fields from the Columns in Browse list.

3. Change the order of the fields in the Columns in Browse list to the order shown in Figure 10-4, then click OK.

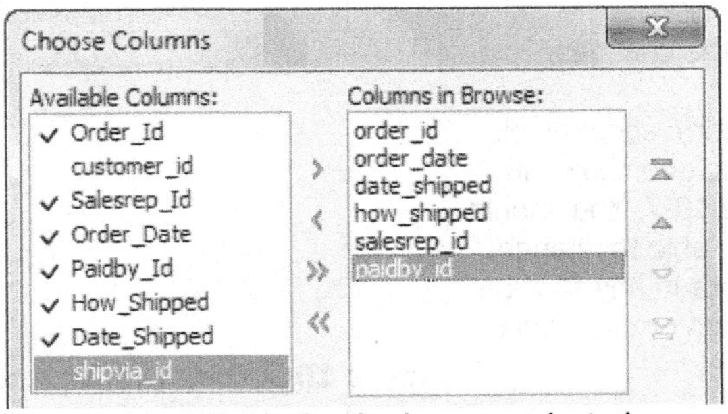

Figure 10-4 Fields for the browse selected

4. Click Finish. Save the form as `Customers Orders`.

Modify The Forms Layout

1. Delete all of the field headings, except for the Note field.

2. Make the Note field smaller, then change the heading to `Comments`.

3. Rearrange the fields so that they look like the form shown in Figure 10-5.

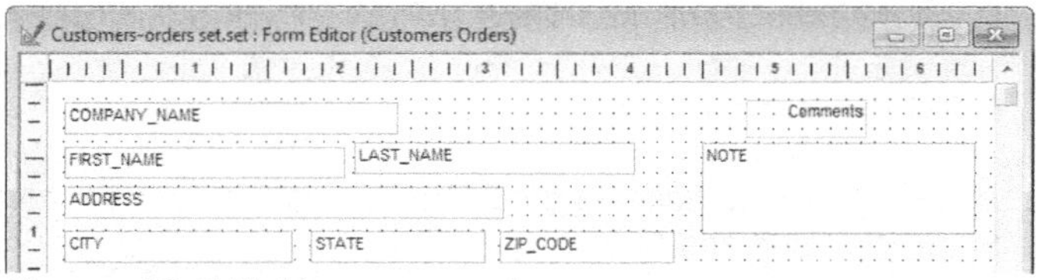

Figure 10-5 Fields rearranged

4. Move the Browse object up. Make the form wider and shorter. Make the Browse object wide enough to display all of the fields.

5. Add a background color to the form, then save the changes.

Make The Form Read Only

I would like to see one option to select to be able to make all fields and objects read only, but currently that is not possible.

1. On the Forms Properties panel, scroll down to the **RESTRICTIONS** section, then check the following options shown in Figure 10-6: Browse, Change, Delete, Edit and Enter.

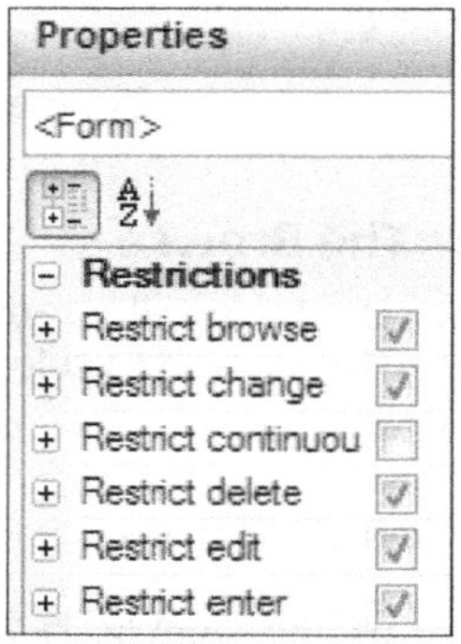

Figure 10-6 Restrictions options

2. Save the changes.

   Your form should look like the one shown in Figure 10-7. You should not be able to change the data in any field on the form or embedded browse.

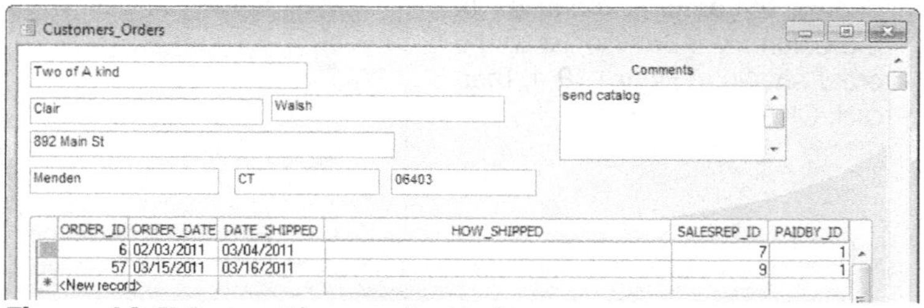

Figure 10-7 Form with an embedded browse

Browse Object Properties Dialog Box

You learned about the Browse Properties dialog box, which is used for a stand alone browse. The form that you just created has an **EMBEDDED BROWSE**. Like other objects on a form, an embedded browse has its own set of properties. Many of the options on this dialog box are the same as the ones on the Browse Properties and Column Properties dialog boxes that were covered in Chapter 9.

To open this dialog box, click on the embedded browse ⇒ Objects menu ⇒ Properties.

Setup Tab

The options shown in Figure 10-8 are used to select general options for the embedded browse. The options specific to an embedded browse are explained on Table 10-1.

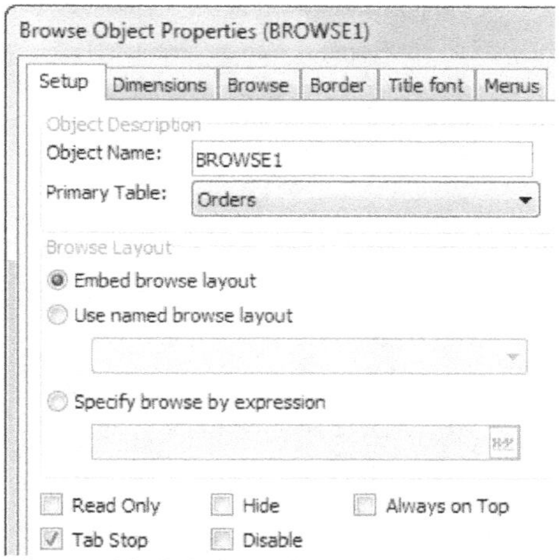

Figure 10-8 Setup tab

Option	Description
Primary Table	The drop-down list contains all of the tables bound to the form. The table displayed by default, is the primary table.
Embedded browse layout	This is the default option because the selected browse is embedded.
Use named browse layout	If you do not want to use the embedded browse, select this option, then open the drop-down list and select the browse that you want to use. The browse forms in the drop-down list were created using the primary table. You may get unexpected results if the browse that you select was not created from the set that the form was created from.
Specify browse by expression	Select this option if you want to create an expression to select the fields that will be displayed in the browse.
Hide	Displays or hides the embedded browse.
Disable	Enables or disables the embedded browse.
Always on Top	If checked, no other object on the form will overlap the embedded browse.

Table 10-1 Setup tab options explained

Dimensions Tab

[See Chapter 8, Field Properties Dialog Box, Dimensions Tab]

Browse Tab

The options shown in Figure 10-9 are used to change the appearance or color of different parts of the embedded browse. In addition to the options that are the same as the stand alone browse, the embedded browse also has the following appearance options. [See Chapter 9, Browse Properties Dialog Box, Browse Tab]

The **VERTICAL SCROLLBAR** and **HORIZONTAL SCROLLBAR** options are used to display or hide the scrollbars.

If checked, the **HIGHLIGHT ROW** option allows the row that is clicked on to automatically be highlighted. To use this option, the embedded browse must be set to read only.

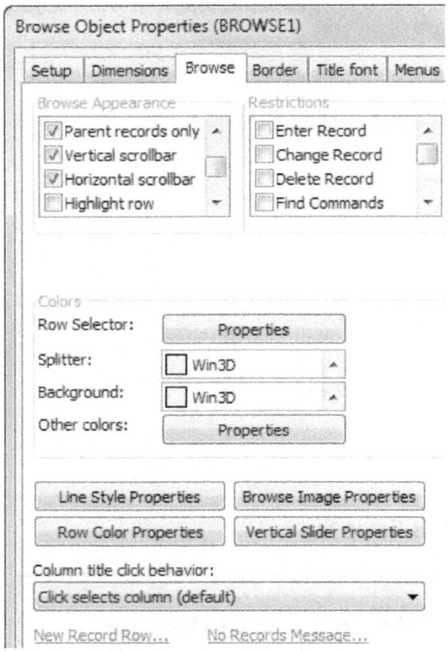

Figure 10-9 Browse tab

Border Tab

[See Chapter 8, Field Properties Dialog Box, Border Tab]

Title Font Tab

[See Chapter 9, Browse Properties Dialog Box, Title Font Tab]

Menus Tab

[See Chapter 8, Field Properties Dialog Box, Menus/Toolbars Tab]

Exercise 10.3: Create A Form With Multiple Embedded Browses

In the previous exercise you learned how to embed a browse in a form. There will probably be times when you need to have more than one embedded browse on a form. An example would be if you needed to see customers, their orders and items for each order. In this exercise you will modify the set used in Exercise 10.2 to add the order detail table and add referential integrity to the set.

Modify The Set

1. Open the Customers Orders set.
2. Click on the arrow on the Orders table and select Add new child.
3. Create a one-to-many link for the Order Detail table. Link the tables on the Order ID field.
4. On the Set Editor, enable the Referential integrity cascade changes/deletes option, for both links.

5. Save the set as `Customers orders and details set.`

   The set should look like the one shown in Figure 10-10.

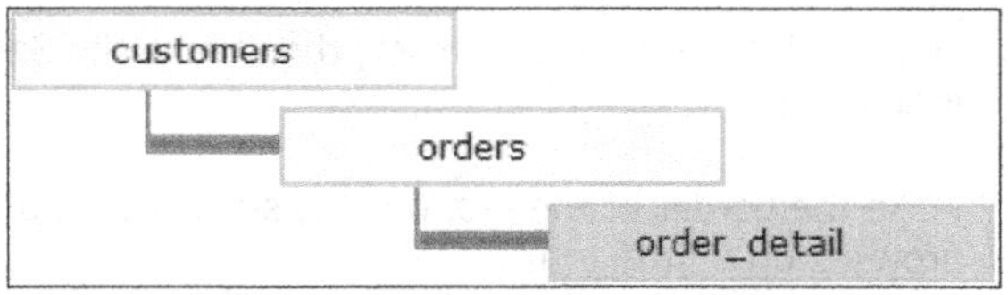

Figure 10-10 Customers orders and details set

Create A Form With Two Embedded Browses

1. On the Forms tab, click the New button. Select the set that you just created, then click Next.
2. Select the Custom Form option, then click Next.
3. Add the following fields from the Customer table to the Fields on Form list: Customer ID, Company Name, First Name, Last Name and State.
4. Scroll down to the bottom of the Available Fields list.

   You should see a browse for the Orders and Order Detail tables.

   Add both of them to the Fields on Form list, as shown in Figure 10-11.

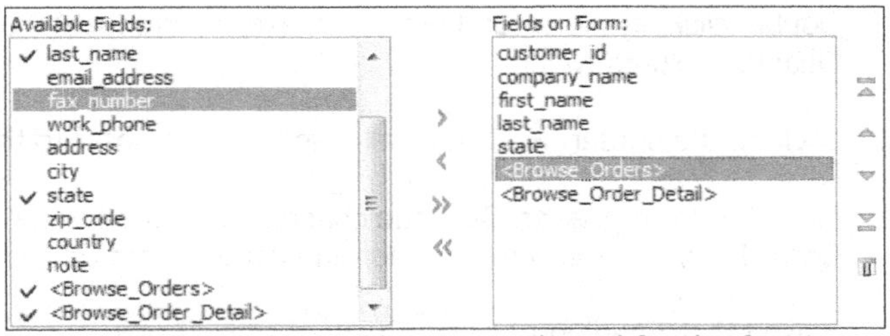

Figure 10-11 Fields and browses selected for the form

5. Click on the Orders Browse. Click the Choose Columns button. Remove the How Shipped field from the Columns in Browse list.
6. Click Finish. Save the form as `Customer Order Details.`

Modify The Forms Layout

Aligning Multiple Objects
I selected all of the field headings thinking that I could align them at the same time. I tried the Arrange ⇒ Align Positions option and on the Properties panel, I tried the Layout Align options. Neither option changed the alignment for all of the selected field headings at one time, so I had to change them one by one.

1. Left align all of the field headings at the top of the form.
2. Rearrange the fields at the top of the form to look like the layout shown in Figure 10-12.

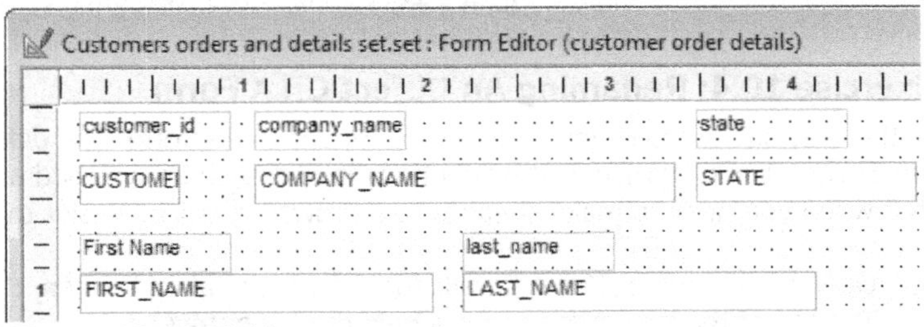

Figure 10-12 Fields rearranged

3. Double-click on the first browse, then make the Salesrep ID and Paid By ID columns smaller, if necessary.

4. Make the border of the first browse smaller so that it is closer to the columns, then move both browses up on the form.

Add A Field To An Embedded Browse

In this part of the exercise you will add a field to the second browse.

1. Scroll down the Drag Drop list. Drag the Order ID field in the Order Detail table to the beginning of the second browse.

2. On the Drop Fields dialog box, select the **VALUE IN THE FIELD** option if it is not already selected, then click OK.

3. Double-click on the second browse, make the Product ID column smaller, then make the Quantity column wider.

4. Click on the border. Make it smaller so that it is closer to the columns.

5. Make the form smaller. Save the changes. If you view the record for Customer ID 2 and select Order ID 9, you will see the order and detail records shown in Figure 10-13.

The reason that I had you display the ID fields on the form is because I wanted you to be able to see that the records from the Orders table belong to the customer displayed at the top of the form and that the order detail records belong to the order that is selected in the first browse.

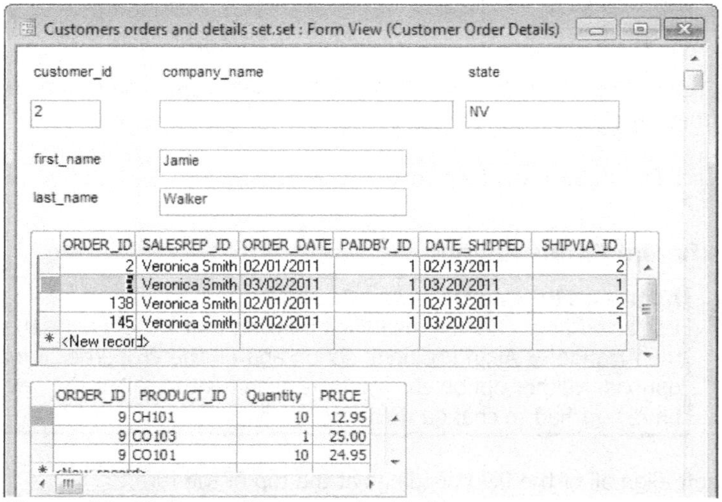

Figure 10-13 Form with two embedded browses

Exercise 10.4: Renaming An Object On A Form

In the previous exercise you added two browses to the form. The default names for these browses are Browse 1 and Browse 2. It would be helpful if each browse had a more meaningful name, so that when you need to make changes to a browse, it will be easier to know which browse is which.

1. Open the Customer Order Details form if it is not already open, then click on the first browse. The top of the Properties panel should display **BROWSE 1**.

2. Scroll down the Properties panel list to the MISC section. On the second Name option, you should see Browse 1. Change this entry to `OrdersBrowse`.

3. Change the same field for the second browse to `OrderDetailBrowse`, as shown in Figure 10-14.

   Save the changes.

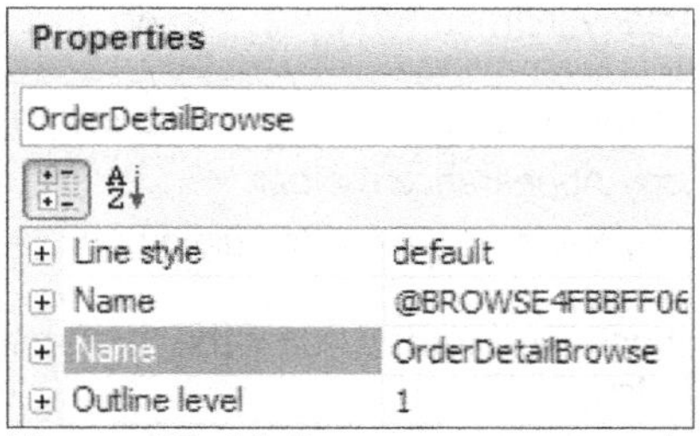

Figure 10-14 Browse name property changed

Exercise 10.5: Add A Text Object To A Form

There will be times when you need to add content to a form that is not in a field. One way to do this is to add a text object to the form and add content to it. An example is if you want to display the name of the form on the form, which is what you will learn how to do in this exercise.

1. Open the Products form, then move all of the fields down about a half an inch.

2. Object ⇒ New. Scroll down the list, select the Text option, then click OK.

3. Select the Heading option shown in Figure 10-15, then click OK.

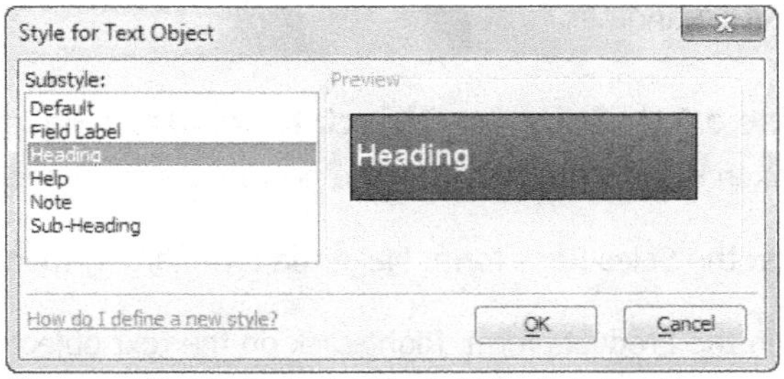

Figure 10-15 Style for Text Object dialog box

4. Make the text object as wide as the fields are spread out.

5. Double-click in the Text box. The green background should have disappeared. Type `Products Form`.

6. Open the Properties dialog box. On the Alignment tab, select Center in the Horizontal list. Click OK.

7. Preview the form.

   It should look like the one shown in Figure 10-16.

   Save the changes.

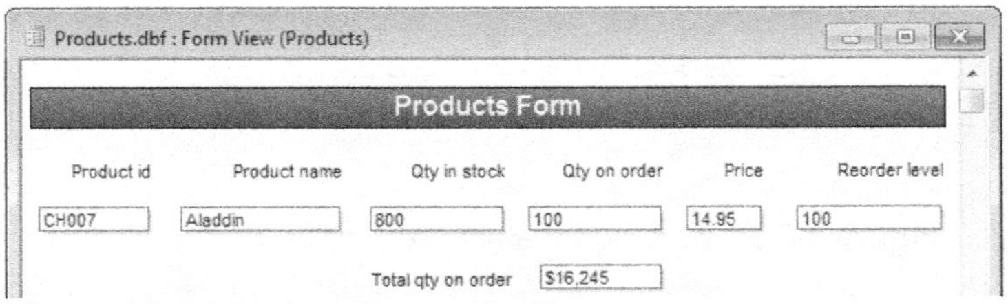

Figure 10-16 Products form with title

Copy Formatting

There may be times when you need to apply the same formatting to some or all of the other objects on the form. You already learned three ways to do this, as explained below.

① Select all of the objects first, then make the changes.
② Use the Copy Appearance toolbar.
③ Use the Copy Selected Properties dialog box.

There is another option if you want to copy the formatting options to all other objects of the same type, as explained below.

1. Add the formatting that you want to copy to one object.
2. Right-click on the object that has the formatting that you want to copy and select **COPY APPEARANCE.**
3. Right-click on the object that you want to apply the formatting to and select **PASTE APPEARANCE.**

Copy And Paste Objects From One Form To Another

Similar to pasting formatting options to other objects, objects can be copied from one form to another. This feature is helpful when you have created formatting for an object and want to use the object on another form.

Exercise 10.6: Copy An Object To Another Form

In this exercise you will copy a text object in one form and paste it in another form.

1. Open the Sales Reps form. Make the form larger, then move the fields down.
2. Open the Products form. Right-click on the text object at the top of the form and select Copy.
3. Display the Sales Reps form. Right-click on the form and select Paste.
4. You will see the text object at the top of the Sales Reps form. Save the Sales Reps form as `Pasted Text Object`.

> If a field that you are pasting is not in the table or set of the form that you are pasting into, Alpha Five will display a message similar to the one shown in Figure 10-17 when you preview the form.

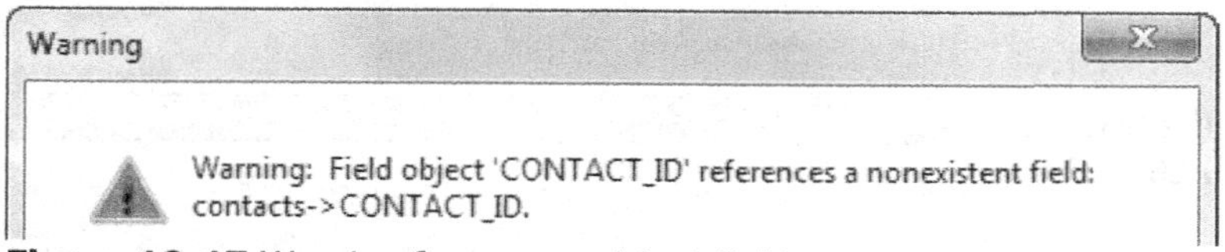
Warning
Warning: Field object 'CONTACT_ID' references a nonexistent field:
contacts->CONTACT_ID.

Figure 10-17 Warning for a non existent field

Copy A Browse To Another Form

In this part of the exercise you will copy and paste a browse from one form to another form.

1. Open the Customer Order Details form, then right-click on the OrderDetail browse and select Copy.
2. Open the Customers Orders form. Paste the browse at the bottom of the form.
3. Click OK when you see the warning message. The reason that you see the message is because the fields in the browse that you pasted are not part of the set that the form is based on. To fix this, you would have to add the Order Detail table to the set.
4. Save the form as `Browse copied to a form`.

Using Long Forms

Some forms that you create will have a lot of fields and other objects. If all of the objects are placed straight down the left column, the user may have to scroll down to see and use the objects at the bottom of the form. If the form also has a header and footer section, the form will be even longer. There may also be a need to keep some objects displayed at the top of the form when you scroll down. Chapter 7 covered the header and footer options on the rulers. They are the options that control the scrolling.

Exercise 10.7: Use The Header And Footer Options On The Ruler

In this exercise you will create a long form, add a text object to the top of the form and select some fields that will always be displayed on the screen, even when you scroll to the bottom of the form.

An Easy Way To Create A Browse Form

So far, all of the forms that you have created used the Form Genie. There is an easier way.

1. On the Tables/Sets tab, select the Customers table. Click the View button, then select the Default Form option.
2. Switch to design mode. Make the form longer, then move all of the fields down about half an inch.
3. Save the form as `Nonscrollable header`. To me, this is much easier then using the Form Genie to create a basic form. What do you think?
4. Add a text object to the top of the form. Type `Customer Form With A Nonscrollable Region`, then format the text object however you want.

Create The Non Scrollable Region

This functionality will remind you of the freeze panes feature in Excel.

1. Right-click on the left ruler and select Header.

   On the left ruler you will see an arrow with a dotted line across the form, as illustrated in Figure 10-18.

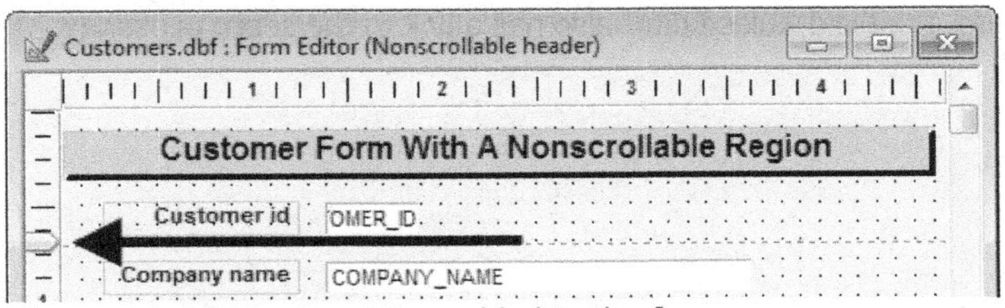

Figure 10-18 Header option added to the form

2. Drag the arrow down until the dotted line is below the Company Name field.

3. Make the form shorter, so that the last field showing is the Address field. Save the changes.

4. Preview the form.

   Scroll down until the Note field is visible. You should still see the text object, Customer ID and Company Name fields, as shown in Figure 10-19.

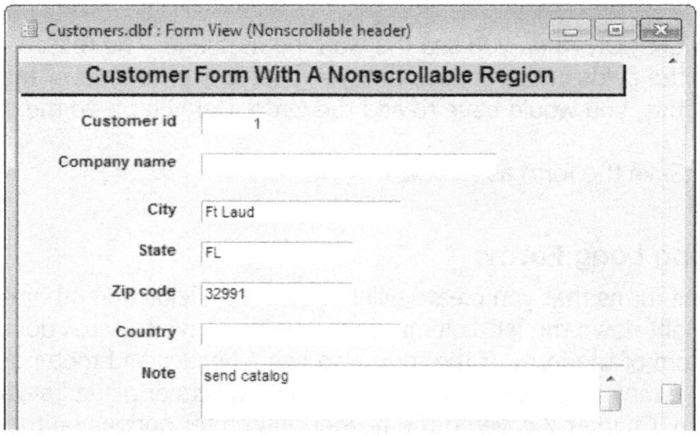

Figure 10-19 Form with nonscrollable region

Form Level Field Rules

In Chapter 4 you learned how to create table level field rules, which are used for all layouts based on the table. While it is very possible that you may not have an immediate need to create field rules at the form level, keep the following in mind. Two rules of thumb that I use when I have to decide where to create a field rule is:

① Does the rule have anything to do with data entry, especially for a required field?
② Does the rule always have to be applied every place the field is used?

If the answer to either of these questions is yes, then I create the rule at the table level. If the rule is only needed for a specific case or if the rule will use a variable, the rule should be created at the form level. Before creating a form level field rule, make sure that there isn't a property that has the functionality that you need. Even though variables are referred to as fields, the difference is that variables are not stored in a table, the value of a variable is often displayed on a layout.

For the most part, table field rules override form level field rules. An exception that I noticed is using decimals in a numeric field. Decimal options set on the **OBJECT PROPERTIES DIALOG BOX** or on the Properties panel, override decimal rules created at the table level in the form. Object Properties also take precedence with **CASE CONVERSION**.

Edit Field Rules From The Form

Not surprisingly, field rules created at the form level have their own editor. The Field Rules Editor dialog box contains some options that the Field Rules dialog box has. In addition to form level field rules, the Field Rules Editor also has a link to the **SPEED GLOSSARY**.

Field Rules Editor

This dialog box is opened from a form in design mode.

On the right side of Figure 10-20 are all of the fields displayed on the form.

Before creating a field rule, make sure that the field that you want to create the rule for is selected. Fields in bold indicate that the field has a form level field rule.

The options on the right side of the dialog box are the rules that can be applied to a field.

Just like table level field rules, form level field rules can only be applied one field at a time, even if multiple fields are selected prior to opening the dialog box.

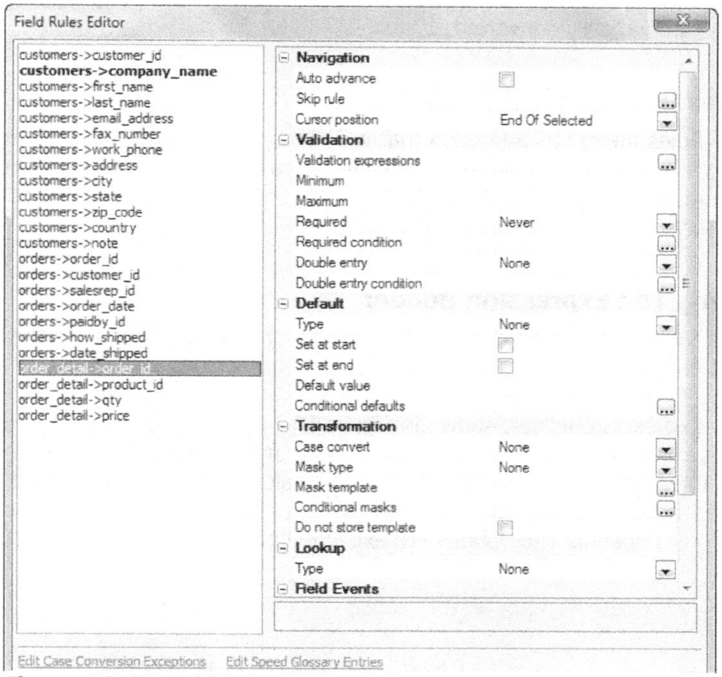

Figure 10-20 Field Rules Editor dialog box

Indicating That Table Level Field Rules Exist

As you saw in Chapter 4, it is not difficult to create a lot of field rules for a table. I don't know about you, but I do not remember all of the field rules that were created in that chapter do you? If this application was going into production, Chapter 4 would have been much longer <smile>. This is why I think that it would be very helpful if these two field rules dialog boxes were connected, so that we could see what rules have already been created for the field or even better, if the two dialog boxes were merged into one dialog box.

While the Field Rules and Field Rules Editor dialog boxes visually display whether or not field rules of that type have been created, there is no cross reference of the rules between the dialog boxes. If there was, we could easily tell what rules and at what level, each field in each table has. Trust me, it is not hard to create a table level field rule and then create a form level field rule and can't figure out why the form level field rule is not working properly.

Exercise 10.8: Create Form Level Formatting Field Rules

In this exercise you will create a rule to force a field to be all capital letters.

1. Open the Customer Order Details form.

2. Right-click on the Company Name field and select Edit Rules for Company Name.

3. Open the Transformation **CASE CONVERT** drop-down list and select Upper, then click OK. If you right-click on the Company Name field again in the form, you will see that the Edit Rules option is bold. The bold is used to indicate that the field has a form level field rule.

4. Save the form as `Form level field rule`. From this point on, all company names entered on this form will be in all capital letters. Company names already in the table are not automatically converted.

Reevaluating Field Rules

The Rules menu has an option that will reevaluate certain types of field rules including converting the case of data in fields. If the reevaluate case conversion that you need to complete cannot be accomplished using the Re-evaluate option on the Rules menu, the **CONVERT CASE OF FIELDS OPERATION** has a lot more options.

Using The Expression Builder

This tool has not been discussed, even though you used it in Chapters 4 and 9. The wait is over. It is briefly explained below.

The Expression Builder, shown in Figure 10-21, is used to create calculated and summary fields. These field types cannot have spaces in the field names. The list on the left side of the dialog box are the tools that you can use to create a calculated or summary field. In addition to using the Insert button or the shortcut key shown after each tool to open it, you can also double-click on the option to open it. The options are explained in Table 10-2.

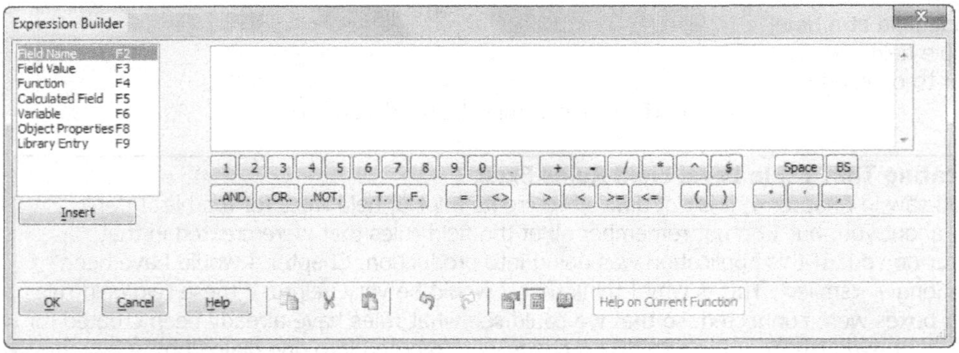

Figure 10-21 Expression Builder

Option	Opens The Dialog Box Shown In . . .
Field Name	Figure 10-22. It displays all of the fields in the table or set.
Field Value	Figure 10-23. It displays all of the values in a field.
Function	Figure 10-24. It is used to select a function to add to the expression.
Calculated Field	Figure 10-25. It lists all of the calculated fields for the layout. It is used to add a calculated field to the expression.
Variable	Figure 10-26. It displays a list of variables associated with the layout. These variables can be used to create the calculated field.
Object Properties	Figure 10-27. It displays all of the objects on the layout and their properties. It will remind you of the Object Explorer.
Library Entry	Figure 10-28. Displays all of the calculated fields associated with the layout. This includes calculated fields that have been created for the database, table, set or global library. Items that are added to the library can be used as often as needed.

Table 10-2 Expression Builder options explained

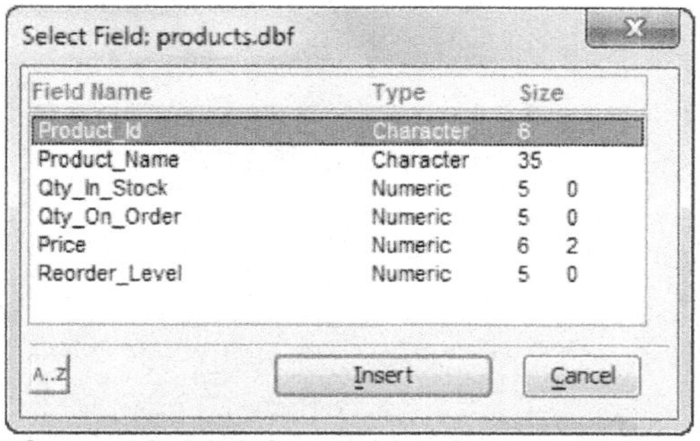

Figure 10-22 Select Field dialog box (Field Name)

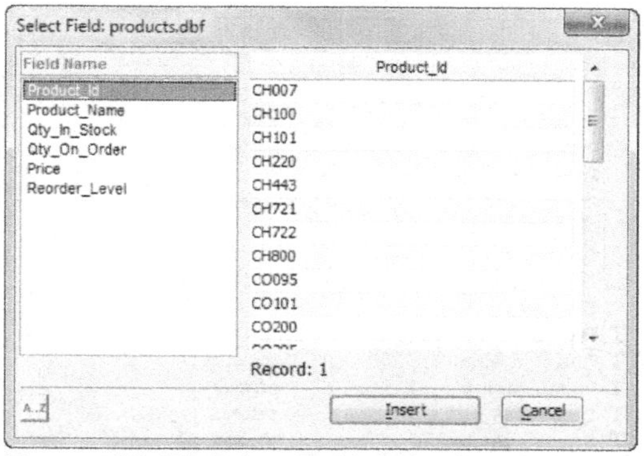

Figure 10-23 Select Field dialog box (Field Value)

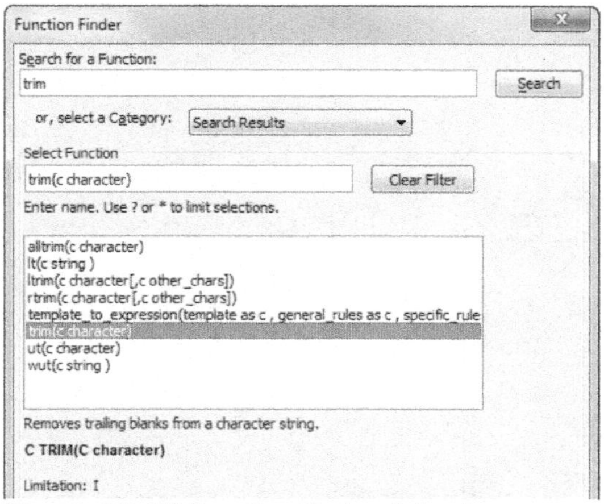

Figure 10-24 Function Finder dialog box

Figure 10-25 Select Calculated Field dialog box

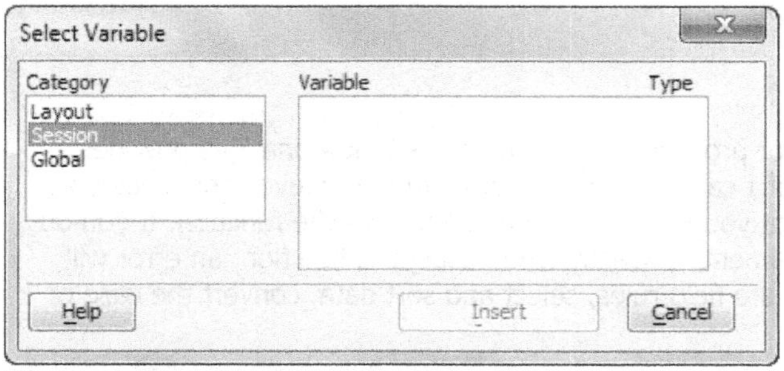

Figure 10-26 Select Variable dialog box

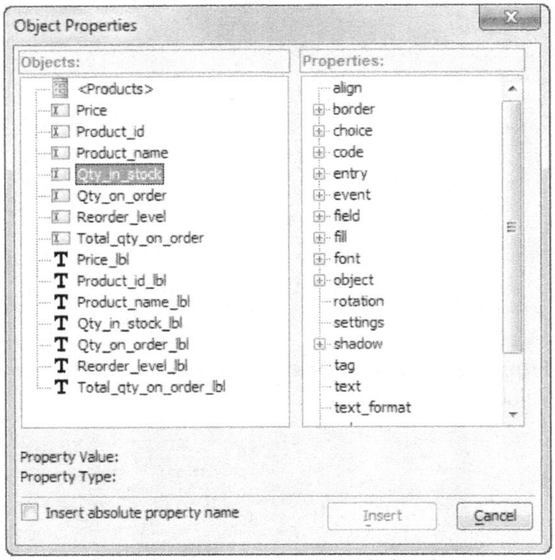

Figure 10-27 Object Properties dialog box

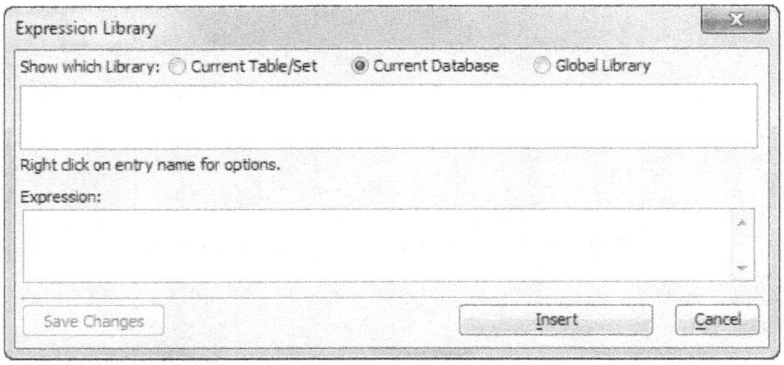

Figure 10-28 Expression Library dialog box

What Are Functions?

Functions are prewritten, built-in formulas or procedures. The functions that Alpha Five provides have been thoroughly tested and from what I can tell, they are error free. However, this does not mean that if there is bad data in a table that you won't have a problem with the function. If you do not follow the syntax rules or fill in the arguments correctly when using the function, an error will be generated. Functions can be used to create field rules, select and sort data, convert the case of data and much more.

Exercise 10.9: Create A Form Level Lookup

In this exercise you will create a basic form for the Contacts table, then add a form level table lookup to the State field.

Add A Table To The Database

Currently, the database does not have a table with the States, so it needs to be added to the database.

1. Right-click on a blank space on the Tables/Sets tab and select Add Table/Set.

2. In the Lookin field, select the CBC APP Data database. Select the States.dbf file, then click OK.

3. The States table should be in the Selected Tables/Sets list. Click OK twice.

Create The Lookup Field

1. Create a basic form for the Contacts table. Save the form as `Form level lookup`.

2. In design mode, open the Field Rules Editor for the State field.

3. In the Lookup section on the right, open the Type drop-down list and select Table.

4. In the Table drop-down list, select the States table.

5. Click the button at the end of the Link field. On the Expression Builder, click the Insert button. Select the State field, then click the Insert field. You should see the word State in the Expression Builder. Click OK.

6. Click the button at the end of the Data field. Add the State field from the list on the left.

> **Edit Table Lookup**
> This dialog box closes un-expectantly. I don't think that this is suppose to happen. If that happens to you, reopen the dialog box.

7. Open the Fill drop-down list on the right and select the State Province field. You should have the options shown in Figure 10-29. Click OK.

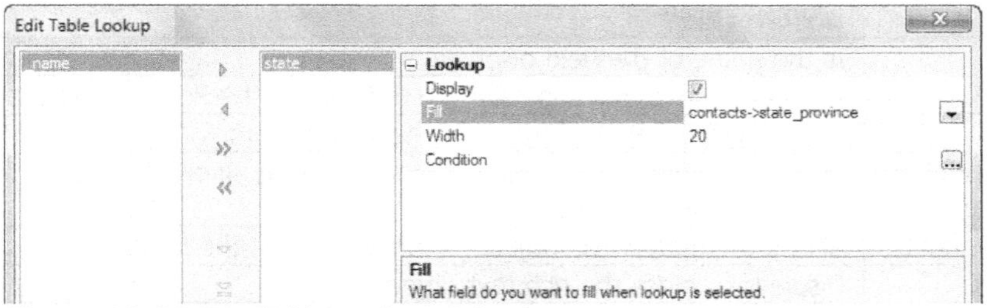

Figure 10-29 Edit Table Lookup dialog box

8. Check the Dropdown option on the Field Rules Editor dialog box.

   You should have the lookup options shown in Figure 10-30.

   Click OK.

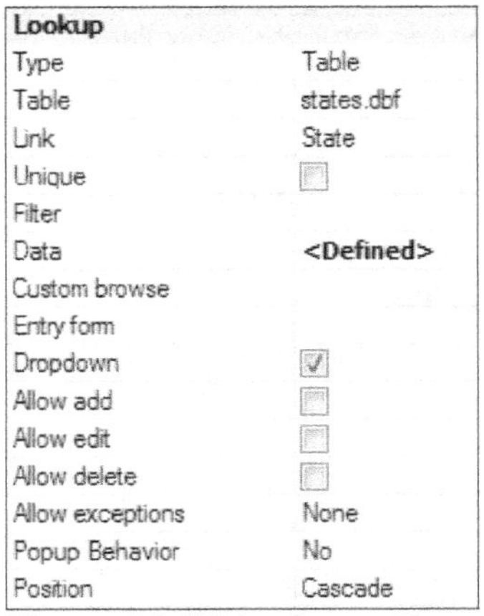

Figure 10-30 Lookup options

9. Save the changes, then test the State drop-down list.

Rich Text Properties Dialog Box

The options on this dialog box are used to customize a rich text object. There is a different Rich Text Properties dialog box for the fields in a rich text object that is covered later in this chapter.

To open this dialog box, right-click on the Rich Text object and select Properties or click on the Rich Text field ⇒ Object ⇒ Properties.

Setup Tab

The options shown in Figure 10-31 are used to select general options for the field. The options are explained in Table 10-3.

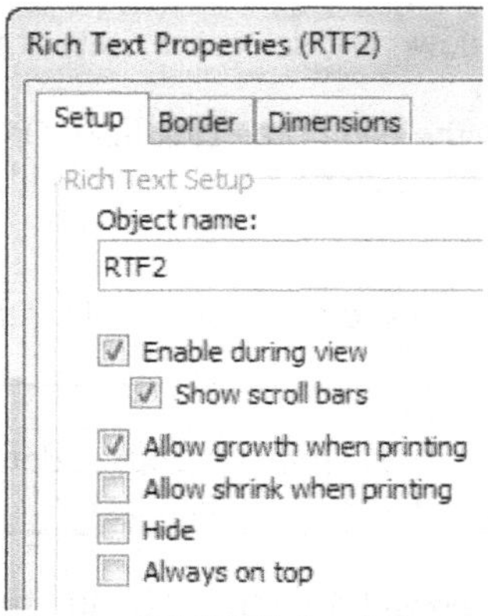

Figure 10-31 Setup tab

Option	Description
Object name	Is the name of the field or object.
Enable during view	If checked, the user can read the RTF text in the Pop up Editor.
Show scroll bars	If checked, the Popup Editor will have scrollbars.
Allow growth when printing	Allows the object to expand if needed, so that all of the data in the object will be printed on the report.
Allow shrink when printing	Allows the data in the object to shrink to fit on the page.
Hide	Displays or hides the rich text object.
Always on top	If checked, no other object on the form will overlap the rich text object.

Table 10-3 Setup tab options explained

Border Tab

[See Chapter 8, Field Properties Dialog Box, Border Tab]

Dimensions Tab

[See Chapter 8, Field Properties Dialog Box, Dimensions Tab]

Text Toolbar (RTF)

The toolbar is helpful when you want to format a Rich Text object on a form. In Chapter 7 you learned about the Text toolbar that is used to format text.

The toolbar shown in Figure 10-32 has more options and is specifically for RTF objects. The additional options are explained below.

Double-clicking on a Rich Text object opens this toolbar.

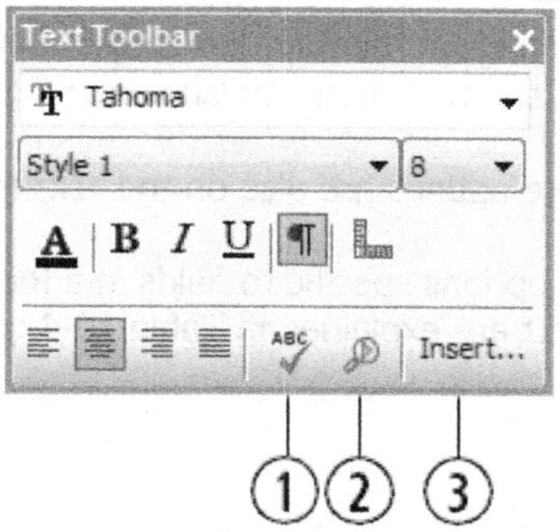

Figure 10-32 Text Toolbar (RTF)

① Opens the dialog box shown in Figure 10-33, which is used to spell check the content in the RTF object.
② Opens the dialog box shown in Figure 10-34, which is used to find or replace text in the RTF object. The options work the same as they do in word processing software that you are probably already familiar with.
③ Opens the toolbar shown in Figure 10-35. The options are used to add more functionality to RTF objects.

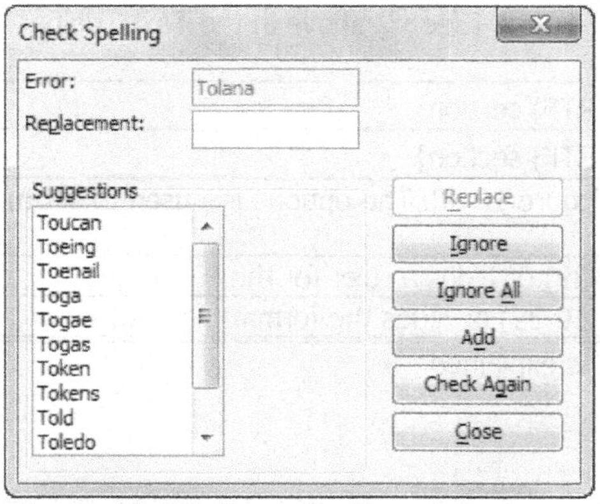

Figure 10-33 Check Spelling dialog box

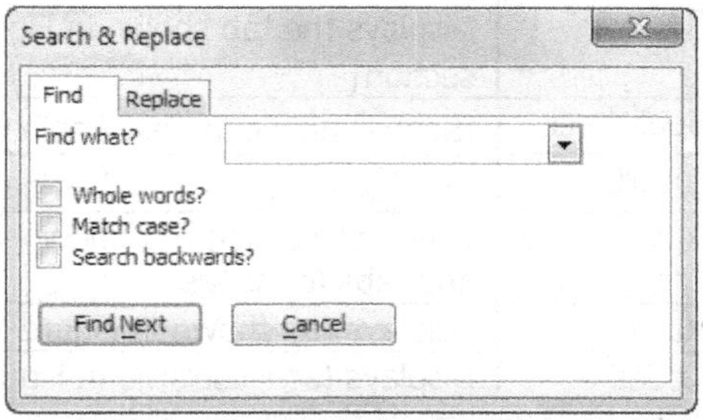

Figure 10-34 Search & Replace dialog box

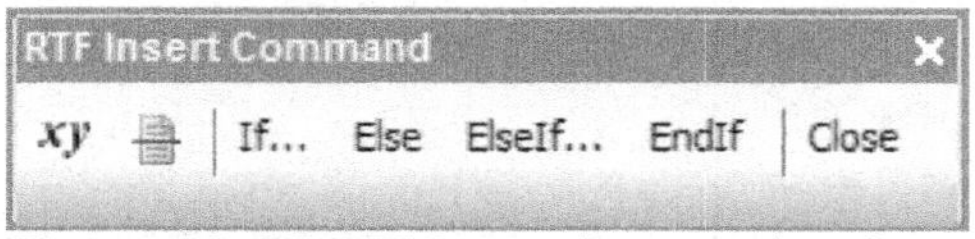

Figure 10-35 RTF Insert Command toolbar

Clicking the Text toolbar button on the design view toolbar does not open this Text (RTF) toolbar. It opens the Text toolbar that you learned about in Chapter 7.

Rich Text Field Shortcut Menu

The fields in the Rich Text object have their own shortcut menu, as shown in Figure 10-36.

These options are also on the **TEXT MENU**.

The options specific to fields in a Rich Text object are explained in Table 10-4.

Figure 10-36 Rich Text field shortcut menu

Option	Description
Properties	[See Rich Text Properties Dialog Box (For Fields), later in this chapter]
Find	[See ② above in Text Toolbar (RTF) section]
Replace	Displays the tab shown in Figure 10-37. [See ② above in the Text Toolbar section]
Spellcheck	[See ① above in Text Toolbar (RTF) section]
Insert	[See ③ above in Text Toolbar (RTF) section]
Rulers	Opens the dialog box shown in Figure 10-38. The options are used to set margins and tabs for styles.
Ruler	Displays (as shown in Figure 10-39) or hides a ruler for the RTF object.
Codes	Displays (as illustrated in Figure 10-39) or hides the formatting marks.

Table 10-4 Rich Text field shortcut menu options explained

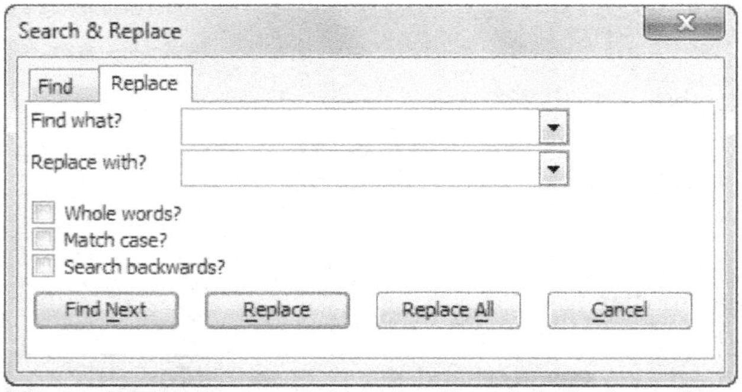

Figure 10-37 Replace tab on the Search & Replace dialog box

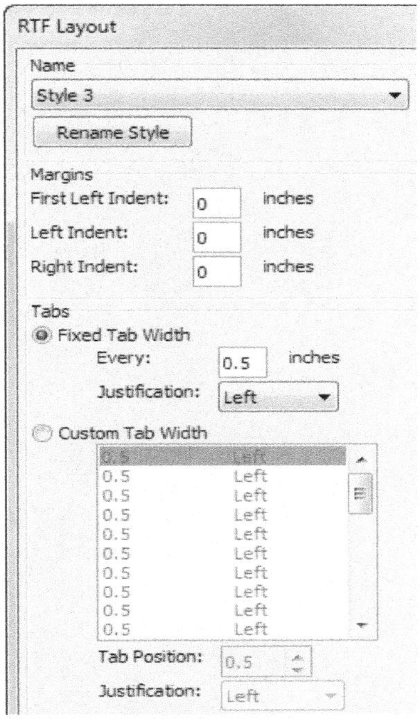

Figure 10-38 RTF Layout dialog box

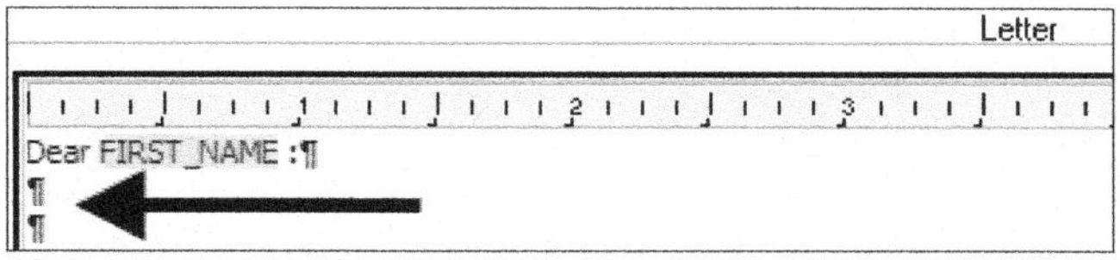

Figure 10-39 Ruler and formatting marks displayed with RTF object

Rich Text Properties Dialog Box (For Fields)

To access the dialog box shown in Figure 10-40, highlight a field (has a shaded gray background) in the Rich Text object, right-click and select Properties.

The options on this dialog box are used to change the font and alignment of the field.

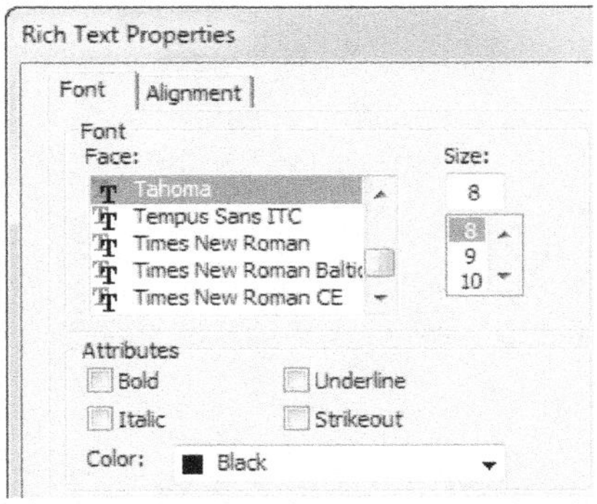

Figure 10-40 Rich Text Properties dialog box (for fields)

Expression Properties Dialog Box

To open the dialog box shown in Figure 10-41, double-click on a field in the Rich Text object.

The options on this dialog box are used to add or change the expression or format style.

The options displayed, depend on the field type.

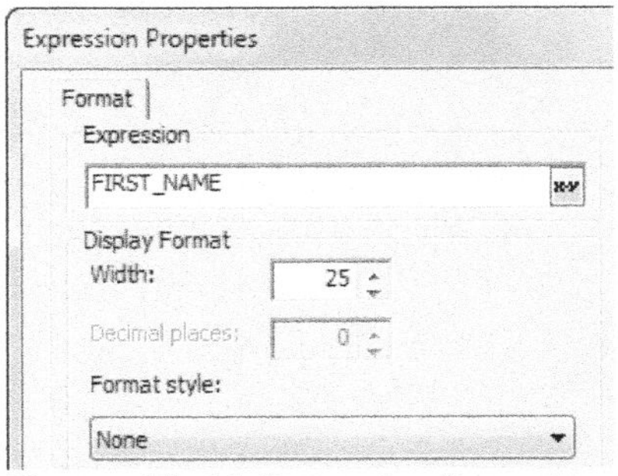

Figure 10-41 Expression Properties dialog box

ENHANCING FORMS PART 2

In this chapter you will learn more techniques including the following, that will help make forms look professional.

☑ Create a form that has tabs
☑ Create a conditional formatting formula
☑ Create and manage styles
☑ Use Smart Fields

CHAPTER 11

Overview

Forms are probably the most used part of an application. Alpha Five provides a lot of options for creating a large variety of forms, which is why at the 11th hour, I decided to include more form features in this book.

Exercise 11.1: Create A Tabbed Form

I personally think that this is a really cool type of form for both entering and viewing data. The form that you will create in this exercise will include a tab for each table in the set. This is not the norm. It is being done for illustration purposes only. The tabbed form will let the user view all of the customers, their orders and each product on each order.

Create The Set

This exercise requires a set with a lot of tables. Instead of creating the set from scratch, you will add tables to an existing set.

1. Save the Customers orders and details set as `Customers tabbed form set`.

2. Add the tables in Table 11-1 to the set.

Link This Table ...	To This Table	Relationship Type	Link Column
Sales Rep	Orders	One-to-many	SalesRep ID/Sales Rep ID
Paid By	Orders	One-to-many	PaidBy ID/Paid By ID
Ship Via	Orders	One-to-many	Shipvia ID/Shipvia ID
Products	Order Detail	One-to-one	Product ID/Product ID

Table 11-1 Tables to add to the set

3. Add cascading referential integrity to the Orders and Order Detail tables.

4. Add the Prevent changes referential integrity option to the Products, Sales Reps, Paid By and Ship Via tables.

   When you are finished, the set should look like the one shown in Figure 11-1.

   Save the changes.

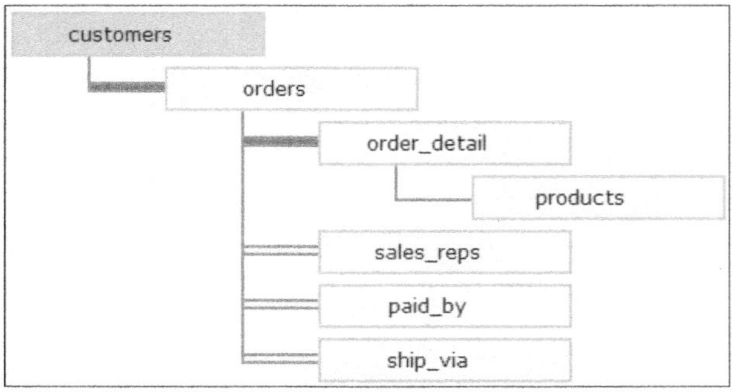

Figure 11-1 Customers tabbed form set

Create The Tabbed Form

1. Open the Form Genie and select the Customers Tabbed form set. Select the Custom Form option, the click Next.

2. Open the Layout Style drop-down list and select Tabbed.

Create The Tabs

By default, Alpha Five only creates two tabs. For this form, six tabs are needed. I prefer to create all of the tabs first, instead of using the default tabs and then adding more. You can decide which method works best for you.

1. Click on the Tabs tab. Select the Page 1 tab and rename it to `Customers`, then click the Change button.

2. Click on the Page 2 tab and rename it to `Orders`.

3. Click on the <New Tab> option. Type `Products`, then click the Add button.

4. Repeat step 3 to create the following tabs: Sales Reps, Ship Via and Paid By.

   You should have the tabs shown in Figure 11-2.

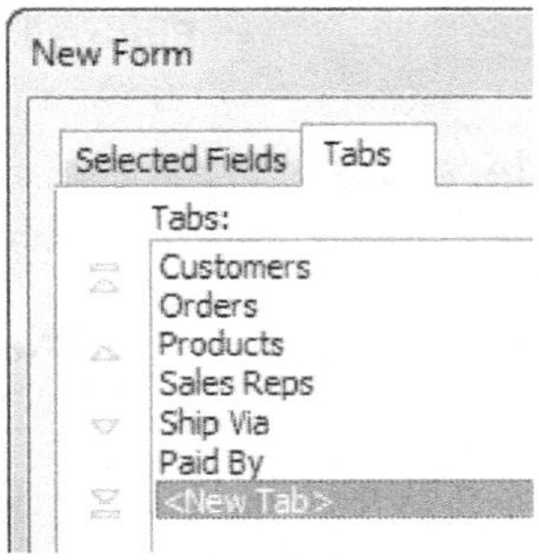

Figure 11-2 Tab names

Add Fields To The Tabs

1. On the Selected Fields tab, add all of the fields in the Customer table, except the Customer ID field to the Customers tab.

2. Add the Browse Orders and Browse Order Detail objects to the Orders tab.

3. Add the remaining browse objects to the corresponding tab.

4. Select the Orders tab, then select the Browse Orders form. Open the Choose Columns dialog box and remove the Salesrep ID, Paidby ID, How Shipped and Shipvia ID fields, then click Finish.

5. Save the form as `Customers tabbed form`.

Modify The Tabbed Form

If you preview the form, you will see that it looks pretty good. There are a few changes that would make the form look better.

Modify The Customers Tab

1. Rearrange the fields to match the layout shown in Figure 11-3.

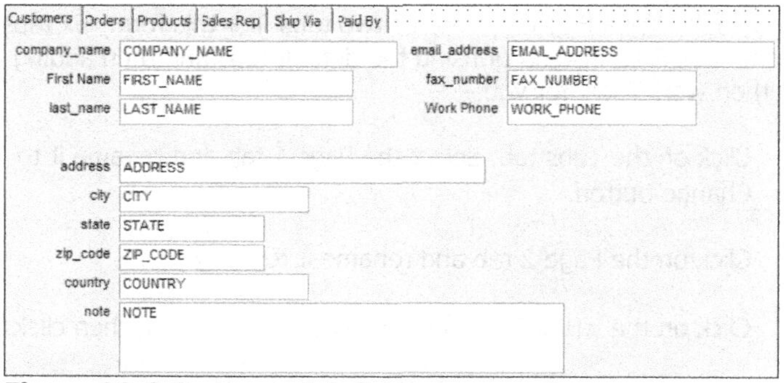

Figure 11-3 Customers tab fields rearranged

Modify The Orders Tab

When you add fields to the browse select the option, Value in the field on the Drop Fields dialog box.

1. Add the Rep First Name and Rep Last Name fields in the Sales Reps table after the Order ID field.
2. Add the Paid By field from the Paid By table after the Order Date field in the browse.
3. Add the How Shipped field from the Ship Via table after the Date Shipped field.
4. Add the Product Name field from the Products table after the Product ID field in the second browse window.
5. Resize the columns in both browse windows as needed, then save the changes.

   Your Orders tab should look similar to the one shown in Figure 11-4.

   To make the Orders tab look more professional, you could change some of the column heading names.

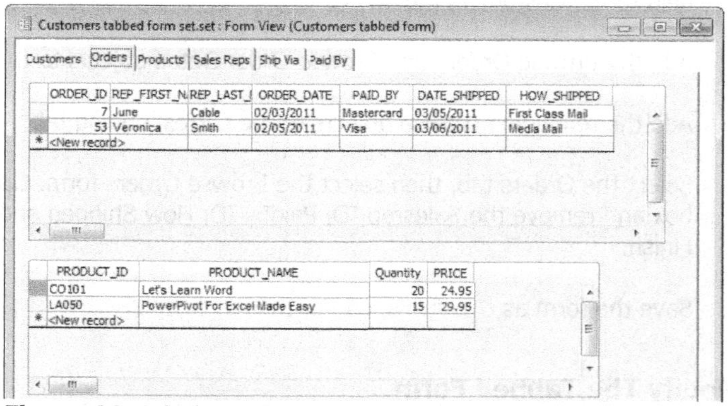

Figure 11-4 Orders tab layout

Tabbed Object Properties Dialog Box

The options on this dialog box are used to customize the tabbed object on the form. Some of the tabs have the same options as other objects.

Setup Tab

The options shown in Figure 11-5 are used to select the general options for the tabbed object. The options are explained in Table 11-2.

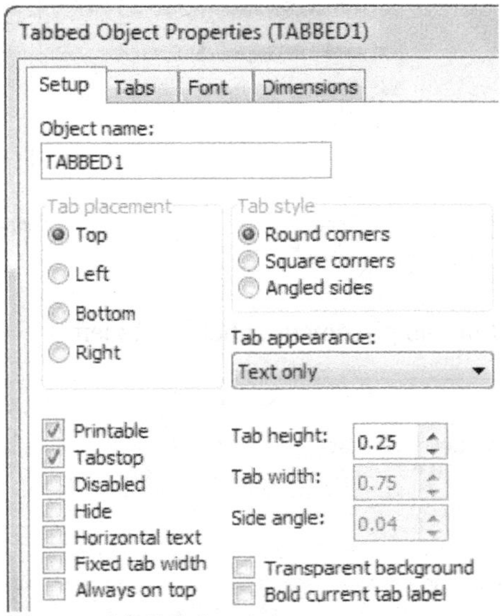

Figure 11-5 Setup tab

Option	Description
Tab placement	The options in this section are used to select where the tabs will be placed. If this option is set to Right or Left, the text on the tabs are displayed vertically, as shown in Figure 11-6.
Tab style	The options in this section are used to select the shape of the tabs.
Tab appearance	The options in this drop-down list are used to select what appears on the tab. In addition to displaying text, images can also be displayed on the tab.
Disabled	If checked, the tabbed control is set to read only and interactive features are disabled.
Horizontal text	If checked and the tab placement is set to Right or Left, the content on the tab is forced to be displayed horizontally, as shown in Figure 11-7. Compare this to Figure 11-6.
Fixed tab width	Must be enabled to use the **TAB WIDTH OPTION**. If enabled, all of the tabs will be the same width as shown in Figure 11-8. Compare this to the tabs shown earlier in Figure 11-4.
Side angle	Is used to slant the tabs.
Transparent background	If checked, the fill color of the tabbed object is set to transparent.
Bold current tab label	If checked, the text on the selected tab is displayed in bold.

Table 11-2 Setup tab options explained

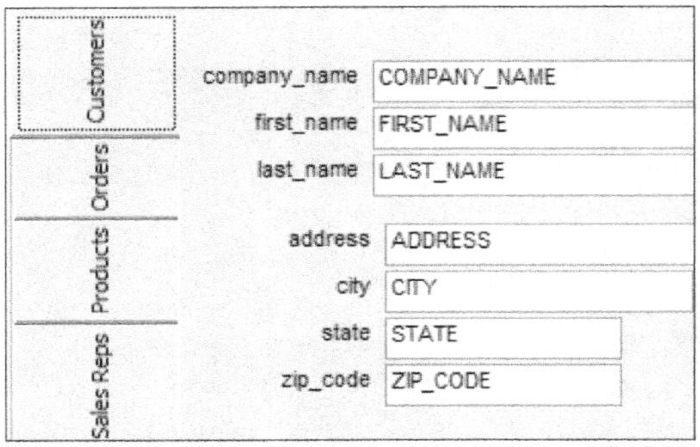

Figure 11-6 Tab placement option set to left

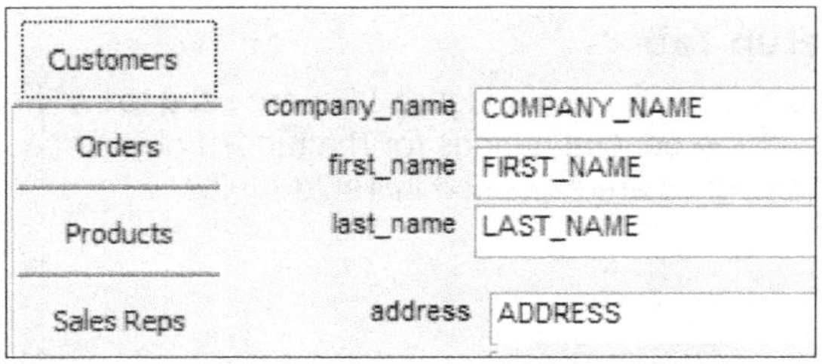

Figure 11-7 Horizontal text option enabled

Figure 11-8 Fixed tab width option enabled

Tabs Tab

The options shown in Figure 11-9 are used to change the order of the tabs, change the text displayed on the tab and select colors for the tabs when they are selected or not selected.

The **CHANGE IMAGE BUTTON** is enabled if the selected tab has an image. Click this button to select a different image.

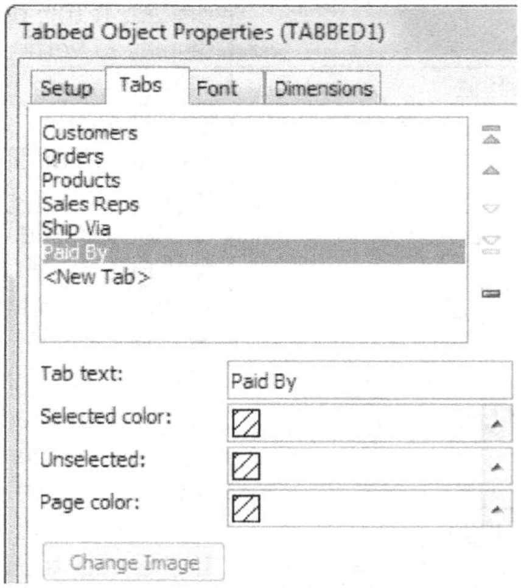

Figure 11-9 Tabs tab

Font Tab

[See Chapter 8, Field Properties Dialog Box, Font Tab]

Dimensions Tab

[See Chapter 8, Field Properties Dialog Box, Dimensions Tab]

Modifying The Tab Object Properties

In this part of the exercise you will change the background color of the tabs and the page. The down side is that the changes have to be done on a tab by tab basis. It would be great if you could apply the same options to more than one tab at the same time.

1. Right-click on the tabbed object and select Properties.

2. On the Setup tab, select the Fixed tab width option, then change the Tab width option to `0.85`.

3. Select the Bold current tab label option.

4. For each tab make the changes in Table 11-3 on the Tabs tab. These are not colors that you would normally put together, but I selected them so that you could easily tell which option displays which color.

Option	Color
Selected color	Pale Blue
Unselected	Light Orange
Page color	Pale Yellow

Table 11-3 Colors for the tabs

5. Save the changes and preview the form.

How The Tabbed Form Works
In this exercise the Customers tab controls the data displayed on the other tabs. When a different customer is selected, the data on the other tabs change to display the data for the new customer.

Restoring A Prior Version Of A Form

Each time that you save a form, a new copy is saved in a backup folder. If you need to go back to a previous version, you can follow the steps below.

What I think would make this feature more helpful is if all of the backup copies of the form displayed a comment. The Comments field displays what was added or changed on the form. The problem is that comments are not added to each version of the form when it is saved.

1. Right-click on the form that you want to restore and select Restore Prior Version.

2. You will see the dialog box shown in Figure 11-10. Select the version of the form that you want to restore. The options are explained below.

RESTORE TO DIFFERENT NAME Select this option if you know that you do not want to over write the current version of the form.

OPEN FOLDER IN EXPLORER This link opens the folder that has all of the previous versions of the form. Each version of the form is stored in its own zip file.

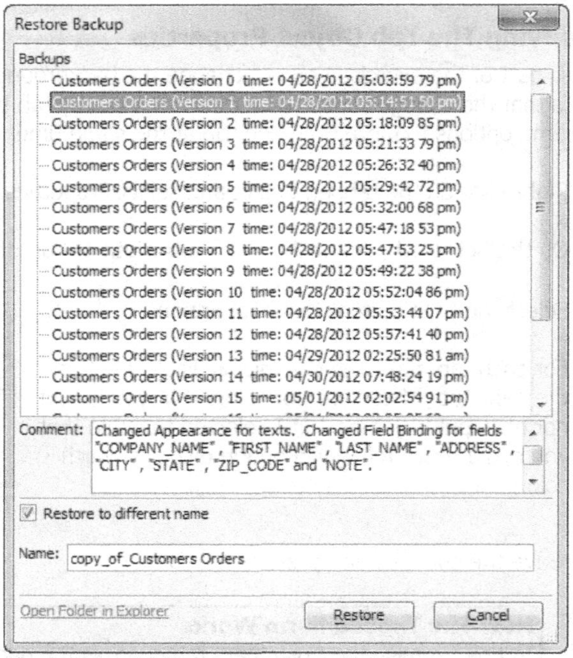

Figure 11-10 Restore Backup dialog box

> **Prior Form Versions Zip Files**
> You can delete these zip files if you know that you will not want to restore the form. It is probably a good idea to delete the majority of these files, once the application is finished. While the file size of a single zip file is not large, if the application has a lot of forms, the overall file size of all of the zip files can be substantial.

3. Decide whether or not you want to restore the form with a different name. If so, type in the new name for the form.

4. Click the Restore button. The form will be restored and available on the Forms tab.

Setting The Forms Tab Order

The tab order is the field to field order on the form that the tab key follows when pressed.
By default, the tab order is the order that the fields are placed on the form. Sometimes the default order will be what you need. If not, there are two ways to change the tab order. Both options can be accessed from the Arrange menu, as explained below.

① **BY EXAMPLE** This option is the easiest to use in my opinion because you click on the tab order buttons in the order that you want the tab key to follow. When using this option, you should only click on fields that will be used for data entry. That means that fields like ID fields that are set to auto increment should not be clicked on when setting up the tab stops. This option can also be accessed from the Arrange toolbar.

② **BY TABLE** Opens the dialog box shown in Figure 11-11. You have to put the fields and browses in the correct order on this dialog box.

As shown, the two browses are at the top of the form, which means that when the form is first opened, the cursor would automatically be placed in the OrdersBrowse, instead of the fields at the top of the form. This probably is not what you want to have happen.

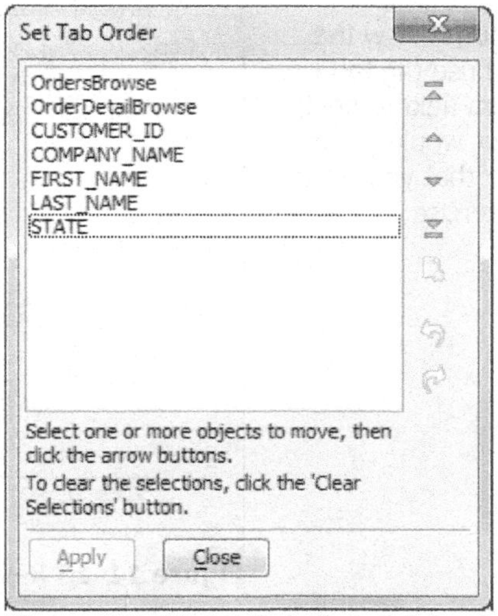

Figure 11-11 Set Tab Order dialog box

Exercise 11.2: Change The Tab Order

In this exercise you will learn how to use the By Example option to set the tab order for the form.

1. Open the Customer Order Details form.

2. Arrange ⇒ Set Tab Order ⇒ Set Tab Order by example. When you see the Setting Tab Order message, click Close.

As shown by the tab stop numbers in Figure 11-12, the two browses are currently set as the first two tab stops. They should be last during data entry.

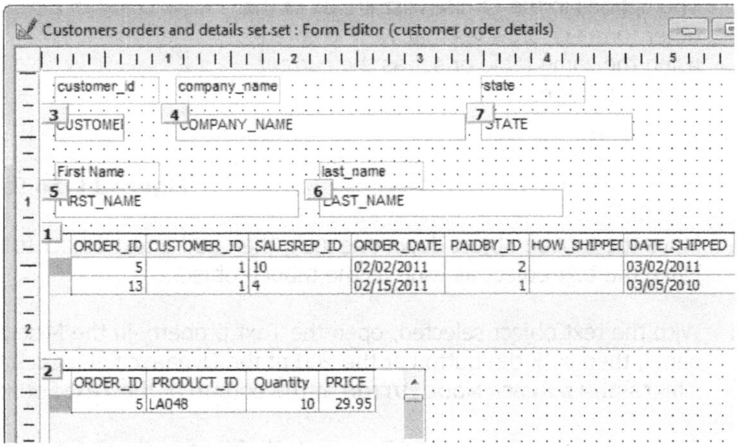

Figure 11-12 Default tab order

3. Click on the fields in this order: Customer Name, First Name, Last Name, State, Orders Browse and Order Detail browse.

4. The tab stops should be numbered as shown in Figure 11-13. The reason that you did not click on the Customer ID field is because the field is set to auto increment and the user will not be entering data in the field. Save the changes.

When you preview the form and use the tab key to go from field to field, the cursor would go in the order that you set up in this exercise.

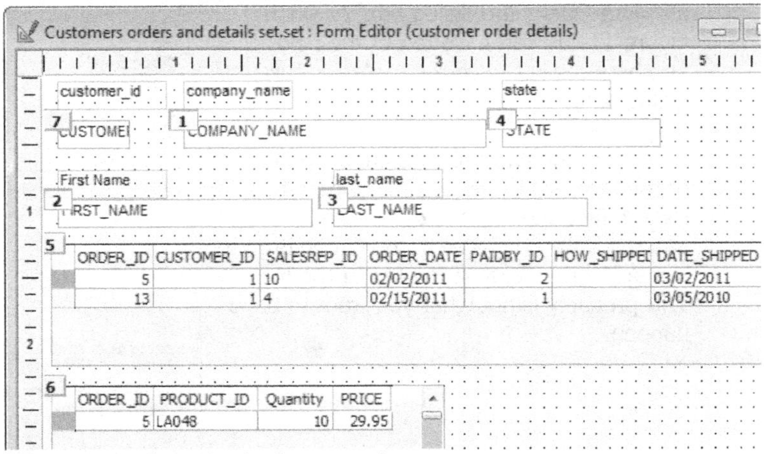

Figure 11-13 Revised tab stop order

Exercise 11.3: Using The Dynamic Property Option

The dynamic option on the Properties panel can be used to display data. In this exercise you will display the customers name and company at the top of the form.

1. Save the Customers tabbed form as `Display customer name.`

   The dialog box shown in Figure 11-14 is used to type in a new name for an existing form. The options in the Choices list are all of the other forms or browses that were created using the same table or set as the current form or browse.

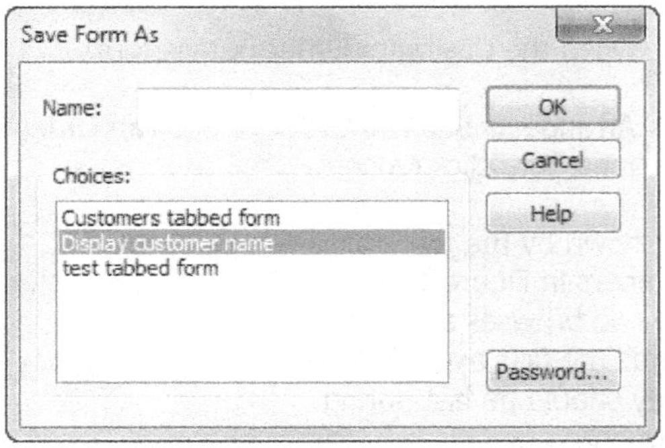

Figure 11-14 Save Form As dialog box

2. Move the tabbed object down one inch, then add a text object to the top of the form. Make the text object as wide as the tabbed object.

3. With the text object selected, open the Text property in the Misc section of the Properties panel, then click the button at the end of the Dynamic field. Click the **SWITCH FROM GENIE TO EXPRESSION BUILDER MODE BUTTON** at the bottom of the Text Equation Genie, then click Yes.

4. Create the formula shown in Figure 11-15. The **TRIM FUNCTION** removes the spaces from the end of the field.

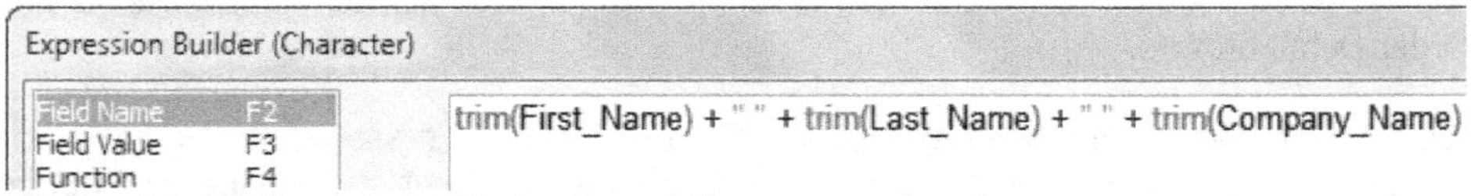

Figure 11-15 Formula to display the customers name and company

5. Change the following properties for the text object: Font size 14, Bold, Center alignment, Fill style solid and Color Light orange.

6. When you preview the form, click on the Orders tab.

   Click the Next button until you see the orders for Stuart Thomas, as shown in Figure 11-16.

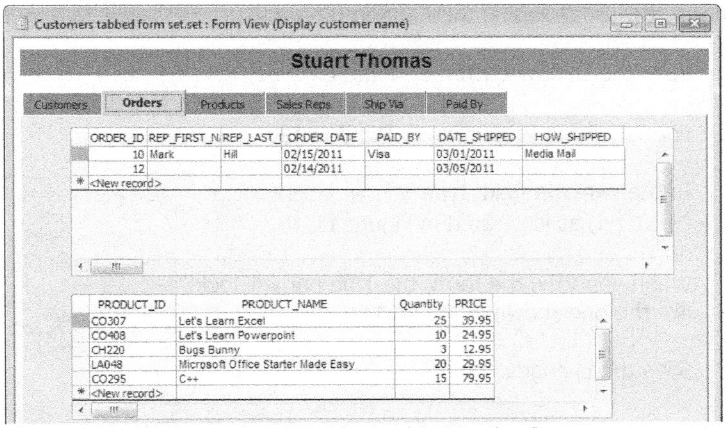

ORDER_ID	REP_FIRST_N	REP_LAST_I	ORDER_DATE	PAID_BY	DATE_SHIPPED	HOW_SHIPPED
10	Mark	Hill	02/15/2011	Visa	03/01/2011	Media Mail
12			02/14/2011		03/05/2011	
<New record>						

PRODUCT_ID	PRODUCT_NAME	Quantity	PRICE
CO307	Let's Learn Excel	25	39.95
CO408	Let's Learn Powerpoint	10	24.95
CH220	Bugs Bunny	3	12.95
LA048	Microsoft Office Starter Made Easy	20	29.95
CO295	C++	15	79.95
<New record>			

Figure 11-16 Dynamic text object added to the form

Form Properties Dialog Box (Tabbed Form)

Overall, this dialog box has the same options as a non tabbed form. [See Chapter 8, Form Properties Dialog Box (Non Tabbed Form)] The difference is explained below.

Filter/Order Tab

In addition to creating filter or order expressions to select records to be displayed on the form, the options shown in Figure 11-17 have more functionality then the options for a form that does not have tabs. These options are applied on a table by table basis.

The **TABLES SECTION** is used to select the table that you want to create a filter or order expression for. This means that the data in each table can be sorted in a different order.

Only tables with a one-to-many relationship are displayed in this section. If you look at Figure 11-1 shown earlier, you will see that Figure 11-17 does not have a link from the Order Detail table to the Products table. That is because the link between those tables is a one-to-one link.

The **LOCK ORDER WHEN EDITING** option is used to stop the records in the browse from being reordered while the sort field is being edited.

The **MAXIMUM NUMBER OF RECORDS TO CACHE** option is used to select how many records from the browse you want to create a local cache of. This is useful when you do not want the records in the browse to be reordered dynamically when they are being edited. It is only enabled if the Lock order when editing option is enabled.

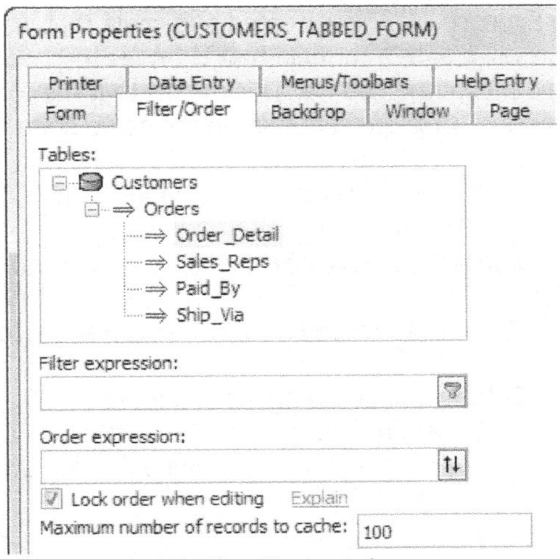

Figure 11-17 Filter/Order tab

Exercise 11.4: Change The Form Name

As shown earlier at the top of Figure 11-16, the set name is displayed in the Title bar. You can change this by changing the Caption property.

1. Save the Display customer name form as `Change title bar caption`.
2. Form ⇒ Form Properties ⇒ Window tab.
3. In the **CAPTION** field, type `View Customer Orders`, as illustrated in Figure 11-18.

   When you view the form, the Title bar will look like the one shown in Figure 11-19.

   Save the changes.

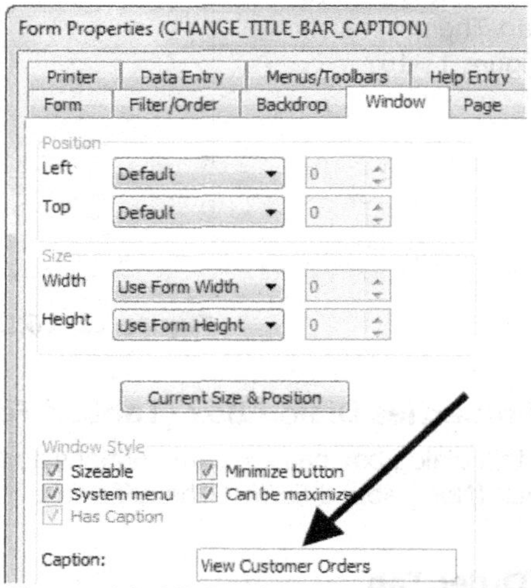

Figure 11-18 Caption property illustrated

Figure 11-19 Modified Title bar

Exercise 11.5: Create A Conditional Property Formula

In Exercise 11.3 you created a formula that was applied to every record in the table. In this exercise you will create a formula that changes the color of the State field on a form when the value in the field meets the criteria. This means that the formula will not be applied to every record in the table, unless all of the records are in the same state that the formula uses.

1. Save the Display customer name form as `Conditional formatting`.
2. Open the Field Properties dialog box for the State field.
3. On the Setup tab check the **COLOR EQUATION** option, then click the button at the end of the field.
4. Select the options shown in Figure 11-20. These options will change the background color of the State field to light orange if the value is FL, otherwise, the options illustrated at the bottom of the figure are applied to the field. Click OK.

The options illustrated in the figure are the default options.

If changed, every record will display one color or the other.

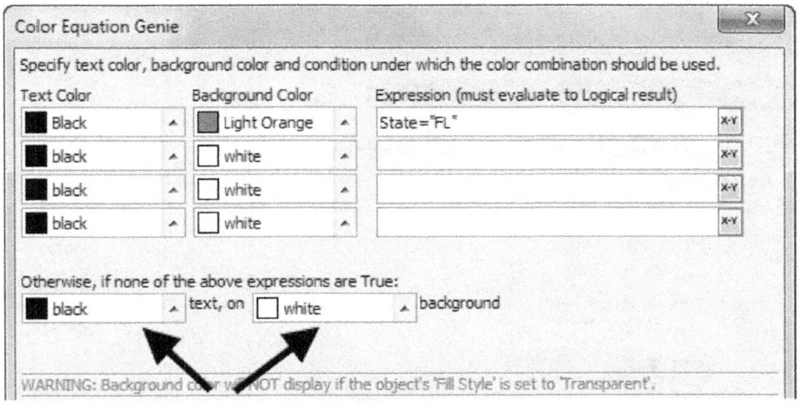

Figure 11-20 Color Equation Genie options

5. Check the **FONT EQUATION** option, then click the button at the end of the field.

   Select the options shown in Figure 11-21.

   Click OK.

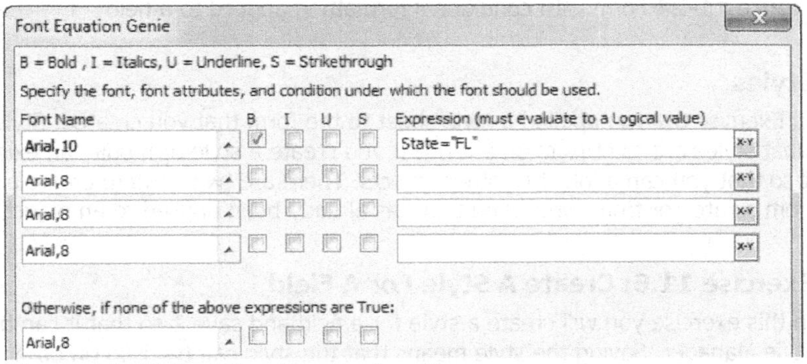

Figure 11-21 Font Equation Genie options

6. The Setup tab should have the equation options shown in Figure 11-22. You can also create these formulas on the Properties panel. Figure 11-23 shows the options on the Properties panel that you would use to create the formulas. Save the changes. When you view the form, the State field will have a light orange background and font formatting if the State = FL, as shown in Figure 11-24.

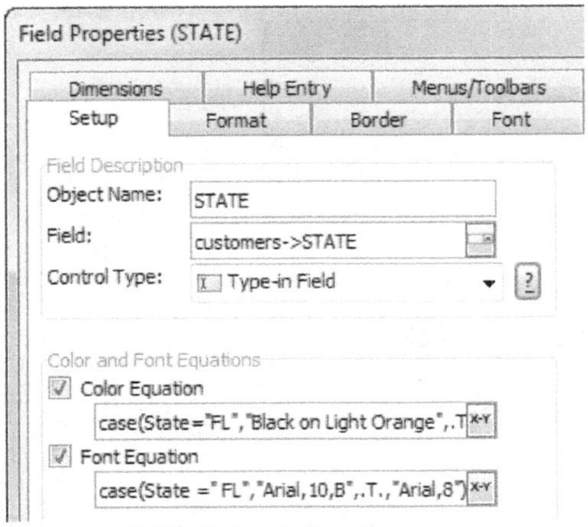

Figure 11-22 Setup tab options

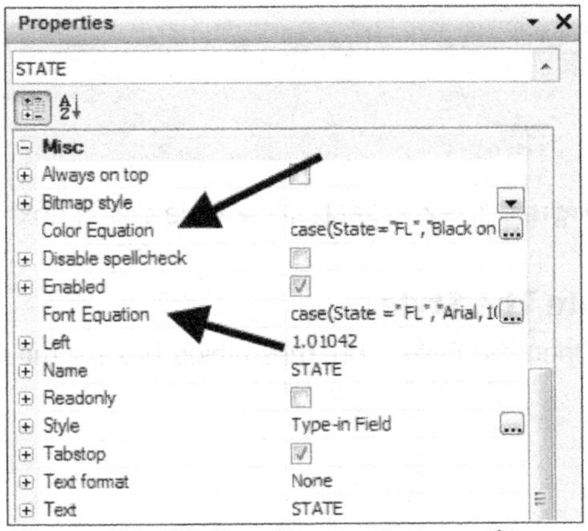

Figure 11-23 Equation options on the Properties panel illustrated

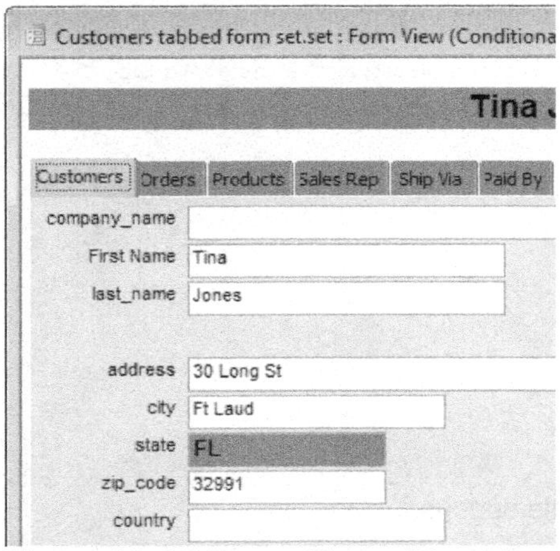

Figure 11-24 Form with conditional formatting applied to a field

Styles

In Exercise 8.1 you applied a style sheet to the form that you created. Style sheets are to the form what styles are to objects on a form. If you create a style or modify an existing style, you can save it so that you can apply it to other objects. There are two ways to create a style. It can be created from scratch or from formatting that has already been applied to an object.

Exercise 11.6: Create A Style For A Field

In this exercise you will create a style for a field and save it so that it can be accessed from the Style Manager. Saving the style means that the style can be used on other objects on the same form. Styles can be used with other forms, as you will see later in Exercise 11.8.

1. Save the Contact Type form as `New field style`.
2. Right-click on the Contact Date field ⇒ Styles ⇒ New Style.
3. In the Style Name field, type `My date style`, as shown in Figure 11-25, then click OK.

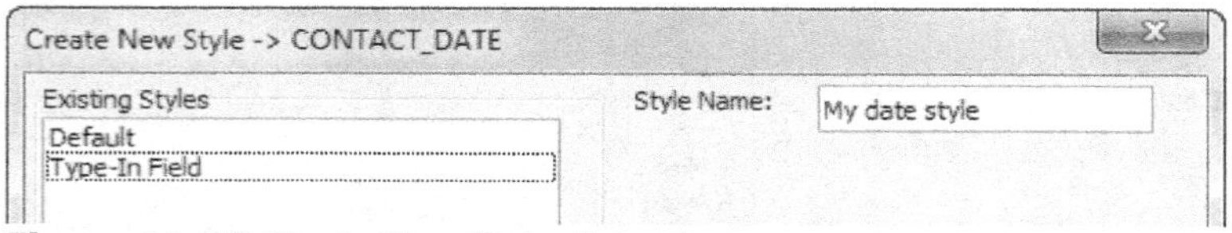

Figure 11-25 Create New Style dialog box

Create The Style

1. Open the Field Properties dialog box for the Contact Date field.

2. On the Border tab, select the following options, as shown in Figure 11-26.

   Border Style - Long Dashes
   Border Color - Lavender
   Shadow Style - Medium
   Fill Style - Gradient Vertical
   Fill Style Color - Light Orange

Figure 11-26 Border formatting options

3. On the Font tab, change the size to 10. Select the bold attribute, then click OK.

4. Save the changes. You will view the style later in this chapter.

Exercise 11.7: Create A Style Based On Existing Formatting

In this exercise you will use the formatting that has been applied to an object to create a new style.

1. Open the Nonscrollable header form.

2. Right-click on the text object at the top of the form ⇒ Styles ⇒ New Style.

3. In the Style Name field type `My purple text field`, then click OK. Save the changes, then close the form.

Managing Styles

There is no direct way to get to the Manage Styles dialog box. You have to go through the Stylesheets dialog box. The steps below show you how to get to the Manage Styles dialog box.

1. Open the New Field Style form.

2. Stylesheets ⇒ Apply or Create a stylesheet ⇒ Manage Styles button.

3. Open the Styles defined on Form section on the left, then click on the My Date Style, as shown in Figure 11-27. From this dialog box you can apply a style saved with the form or a style from the style sheet that is attached to the form. You can also create a new style, update the selected style or delete a style. The Properties tab shown in Figure 11-28 contains the properties for the selected style.

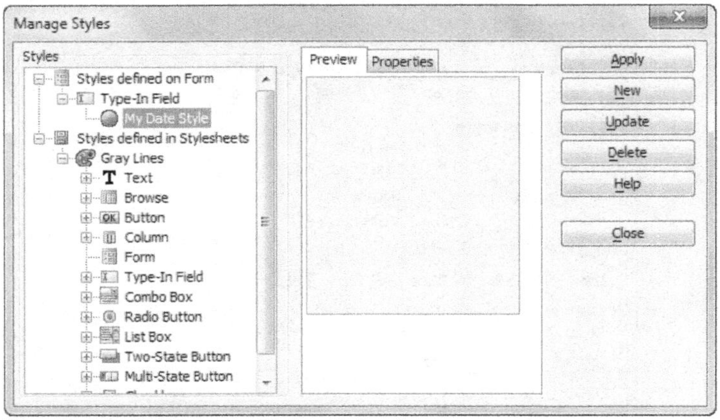

Figure 11-27 Manage Styles dialog box

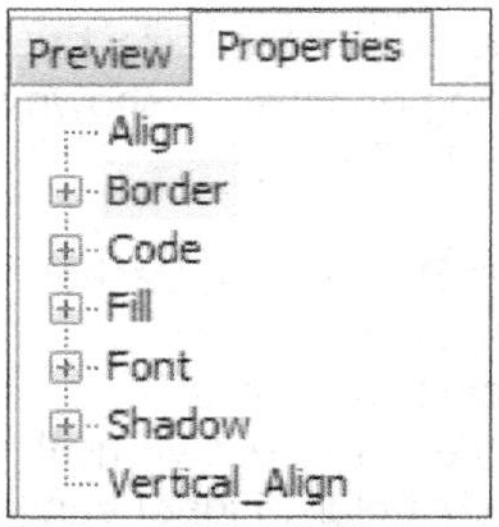

Figure 11-28 Manage Styles dialog box Properties tab

How To View Your Style Sheet
To view your style sheet, follow the steps below.

1. Open the Styles defined in Stylesheets section on the Manage Styles dialog box.
2. Open the section for your style sheet. In this case, the Type-In-Field section.
3. Click on your style. It will be displayed on the Preview tab on the right.

Styles Submenu Options

As shown in Figure 11-29, the styles available for the selected object are listed. You can select a style from this submenu. The option with the check mark is the style currently applied to the object.

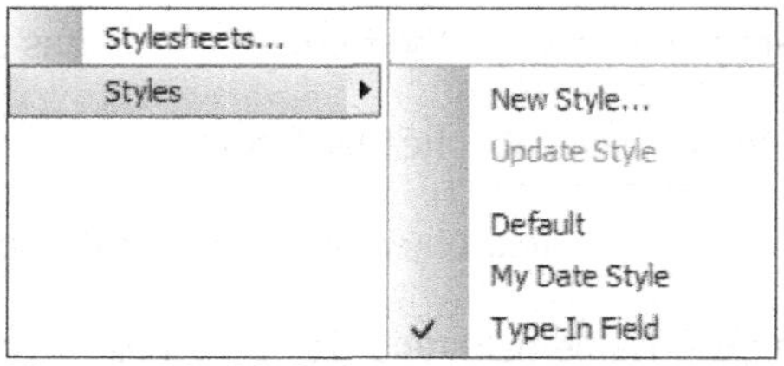

Figure 11-29 Styles submenu

Duplicating A Style Sheet

In Exercise 11.6 you created a style for a field. As you saw earlier in Figure 11-27, the style that you created is only available in the form that it was created in. If you want a style that you create to be available for other forms, you have to duplicate the style sheet currently attached to the form, save it with a new name, then update the style sheet. It would be very helpful if styles were not linked to an object. To me, styles would be more useful if they were saved outside of the database, so that they were global and could be used by any form in any database that you need.

Exercise 11.8: Duplicate And Update A Style Sheet

In this exercise you will duplicate the style sheet that is attached to the New field style form, then update it so that the style is part of the style sheet.

1. Save the New field style form as `Updated style sheet.`

2. Right-click on a blank space on the form and select Stylesheets.

3. The Gray Lines style sheet should be selected. If not, select it now. Click the Duplicate button. Type `My gray lines style sheet` as the Style name, then click the Duplicate button.

4. On the Stylesheets dialog box, click the Update button. Click Yes when prompted to update the style sheet.

5. Click the Manage Styles button.

   In the Styles defined in Stylesheets section, open the Type-In field section.

   You will see your date style, as illustrated in Figure 11-30.

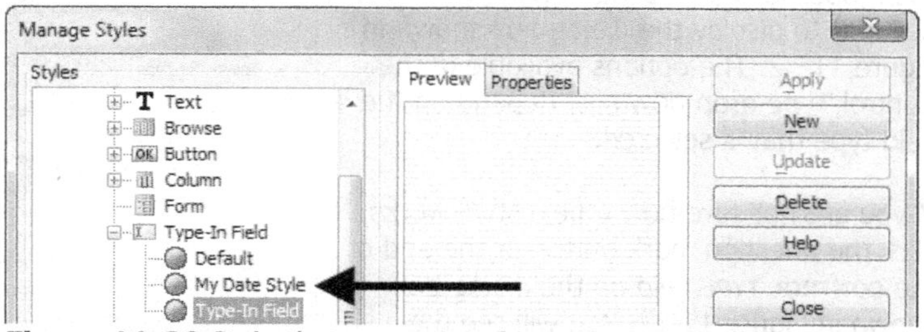

Figure 11-30 Style that you created is now part of a style sheet

6. Click the Close button twice, then save the form.

What Is A Smart Field?

Smart Fields are fields that have a button at the end of the field. Clicking on one of these buttons provides an application or tool. Smart Fields are automatically added to date and time fields in forms and browses. There are two locations for smart fields, as explained below.

① The Color Equation field shown earlier in Figure 11-22 has a button that opens the Color Equation Genie. The Expression field on the Color Equation Genie has a button that opens the Expression Builder.
② Fields that you create and place on a form. These smart fields have specific data entry features that make data entry easier and more accurate.

Smart Field Options Explained

In Chapter 9, Figure 9-31 you saw the **CONTROL TYPE** field on the Column Properties dialog box Setup tab.

The options in the drop-down list shown in Figure 11-31, except the Type-In Field option is a Smart Field. The options in the drop-down list are explained below.

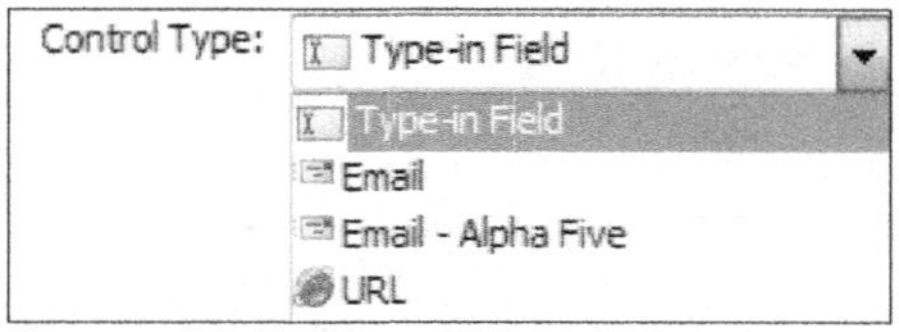

Figure 11-31 Smart Field options

① **EMAIL** Opens a new email window in HTML format in your default email software. (1)
② **EMAIL-ALPHA FIVE** Opens the Alpha Five email software. (1)
③ **URL** A web browser icon is added to the end of the field. Clicking on the icon opens the web browser and displays the web site listed in the field if the computer is connected to the Internet.

(1) Adds an email icon at the end of the field. Actually, the icon is displayed in the field to the right. The icon is very small, so it is possible that you may not see it.

Using Smart Fields

By default, fields in a table use the **TYPE-IN FIELD STYLE**. Some of these styles are options in the Toolbox. Click the ellipsis button on the Properties Panel Style option (in the Misc Section) to display the dialog box shown in Figure 11-32. The options available in the Control Type drop-down list depend on the field type that is selected.

If you are not sure how a field style works, click the question mark button at the end of the **CONTROL TYPE** field on the dialog box shown in Figure 11-32. You will see the dialog box shown in Figures 11-33 and 11-34. The purpose of this dialog box is to let you test the different control styles. I think that being able to test the options is a really cool feature. Click on the tabs and test a few of the options.

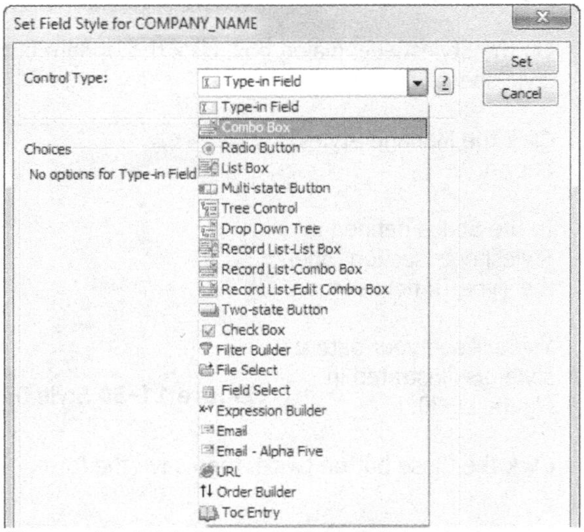

Figure 11-32 Set Field Style For dialog box

Alpha Five refers to these as **SMART CONTROLS**. To the right of the Order Date field is a button. When you click on the button, the calendar shown in Figure 11-35 appears.

> **Automatic vs Manual Smart Fields**
> The way to tell the difference between the types of Smart Fields is that the button is outside of the field for **AUTOMATIC SMART FIELDS** and inside the field for **MANUAL SMART FIELDS.**

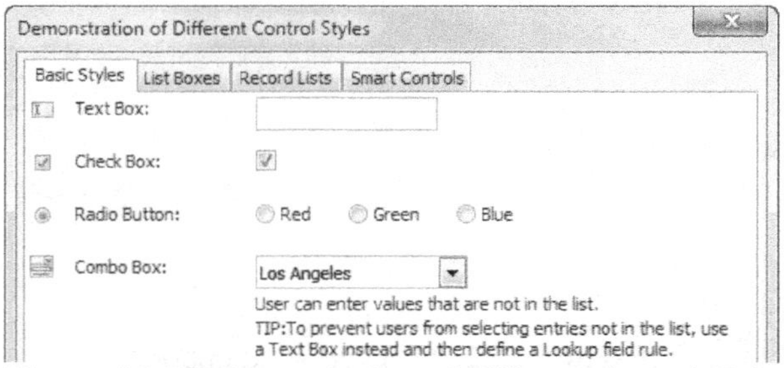

Figure 11-33 Demonstration of Different Control Styles dialog box

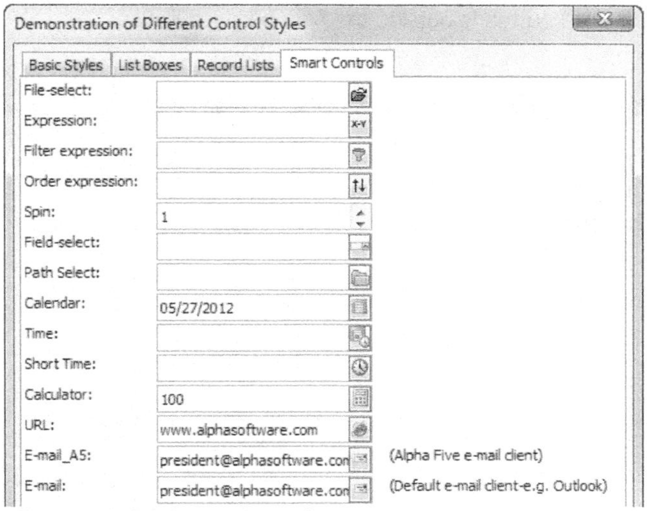

Figure 11-34 Smart Controls

Figure 11-35 Smart field options for a date field

Exercise 11.9: Create Smart Fields

In this exercise you will view automatic smart fields and create several types of smart fields.

1. Add the Smart Fields table from the CBC APP Data folder to your database.

2. View the Smart Fields table in the Default form, then save the form as `Smart Fields`.

3. Select all of the objects on the form, then click the Un-Group button on the toolbar.

Change The Control Type To Calculator For A Numeric Field

In this part of the exercise you will add a calculator to the Order Total field.

1. Click on the Order Total field, then scroll down the Properties panel to the Misc section.

2. Click the button at the end of the Style property. Open the Control Type drop-down list and select Calculator.

3. Click the Set button.

Change The Control Type For Other Fields

1. Follow the steps above to create the Smart Fields in Table 11-4, then save the changes.

Field	Control Type
Ship Date	Calendar
Ship Time	Short Time
Home Email	Email
Web site	URL

Table 11-4 Smart Fields to create

2. View the Smart Fields form.

3. Click in the Order Date field. The Smart Field button is outside the field because it was automatically created.

4. Click in the Ship Date field. The Smart Field button is in the field because it was created manually.

5. Click in the Ship Time field, then click the Smart Field button. You should see the clock shown in Figure 11-36.

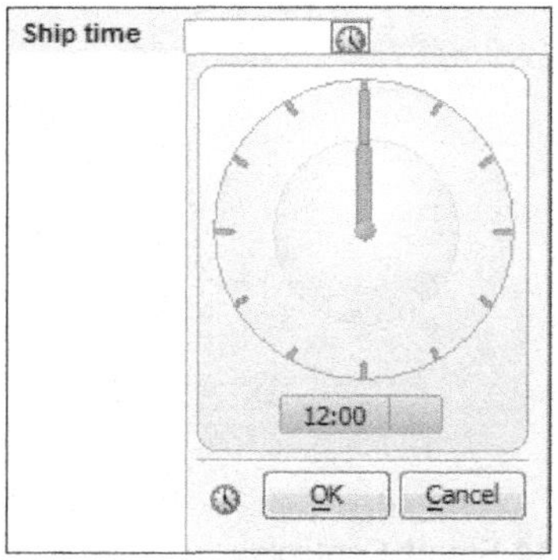

Figure 11-36 Time smart control

6. Click in the Home Email field, then click the Smart Field button. Your email software will open.

7. Click in the Website field, then click the Smart Field button. Your web browser software will open.

Copying Records

If you have the need to copy records in one table or set to a new table or to an existing table you can. The existing table must have the same field names as the table that you are copying from. The difference between this option and duplicating a table is that the Copy Records option does not require you to copy all of the fields in the table. If you use a form that is based on a set, you can select fields from any table in the set to copy data to.

Exercise 11.10: Copy Records To A New Table

In this exercise you will learn how to copy records in a set to a new table.

1. Display the Customers tabbed form in form view.

2. Records ⇒ Copy Selected Records.

3. In the Table Name field type `Customer-Order-Merge`.

4. Select the **SELECTED FIELDS** option, then click the **SELECT FIELDS** button.

5. Select the following fields in the Customers table: Customer ID, Company Name, First Name, Last Name, City and State.

6. Select the following fields in the Orders table: Order ID, Order Date and Date Shipped.

7. Add the Qty and Price fields from the Order Detail table.

8. Add the Product Name field from the Products table.

9. Add the Rep First Name and Rep Last Name fields from the Sales Reps table.

10. Add the Paid By field from the Paid By table.

11. Add the How Shipped field from the Shipvia table, then click OK.

12. You should have the options shown in Figure 11-37. Click OK.

    The Notice message lets you know how many records will be copied.

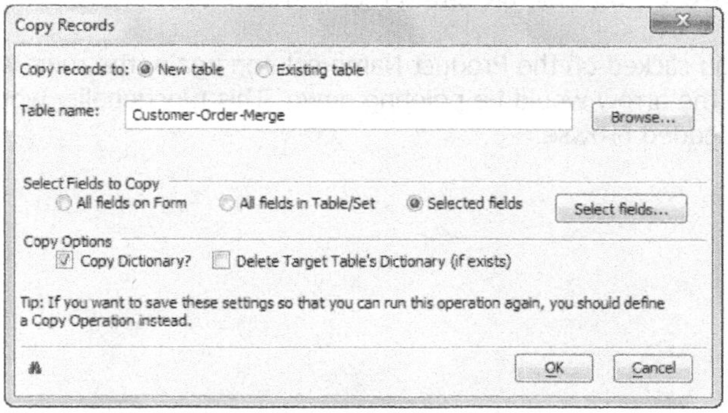

Figure 11-37 Copy Records dialog box

13. Click Yes to copy the records to the new table. Click Yes to view the copied records.

14. Click Cancel to close the Copy Records dialog box.

Sort Data In An Embedded Browse By Column

In Chapter 9, Exercise 9.9 you created what I call a "hard coded" sort for the data that will be displayed in a stand alone browse. You can let the user select the column to sort on (in ascending or descending order) by clicking on the column heading in an embedded browse.

Exercise 11.11: How To Sort An Embedded Browse By Column

In this exercise you will modify an embedded browse so that it can be sorted by column.

1. Save the Customers tabbed form as `Sort by column`.

2. On the Orders tab, right-click on the second browse window and select Properties.

3. On the Browse tab, open the **COLUMN TITLE CLICK BEHAVIOR DROP-DOWN LIST** shown in Figure 11-38 and select Click sorts by column.

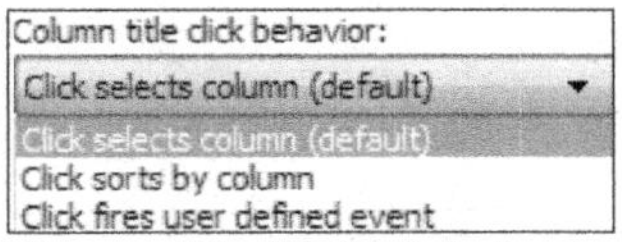

Figure 11-38 Click behavior options

4. Click OK, then save the changes. Preview the customer Stuart Thomas. On the Orders tab, click on the row for Order ID 10.

5. In the second browse, click on the Product Name column. The rows are now sorted by the product name. You will see a ▲ after this column heading, as illustrated in Figure 11-39. This lets you know that the rows are sorted and on which column.

PRODUCT_ID	PRODUCT_NAME	Quantity	PRICE
CH220	Bugs Bunny	3	12.95
CO295	C++	15	79.95
CO307	Let's Learn Excel	25	39.95
CO408	Let's Learn Powerpoint	10	24.95
LA048	Microsoft Office Starter Made Easy	20	29.95

Figure 11-39 Column sorted on illustrated

If you clicked on the Product Name column again, the rows would be sorted in descending order and the arrow would be pointing down. This functionality works for all columns displayed in the embedded browse.

DATA ENTRY TIPS AND TOOLS

This chapter takes a slightly different perspective because it covers topics from a users perspective of viewing and entering data on forms and browses. The following topics are covered:

- ☑ Form view menu and toolbar
- ☑ Form keyboard shortcuts
- ☑ Finding records
- ☑ Speed Typing Glossary

> **Shameless Book Plug**
> If you have enjoyed this book and want to learn more about Alpha Five, check out my other Alpha Five books on www.tolana.com.

CHAPTER 12

Overview

You have come a long way towards learning about the core features in Alpha Five from a developers perspective to build an application. As the developer of the application, other then during the testing phase, you probably will not have the need to use the features covered in this chapter, but you can pass the topics covered in this chapter that are appropriate to the people that will use the application that you developed.

Form Data Entry Tips And Tools

The topics covered in this section will aid users when they are doing data entry on forms, as well as viewing data, creating queries and sorting records.

Form View Menu

While you are designing and testing forms, you will use the Form view menu and toolbar options often. When you are finished, you will hand the application over to the users. They will have the need to use many of the options on this menu and toolbar.

When you view a form different options are on the menu, as shown in Figure 12-1, compared to what is on the menu when the form is in design mode. Many of the options on the Form view toolbar are explained in later in Table 12-10. Tables 12-1 to 12-9 explain the menu options that are specific to viewing forms.

Figure 12-1 Form view menu

> A browse has the same View menu. The only difference is that a browse displays the Browse menu instead of the Form menu shown above in Figure 12-1. On some of the menus, there are fewer options when viewing a browse.

File Menu

The File menu is shown in Figure 12-2.
The options for forms are explained in Table 12-1.

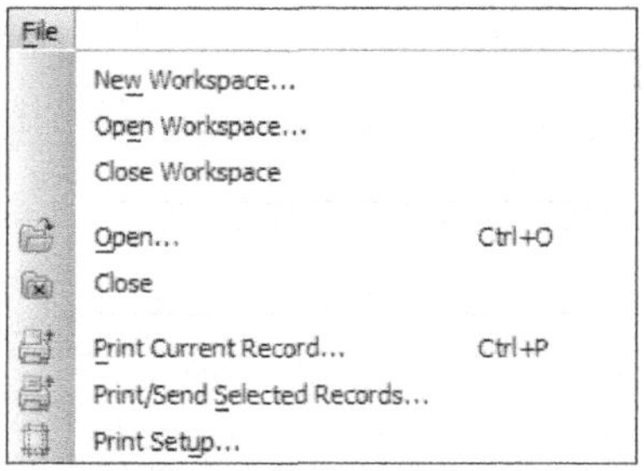

Figure 12-2 File menu

Option	Description
Print Current Record	Opens the dialog box shown in Figure 12-3. The options are used to select the layout type and how the form and data currently displayed will be printed or sent. These are the same options that are available for reports. The options are explained below. Figure 12-5 shows what the Contact Type form will look like when printed.
Print/Send Selected Records	Opens the genie shown in Figure 12-6. This genie is used to customize how the form will be printed.

Table 12-1 File menu options explained

① Clicking the **SHOW XBASIC** button opens the dialog box shown in Figure 12-4, to let you view or paste the code.

② Clicking this button saves the current print selections so that you do not have to select them the next time that you want to print the form.

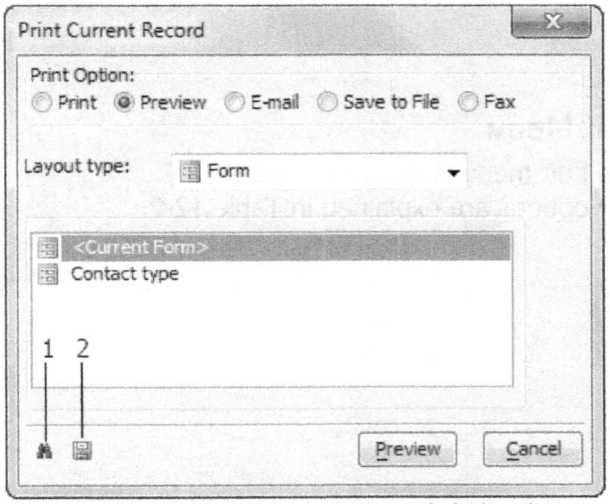
Print Current Record
Print Option:
Print
Preview
E-mail
Save to File
Fax
Layout type:
Form
<Current Form>
Contact type
1
2
Preview
Cancel

Figure 12-3 Print Current Record dialog box

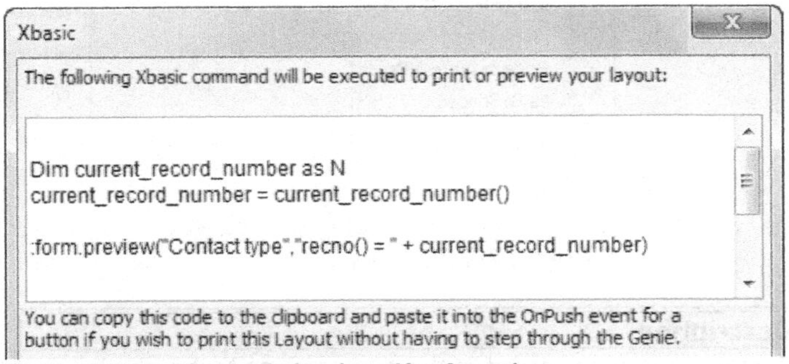
Xbasic
The following Xbasic command will be executed to print or preview your layout:
Dim current_record_number as N
current_record_number = current_record_number()
:form.preview("Contact type","recno() = " + current_record_number)
You can copy this code to the clipboard and paste it into the OnPush event for a button if you wish to print this Layout without having to step through the Genie.

Figure 12-4 Xbasic dialog box (for forms)

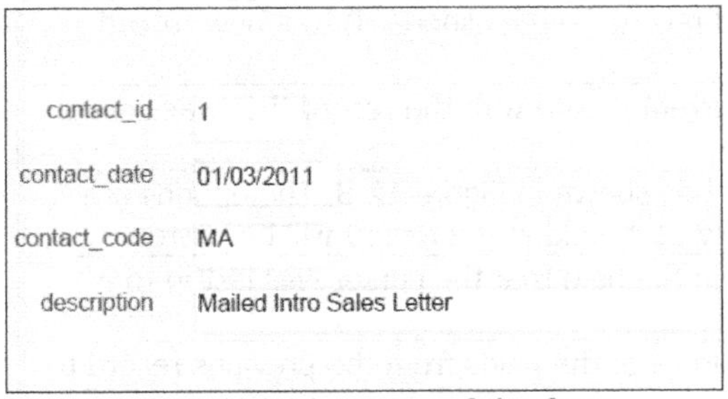
contact_id 1
contact_date 01/03/2011
contact_code MA
description Mailed Intro Sales Letter

Figure 12-5 Printed version of the form

Print Layout Genie

The options shown in Figure 12-6 are used to print, preview or send a layout. Select the layout type from the drop-down list.

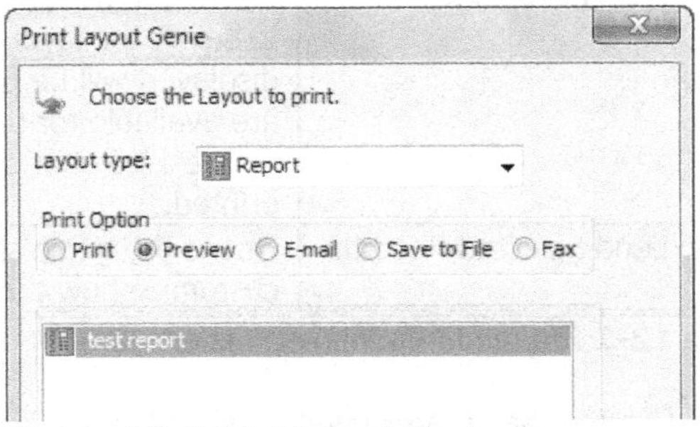

Figure 12-6 Print Layout Genie

Edit Menu

The Edit menu is shown in Figure 12-7. The options are explained in Table 12-2.

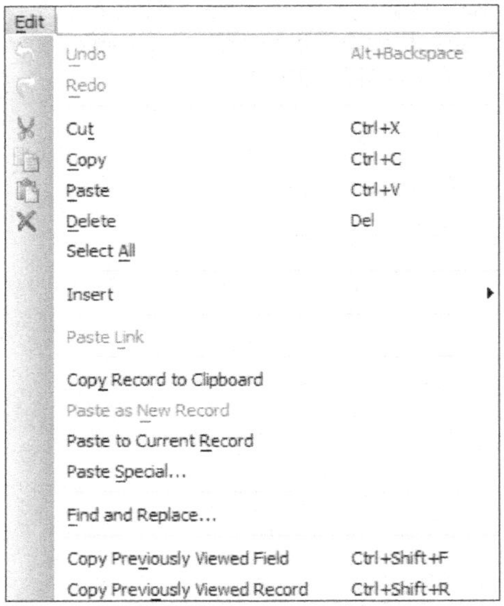

Figure 12-7 Edit menu

Option	Description
Copy Record to Clipboard	Copies the current record to the clipboard, so that it can be pasted someplace else.
Paste as New Record	Pastes the copied record (in the clipboard) to a new record in the table or set.
Paste to Current Record	Overwrites the current record with the record that was copied to the clipboard.
Paste Special	Opens the dialog box shown in Figure 12-8. The options are used to select how each field in the record will be pasted.
Copy Previously Viewed Field	Copies the value in the field that the cursor was last in to a new record.
Copy Previously Viewed Record	Copies the value in all of the fields from the previous record to a new record.

Table 12-2 Edit menu options explained

Figure 12-8 Alpha Five Record Clipboard dialog box

View Menu

[See Chapter 2, Table 2-2]

Form Menu

The Form menu is shown in Figure 12-9. The options are explained in Table 12-3.

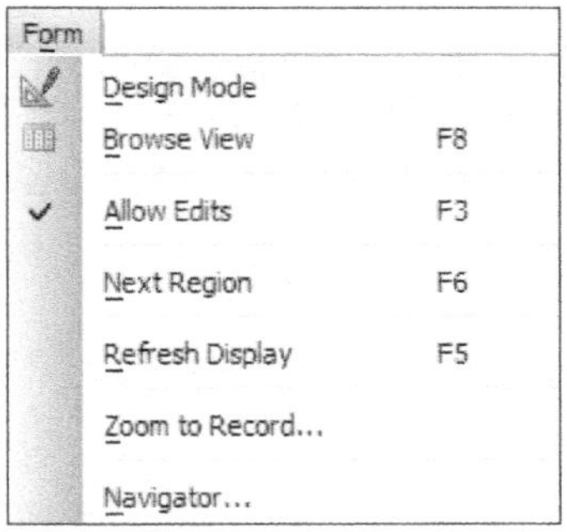

Figure 12-9 Form menu

Option	Description
Design Mode	Displays the form in design mode.
Browse View	Displays the data in the form in the default browse window, as shown in Figure 12-10.
Allow Edits	Toggles on and off to allow the data to be changed.
Next Region	When selected, this option causes the cursor to go from the form to the browse section of the form. (1)
Refresh Display	Redisplays the current record in the form.
Zoom to Record	When selected, a default form (unless you create a form for the browse) opens and displays the fields for the selected record in the browse in a different form. (1)

Table 12-3 Form menu options explained

Option	Description
Navigator	Displays the dialog box shown in Figure 12-11. It is used to find a field on the form. This is helpful if a form has a lot of fields or has a browse on the form.

Table 12-3 Form menu options explained (Continued)

(1) This option only works with a form that has a browse embedded in the form. The mouse pointer must be in the browse on the form for this option to work. This option is not available when viewing a stand alone browse.

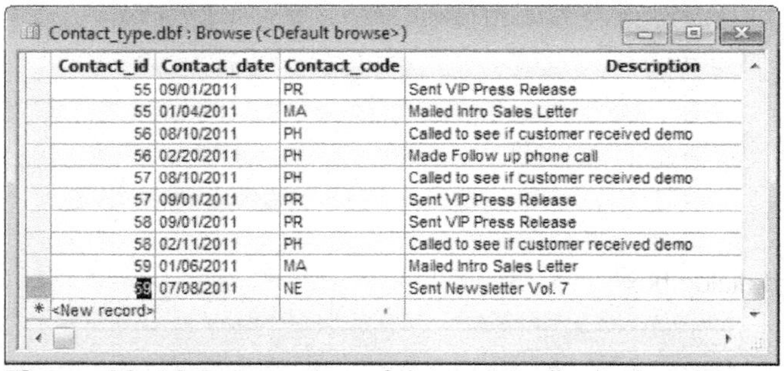

Figure 12-10 Browse view of data originally displayed in a form

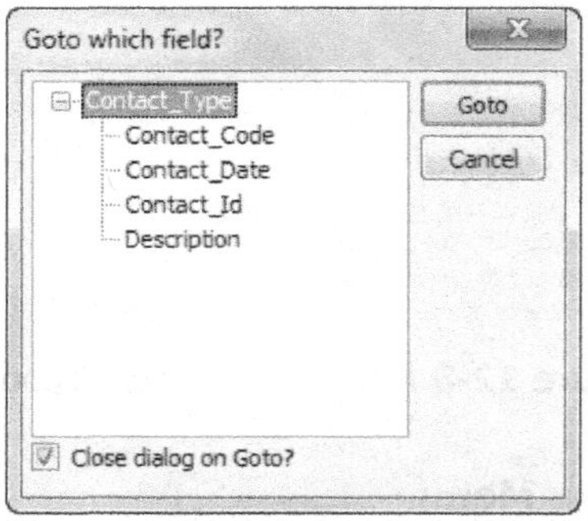

Figure 12-11 Goto which field dialog box

Records Menu

The Records menu is shown in Figure 12-12. The options are explained in Table 12-4.

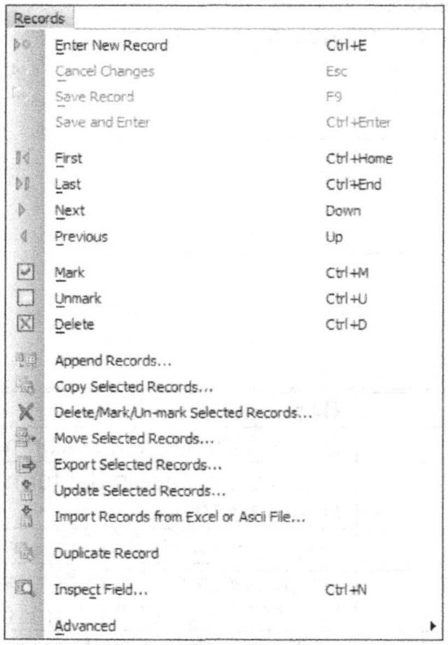

Figure 12-12 Records menu

Option	Description
Enter New Record	[See Table 12-10, Button 9]
Cancel Changes	[See Table 12-10, Button 12]
Save Record	[See Table 12-10, Button 11]
Save and Enter	Saves the current record, then displays a new record.
First	[See Table 12-10, Button 4]
Last	[See Table 12-10, Button 8]
Next	[See Table 12-10, Button 7]
Previous	[See Table 12-10, Button 5]
Mark	Is used to select records manually or by using an expression to find records to perform an action like updating a field on all of the marked records or deleting the marked records.
Unmark	Clears the marked record option from a record.
Delete	Deletes the selected record(s).
Append Records	Opens the **APPEND RECORDS DIALOG BOX**, which is used to add records to the current table or set. You learned how to use this operation in Chapter 5. (2)
Copy Selected Records	Opens the **COPY RECORDS DIALOG BOX**, which is used to copy records in the current table to new table or to an existing table. [See Chapter 11, Copying Records] (2)
Delete/Mark/Un-mark Selected Records	Opens the **DELETE/MARK/UN-MARK RECORDS DIALOG BOX**, which is used to mark, unmark or delete records. (2)
Move Selected Records	Opens the **MOVE RECORDS DIALOG BOX**, which is used to move records from the current table to another table in the current database.
Export Selected Records	Opens the **EXPORT RECORDS DIALOG BOX**, which is used to export records to one of the formats illustrated in Figure 12-13. (2)
Update Selected Records	Opens the **UPDATE FIELDS DIALOG BOX**, which is used to change the data value in fields in the table. For example, if the wrong year was entered into a date field, you could update all of the records that have the wrong date using this dialog box. (2)
Import Records from Excel or ASCII File	Opens the **IMPORT RECORDS INTO CURRENT TABLE DIALOG BOX**, which is used to import data from Excel or form a comma delimited ASCII file into the current table. (2)
Duplicate Record	Creates a copy of the current record and adds the copy to the end of the table.
Inspect Field	This option is only enabled in a memo field that has data. It opens the Memo dialog box, which looks like the Memo Editor, so that you can view or change the contents of the memo field.
Advanced	Displays the submenu shown in Figure 12-14. The **APPLY RANGE** option opens the **RANGE DIALOG BOX**, which is used to order and filter records. The **FOLLOW CHANGES/ENTERS** option is enabled by default. After the current record has been entered, the next record (based on the primary index order) will be displayed.

Table 12-4 Records menu options explained

(2) This is known as an Ad-Hoc Operation. It has a subset of the features that the corresponding option on the Operations tab has. The biggest difference is that Ad-Hoc operations cannot be saved.

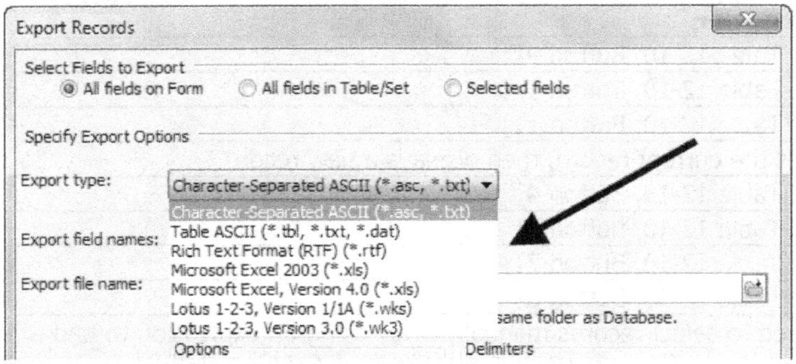

Figure 12-13 Export format options illustrated

Figure 12-14 Advanced submenu options

Find Menu (Before Search)

The Find menu shown in Figure 12-15 is available before you search for records. The options are explained in Table 12-5.

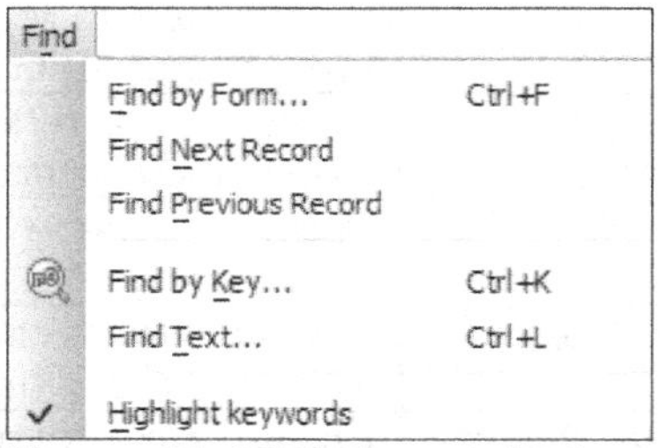

Figure 12-15 Find menu (before search)

Option	Description
Find by Form	[See Find By Form, later in this chapter]
Find Next Record	Displays the next record from the Find by Form search. (3)
Find Previous Record	Displays the previous record from the Find by Form search. (3)
Find by Key	[See Find By Key, later in this chapter]
Find Text	[See Find Text, later in this chapter]
Highlight keywords	Is enabled by default. It highlights the value in the field that the cursor is in. Clearing the check mark does not remove the highlighting, as expected.

Table 12-5 Find menu options explained

(3) This option is only available after using the Find by Form search option.

Query Menu

The Query menu is shown in Figure 12-16. The majority of options on this menu are used to find specific records. The options are explained in Table 12-6.

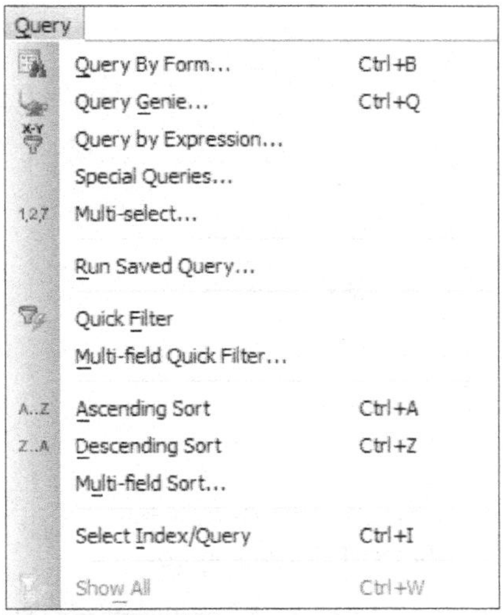

Figure 12-16 Query menu

Option	Description
Query By Form	[See Table 12-10, Button 15]
Query Genie	[See Table 12-10, Button 16]
Query by Expression	Opens the **QUERY BY EXPRESSION DIALOG BOX**, which is used to create a filter or order expression to find records in the table or set.
Special Queries	[See Select Filter Dialog Box below]
Multi-select	Opens the **MULTI-SELECT RECORDS DIALOG BOX**, which is used to select records and then create a query.
Run Saved Query	Opens the **SELECT QUERY DIALOG BOX**, which is used to select an existing query to run.
Quick Filter	[See Table 12-10, Button 17]
Multi-field Quick Filter	Opens the **MULTI-FIELD QUICK FILTER DIALOG BOX**, which is used to create a filter based on fields in the table or set.
Ascending Sort	[See Table 12-10, Button 13]
Descending Sort	[See Table 12-10, Button 14]
Multi-field Sort	Opens the **CUSTOM SORT DIALOG BOX**, which is used to select field(s) in the table or set to sort on and to select the sort order (ascending or descending).
Select Index/Query	[See Table 12-10, Button 20]
Show All	[See Table 12-10, Button 18]

Table 12-6 Query menu options explained

Select Filter Dialog Box

The options on the top portion of the dialog box shown in Figure 12-17 are used to select a query that will retrieve the records that will be displayed on the form. The options are explained in Table 12-7.

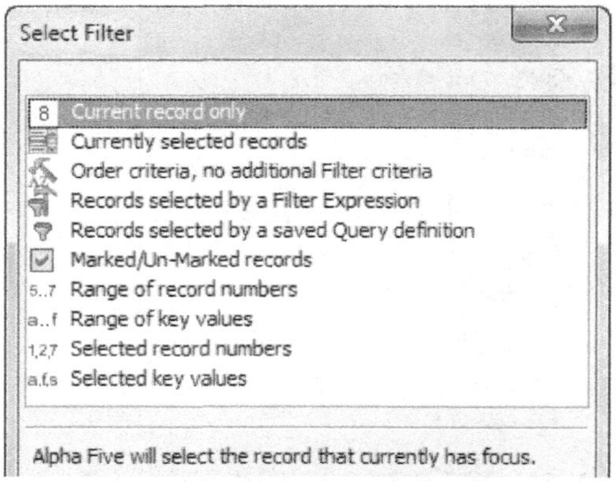

Figure 12-17 Select Filter dialog box

Option	Creates A Query That . . .
Current record only	Only returns the current record. I don't see the value of this option.
Currently selected records	Is based on all of the records in the current query list or current index. (4)
Order criteria, no additional Filter criteria	Is based on the order expression that you create. Filter criteria will not be applied.
Records select by a Filter Expression	Uses a filter or order expression. (4)
Records selected by a save Query definition	Uses an existing query. (4)
Marked/Un-Marked records	Uses marked or un-marked records from the entire table or the records that are currently selected.
Range of record numbers	Retrieves all records that have a record number in the range that you select.
Range of key values	Retrieves records that have the key value(s) in the range that you select. Figure 12-18 shows the options. This option has the same functionality as the **IS BETWEEN OPERATOR**.
Selected record numbers	Retrieves the records that have the record numbers that you select. In addition to being able to select non consecutive record numbers, this option is also used to select a range of record numbers.
Selected key value	Retrieves all of the records that have one of the values that you select. This option has the same functionality as the **IS ONE OF OPERATOR**.

Table 12-7 Select Filter dialog box options explained

(4) This option can also be used to create a **TOP N, BOTTOM N** or an **N PERCENT QUERY**.

Range Of Key Values

The **KEY BUTTON** is used to select the index or query list. You can also select a specific field.

The **FIRST BUTTON** is used to select the beginning value of the range.

The **LAST BUTTON** is used to select the ending value of the range.

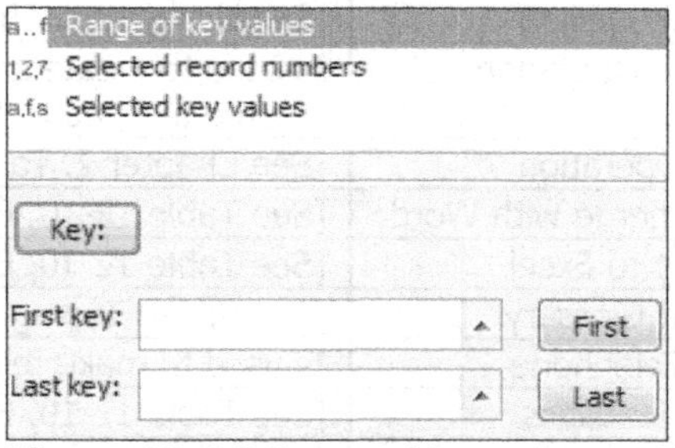

Figure 12-18 Range of key values options

Scripts Menu

The Scripts menu is shown in Figure 12-19. The options are explained in Table 12-8.

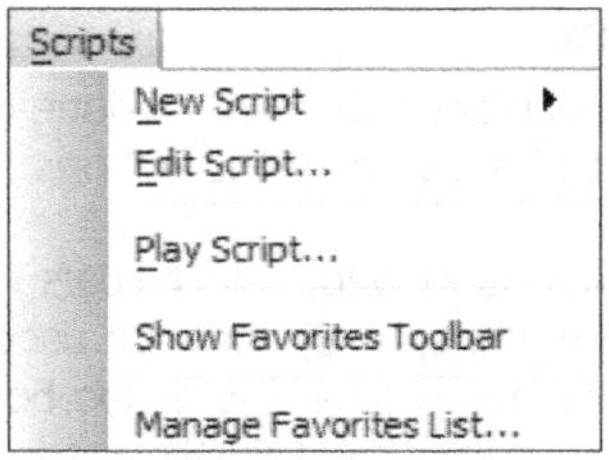

Figure 12-19 Scripts menu

Option	Description
New Script	Opens the **CREATE NEW SCRIPT OR FUNCTION DIALOG BOX**, which is used to create a script using the **SCRIPT GENIE** or Xbasic.
Edit Script	Opens the **SELECT SCRIPT OR FUNCTION TO EDIT DIALOG BOX**, which is used to edit an existing script.
Play Script	Opens the **PICK THE SCRIPT TO PLAY DIALOG BOX**, which is used to select a script to run.
Show Favorites Toolbar	Displays a toolbar that has scripts that you have added to it.
Manage Favorites List	Opens the **MANAGE FAVORITES DIALOG BOX**, which is used to add scripts to a custom toolbar or to a submenu.

Table 12-8 Scripts menu options explained

Tools Menu (Form/Browse View)

The Tools menu is shown in Figure 12-20. The options are explained in Table 12-9.

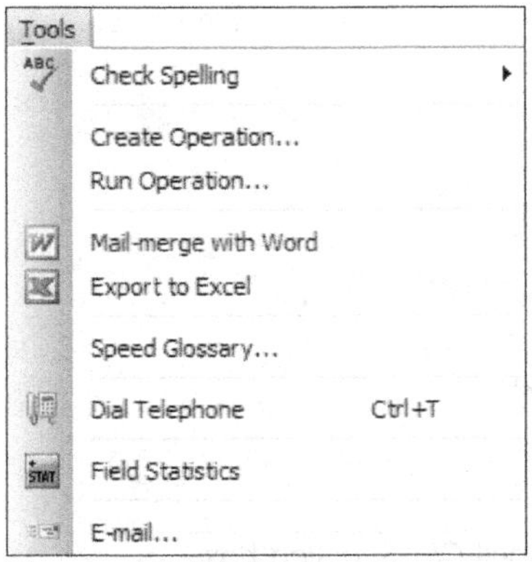

Figure 12-20 Tools menu

Option	Description
Check Spelling	[See Using Spell Check below]
Create Operation	Is used to create an operation, like the append operations that you created in Chapter 5.
Run Operation	[See Chapter 2, Table 2-11, Run Operation]
Mail-merge with Word	[See Table 12-10, Button 23]
Export to Excel	[See Table 12-10, Button 22]
Speed Glossary	[See Speed Typing Glossary Dialog Box, later in this chapter]
Dial Telephone	Is used to make telephone calls from inside of Alpha Five.
Field Statistics	[See Table 12-10, Button 21]
E-mail	Is used to send an email that contains the data in the form.

Table 12-9 Tools menu options explained

Using Spell Check

I am not sure how much spell checking is done during data entry, other then in note and memo fields, but I wanted to briefly cover the options.

When a form or browse is viewed, select Tools ⇒ Check Spelling. You will see the submenu shown in Figure 12-21. The majority of options are used to select what you want to spell check. The first four options on the submenu open the dialog box shown in Figure 12-22.

The **EDIT USER DICTIONARY** option on the submenu and the pencil icon illustrated on Figure 12-22 open the dialog box shown in Figure 12-23. This dialog box is used to add words that you use that the spell checker does not recognize.

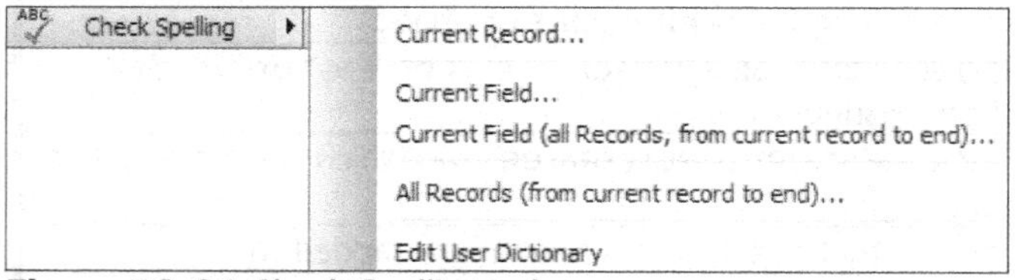

Figure 12-21 Check Spelling submenu

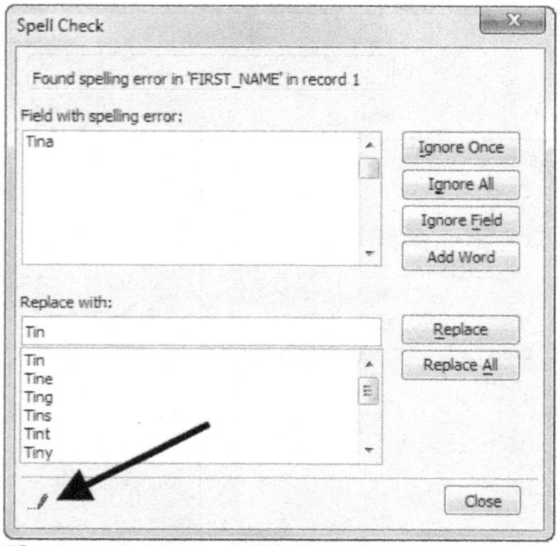

Figure 12-22 Spell Check dialog box

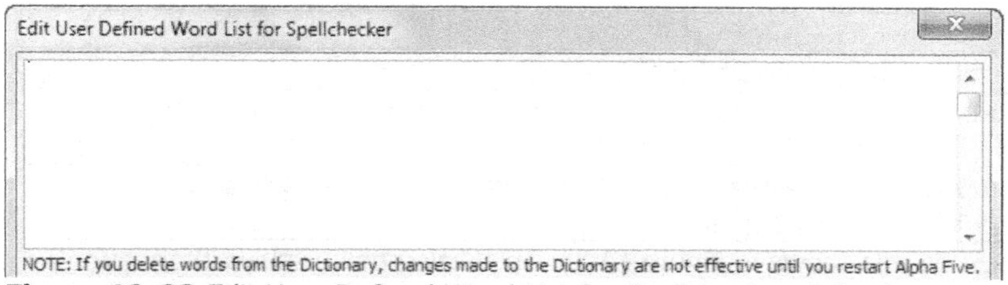

Figure 12-23 Edit User Defined Word List for Spellchecker dialog box

Form View Toolbar

The toolbar shown in Figure 12-24 has the options that you will probably use the most. This toolbar is available when viewing a form. The options are a subset of the options on the menu that was just covered. The options are explained in Table 12-10.

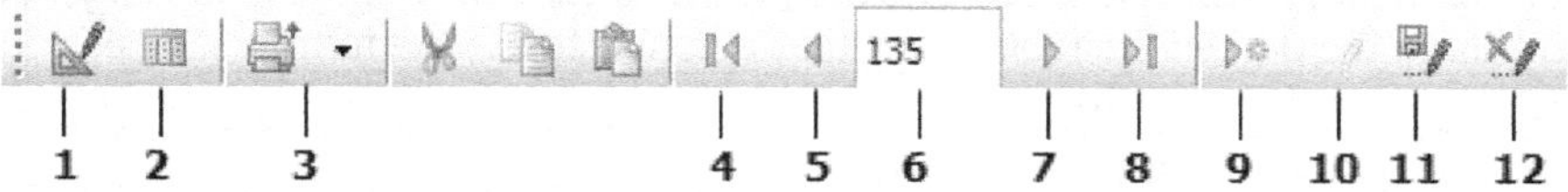

Figure 12-24 Form view toolbar - Buttons 1-12

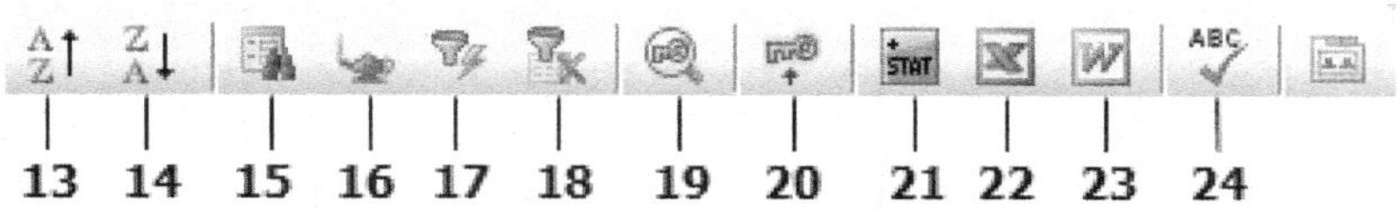

Figure 12-24 Form view toolbar (Continued) - Buttons 13-24

Button	Description
1	Displays the form in design mode.
2	Displays the data (currently displayed on the form) in the default browse for the table.
3	Prints the current record or send it via email, fax or save it to a file.
4	Displays the first record in the table.
5	Displays the previous record in the table.
6	Displays the record number in the table of the record currently displayed.
7	Displays the next record in the table.
8	Displays the last record in the table.
9	Displays a new record.
10	The **CHANGE RECORD BUTTON** is used to make changes to the current record if the form or browse has the **MODAL DATA ENTRY** option enabled, otherwise, the button is not enabled.
11	Saves the current record.
12	Cancels the changes to the record.
13	Sorts the records in ascending order based on the field that the cursor is in.
14	Sorts the records in descending order based on the field that the cursor is in.
15	Opens the **QBF HELPER DIALOG BOX.** (5)
16	Opens the **QUERY GENIE.** (5)
17	The **QUICK FILTER BUTTON** displays all records that have the value in the field that the cursor is in before you click this button.

Table 12-10 Form view toolbar buttons explained

Button	Description
18	Removes the filters and displays all of the records in the form.
19	Opens the **FIND BY KEY DIALOG BOX**, which is used to search for a value in the selected field on the form.
20	Opens the **PRIMARY INDEX OR QUERY DIALOG BOX**, which is used to select or view indexes, query lists and saved queries.
21	Displays the dialog box shown in Figure 12-25. This dialog box displays information about the fields on the form. If the field is used in an expression, the expression will be on the Expression tab. Expressions can also be created on this dialog box.
22	Automatically exports the records in the table or set that the form is based on to Excel, then opens Excel. The spreadsheet is automatically saved with the same file name as the table or set. In Windows 7, the export file is stored in this location, by default. C:\Users\<your account>\AppData\Local\Temp\. You can change this default folder. [See Chapter 2, System Directories]
23	Opens the **MICROSOFT WORD MERGE DIALOG BOX**, which is used to create a mail merge document using the data in the table or set that is connected to the form.
24	This button only spell checks the current record.

Table 12-10 Form view toolbar buttons explained (Continued)

(5) This dialog box is used to create a query to find records in the table or set.

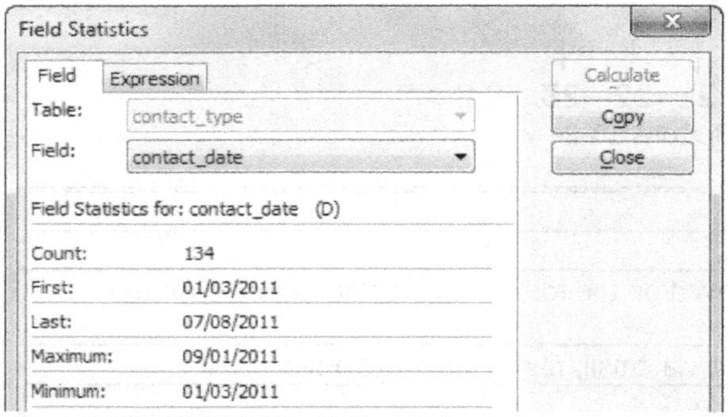

Figure 12-25 Field Statistics dialog box

Preview Mode Form Field Shortcut Menu

The fields on the form will display the shortcut menu shown in Figure 12-26 in preview mode. The options are explained in Table 12-11.

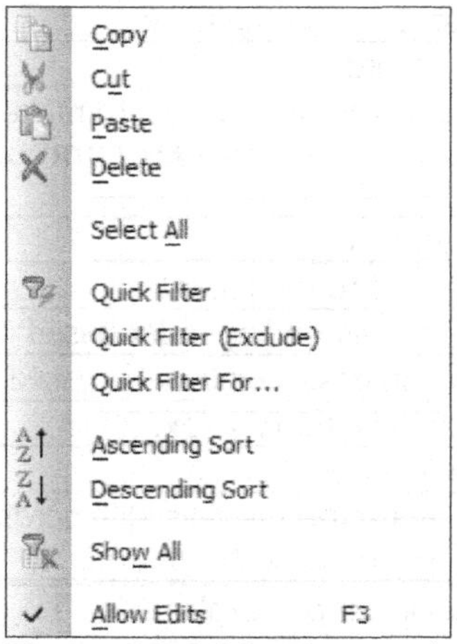

Figure 12-26 Preview mode form field shortcut menu

Option	Description
Select All	Selects the contents of the field.
Quick Filter	[See Using The Quick Filter section, later in this chapter]
Quick Filter (Exclude)	[See Using The Quick Filter (Exclude) section, later in this chapter]
Quick Filter For	Opens the **FILTER FIELD DIALOG BOX** shown in Figure 12-27, which is used to select what you want to search for in the field.
Ascending Sort	[See Table 12-10, Button 13]
Descending Sort	[See Table 12-10, Button 14]
Show All	[See Table 12-10, Button 18]
Allow Edits	[See Table 12-1]

Table 12-11 Preview mode form field shortcut menu options explained

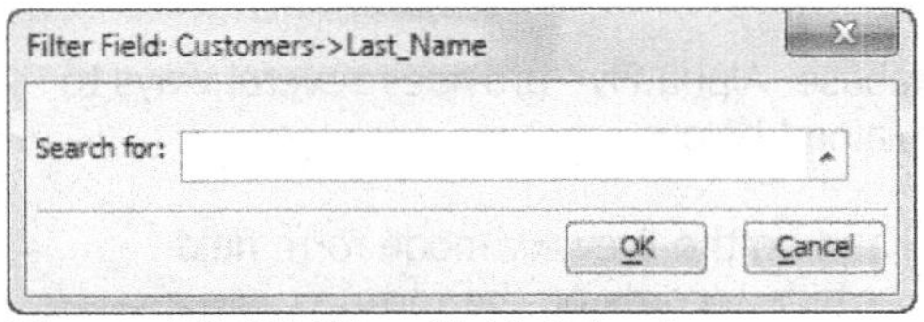

Figure 12-27 Filter Field dialog box

Form Keyboard Shortcuts

Using some or all of the keyboard shortcuts when entering data on a form can make the process easier. Keep in mind that these shortcuts take into consideration the tab stop order of the form.

Form Navigation Shortcuts

The keyboard shortcuts explained in Table 12-12 are used to move around the form.

Key	Moves . . .
Tab	To the next field. (6)
Enter	To the next field. If a button is the next field, it pushes the button. (6)
Shift + Tab	To the previous field. (6)
Page Up	To the previous field. (6)
Page Down	To the next field. (6)
Left	One field to the left. (6)
Right	One field to the right. (6)
F6	From the browse on the form to fields on the form. (7)
Shift + F6	Up to the next browse or field on the form.
Ctrl + Tab	From the active browse to the next browse on the form. (7)

Table 12-12 Form navigation keyboard shortcuts explained

(6) This option will also move to objects, like a button.
(7) If the form has more than one browse and the cursor is in the last browse on the form, pressing this key moves to the first field on the next record.

Data Entry Shortcuts

The keyboard shortcuts explained in Table 12-13 are used in a field when adding or editing data in a form or browse.

Key	Description
Left	Moves left one character.
Right	Moves right one character.
Delete	Removes characters to the right of the cursor.
Backspace	Removes characters to the left of the cursor.
Ctrl + Left	Moves left one word.
Ctrl + Right	Moves right one word.

Table 12-13 Data entry navigation keyboard shortcuts explained

Finding Records

Users will have the need to search for records in the database. Alpha Five provides several ways to search for records. The two main ways to search are explained below.

① The **QUERY FILTER OPTIONS** on the Query menu and on the Preview mode form field shortcut menu provide an easy way to display or hide records on the form.
② Use the **FIND OPTIONS** on the Find menu.

Using The Quick Filter

This tool is used to find records that have the value of the field that you click in on the form. The steps below explain how to use this filter option.

1. Display the form that you want to filter on, then click in the field of a record that has the value that you want to filter on.

2. Click the **QUICK FILTER BUTTON** on the toolbar or right-click in the field and select Quick Filter.

3. The only records displayed on the form will be those that have the value in the field that you selected. Click the **SHOW ALL BUTTON** on the toolbar to display all of the records.

> **CTRL+W**
> This keyboard shortcut removes the active filter, which is the equivalent of using the Show All button on the Form view toolbar.

Using The Quick Filter (Exclude) Option

As you may have guessed, this option works the opposite of the Quick Filter option discussed above. It displays records that do not have the value in the field that you select. The steps below explain how to use this filter option.

1. Display the form that you want to filter on, then click in the field of a record that has the value that you want to use to exclude records.

2. Right-click in the field that has the value that you want to exclude, then select **QUICK FILTER (EXCLUDE)**.

3. The only records displayed on the form will be those that do not have the value in the field that you selected.

Find Menu (After Search)

Figure 12-28 shows the Find menu that is available after you have run a search. The options are the same as the options explained below in Table 12-14.

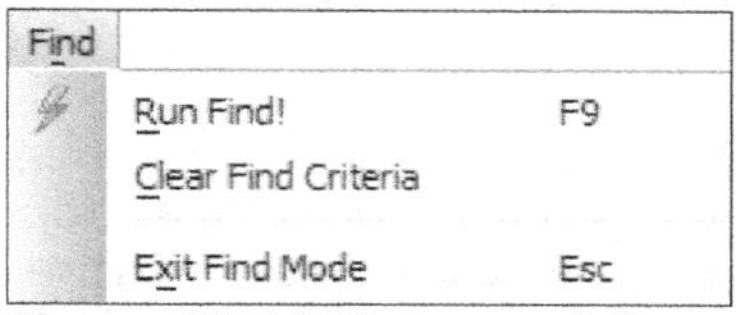

Figure 12-28 Find menu (after search)

Exercise 12.1: Use The Find Menu Options

In this exercise you will learn how to use the search options on the Find menu.

Find By Form

This option is used to enter values on an empty form that you want to search for. If the form is based on a set, the parent and child records are searched. When I entered the criteria, I expected to see all records that match the criteria. Instead, it only returns the first record that matches the criteria is returned. Below are the menu and toolbar options that are available after you select the Find by form option.

Figure 12-29 shows the toolbar. The buttons are explained in Table 12-14.

Figure 12-29 Find by Form toolbar

Button	Description
Run Find	Is used to search for the first record in the table or set that matches the criteria that you entered.
Clear Criteria	Is used to remove the current criteria from the search form.
Exit Find Mode	Closes the toolbar and displays the form with data.

Table 12-14 Find by Form toolbar buttons and Find menu options explained

1. View the form that you want to find records in, then Find ⇒ Find by Form.

2. Click in the field that you want to create criteria for, then type in the criteria, similar to what is shown in Figure 12-30.

   If you need to enter criteria for more than one field, you can.

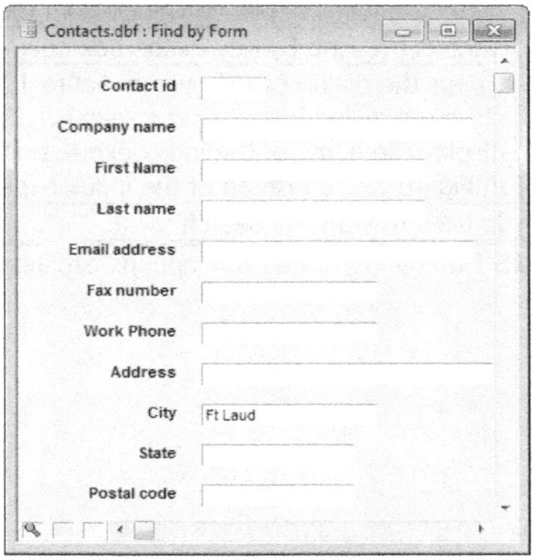

Figure 12-30 Find by Form dialog box

3. Click the Run Find button. The record that you see is the first record in the table that matches the criteria that you selected.

Find By Key

This option finds a record by searching a field, index or query list. This search option can also be used on a browse. The search is case sensitive. If you want to search in two fields like First and Last name, an index needs to be created. The downside of this search tool is that it only retrieves the first record that matches exactly or is the closest match to the selection criteria.

Figure 12-31 shows the dialog box for this search. The options are explained in Table 12-15.

There are three ways to open this dialog box, as explained below.

① Click the Find by Key button on the Browse view toolbar.
② Find ⇒ Find by Key.
③ Press Ctrl+K.

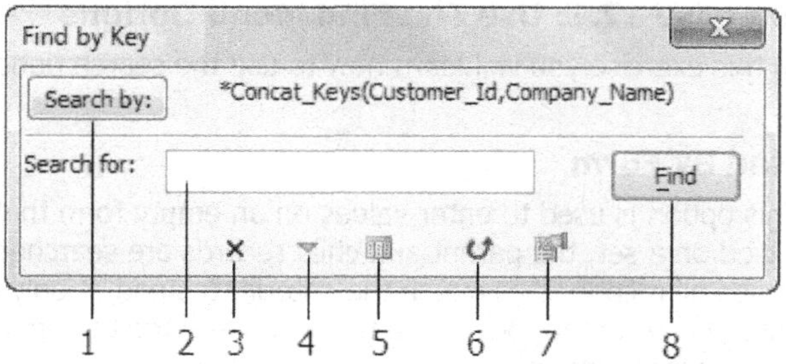

Figure 12-31 Find by Key dialog box (for forms)

Option	Description
1	The **SEARCH BY BUTTON** opens the dialog box shown later in Figure 12-37. The options on this dialog box are used to select a different field, index or query list that will be used as the search criteria.
2	Is used to type in the value that you want to search for in the selected field. This field has auto fill functionality, which means that as you are typing, the record with the closest match fills in the field. If the auto fill value is not the value that you need, keep typing. This option did not work with a date field when I tested it.
3	Closes the dialog box.
4	Displays a list of the previous criteria entered in the Search for field, as shown in Figure 12-32, since the dialog box was opened.
5	Displays the list of values in the field being searched, as shown in Figure 12-33. You can select one to perform another search. If checked, the **UNIQUE KEYS ONLY** option removes duplicate values from the list.
6	Shrinks the Find By Key dialog box down to a button, as shown in Figure 12-34.
7	Opens the dialog box shown in Figure 12-35. The **CLOSE THE FIND BY KEY . . .** option will close the dialog box after the search. The **DISPLAY INDEX NAME . . .** option is used to display the name of the index expression across from the Search by button, as shown in Figure 12-36 instead of the index expression formula shown earlier in Figure 12-31.
8	Is used to start the search.

Table 12-15 Find by Key dialog box options explained

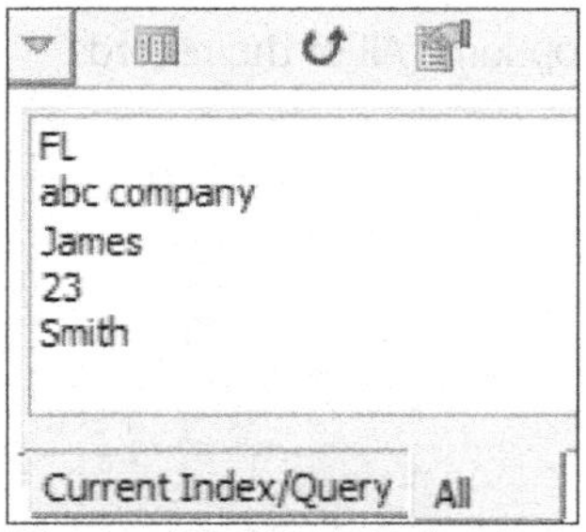

Figure 12-32 List of values searched for

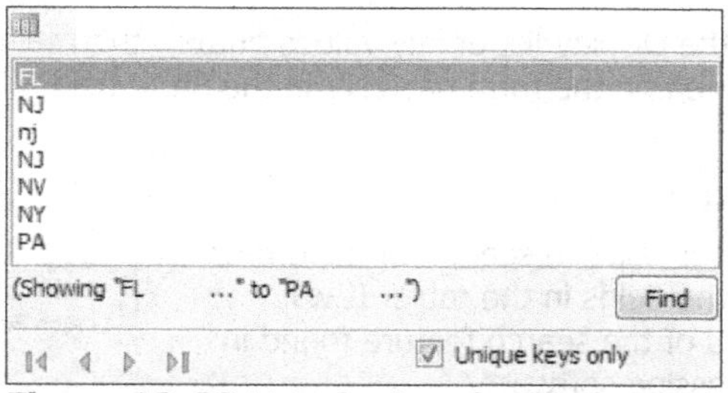

Figure 12-33 List of values for the Search by option

Figure 12-34 Find By Key dialog box shrunk down to a button

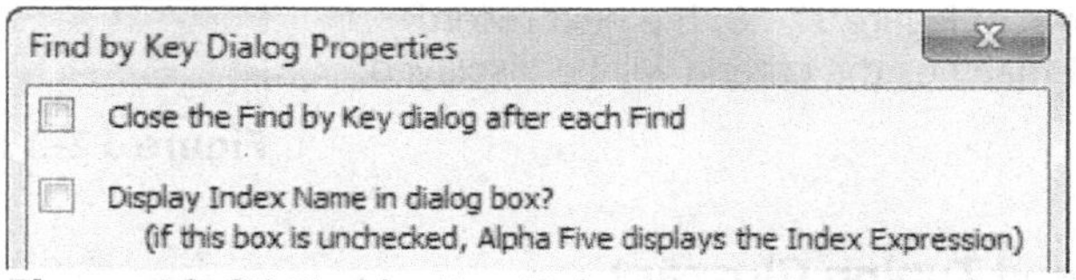

Figure 12-35 Find by Key Dialog Properties dialog box

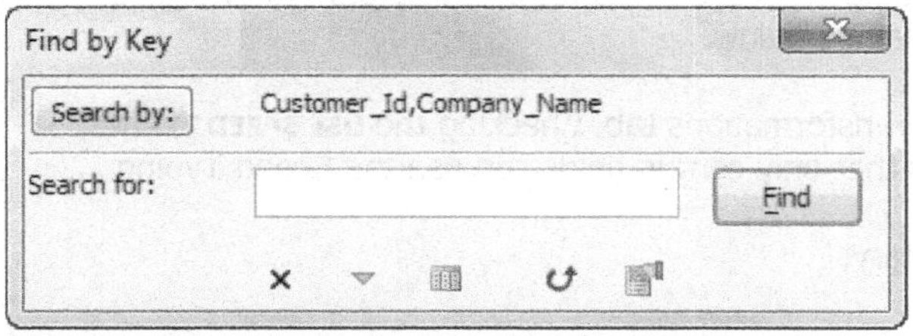

Figure 12-36 Display Index Name option enabled

Find A Record By The (Index) Key

In this part of the exercise you will search for a record in the state of Nevada.

1. View the Change title bar caption form.

2. Find ⇒ Find by Key, then click the Search by button.

   You will see the dialog box shown in Figure 12-37.

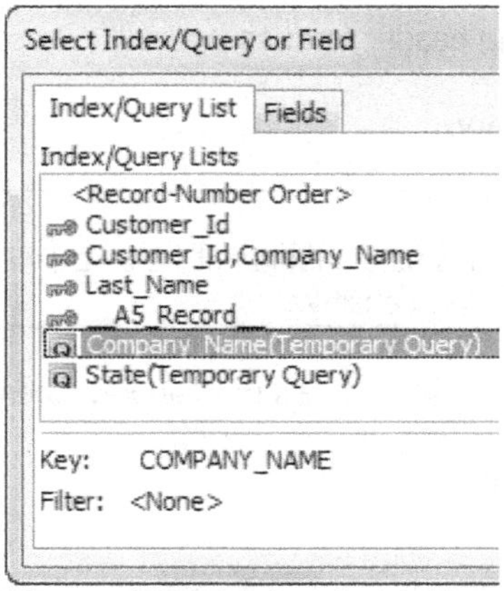

Figure 12-37 Select Index/Query or Field dialog box

3. On the Fields tab, click on the State field, then click OK.

4. Click the Display list of key values button, then select one of the NV options. All of the records displayed on the form have NV in the State field.

Find Text

This option is used to search for a word or phrase in the fields in the table. It will remind you of the search feature found in word processing software.

Each time that you click the Find button shown in Figure 12-38, the next record that matches the criteria will be displayed.

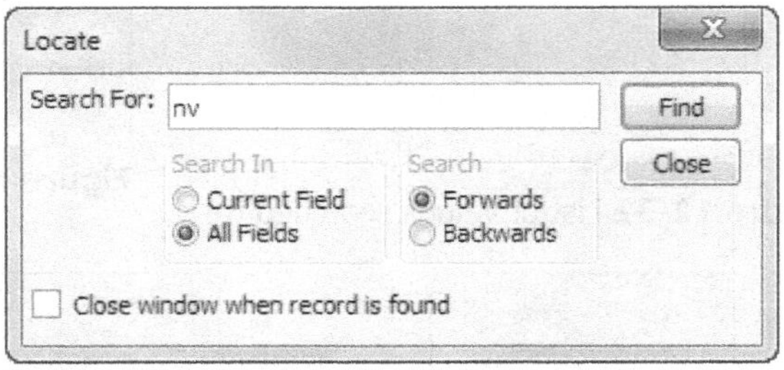

Figure 12-38 Locate dialog box

Speed Typing Glossary

In Chapter 4 you learned about this option and how it can be used to make data entry faster because you can use a keyword instead of typing an entire sentence or paragraph. Keywords can be set up by selecting one of the options explained below.

① The Field Rules dialog box on the Transformations tab. Checking the **USE SPEED TYPING GLOSSARY** option on this tab means that only certain fields can use the Speed Typing Glossary.
② In Form view, Tools ⇒ Speed Glossary.

The Speed Typing Glossary dialog box works like the Auto Correct and Auto Text options in Microsoft Word.

Exercise 12.2: Use The Speed Typing Glossary

In this exercise you will create a glossary entry for a city name. You will also create an entry that is often used for a closing sentence in a letter.

1. Save the Nonscrollable header form as `Speed glossary entries`, then view the form.

2. Tools ⇒ Speed Glossary.

Replace Field
What you enter in this field should not be a real word. This field is not case sensitive. The **WITH FIELD** is case sensitive.

3. In the Replace field type `atl`. Press the Tab key, then type `Atlanta` in the With field.

4. Click the **ADD WORD** button.

5. In the Replace field type `s2`.

   In the With field type
   `Hope to hear from you soon.`

   The dialog box should look like the one shown in Figure 12-39.

   Click the Add Word button.

   Click the Close button.

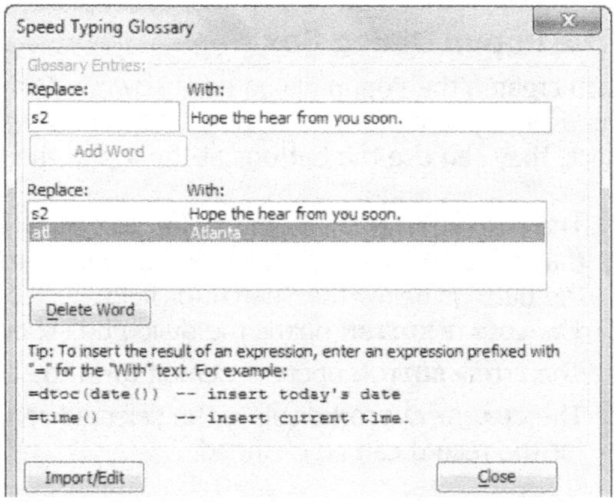
Speed Typing Glossary
Glossary Entries:
Replace:
With:
s2
Hope the hear from you soon.
Add Word
Replace:
With:
s2
Hope the hear from you soon.
atl
Atlanta
Delete Word
Tip: To insert the result of an expression, enter an expression prefixed with "=" for the "With" text. For example:
=dtoc(date()) -- insert today's date
=time() -- insert current time.
Import/Edit
Close

Figure 12-39 Speed typing entries created

6. Display a new record on the form.

7. In the City field type `atl`.

   You will see the word that will be filled in the field, as shown in Figure 12-40.

City
atl
Atlanta

Figure 12-40 Glossary entry

8. Press the Enter key.

9. In the Note field type `s2`, then press the Enter key. You should see the sentence shown in Figure 12-41. Save the changes.

Note
Hope the hear from you soon.

Figure 12-41 Glossary entry added to the field

Importing And Editing Multiple Glossary Entries At The Same Time

Earlier in Figure 12-39, you saw the **IMPORT/EDIT BUTTON**. This button opens the dialog box shown in Figure 12-42. As shown, the entries that were already created are in the list. You can edit or delete entries, as well as, add new entries. To add an entry, follow the steps below.

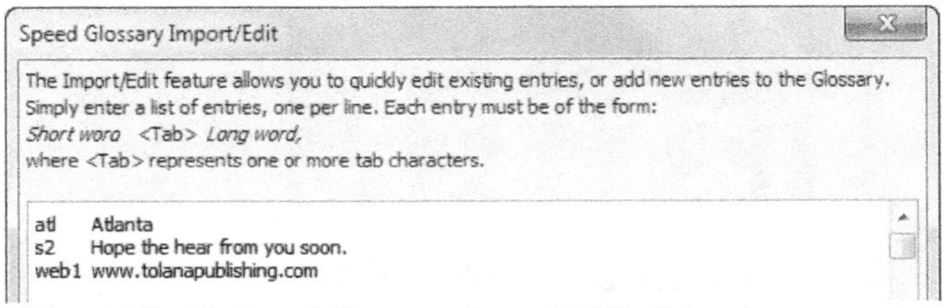
Speed Glossary Import/Edit
The Import/Edit feature allows you to quickly edit existing entries, or add new entries to the Glossary.
Simply enter a list of entries, one per line. Each entry must be of the form:
Short word <Tab> Long word,
where <Tab> represents one or more tab characters.
atl Atlanta
s2 Hope the hear from you soon.
web1 www.tolanapublishing.com

Figure 12-42 Speed Glossary Import/Edit dialog box

1. Move the cursor to a new line.

2. Type in what you would enter in the Replace field on the Speed Typing Glossary dialog box, then press the Tab key.

3. Type in what you would enter in the With field, then click OK. Close to close the Speed Typing Glossary dialog box.

Using The Popup Dialog Box

Earlier, you created the Popup dialog box shown in Chapter 4, Figure 4-42. This popup dialog box allows the user to search for the product. If the user does not want to scroll down the list to find the product, they can use the buttons at the top of the dialog box, as explained below.

① The **FIND BUTTON** opens the dialog box shown earlier in Figure 12-31. The difference is that the Find By Key dialog box that opens from the popup dialog box does not have the buttons below the Search for field.
② The **LOCATE BUTTON** opens the dialog box shown earlier in Figure 12-38.
③ The **ENTER BUTTON** opens a default form to allow more products to be added.
④ The **CHANGE BUTTON** displays the selected record on the popup dialog box so that the data for the record can be changed.

Date Field Tips

There are a few shortcuts that you can use to enter a date in a date field in a browse or a form. The options are explained below. After you type in one of these shortcuts, press the Tab key to leave the field.

① Typing `6/24/99` will display 6/24/1999 in the date field.
② Typing `092416` will display 9/24/2016 in the date field.
③ Typing `0624` will display 6/24/2012 in the date field or whatever the current year is.
④ Clicking the button at the end of a date field displays the calendar control shown in Figure 12-43. You can select the date in the calendar.

Figure 12-43 Date field calendar control

Browse Data Entry Tips And Tools

The topics covered in this section will aid users when they are doing data entry on a browse, as well as viewing data, creating queries and sorting records in a browse.

Creating A Quick Sort

In addition to being able to sort by using the Order Builder, records in a browse can be sorted on one column, by using the **ASCENDING SORT** or **DESCENDING SORT BUTTONS** on the Browse view toolbar or by right-clicking on the column header or in a cell and selecting a sort option. The main difference between this sort method and the Order Builder is that this sort cannot be saved.

Finding Records In A Browse By Key

This tool is used to find and display records, similar to filtering records. It searches and sorts the records at the same time. If you are using this tool on a set, the records in the child table that match the selected records in the parent table are also retrieved. The default key is the record number order, which is the order that the records were entered into the table.

Find By Key Dialog Box

Figure 12-44 shows the options that are available to find records in a browse. All of the options except one were explained earlier in Table 12-15.

The **SCROLL FOUND RECORD TO TOP OPTION** if checked, forces the record(s) that match the criteria to be displayed at the top of the browse.

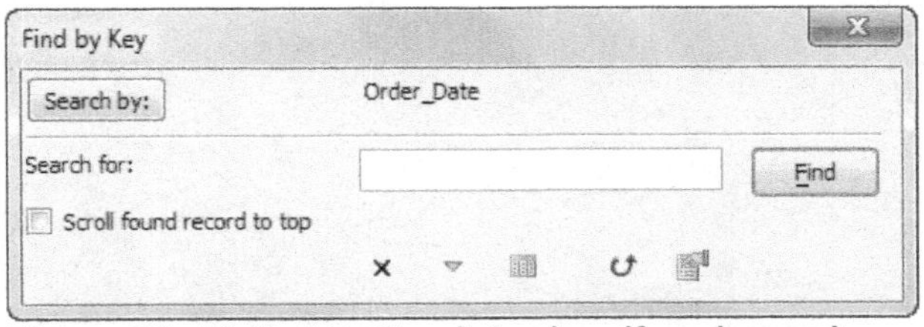

Figure 12-44 Find by Key dialog box (for a browse)

Exercise 12.3: Find Records By Key Using A Browse

In this exercise you will use a set to find all orders that were shipped on a specific date.

1. View the Orders multi table set browse.
2. Open the Find by Key dialog box. Click the Search by button, then select the Date Shipped field. Select the Scroll found record to top option.
3. Click the Display list of key values button, then select the date 4/11/2011. You should see the records with the date 4/11/2011 at the top of the browse.

USING POWERPIVOT

In this bonus chapter you will learn how to use PowerPivot For Excel. This free tool will let you create Pivot Tables and Pivot Charts with data from your Alpha Five database after you export it to Excel.

This chapter comes from my book, Getting Started With PowerPivot for Excel. For more information, go to www.tolana.com/books/2011/powerpivot/powerpivot2010.html.

CHAPTER 13

What Is PowerPivot And What Can I Use It For?

PowerPivot is a free tool that is used to pull data from multiple sources into one PowerPivot database that is part of an Excel 2010 or higher workbook. This functionality is used to enhance data analysis done in pivot tables and pivot charts in Excel. PowerPivot workbooks, as I call them, can also be shared with other users if the workbook is published on a SharePoint server. PowerPivot is Microsoft's first self-service business intelligence tool. Business Intelligence (also known as BI) tools and analysts are in great demand in companies of all sizes, in all types of industries.

The standard business intelligence approach to data is to place the data in a data warehouse for staging and then import the data into an Online Analytical Processing (OLAP) database. PowerPivot allows the data to bypass the data warehouse staging area step and be imported directly into the software that will be used to process the data. This means that the data that you use to create pivot tables in Excel, that are based on data in PowerPivot tables, can actually be saved on your computers hard drive, opposed to being saved on a server.

PowerPivot for Excel is a Visual Studio Tools for Office (VSTO) add-in. Specifically, PowerPivot is an add-in for the pivot table and pivot chart functionality in Excel. While you will see the software referred to as PowerPivot for Excel, its official name is **MICROSOFT SQL SERVER POWERPIVOT FOR EXCEL**. This is because PowerPivot is included in SQL Server 2008 R2, which includes major enhancements for business intelligence.

PowerPivot is used to import millions and millions of rows of data that will be used to create pivot tables. In addition to spreadsheet data, data can be imported from a variety of sources including databases, like Access, text files, Oracle, Atom data feeds and more. PowerPivot has a database that is embedded in the workbook. Once the data is imported into PowerPivot, it can be analyzed by creating pivot tables in Excel. PowerPivot puts the data into OLAP format behind the scenes. To take PowerPivot to the next level, which includes enterprise collaboration, PowerPivot for SharePoint can be used.

The purpose of PowerPivot for Excel is to help Excel end users access data in multi-dimensional databases without having extensive training and knowledge of this type of data modeling. Usually, only IT professionals have data modeling knowledge.

Additionally, PowerPivot has a new programming language called Data Analysis Expressions (DAX). This language adds data manipulation functionality to Excel formulas, including analysis and complex grouping that is above the formula capabilities that are available in Excel. DAX takes the formulas that you are use to creating for pivot tables and pivot charts in Excel to a whole new level.

The DAX programming language was created based on the formulas and functions that are already available in Excel, in hopes of making it easier for Excel users to create more advanced formulas to help resolve business intelligence needs. PowerPivot for Excel allows non programmers to access enterprise data to perform a higher level of analysis in one of Excels most popular analysis tools - PivotTables, then is available in Excel.

As I mentioned earlier, PowerPivot can be used to analyze millions of records. The Table Import Wizard is the primary tool used to import data into PowerPivot. The data is imported as tables and stored on separate tabs in the PowerPivot window. Believe it or not, data can also be pasted into a PowerPivot table. Really? That's what I thought when I first found that out. PowerPivot stores the data that is imported in a database that is saved in the Excel workbook. The local (database) engine is used to load, query and update the database in the Excel workbook.

This data analysis tool adds a lot of functionality to Excel pivot tables. Once the data is imported into PowerPivot, relationships between the tables of data can be created, very similar to how relationships between tables in a database are created, without using **VLOOKUP**.

PowerPivot Workbooks vs Excel Workbooks

In addition to how PowerPivot and Excel handle data differently, there are other differences between these types of workbooks that you should be aware of, as discussed below.

① The biggest difference between these workbooks is that a PowerPivot workbook stores data in a database that is embedded in the workbook. Keep in mind that PowerPivot is an add-in application for Excel, not a stand alone application, which means that PowerPivot cannot run on its own.

② The second biggest difference is that PowerPivot tables can store more than one million rows of data, which is the maximum in Excel. While one million rows may sound like a lot of data, in BI analysis, one is often working with tens of millions of rows of data. Two scenarios that come to mind are the number of tests run on patients in a hospital over the last five years or the number of transactions for a major credit card company over the last year.

③ PowerPivot does not support **VISUAL BASIC FOR APPLICATIONS (VBA)**, but VBA can be used on the Excel side of a PowerPivot workbook to enhance pivot tables if needed.

④ PowerPivot lets you build the data model that you need, whether the data comes from one database or 20 databases.

⑤ PowerPivot workbooks can save up to 2GB of data and can support up to 4GB of data in memory.

2GB File Size
While 2GB may not seem like a lot of space for a single workbook, keep in mind that .xlsx workbook files are really zip files. This means that it can store more than 2GB of raw data because of the data compression that zip files have and the **COLUMNAR DATABASE** that PowerPivot uses.

Using Excel 2007
Excel 2007 can be used to open a PowerPivot workbook to change the formatting and style of a pivot table in the PowerPivot workbook. Excel 2007 cannot be used to interact with pivot tables and pivot charts that use PowerPivot data or change the data.

Attention Windows XP Users
In Windows Vista and higher, the PowerPivot options are available on a ribbon. In Windows XP, the PowerPivot options are available on a set of menus. The link below shows the correlation between the options on the ribbon in Windows Vista and higher and their menu counterparts in Windows XP. http://technet.microsoft.com/en-us/library/ff452230.aspx

What Is The Difference Between The 32 And 64-Bit Versions Of PowerPivot?

The version of PowerPivot that you install must match the version of Excel 2010 or higher that is installed. The difference between these versions is that the 32-bit version only supports up to 2GB of data in memory. The 64-bit version supports up to 4GB of data in memory.

How To Verify That PowerPivot Is Installed Correctly

After you have installed all of the components and PowerPivot for Excel, open Excel. On the Excel splash screen you should see the message shown in Figure 13-1 indicating that the PowerPivot add-in is being loaded.

Once Excel is open, you should see the PowerPivot tab on the Excel ribbon. Click on this tab, then click the PowerPivot Window button. An empty PowerPivot window will open. Seeing this window lets you know that PowerPivot is installed correctly.

Figure 13-1 Excel splash screen showing the PowerPivot add-in loading

As you will see, PowerPivot for Excel has two components, as explained below.

① The **POWERPIVOT WINDOW** is primarily used to import the data into PowerPivot, create relationships and to create calculated columns.
② The **POWERPIVOT FIELD LIST** is used to select the fields to create a pivot table, as well as create DAX measures.

Download Sample Data

The next section describes the sample database that will be used in this chapter and will show you where to download it from.

Adventure Works Database This database is for a fictitious company named Adventure Works. The company makes and sells bicycles globally. This is the Microsoft Access version of the popular SQL database by the same name, that has been around for years. The database has 67 tables.

I decided to use the Access version of the database because I did not want people to have to download and install SQL Server or upgrade the version that they may already have installed. If something went wrong with that installation or upgrade, your computer is not powerful enough to support it, you would be stuck. The Access version does not require you to install any other software, not even Microsoft Access.

1. Go to http://adventureworksaccess.codeplex.com/releases/view/44496.
2. Click on the **ADVENTURE WORKS IN ACCESS 2010 FORMAT (ZIPPED)** link.
3. Download this file to your folder, then extract the database to the folder. In this chapter, you will not see this database in the Alpha Five folder. It is shown in the folder for the PowerPivot book.

Exercise 13.1: Let Me See What PowerPivot Can Do

In this exercise you will learn the basic steps of creating a pivot table that uses PowerPivot data. By the end of this exercise you will have used many of the core features of PowerPivot.

Step 1: Open The PowerPivot Window

This step covers opening the PowerPivot window and selecting a data source to connect to.

1. Open a new Excel workbook.

2. PowerPivot tab ⇒ PowerPivot Window button.

Welcome To PowerPivot! As you can see, PowerPivot has its own window, separate from the Excel window. Behind the scenes, the PowerPivot window is connected to the Excel workbook. If you have several Excel workbooks open, some with PowerPivot windows open and others not, Excel still knows which workbooks have PowerPivot windows open. It can get confusing looking at the Windows taskbar if you have multiple Excel workbooks and PowerPivot windows open, so you may find it helpful to close all open windows before starting an exercise, but that is up to you.

3. Home tab ⇒ Get External Data group ⇒ From Database button ⇒ From Access, as shown in Figure 13-2.

   The **TABLE IMPORT WIZARD** dialog box will open.

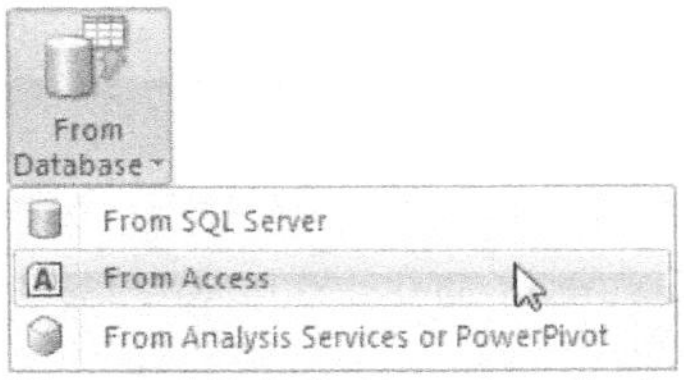

Figure 13-2 Options to select a Microsoft database

Step 2: Select The Data Source

This step covers selecting the data source and connecting to it. As you will learn, data from different sources including text files, spreadsheets, data feeds, as well as enterprise databases can be used to get the data for your analysis needs. This process is known as establishing a connection to a data source. Regardless of the data source, all data is imported as a table. Each table is placed on a different tab in the PowerPivot window, like worksheets in an Excel workbook.

1. On the Table Import Wizard dialog box, in the Friendly connection name field type `First PowerPivot Project.`

Using The Friendly Connection Name Field
It is not a requirement to use this field. By default, the type of database and database file name will automatically be filled in once data is imported from the database. It will be helpful to enter a name for the connection if you are going to import data from more than one data source into the same PowerPivot workbook. For example, if you are going to import data from different databases of the same type (like SQL or Access), using a descriptive name in this field will help you know which types or tables of data came from which database. PowerPivot has an option to display all of the connections in the workbook. The name entered in the Friendly connection field is also displayed, as illustrated in bold in Figure 13-3. All of the databases in the figure are Access databases. What helps to distinguish them is the Friendly connection name.

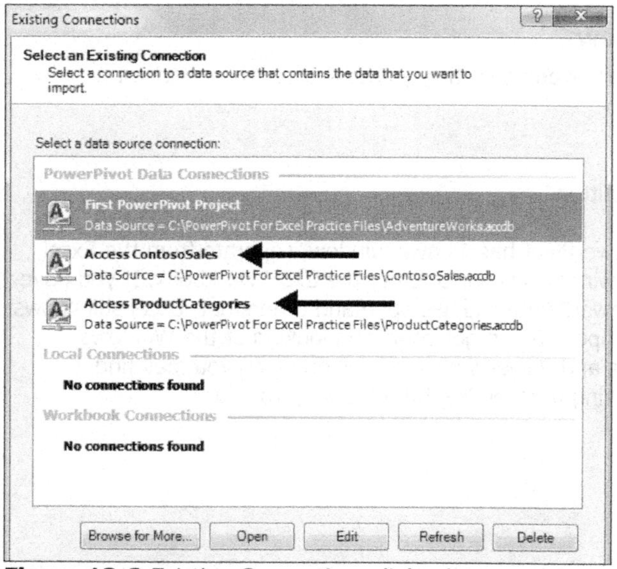

Figure 13-3 Existing Connections dialog box

2. Click the Browse button.

   Navigate to your folder, then double-click on the Adventure Works database.

   You should have the options shown in Figure 13-4.

   Click Next.

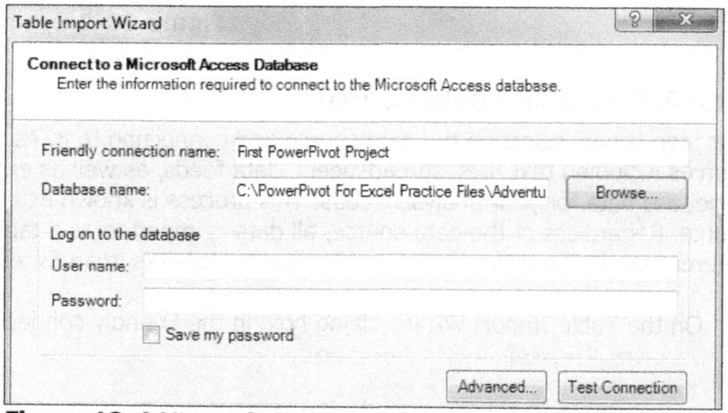

Figure 13-4 Microsoft Access database connection options

Step 3: Select The Tables Of Data To Import

Data sources, in particular databases, often have a lot of tables. There will be times when you will not need all of the tables in a database. The steps below show you how to select the tables that you need. All of the tables and views in the database are displayed on the Select Tables and Views screen on the Table Import Wizard dialog box. Only importing the tables and data in the tables that you will use will keep the size of the PowerPivot workbook small.

For example, if a database has tables in the following categories; employees, products, financial, orders, car leases and retail stores and your goal is to create pivot charts on product sales, you can skip importing the financial and car leases tables. Remember that there is a workbook file size limitation.

1. Select the first option on the screen shown in Figure 13-5, then click Next.

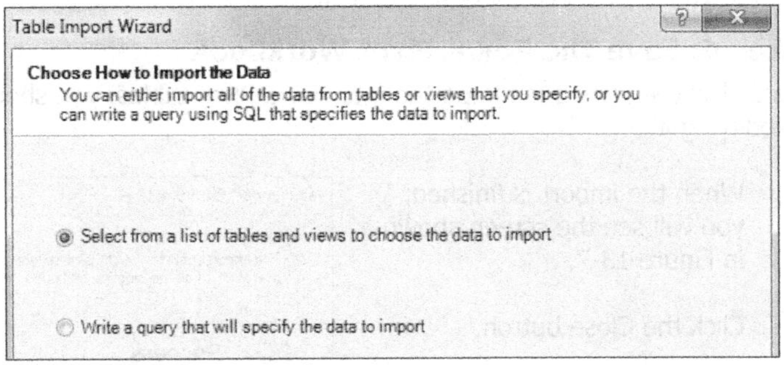

Figure 13-5 Import options

2. On the Select Tables and Views screen, click in the box in front of the following tables to select them: HumanResources_Employee, Person_Contact, Sales_SalesOrderHeader, Sales_SalesPerson and Sales_SalesTerritory, as shown in Figure 13-6.

> **Resizing Columns**
> If you need to see more of the Source Table name then is visible, the columns on the Table Import Wizard dialog box can be resized by placing the mouse pointer on the vertical line after the column that you need to resize and dragging the line to the right.

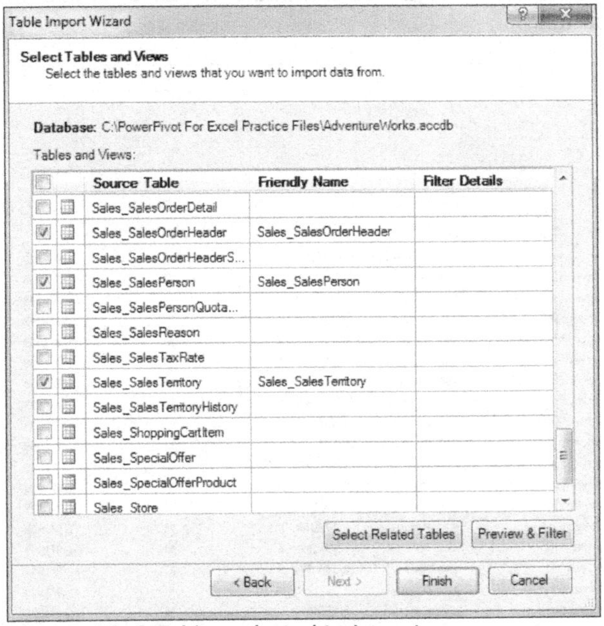

Figure 13-6 Tables selected to import

> **Selecting Records To Import**
> If you do not need to import all of the records and fields in a table, click the **PREVIEW & FILTER** button on the screen shown above in Figure 13-6. This is where you would create a filter to select the records and fields that you do not want to import.

3. Click Finish. The data will now be imported from the Access database into tables in the PowerPivot window.

Step 4: Save The PowerPivot Workbook

Once the data has been imported into PowerPivot tables, you should save the workbook before modifying it.

1. When the import is finished, you will see the screen shown in Figure 13-7.

   Click the Close button.

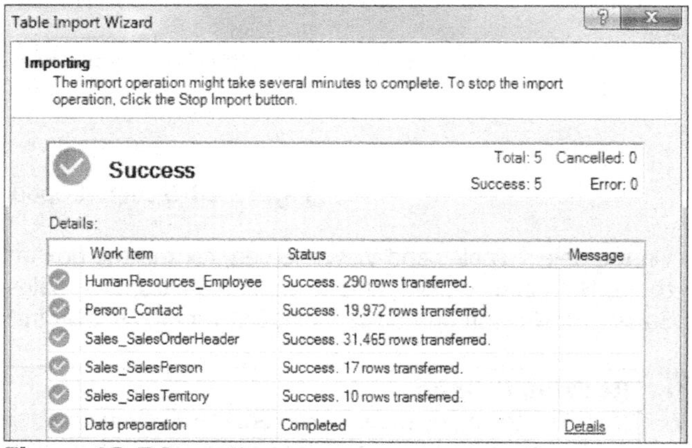

Figure 13-7 Importing screen

2. When you see the PowerPivot window shown in Figure 13-8 with the five tables of data that you just imported, click the Save button.

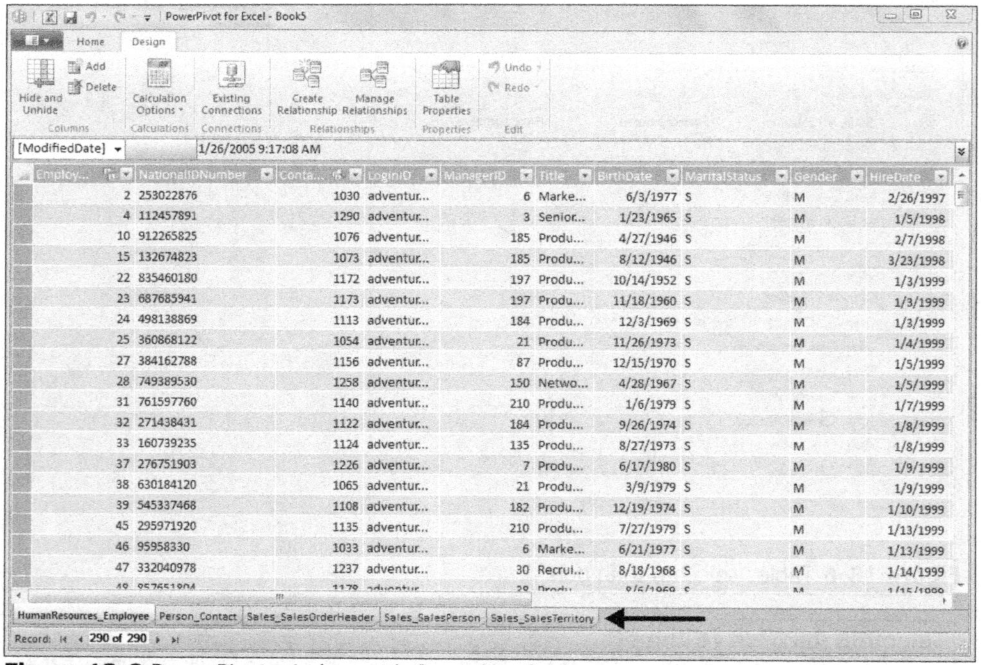

Figure 13-8 PowerPivot window with five tabs of data

3. Navigate to your folder if necessary, then type `First PowerPivot Workbook` as the file name, then press Enter.

Using The PowerPivot Field List

When you select the type of pivot table or pivot chart that you want to create, you will see the Create PivotTable or Create PivotChart dialog box. This is how you select where on the worksheet the pivot table or pivot chart will be placed. You can move the pivot table or pivot chart later if necessary.

You will also see the PowerPivot Field List. The top section lists all of the tables and fields that are in the PowerPivot window. This section is used to select and add the fields to the pivot table. You can also use the top section to rename fields for the pivot table.

The bottom section of the PowerPivot Field List is the **DROP ZONE** section. It is used to select where the fields are placed on the pivot table.

> **Excel PivotTable Option**
> Excel has options on the Insert tab to create pivot tables and pivot charts. You cannot use these options because they are not connected to the PowerPivot data.

Step 5: Create The Pivot Table

In this step you will learn how to create a pivot table using the data that you imported into PowerPivot. The pivot table that you create will show the total sales amount by region for each sales rep.

1. In the Excel window, PowerPivot tab ⇒ Report group ⇒ PivotTable button ⇒ PivotTable.

2. Select the **EXISTING WORKSHEET** option on the Create PivotTable dialog box, then click OK. The PowerPivot Field List should appear on the right side of the Excel worksheet.

3. In the Sales_SalesOrderHeader table in the PowerPivot Field List, right-click on the SalesPersonID field and select the **ADD TO ROW LABELS** option, shown in Figure 13-9.

   This option will create the row of data for the left most column in the pivot table.

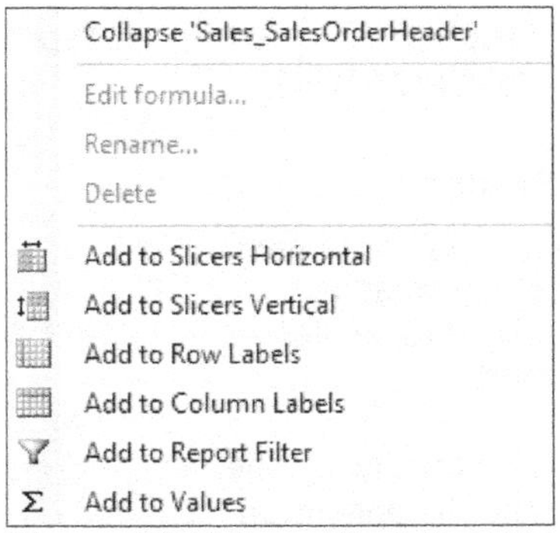

Figure 13-9 PowerPivot Field List shortcut menu

4. In the Sales_SalesTerritory table, right-click on the Name field, then select the Add to Column Labels option. This will create the column headings across the top of the pivot table.

5. In the Sales_SalesOrderHeader table, right-click on the SubTotal field, then select the Add to Values option. This will calculate the values that will be displayed in the middle of the pivot table.

6. The drop zone section of the PowerPivot Field List should look like the one shown in Figure 13-10.

   The pivot table should look like the one shown in Figure 13-11.

   Save the changes.

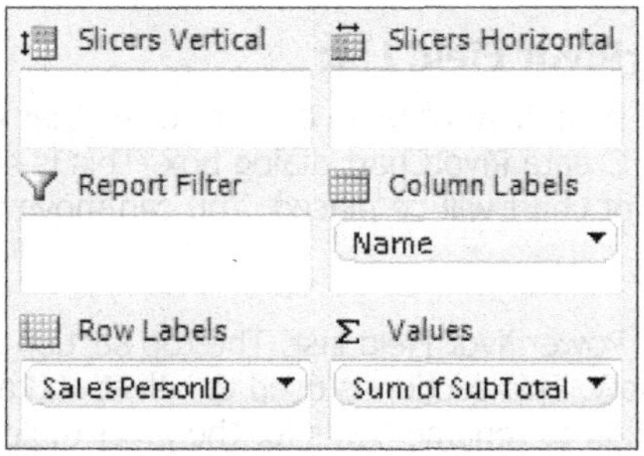

Figure 13-10 PowerPivot Field List drop zone options

Did you notice that you used fields from more than one table to create the pivot table without writing a formula or selecting any additional options? That is one of the features that makes PowerPivot rock in my opinion.

	A	B	C	D	E	F	G	H	I	J	K	L
1	Sum of SubTotal	Column Labels										
2	Row Labels	Australia	Canada	Central	France	Germany	Northeast	Northwest	Southeast	Southwest	United Kingdom	Grand Total
3		9061000.584	1977844.862	3000.8296	2644017.714	2894312.338	6532.4682	3649866.551	12238.8496	5718150.812	3391712.211	29358677.22
4	268		264867.0069	43824.0227			100165.0377	279997.5919	181804.2136	498966.7766		1369624.649
5	275			3127053.025			3547034.396		347730.2939	4230221.05		11252038.77
6	276			2225871.149				2562534.431		7859324.248		12647729.83
7	277			3543660.984			4735174.261		309496.8021	3569595.145		12157927.19
8	278		4380714.255									4380714.255
9	279								8714865.97			8714865.97
10	280							4029938.356				4029938.356
11	281			621258.9399				936689.47		6371216.557		7929164.967
12	282		2532500.913								4678149.585	7210650.498
13	283							4551897.661				4551897.661
14	284				118890.3863	239835.1362					533258.121	891983.6435
15	285		10302726.69									10302726.69
16	286				5505602.675							5505602.675
17	287							2814958.894				2814958.894
18	288	219088.8836										219088.8836
19	289					2241204.042						2241204.042
20	290	1758385.926										1758385.926
21	Grand Total	11038475.39	19458653.72	9564668.951	8268510.775	5375351.517	8388906.163	18825882.96	9566136.129	28247474.59	8603119.917	127337180.1

Figure 13-11 PowerPivot pivot table

Using The Pivot Table

At this point, PowerPivots job is finished, unless more data needs to be added to the pivot table or you need to create more calculated columns.

From this point on, you primarily use the PowerPivot Field List and the options on the PowerPivot tab to add pivot table and pivot chart functionality.

As shown above in Figure 13-11, the pivot table that is using data from PowerPivot can be used just like pivot tables that are created from data in an Excel worksheet. That means that you can use the Excel filter options shown in Figure 13-12.

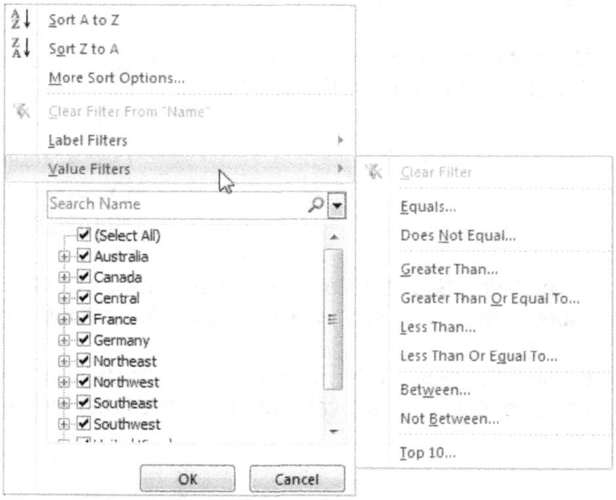

Figure 13-12 Excel filter options

If you find that you are using the same filter options over and over, you can add the field or fields to the **REPORT FILTER** drop zone on the PowerPivot Field List. That is what you will do in the next exercise.

Exercise 13.2: Modify A Pivot Table

In this exercise you will modify the pivot table that you created in the previous exercise to have a report filter. The filter that you add will let the pivot table display the sales data by shipping method.

If you look in the Sales_SalesOrderHeader table, you will see the ShipMethodID field. While you can use the ID field (which is a number) for the shipping method filter, it may be difficult to remember what each number means. None of the tables that you imported in Exercise 13.1 have the field with the shipping method names. These values are stored in the Purchasing_ShipMethod table. This is when it would be helpful to have the data dictionary or a print out of all of the fields in each table in the database. Having that would make it easier to find the field that you need. As you read, the Adventure Works database has 67 tables. Aren't you happy that this bonus chapter has step-by-step instructions? <smile>

Step 1: Add Another Table Of Data To The PowerPivot Workbook

In this step you will import the data from the table that has the shipping method names that you will use for the report filter.

1. Save the First Powerpivot workbook as `Modify pivot table`.
2. PowerPivot tab ⇒ PowerPivot Window button.
3. Design tab ⇒ Existing Connections button.
4. Select the Adventure Works database, then click the Open button.
5. Click Next on the Import Data screen.
6. Select the Purchasing_ShipMethod table, then click Finish. The table will now be imported into PowerPivot.
7. Click Close after the data has been imported, then save the changes.

Refreshing Data

PowerPivot pivot tables and PowerPivot pivot charts are based on the data in PowerPivot tables at the time that the pivot table or pivot chart was created. After the pivot tables and pivot charts are created, more than likely the data in PowerPivot tables will be updated. This means that the data in the underlying tables of the pivot table or pivot chart are out of sync, which causes the data displayed in the pivot table or pivot chart to not be current.

When the data is updated in the PowerPivot window, you will see the message shown below in Figure 13-13 at the top of the PowerPivot Field list. Click the **REFRESH** button to update the data in the pivot table or pivot chart, as well as, update the tables in the PowerPivot Field List if you imported more tables, appended data to an existing PowerPivot table or created more calculated fields.

If you created a pivot table and then create a measure or relationship, the message shown in Figure 13-13 will also be displayed in the PowerPivot Field List.

Step 2: Create The Report Filter

1. Display the pivot table.

At the top of the PowerPivot Field List you should see the message shown in Figure 13-13.

Figure 13-13 PowerPivot data was modified message

This message lets you know that data in the PowerPivot workbook has changed. In this case, the change was that a table was added to the workbook.

2. Click the Refresh button shown above in Figure 13-13.

3. Scroll to the bottom of the list of tables in the PowerPivot Field List pane. You will see the Purchasing_ShipMethod table. Add the Name field from this table to the Report Filter drop zone.

4. When you see the message at the top of the PowerPivot Field List that a relationship may be needed, as shown in Figure 13-14, click the Create button. You will see the dialog box shown in Figure 13-15.

Figure 13-14 PowerPivot relationship message

Relationship Detection And Creation

PowerPivot displayed the message shown above in Figure 13-14 because there may be a relationship that needs to be created between tables, based on the data that was modified in the workbook.

In the previous section you imported data after the pivot table was created and are now adding a field from the new PowerPivot table to the pivot table. Clicking the Create button tells PowerPivot to look for and create any relationships that it thinks should be created. The result of the search for new relationships is what is displayed in Figure 13-15. In this case, PowerPivot found at least one relationship that needed to be created and created it. This is not always the case. Sometimes when you see this message and click the Create button, the dialog box in Figure 13-15 will display a message indicating that no relationships were detected.

If you click on the DETAILS link across from the Relationship detection item, you will see the dialog box shown in Figure 13-16. This lets you know how many relationships PowerPivot found that could be created. If you click on the Details link across from the Relationship creation item, you will see the dialog box shown in Figure 13-17. You will see the relationships that were created.

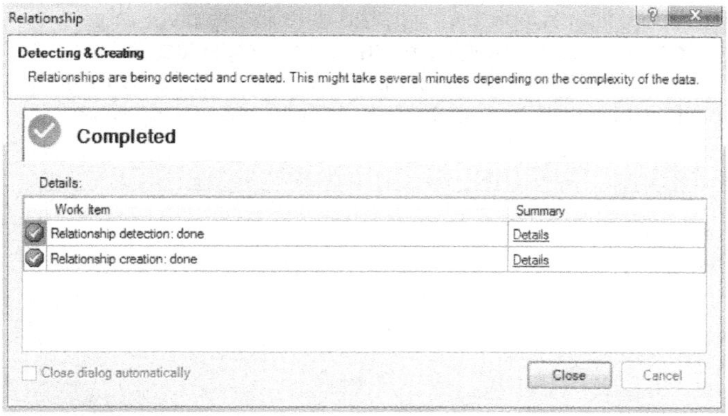

Figure 13-15 Relationship dialog box

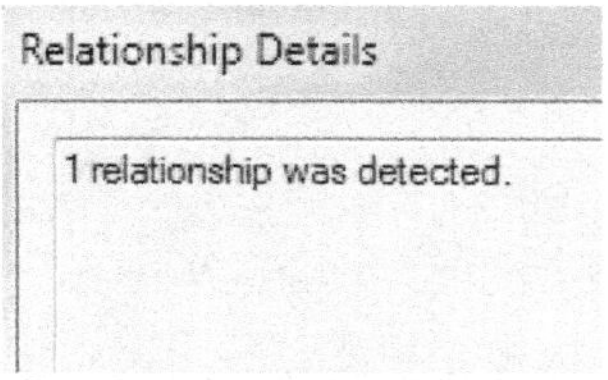

Figure 13-16 Relationship Details dialog box for the relationship detection option

Figure 13-17 Relationship Details dialog box for the relationship creation option

5. Click the Close button on the Relationship dialog box shown earlier in Figure 13-15. If the relationship that was needed for the field that you selected was created, the field will be added to the drop zone.

How To Rename A Report Filter

By default when a field is added to the Report Filter drop zone or any drop zone for that matter, the field name is displayed for the filter above the pivot table or pivot chart. Sometimes, this name is not the best option to be displayed with the pivot table. When that is the case, you can rename the Report Filter. The steps below show you how.

6. Click on the Name field in the Report Filter drop zone, then select the Field Settings option on the shortcut menu.

7. In the Custom Name field type `Shipping Method`, as shown in Figure 13-18, then click OK.

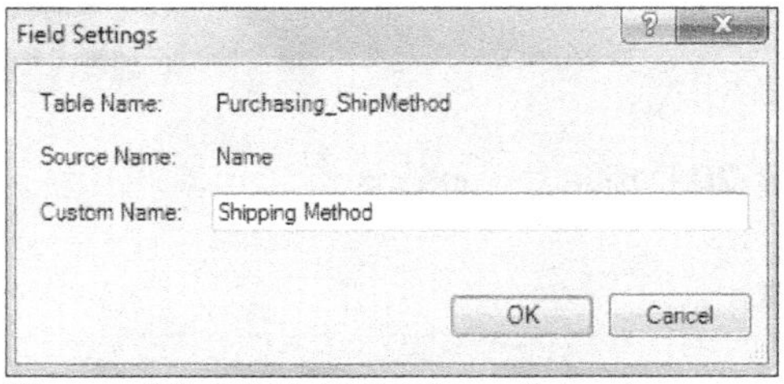

Figure 13-18 Field Settings dialog box

8. You will see that the name of the filter in the upper left corner of the worksheet has changed from "Name" to "Shipping Method". Save the changes.

If you select a shipping method from the report filter drop-down list, the data in the pivot table will only display totals for orders that were shipped with the shipping method that you selected, as shown in Figure 13-19. Compare this to the pivot table shown earlier in Figure 13-11. Being able to use a field in one table as the filter for data in multiple other tables should demonstrate how powerful PowerPivot is.

Shipping Method	CARGO TRANSPORT 5										
Sum of SubTotal	Column Labels										
Row Labels	Australia	Canada	Central	France	Germany	Northeast	Northwest	Southeast	Southwest	United Kingdom	Grand Total
268		264867.0069	43824.0227			100165.0377	279997.5919	181804.2136	498966.7766		1369624.649
275			3127053.025			3547034.396		347730.2939	4230221.05		11252038.77
276			2225871.149				2562534.431		7859324.248		12647729.83
277			3543660.984			4735174.261		309496.8021	3569595.145		12157927.19
278		4380714.255									4380714.255
279								8714865.97			8714865.97
280							4029938.356				4029938.356
281			621258.9399				936689.47		6371216.557		7929164.967
282		2532500.913								4678149.585	7210650.498
283							4551897.661				4551897.661
284				118890.3863	239835.1362					533258.121	891983.6435
285		10302726.69									10302726.69
286				5505602.675							5505602.675
287							2814958.894				2814958.894
288	219088.8836										219088.8836
289					2241204.042						2241204.042
290	1758385.926										1758385.926
Grand Total	1977474.81	17480808.86	9561668.121	5624493.061	2481039.179	8382373.695	15176016.4	9553897.279	22529323.78	5211407.706	97978502.89

Figure 13-19 Pivot table with filtered data

What Is A Pivot Chart Report?

A pivot chart report is like a pivot table report, because they have filters and slicers. Keep in mind that changes made to the pivot table that the pivot chart is linked to, are automatically made to the pivot chart. Pivot charts can be interactive and display data the same way that standard charts do because they display data series, data markers, axis and categories.

PivotChart Tools Contextual Tabs

Like pivot tables, there are tools in Excel specifically for pivot charts. Figures 13-20 to 13-23 show the pivot chart tools. If you have created standard charts in Excel, you may have already used some of these options.

Design Tab

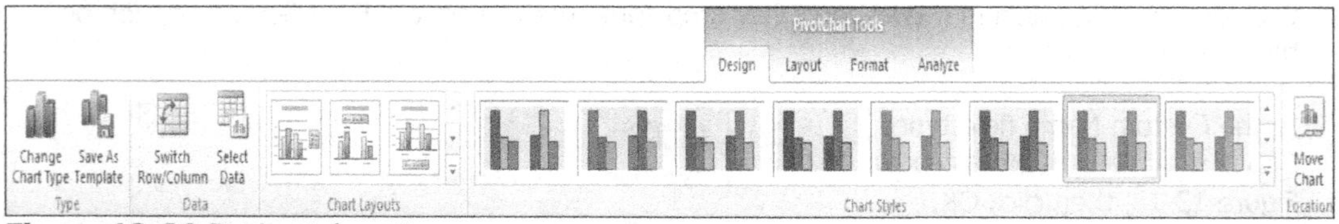

Figure 13-20 Design tab options

Layout Tab

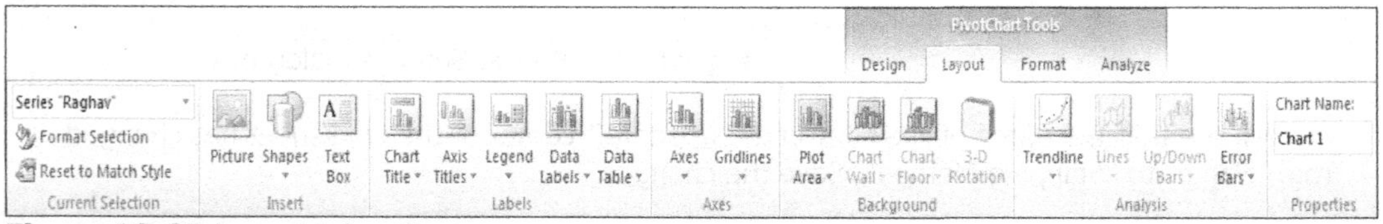

Figure 13-21 Layout tab options

Format Tab

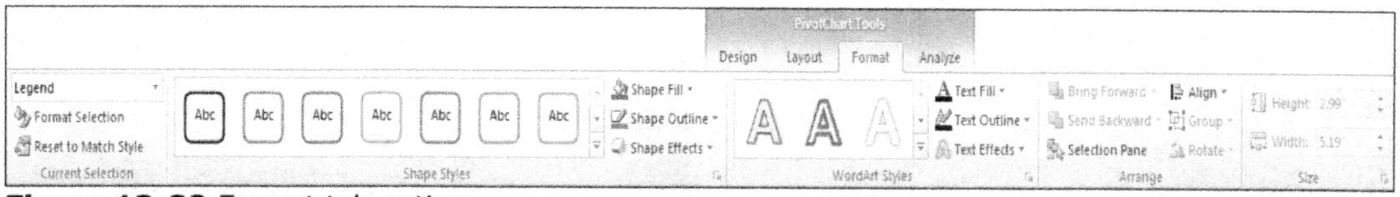

Figure 13-22 Format tab options

Analyze Tab

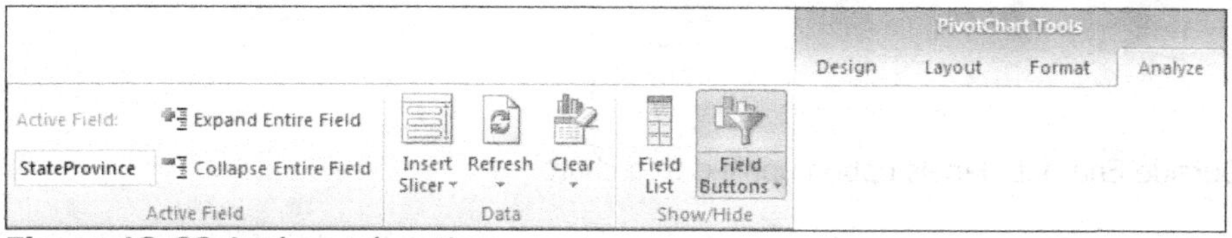

Figure 13-23 Analyze tab options

Pivot Chart Tools That You May Find Helpful

Below are a few options that you may find helpful to enhance your pivot charts.

The **CHART LAYOUTS** options on the Design tab shown in Figure 13-24 are used to rearrange chart objects like the position and style of the legend and the grid style.

The **DATA LABELS** options on the Layout tab shown in Figure 13-25 are used to display the actual value that the slice of a pie chart, a bar or line represents. Figure 13-26 shows the **OUTSIDE END** option applied to the chart.

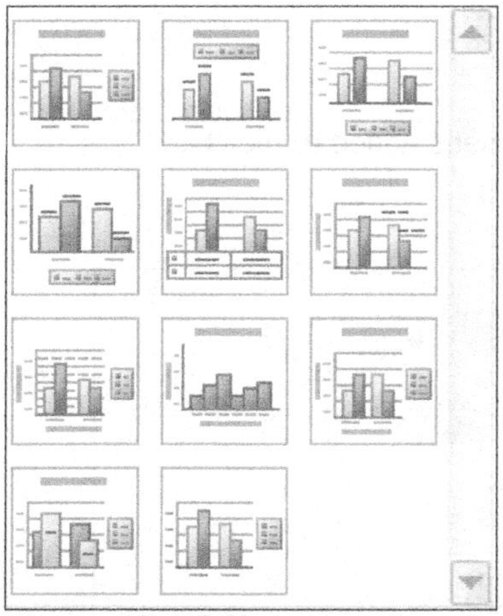
Figure 13-24 Chart Layouts options

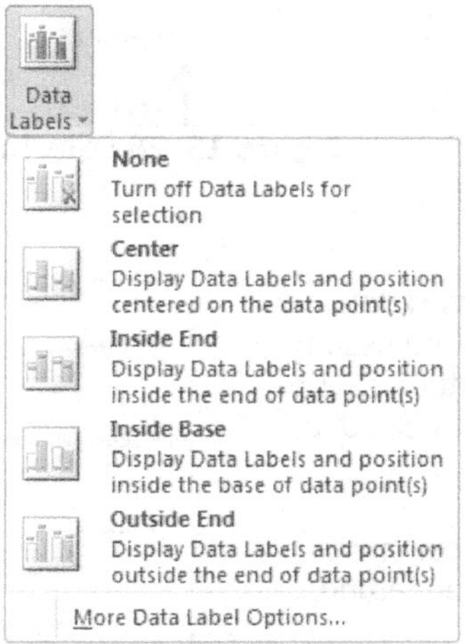

Figure 13-25 Data Labels options

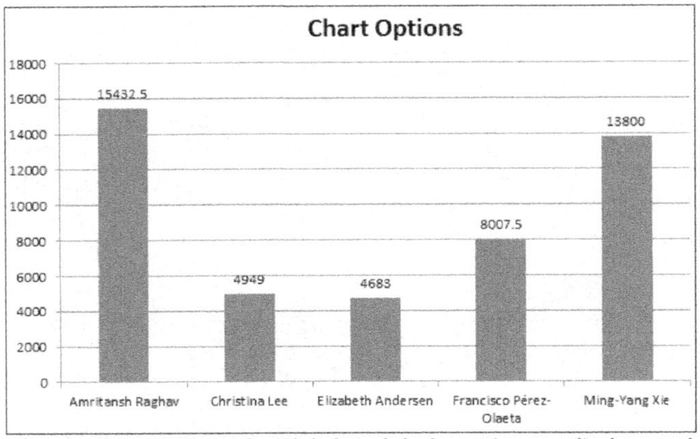

Figure 13-26 Outside End data labels option applied to a chart

The **DATA TABLE** options on the Layout tab shown in Figure 13-27 are used to add a table to the bottom of a chart. The values in the table are the values displayed in the chart. Figure 13-28 shows the pivot chart with a data table and legend keys at the bottom of the chart. If the chart displays a lot of data, this option can be used instead of placing the actual values on the chart, which would make the chart easier to read.

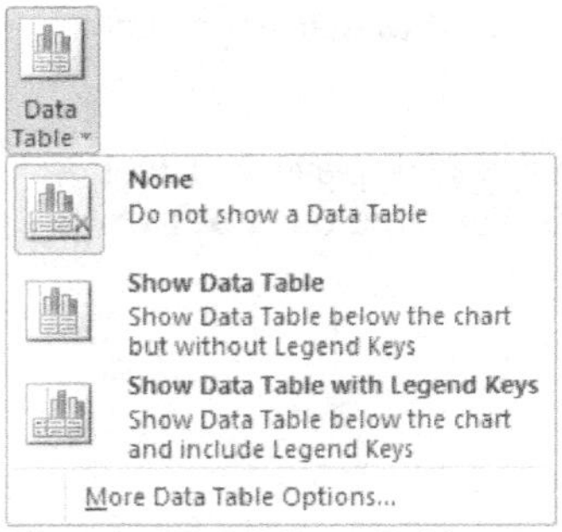

Figure 13-27 Data Table options

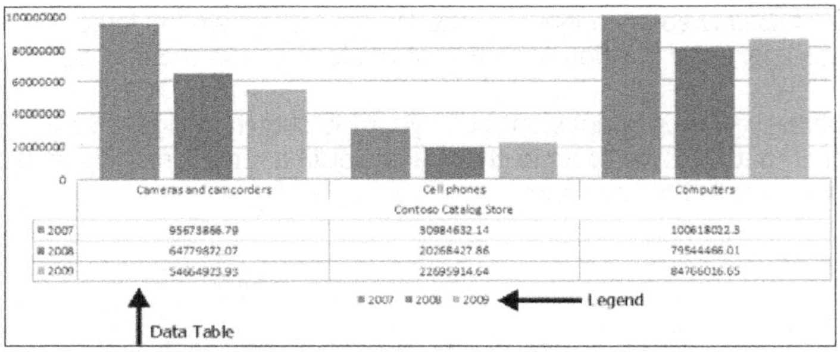

Figure 13-28 Data Table and legend added to the chart

The **CHART WALL** and **CHART FLOOR** options on the Layout tab are used to add a solid color or fill pattern color to the background of certain areas of a 3D chart.

Figure 13-29 shows a 3D bar chart without any background formatting.

Figure 13-30 shows the Format Walls fill pattern options that can be applied to the chart.

Figure 13-31 shows the chart with the fill pattern for the chart walls applied.

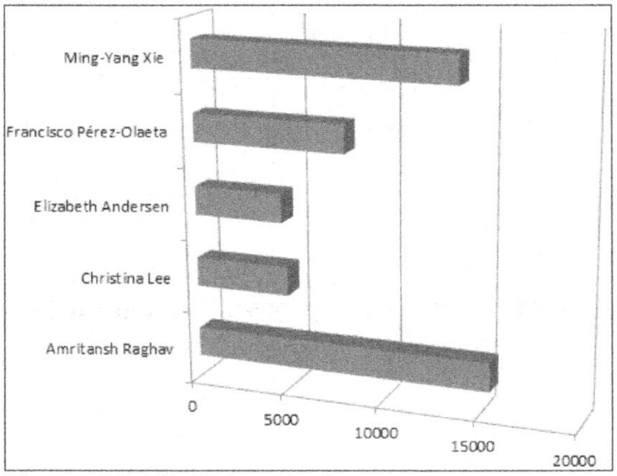

Figure 13-29 3D bar chart

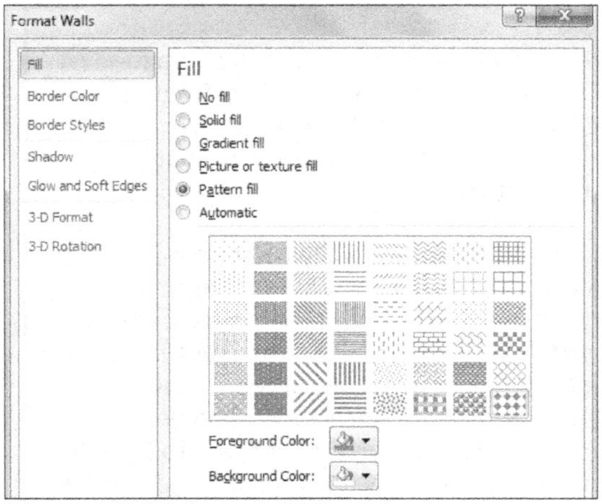

Figure 13-30 Format Walls dialog box

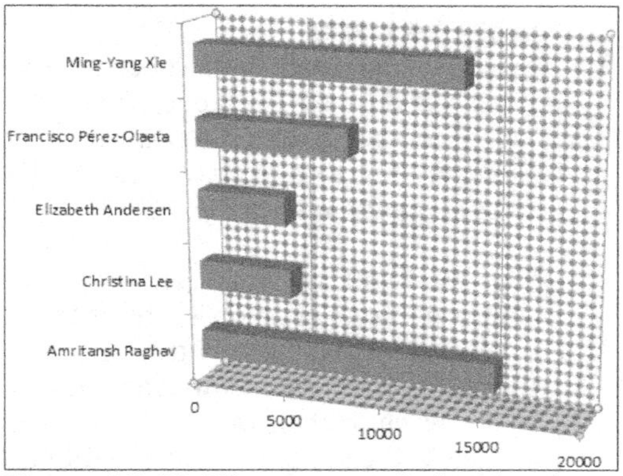

Figure 13-31 Fill pattern applied to the chart

Differences On The PowerPivot Field List For Pivot Charts

Figure 13-32 shows the PowerPivot Field List when a pivot chart is selected.

The Row Labels and Column Labels drop zones are not available for pivot charts. Instead, pivot charts have the drop zones explained below.

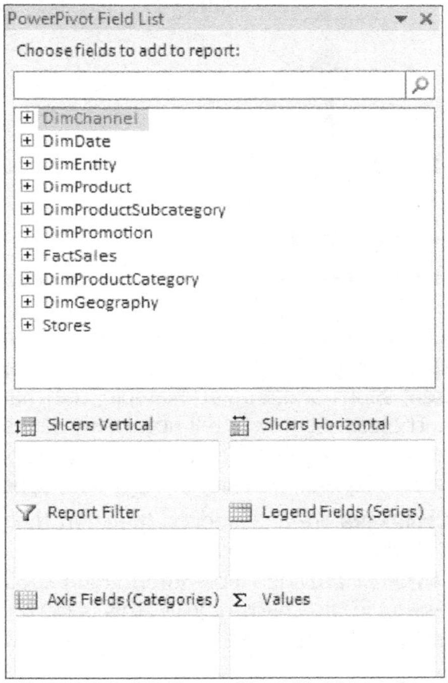

Figure 13-32 PowerPivot Field List for pivot charts

① **AXIS FIELDS (CATEGORIES)** The fields placed in this drop zone are displayed across the bottom of the chart. If a text field is checked at the top of the PowerPivot Field List, by default it is placed in this drop zone. This drop zone replaces the Row Labels drop zone that pivot tables have.

② **LEGEND FIELDS (SERIES)** The fields placed in this drop zone are displayed vertically on the left side of the chart. If a text field is added to this drop zone, each item becomes a new series in the chart. This drop zone replaces the Column Labels drop zone that pivot tables have. Like the Column Labels drop zone, the Legend Fields drop zone can be used to filter the data.

Pivot Chart Data
If you are only creating a pivot chart, PowerPivot needs a place to store the data for a pivot chart, just like Excel does. The difference is that creating a pivot chart from PowerPivot data does not require you to select a range of cells. PowerPivot will automatically create the pivot table for the pivot chart, based on the options that you select in the PowerPivot Field List to create the pivot chart.

When the PivotChart option is selected, PowerPivot will automatically create a worksheet and place a pivot table on it. This is the data that the pivot chart will be created from. The syntax for the name of the tab that the pivot chart will be placed on is **DATA FOR <SHEET NAME> CHART <NUMBER>**, as illustrated in Figure 13-33. The name of the tab lets you know which chart the pivot table is for. Why the new (pivot table) worksheets are inserted to the left of the worksheet that it is connected to is a mystery to me because new worksheets are added to the right in Excel, by default. If you do not plan to hide the tab that has the pivot table for the pivot chart, rename the Sheet 1 tab before you add a pivot chart to it so that you and anyone else that uses the workbook will understand what the pivot table is for.

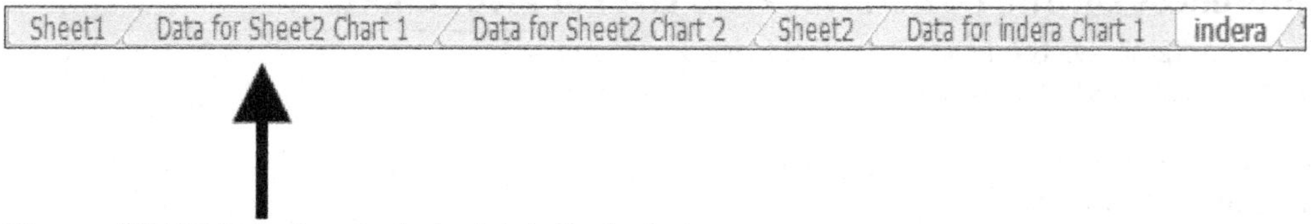

Figure 13-33 Data for pivot chart tab illustrated

Pivot Chart Components

Pivot charts have features that pivot tables do not have. These features are explained below.

① **DATA SERIES** are related points of data that are plotted on a chart. More than one data series can be plotted on a chart, except for pie charts. Each color on a chart represents a different series of data. For example, the chart shown in Figure 13-34 has three series of data. The easiest way to tell how many series of data a chart has is to count the number of items in the legend. The legend contains one item for each series of data.

② A **LEGEND** displays the color of each data series in the chart.

③ **DATA MARKERS** are a symbol on the chart that represents a single value on the chart. Data markers that are related, create a data series.

④ A **DATA LABEL** provides more information about the data point that the data marker represents in the chart. Usually, this is the value of the data point because it can be difficult to tell what the exact value of the data point is.

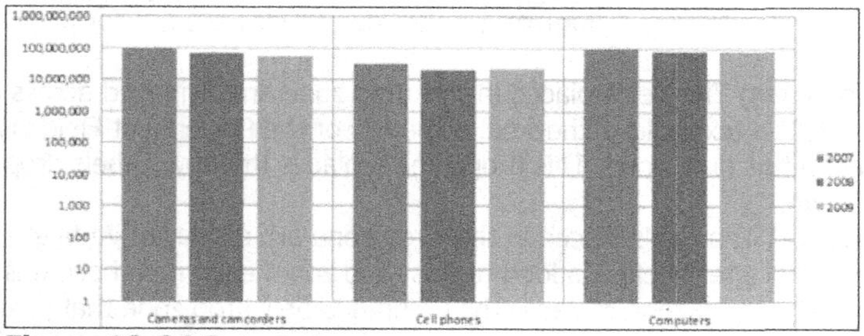

Figure 13-34 Data series

Pivot Chart Creation Tips

① In the pivot chart exercise, you will see the dialog box shown in Figure 13-35 after you select a pivot chart option from the PivotTable button on the PowerPivot tab. Select the Existing Worksheet option, then click OK.

② Often, the default size of charts is small. You can make them larger as needed.

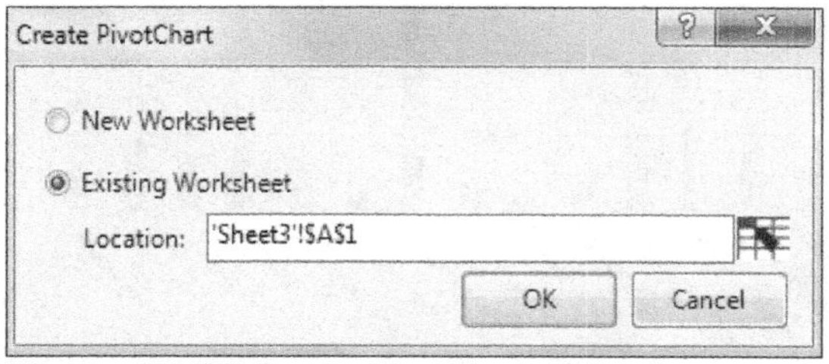

Figure 13-35 Create PivotChart dialog box

Exercise 13.3: Create A Customer Order Subtotal Pivot Chart

In this exercise you will create a pivot chart that displays customer order subtotal information.

1. Save the PivotChart Bonus workbook as `Customer order subtotal pivot chart.`
2. PowerPivot tab ⇒ Report group ⇒ PivotTable button ⇒ PivotChart.
3. Add the Ship Name field in the Orders table to the Axis Fields drop zone.
4. Add the Subtotal field in the Order Subtotals table to the Values drop zone.

   The bottom of the PowerPivot Field List should look like the one shown in Figure 13-36.

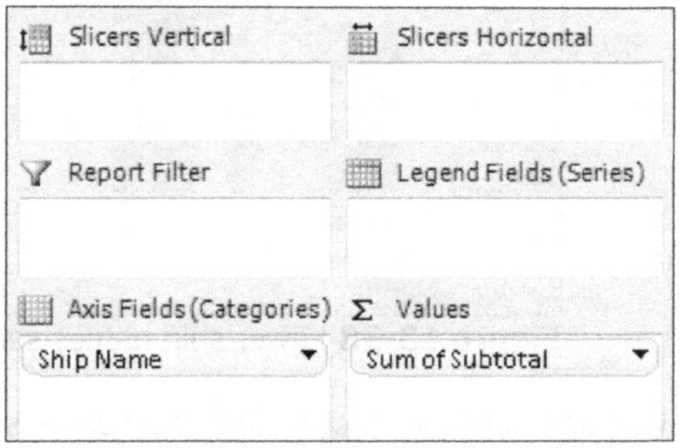

Figure 13-36 PowerPivot Field List drop zone options for a pivot chart

5. Save the changes.

   The pivot chart should look like the one shown in Figure 13-37.

   This chart layout works because there are not a lot of customers.

   If there were thousands of customers, the pivot chart would need filters and/or slicers to reduce the number of customers displayed in the chart.

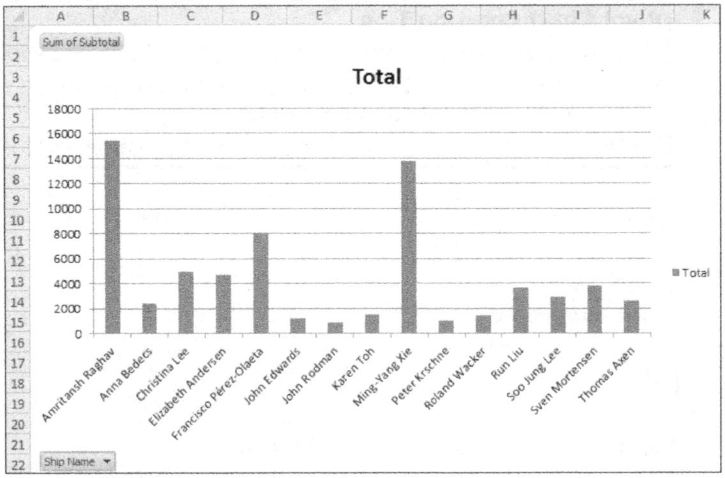

Figure 13-37 Pivot chart

Selecting fewer names in the Ship Name filter would cause the chart to look like the one shown in Figure 13-38.

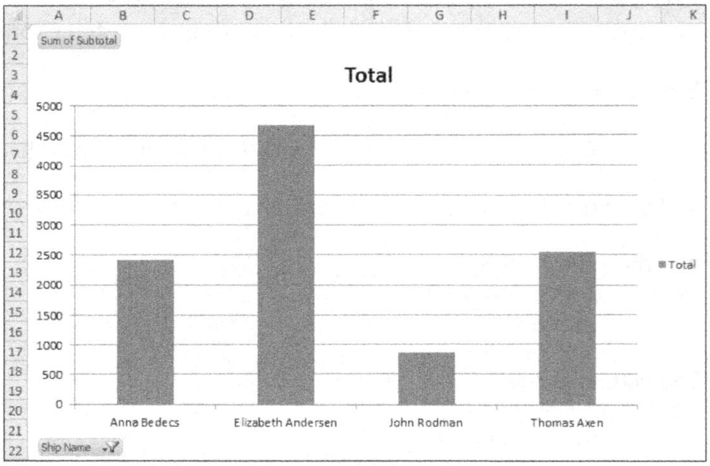

Figure 13-38 Fewer ship names selected

If the Employee ID field was added to the Report Filter drop zone, sales reps could be selected to only display their orders on the pivot chart. Selecting the Employee ID filter options shown in the upper left corner of Figure 13-39 would display the chart shown in the figure.

If the Employee ID field was added to the Legend Fields drop zone, the pivot chart would look like the one shown in Figure 13-40.

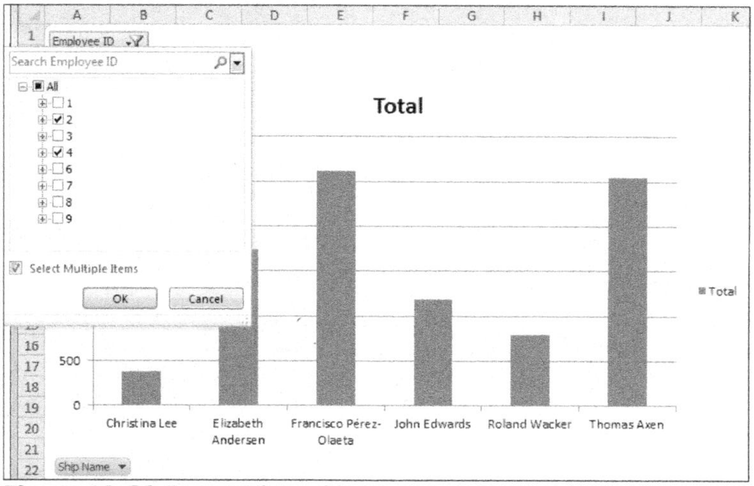

Figure 13-39 Report Filter added to a report

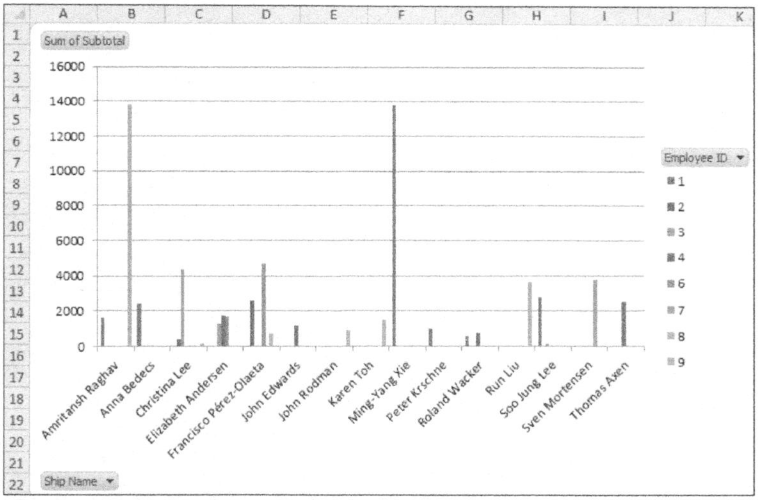

Figure 13-40 Employee ID field added to the Legend Fields drop zone

If you click on the Data for Sheet 1 Chart 1 tab, you will see the pivot table that was automatically created when you created the pivot chart in this exercise. This pivot table is linked to the pivot chart.

INDEX

C

D

E

F

M

N

O

P

Q

R

S

T

U

V

W

X

Z

Made in the USA
Monee, IL
08 November 2026

68106868R00177